Phillip Kerman

{MACROMEDIA® FLASH™ MX 2004 FOR RICH INTERNET APPLICATIONS}

New Riders

800 East 96th Street, 3rd Floor, Indianapolis, IN 46240
An Imprint of Pearson Education
Boston • Indianapolis • London • Munich • New York • San Francisco

Copyright © 2004 by Phillip Kerman

All rights reserved. No part of this book shall be reproduced, stored in a retrieval system, or transmitted by any means—electronic, mechanical, photocopying, recording, or otherwise—without written permission from the publisher, except for the inclusion of brief quotations in a review.

International Standard Book Number: 0-7357-1366-9

Library of Congress Catalog Card Number: 2003111727

Printed in the United States of America

First printing: October 2003

08 07 06 05 04 03   7 6 5 4 3 2 1

Interpretation of the printing code: The rightmost double-digit number is the year of the book's printing; the rightmost single-digit number is the number of the book's printing. For example, the printing code 03-1 shows that the first printing of the book occurred in 2003.

Trademarks

All terms mentioned in this book that are known to be trademarks or service marks have been appropriately capitalized. New Riders Publishing cannot attest to the accuracy of this information. Use of a term in this book should not be regarded as affecting the validity of any trademark or service mark.

Macromedia is a registered trademark of Macromedia, Inc. Flash is a trademark of Macromedia, Inc.

Warning and Disclaimer

Every effort has been made to make this book as complete and as accurate as possible, but no warranty of fitness is implied. The information is provided on an as-is basis. The authors and New Riders Publishing shall have neither liability nor responsibility to any person or entity with respect to any loss or damages arising from the information contained in this book or from the use of the CD or programs that may accompany it.

Publisher
Stephanie Wall

Production Manager
Gina Kanouse

Senior Acquisitions Editor
Linda Anne Bump

Senior Development Editor
Jennifer Eberhardt

Project Editor
Jake McFarland

Copy Editor
Keith Cline

Indexers
Angie Bess
Christine Karpeles

Proofreader
Jessica McCarty

Composition
Amy Hassos

Manufacturing Coordinator
Dan Uhrig

Interior Designer
Alan Clements

Cover Designer
Alan Clements

Marketing
Scott Cowlin
Tammy Detrich
Hannah Onstad Latham

Publicity Manager
Susan Nixon

Contents at a Glance

Introduction   1

Part I   Development
1   Replacing Web Pages with Applications   11
2   Designing Flash Applications   29

Part II   Technology
3   Technology Overview   61
4   Working with Complex Data   91
5   Presenting Data   115
6   Basic Data Exchange   135
7   Exchanging Data with Outside Services   187
8   Foundation Communication Server   227
9   Advanced Communication Server   275

Part III   Productivity
10   Production Techniques   313
11   Quality Assurance and Debugging   339
12   Using Components   371
13   Building a Code Library   401

Dedication

Dedicated to my Mom who—in addition to being right most of the time—always has faith in me.

Table of Contents

Introduction 1

Part I Development 9

1 Replacing Web Pages with Applications 11

The End of Web Pages 12
A Short History of Internet Applications 13
    Milestones and Killer Apps 13
    Flash's Standing 16
    Flash's Coming of Age 19
Glossary 22
    Places or Times 22
    Things 22
    Technologies 23
    Hot Words 23
Makeovers 24
    Broadmoor Hotel 24
    XML News Aggregator 25
    Stampede Cattle 27
Summary 28

2 Designing Flash Applications 29

Identifying the User Benefit 30
    Objectives 30
    Measuring Success 31
    Considering Alternatives 32
    Rationalizing "Rich Media" 34
Selecting Technologies 35
    Tools 36
    Media Formats 38
    Deployment 41
Using Macromedia Central to Target Occasionally Connected
Computers (OCCs) 49
Designing for Accessibility 52
    General Issues 52
    Vision 53
    Motor Skills 55
    Hearing 56
Summary 57

Part II Technology 59

3 Technology Overview 61

Data Handling 62
    Separating Code and Data 62
    Structuring Data 64
    Presenting Data 65
Data Exchanging 66
    Loading 66
    Parsing 69
    Writing 69
    Synchronizing 70
    Ensuring Successful Data Exchange 71
    Web Services 72
Application Servers 73
    Basics 73
    Concepts 76
    Integrating Flash 78
Components 79
    Using Components 79
    Providing Data to Components 81
    Data Components 81
How Flash Communication Server Works 82
Technology Map 84
Configuring Your Work Environment 85
    Configuration Folders 85
    Players 87
    Understanding *localhost* 88
    Publishing 89
Summary 90

4 Working with Complex Data 91

Structuring Data 92
    Data Types 93
    Homemade Objects Versus Arrays 95
    Using Objects Like Arrays 100
    Associating Functions with Event Properties 102
    Comparison to DataProvider Object 104
    Sorting Data 105
    Building a Slide-Show Maker 108
Summary 113
Project Ideas 114

5 Presenting Data 115

- Formatting Text 116
  - Using HTML Text 116
  - Using CSS (Cascading Style Sheets) 122
  - Using the TextFormat Object 126
  - Additional Layout Options 129
- Summary 134

6 Basic Data Exchange 135

- Saving Data with the Local Shared Object 137
  - Using the Local Shared Object 138
  - Practical Examples Involving Local Shared Objects 143
  - Limitations of the Local Shared Object 148
- Sharing Data Using the Local Connection Object 149
  - Local Connection Fundamentals 150
  - Creating a Guided Tour Help Feature 151
  - Downloading Media into a Single Window 154
  - A Better Back Button 158
- Flat Data 165
  - Formatting 166
  - Importing 167
  - LoadVars Object Fundamentals 167
  - Advanced LoadVars Examples 168
  - Server Interaction 172
- XML Structured Data 177
  - Loading XML 178
  - Parsing XML 179
- Summary 185

7 Exchanging Data with Outside Services 187

- Flash Remoting 188
  - How It Works 189
  - Basic Remoting 190
  - Writing the Remote Method 194
  - Remoting Tips 195
- Data Management Components 197
  - The Data Component Concept 198
  - DataSet Component 210
  - Resolvers 216
  - Formatting Data 218
  - Additional Details 223
- Summary 226

8 Foundation Communication Server 227

- Configuration 228
  - Configuration Folders 229
  - Production Techniques 232
- NetConnection 236
  - Basic Connecting 236
  - NetConnection Object Details 237
- Remote Shared Objects 240
  - Setting and Accessing Data in Remote Shared Objects 240
  - Synchronizing Values 242
  - Architectural Decisions 247
  - Practical Examples 250
- Streams 255
  - A Channel Inside Your NetConnection 256
  - Playing FLV Videos and MP3s 258
  - Publishing 267
  - Miscellaneous Tips When Publishing 271
- Why Server-Side ActionScript 274
- Summary 274

9 Advanced Communication Server 275

- Managing Connections 276
  - Key Events 277
  - Application Object's Additional Features 283
  - Additional Client Object Information 286
- Accessing Remote Shared Objects from the Server Side 286
  - Syntax Differences 287
  - Locking 289
  - Sending Messages on RSOs 289
- Messaging 290
  - Using *SharedObject.send()* 290
  - Using *NetConnection.call()* 293
- Optimizing 296
  - It's Still ActionScript 296
  - Using Messaging Sparingly 298
- Server-Side Stream Object 299
  - Publishing Existing Streams from the
    Server Side 299
  - Republishing Portions of Client Streams 301
  - Using Server-Side Streams to Log Events 303
- Integrating the Communication Components 307
- Summary 309

Part III Productivity 311

10 Production Techniques 313

Exploiting Flash MX 2004 Features 314
    Find and Replace 314
    Actions Panel Tricks 314
    Commands 318
    Project Panel 320
Library Management 324
    Shared Library Items 325
    Runtime Shared Libraries (RSLs) 326
Prototyping 329
    Being Sloppy 330
    Using Components 330
Staging and Deployment 330
    Multimode Applications 332
    Creating Dummy Data 335
Summary 337

11 Quality Assurance and Debugging 339

Evaluating Quality 340
    Benefits to Client and Developer 340
    Finding and Assessing Bugs 340
    Taking a Deliberate Approach 343
    Client Management 344
Ensuring Quality 345
    Building Proofing Systems 345
    Leaving Tracks As You Go 350
    Defining Testing Procedures 353
Practical Debugging 354
    Basic Approaches 354
    Homemade Debuggers 357
    Using the Debugger Panel 361
The Error Object 367
Summary 370

12 Using Components 371

V2 Components 372
Foundation Skills 373
    Populating Manually 374
    Populating with Script 375
    Triggering Code 381
Applied Examples Using Components 385
    Text (Label, TextArea, and TextInput) 386
    ComboBox 387

Using the List 388
Advanced Components 390
Styles, Skinning, and Themes 392
Setting Styles 393
Replacing Skins 396
Summary 399

13 Building a Code Library 401

Homemade Components 402
Designing a Component 402
Making a Component 403
Enhancing Components 404
Distributing Components (MXI) 406
Your Script Style 408
Think Modularly 409
Advanced Techniques 410
Storing Scripts 414
AS Text Files 414
Homemade Behaviors 415
Beyond Flash 418
Intro to JSFL (JavaScript Flash) 418
Homemade Commands 419
WindowSWF Custom Panel 421
Other Uses for JSFL 422
Basic Class Packages in AS2 423
Structure 424
Basic Skeleton 426
Summary 430

Index 431

About the Author

Phillip Kerman is an independent programmer, teacher, and writer specializing in Macromedia products. His degree in Imaging and Photographic Technology from the Rochester Institute of Technology was earned back when "multimedia" had a different meaning from today. One of Phillip's internships, for example, involved programming multiple slide projector presentations with dissolves synchronized to a sound track—the multimedia of the 1980s. In 1993, he found Macromedia Authorware a natural fit for his interests and skills. After getting his start at The Human Element, Inc., he moved back to Portland, Oregon, to work on his own.

Phillip has transitioned his expertise from Authorware to Director, and now to Flash. Over 10 years, he has had to adapt to countless version upgrades—Flash MX 2004 being the most significant of them all! In addition to retooling and building his own skills, Phillip finds teaching the biggest challenge. He has trained and made presentations around the world, in such exotic locations as Reykjavik, Iceland; Melbourne, Australia; Amsterdam, Holland; and McAlester, Oklahoma. He also wrote *Sams Teach Yourself Macromedia Flash MX 2004 in 24 Hours* and *ActionScripting in Flash MX*. His writing has also appeared in such publications as *Macworld*, Macromedia's DevNet resource site, on quarterly Developer Resource Kit CDs, and in his self-published The Phillip Newsletter (www.phillipkerman.com/newsletter).

In addition to showing others how to create multimedia, Phillip has had plenty of opportunities to get his hands dirty in programming. He programmed the Flash interface for the real-time cattle auction site stampedecattle.com using Flash Communication Server and Flash Remoting. Feel free to email Phillip at ria@phillipkerman.com.

About the Technical Reviewers

These reviewers contributed their considerable hands-on expertise to the entire development process for *Macromedia Flash MX 2004 for Rich Internet Applications*. As the book was being written, these dedicated professionals reviewed all the material for technical content, organization, and flow. Their feedback was critical to ensuring that *Macromedia Flash MX 2004 for Rich Internet Applications* fits our readers' need for the highest-quality technical information.

Larry Drolet is a developer and dreamer, one of those people who, when "well caffeinated," has about an idea a minute. While in graduate school, he wrote a paper on Internet law, and wouldn't you know it this developed into a hobby and a passion that ultimately led him to starting a dot-com. Sounds all too familiar! Currently he is working at Arizona State University with the Business Information Technology group, developing applications for the online MBA program. When not working or in class for another degree, Larry can be found speaking at user groups in southern California and Arizona, or surfing near San Diego.

Matt Manuel has worked in multimedia since 1993, when he started with Sanctuary Woods. Two more tours of duty included time at Disney Interactive and Creative Capers, both in Los Angeles. Now returning to his roots, Matt recently took a job with a big game company in Vancouver, Canada.

Acknowledgments

I didn't really write this entire book. Well, I typed it all in, but without the guidance, inspiration, and critical input from many other people this book would be nothing like it is. A ton of people also helped in indirect ways.

There are countless correspondents with whom I've learned a lot about Flash. Instead of naming several and inadvertently neglecting many, let me just say that participating in local user groups and online forums is a great way to expand your knowledge and build your business—they've helped me and helped this book.

Macromedia is the most approachable software company I know. Without the following current and former Macromedia employees (and countless others I can't name), this book wouldn't be what it is (nor would Flash be the product that it is): Jeremy Allaire, Allen Ellison, Lucian Beebe, Brad Bechtel, Jody Bleyle, Greg Burch, Damian Burns, David Calaprice, Mike Chambers, Jeremy Clark, Henriette Cohn, Karen Cook, Jim Corbett, John Dowdell, Joel Dreskin, Troy Evans, Vera Fleischer, Craig Goodman, Gary Grossman, Giacomo "Peldi" Guilizzoni, Rebekah Hash, Barbara Herbert, Chris Hock, Jeff Kamerer, Forest Key, Lily Khong, San Khong, Sean Kranzberg, Kevin Lynch, Sasha Magee, David Mendels, Erica Norton, Chris Nuuja, Nigel Pegg, Peter Santangeli, Sharon Selden, Mark Shepherd, Mark Schroeder, Ed Skwarecki, Tracy Stampfi, Joan Tan, Christopher Thilgen, Tinic Uro, Chris Walcott, Matt Wobensmith, Michael Williams, Eric J. Wittman, Edwin Wong, Greg Yachuk, Lisa Young, and Jody Zhang.

Special thanks also to Chafic Kazoun.

Tell Us What You Think

As the reader of this book, you are the most important critic and commentator. We value your opinion and want to know what we're doing right, what we could do better, what areas you'd like to see us publish in, and any other words of wisdom you're willing to pass our way.

As an editor for New Riders Publishing, I welcome your comments. You can fax, email, or write me directly to let me know what you did or didn't like about this book—as well as what we can do to make our books stronger. When you write, please be sure to include this book's title, ISBN, and author, as well as your name and phone or fax number. I will carefully review your comments and share them with the author and editors who worked on the book.

Please note that I cannot help you with technical problems related to the topic of this book, and that due to the high volume of email I receive, I might not be able to reply to every message.

Fax: 317-428-3280

Email: jennifer.eberhardt@newriders.com

Mail: Jennifer Eberhardt
         Senior Development Editor
         New Riders Publishing
         800 East 96th Street, 3rd Floor
         Indianapolis, IN 46240 USA

{ Introduction }

I really wanted to call this book *Replacing Web Pages with Applications*. Or, something even more provocative such as *The End of Web Pages*. Considering that Macromedia Flash is the tool that will bring such changes, I suppose it's only fair it's in the title. But I still think we're at the beginning of a real change.

When new technologies arise, people tend to impress old metaphors onto them. If you look at the first motion pictures, they're little more than a camera pointed at a stage play. When D. W. Griffith decided to move the camera to different positions and insert carefully timed edits, it was a major revolution. In the case of the web, the whole concept of "pages" comes from books. Books are good at what they do, so there's no point trying to re-create books on the web. Instead, we need to exploit the computer for what *it* is good at. In many ways, we still don't know what that is. I'm convinced, however, that the computer's calling is certainly more than just displaying "pages."

Even Flash's short history is marked by mini-milestones. The original gabocorp.com site convinced a generation of Flash developers that a site with little more than an interface and natural transitions could be really cool. Then, yugop.com (built in Flash 4 no less) blew everyone away by showing that you can use math to animate. And then the first examples shown on wireframe.co.za demonstrated practical ways to apply isometric math to make things look realistic. You can also find countless cases where Flash cartoons using sophomoric humor rose to cult status.

The point about many such examples is that although they certainly help Flash advance, they don't necessarily offer something better than an alternative. That is, they're cool and there's nothing like them, but it's not as though average folks say "ah, now *that's* going to help me do this better." Flash users might say "wow, someone's going to use this for something practical—eventually." I suppose this is part of the reason another milestone in Flash history was Dr. Jakob Nielsen's article, "Flash: 99% Bad." My point here is only that Flash needed a push toward usability; otherwise, it would have continued to chart its own course as just a cool animation tool.

{ Note }

To be fair to the revolutionaries responsible for the sites mentioned previously, I should add this note: I know for a fact that they have gone on to make practical and usable applications.

Also, I don't want to ever suggest that animation is only useful for entertainment or eye-candy. In fact, it's as important and unique a communication medium as pictures or words.

Although Dr. Nielsen may have pushed Flash toward usability, we still aren't to the point where people immediately think of Flash when they need to solve a problem. It would seem the obvious goal for Flash would be to replace existing applications that use traditional technologies such as HTML. However, this makes sense only if Flash could do something notably better. That is, if I could replace your email software with Flash, would you be any better off? You wouldn't, unless my Flash emailer was markedly better in some way. Just "spicing up" an application by redoing it in Flash is no better than colorizing a black-and-white movie. The target for Flash applications needs to be solving otherwise unresolved problems. In a way, this takes more creativity because you have to think of new ideas. On the other hand, if Flash is well-suited to solve the problem, it'll be easy to make a case for your application because it won't compete with other technologies.

Flash Comes of Age

The idea of this book is that Flash has come of age. It's obviously capable of employing sophisticated programming. It's also a rich medium that integrates sound, graphics, text, animation, and video (elements that can actually aid in communication, not just add gratuitous distractions). The infrastructure is ready too, because nearly every personal computer has Flash installed. Finally, it's about to come together because the Flash developers are aware of what they need to do: build applications.

Luckily for you, this book isn't filled with many more of my predictions for the future or analyses of the past. I'll try to be persuasive where necessary, but I'm going to assume you're on board with the idea of using Flash for rich Internet applications (RIAs). When it comes down to it, this book is really just about how to use the powerful features in Flash. I invested a lot of time studying, testing, and even helping to improve Flash MX 2004. My hope is this investment will reduce the time you spend getting up to speed.

Flash MX 2004 Versus Flash MX Professional 2004

Although this book focuses on Flash MX 2004, I refuse to ignore compelling features found only in Flash MX Professional 2004. (For that matter, you'll also find two chapters on still another product—the Flash Communication Server.) It's impossible for me to say whether the Pro version is worth the price for you. However, you can't really say whether it's worth it either—not until you really know the difference. In the places where I cover Flash Pro features, I make a note of it. Having said this, it's fair to assume that I can't cover either version in complete detail. This book is just about using Flash to create applications. You'll learn what's necessary to reach that goal.

The Parts of This Book

The 13 chapters in this book are broken into 3 parts: Development, Technology, and Productivity. Here's a quick overview of each.

Part I: Development (Chapters 1 and 2)

This first part of the book concentrates on identifying where Flash applications fit. If you're not already convinced that the time for Flash applications is now, you will be a believer after reading the first chapter. It's not so much that I need to persuade you, but perhaps by positioning Flash and ensuring it's given the respect it deserves, we can help continue to grow Flash's acceptance. That is, I know it's cool and you know it's cool, but how can others be convinced? You should have the answers after reading Chapter 1, "Replacing Web Pages with Applications."

Chapter 2, "Designing Flash Applications," steps back and analyzes how to most appropriately use Flash. It forces you to justify the use of Flash. You will also look at various alternatives to ensure that you're using Flash for the right reasons.

I suppose this part of the book puts Flash in perspective.

Part II: Technology (Chapters 3 Through 9)

If this book were a sandwich, this part would be the meat. And the sandwich would be one of those stacked high with meat. If it's a technical detail, it's probably in this part of the book.

Instead of looking at building an application in a linear or project-based manner, this part of the book focuses on data. How to organize data, how to get data into Flash, how to process data and present it to the user, and how to get data back out of Flash if needed. Some applications you build will need to do all of this, but sometimes you'll only need to perform some of these tasks. I do think a key attribute of any application is that it can manage data.

You'll also see a lot of the new features in Flash MX 2004. On the surface, this book is about building apps. But when I look back, this book is also about the new features in Flash. Interestingly, that's nearly the same thing. Flash has grown in areas to enable people to make rich Internet applications. Therefore, it makes sense to concentrate on the new features.

Finally, I've condensed everything I know about Flash Communication Server down to two chapters. Although this product is sold separately, there is a free developer version. So you can definitely follow along. (Note, however, that you won't be able to deploy any Flash Communication Server apps on Macintosh.) The primary reason I included these chapters is that the product is so amazingly cool. But really, I just want you to have a good grasp on what's possible and what's involved in adding Communication Server features to your app. On the surface, the cost of Communication Server can appear high; however, only after you have an idea of the exact value the product offers will you be able to accurately assess whether it's appropriate for your app (and worth the price). In any event, I'll bet most people will get hooked. (I know I did.)

When you start this part, be ready to sink your teeth in. And don't forget to take breaks—not to rest, but to go try this stuff out!

Part III: Productivity (Chapters 10 Through 13)

This part of the book covers specific techniques, as well as how to develop a general attitude that can help reduce work. Yes, programmers are lazy. We look for ways to avoid work.

Although this part of the book is just as technical as any other, it doesn't flow from one chapter to the next the way the rest of the book does. In fact, I think of these chapters almost like appendixes. You'll find collections of tips concentrating on production, debugging, and building a code library. Chapter 12, "Using Components," is probably the most cohesive because it covers just one topic. Because there are so many different components, however, the chapter is like others in this section: a list of specific ideas on a single topic.

Don't worry; the chapters in this part should be easy enough to follow. I just suspect if you revisit these chapters later it will be for reference.

Who Should Read This Book

On the surface I'd like to think everyone loves Flash and everyone loves to read what I write. However, I do think there are a few prime candidates to read this book.

Ideally, this book is for any Flash developer comfortable in Flash who wants to develop more advanced programming skills—specifically to create applications. You should understand basic ActionScript, such as variables and events. There's something to be said for learning by experience, so I believe even a Flash novice could still learn from this book. However, the person with even just a little scripting experience will gain more than the novice because that person can better appreciate the content in this book.

Another target reader is a technical person who is transitioning to Flash. It's only a slight stretch to imagine readers whose bosses say, "Go learn how to make an RIA." They are indeed target readers, too. If that's you, however, you will want to develop your basic Flash skills in parallel with this book. I can't help you get around the Flash interface, for example. However, I believe it's possible to learn the "why" of RIAs from this book even if you can't immediately apply the "how." (That said, a reasonable goal of this book is that you'll actually be able to produce an RIA, too.)

Finally, because I have written two other books, I can place this book in a relative position. Compared to *Sams Teach Yourself Flash MX 2004 in 24 Hours*, this book is significantly more script oriented. That book starts at the ground level and moves up, mainly toward making Flash animations and presentations. I think it's fair to say this book is more advanced, but I don't believe programming is necessarily easier or harder than anything else.

My book *ActionScripting in Flash MX* is closest to this book, although you'll find very little overlap. If I had revised that book for Flash MX 2004, you would definitely see more overlap. It's just that this book doesn't cover general programming theory the way that book does. Also, this book is all about making RIAs. So whereas *ActionScripting in Flash MX* teaches you both programming and how to apply it to all of Flash, this book teaches you Flash programming and how to apply it to RIAs.

One last note. In many ways, I wrote this book for me. I guess I should rephrase that as, "I wrote it the way I like to learn." Even during production, I found occasions when I needed a reminder about how to do something (and I could find it in the example scripts or sample files). Writing involves studying topics and organizing a clear presentation of information. I know that I've included the information I think is important.

Who This Book Is Not For

Again, I would like to believe this book is perfect for everyone. Because Flash is such a large topic, however, it's really easy to point to what this book isn't:

- **It's not about animation.** Although there are a few mentions of where animation can be particularly effective, we don't make a single tween in this book.

- **It's not about object-oriented programming (OOP) theory.** Although I tried to make the example code as clean as possible, I definitely put a higher priority on communicating one point at a time instead of building the most elegant object-based code. That said, you will find some OOP in here—it just won't be highlighted. Branden Hall and Samuel Wan have a fine book on OOP called *Object-Oriented Programming with ActionScript*, also from New Riders.

- **It's not a reference book.** Although typing 400+ pages has made my hands sore, I haven't scratched the surface of ActionScript—let alone Flash. Check out titles from Robert Reinhardt and Colin Moock for more complete references.

- **It's not a cookbook, case study, or tutorial.** However, it has elements of those book styles. You won't find a ton of code samples that you can just cut and paste into your apps. Also, I mention a few projects I've been on; they're just there to put things in perspective. Finally, the only places where you'll find specific step-by-step directions relate to using some of the newer features in a Flash MX 2004 work environment.

- **It's not the last word.** No doubt you can find other books concentrating on RIAs. This book is all me (plus the insightful input from several creative editors). There are plenty of objective details, but also lots of subjective ideas. In fact, the selection of what information to exclude from this book is a subjective editorial decision. I guess what I'm saying is that this is just one book. I'm very proud of it and I think you'll be happy, but it's still just one book. I'm sure there are lots of other books that will supplement it well.

Conventions

It's not like you need a special decoder to read this book. However, there are a few typographical conventions worth noting:

- Program text, functions, variables, and other "computer language" are set in a fixed-pitch font—for example, `var propCount=0;`.

- Code lines that do not fit within the margins of the printed page are continued on the next line and are preceded by a code continuation character ➥.

- Special notes or side discussions are offset as a way to both diverge from the main flow and offer a bit of a break to the topic at hand.

Last First Word

I'll remind you again at the end of the book, but I really do want you to send links to the RIAs you build. Use the email ria@phillipkerman.com. I think I'm pretty good at replying to email, so also feel free to send pointed questions and suggestions, as well as errors. For this book in particular, I expect it to live on long past the initial printing through the companion site: www.phillipkerman.com/rias. There you'll find any additional information that I think of plus all the source files for the examples in this book. Now that the book is printed and in your hands, it's up to you to get as much as you can out of it. If you can learn what I've learned writing it, I'm sure you'll be satisfied.

{ Part I }

Development

1 Replacing Web Pages with Applications   11
2 Designing Flash Applications   29

{Chapter 1}

Replacing Web Pages with Applications

What's the difference between a web page and a web application? Put simply, a web page is a *presentation*, whereas an application is a *tool*. However, don't let that distinction diminish your respect for the value of web pages. As anyone in web development knows, it is definitely a challenge (albeit a worthy one) to "present" ideas clearly.

Macromedia Flash MX 2004 enables you to build engaging applications that you can deliver via the web, and this book shows you how. It's not as though some line has been crossed and only *now* is it finally possible to make rich Internet applications. However, the demand has grown recently.

This chapter covers the following topics:

- A short history of Internet applications
- The state of the art available today
- A perspective on the future

This chapter really just answers, "Why this book?"

The End of Web Pages

Web pages that present information in novel and effective ways won't really go away. However, the real Internet growth area is in applications running on the web. Although there are plenty of popular applications today, they're just not geared to web delivery. For example, a lot of people have digital cameras that include basic image-manipulation applications. Often these apps get "webified" with certain features (such as those that automatically publish JPGs to a web page). Such apps might even upload the files for you. However, this sort of web feature is an add-on—the app still runs on your computer.

Just having applications installed on your hard drive is not necessarily a bad thing. If you consider what the core task of a particular application is supposed to achieve, however, you will find some apps that are much better suited for Internet delivery. Perhaps a photo editor is most appropriate for the desktop. But what about a calendar application? If you're out of the office and want to check your schedule, you have to perform some minor technical miracle to get access to the calendar on you desktop computer. Wouldn't it be cool if you could connect to your calendar from anywhere—from a laptop, handheld, or even an Internet cafe? That's not to justify Internet applications with just "think how cool it would be." Instead, as you can understand from this example, some of the problems applications intend to solve are best addressed using the benefits of an Internet application.

Keep in mind that although it would be nice to solve all the world's problems, an application need only solve one specific problem. A lot of applications attempt to be the new "everything app." However, as discussed in Chapter 2, "Designing Flash Applications," it's much easier to design, build, and deliver an app that does one thing really well than one that attempts to do everything (and fails to do any of it well). Simply put: Applications are tools that help you achieve a *specific* task or solve a *specific* problem.

This book is all about fashioning effective applications using Flash. The reason to use Flash is much more than "because you can." You'll learn in the next couple chapters how Flash is perfectly suited to deliver Internet applications with compelling interactivity, rich media, and advanced data control. Then, in the rest of the book, you'll learn how to actually build such apps.

A Short History of Internet Applications

Not only will this be a short history, but the history on which this history is based (the Internet) is short. In fact, personal computers have only been around for a few years. I have to mention the story of a student of mine who was previously unaware of the fact that personal computers were relatively new. He just figured they had been around forever—relative to his young age, they had been. Apparently, he had seen a television program about the start of Apple and Microsoft and was amazed that these machines he had grown up with were scarcely older than he was. The point of this digression is that I don't know your background. As a way to show where Flash fits, I'm going to lay down some historical markers—many of which you may already be familiar with.

Milestones and Killer Apps

Considering that an Internet application intends to achieve many of the same tasks as any computer application, it's probably good to look at software history generally. The concept of a "killer app" is worth mentioning here. The idea is that any system (for instance, hardware or operating system) will only succeed provided there's some *killer app*—an application so desirable that it warrants investing in the underlying operating system. A perfect example is Visicalc (the first computer spreadsheet program shown in Figure 1.1). Visicalc helped make the Apple II an attractive system. Perhaps even more profound is how various systems or standards have fallen by the wayside—not because the technology was lacking, but because no software attracted people. For instance, several video game consoles have failed because they lacked good games.

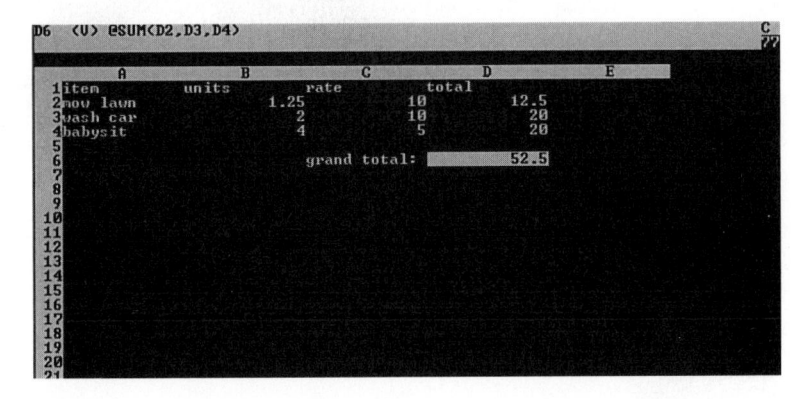

Figure 1.1 *The visual calculator (VisiCalc), also known as the killer app that made the Apple II a success.*

The Multimedia Computer

This discussion returns to killer apps as applied to the Internet shortly, but first it's important to consider a minor revolution that preceded the Internet's popularity. In the early 1990s, the multimedia computer was born. While trade associations were attempting to define exactly what qualified as a multimedia-capable computer, the following few basic technologies were making it happen:

- Sound cards
- Color video displays capable of displaying 16 or even 256 colors
- CD-ROMs that not only contained (what was considered) mass quantities of data but could stream data in factors of 300 kilobits (double-speed or 2X)

These three hardware features, coupled with Apple's digital video format QuickTime (and later, Microsoft's Video for Windows), made many believe that "multimedia" might become the next "plastics" (that is, a sure bet for a money-making industry). Considering the CD-ROM title *Myst* sold millions of copies, you could say there *was* a multimedia revolution.

This information is useful for more than just boring future grandkids. It's mentioned here because it defines what makes a compelling experience. Notice the three big factors that defined a multimedia computer: sound, color graphics, and data access. (I know that I was hooked when I first saw the CD-ROM *Just Grandma and Me* come to life before my eyes.)

Multimedia (now, replaced by the term *rich media*) is effective because it uses multiple channels to communicate. This makes it easier to fashion the appropriate message and increases the likelihood that the message will be understood (because different people respond to different stimuli). Some people are visual learners, others auditory, and still others are tactile. Naturally, Flash can communicate in all of these ways.

Chapter 1 Replacing Web Pages with Applications 15

> **{ Note }**
>
> **MPC Standard** For even more nostalgia, you may find the Multimedia Personal Computer standards (MPC, MPC-2, and MPC-3) interesting. The idea was for hardware manufacturers to include a minimum set of features so that software makers could easily require minimum system configurations. I don't even know what the MPC standard was, but for kicks here are MPC-2 and MPC-3 standards.
>
> | MPC-2 | MPC-3 |
> |---|---|
> | 4MB RAM | 8MB RAM |
> | 25MHz Intel 486SX | 540MB disk drive |
> | VGA (256 colors) | 75MHz Pentium |
> | 2X CD-ROM | 4X CD-ROM |

Everyone on the Internet

Although I'm told it's not true, it sure seems like everyone is "on" the Internet. It's unclear whether the killer app that made the Internet what it is was email or the browser (although it sure wasn't pop-up ads). The important fact is that you can usually depend on users being connected.

Another reasonable expectation is that users have a modern browser. Each generation of browser has additional features making it possible to perform more and more tasks. Believe it or not, the first browsers couldn't even display JPGs without a plug-in. The idea of a plug-in is that if some third party wants to employ a currently unsupported technology or media type, the third party can write a plug-in that the user then needs to install. The bad part is the plug-in must be distributed and users have to manually install it; the good part is that popular plug-ins may eventually get native support by the browser. At the core, media displayed by a plug-in is effectively running like a separate application—it just happens to appear in the browser's window.

Macromedia prefers to call it the Flash Player, but it's basically a plug-in. Unlike any other plug-in in history, however, the Flash Player has reached more than half a billion users. By far, the Flash Player is the most accepted plug-in. Although the claim of "98 percent of all Internet users" includes older versions of the Flash Player, the adoption rate is very fast. For example, Flash Player 6 reached more than 80 percent in only 12 months. It's a snowball effect the way the new player's growth rate continues to accelerate. With more compelling Flash applications (oh, and traditional sites), there's a greater demand for the software necessary to run them. That is, your killer Flash application could very well fuel the demand for the free Flash Player.

If you want statistical evidence of these claims, just check out www.macromedia.com/software/player_census/flashplayer. For a sense of just how frequently the Flash Player gets installed, go ahead and visit that page now to see the growth since the day I wrote this chapter and grabbed Figure 1.2 from the Macromedia site.

```
WORLDWIDE USERS OF MACROMEDIA FLASH PLAYER

              544,484,706
             as of July 24, 2003
```

Figure 1.2 *By the time you visit the Macromedia survey page, I'm sure thousands more will have downloaded the Flash Player.*

Other plug-ins have also contributed to making browsing a better experience—for instance, Adobe Acrobat Reader for viewing documents, Apple QuickTime Player for high-quality video, and RealMedia Real Player for streaming video. There's also Macromedia Shockwave to play Director MX applications, which, despite being underappreciated, has as a better penetration than Real Player or QuickTime. Perhaps the interesting fact is that Flash isn't replacing these other technologies, but is instead slowly picking away at some of their unique advantages (video and streaming video to name just two).

Flash's Standing

Flash has been typecast as an animation tool. Although it is great for that, with more and more sophisticated functionality being added, it's trying to break away from that reputation. Attempting to become the *rich Internet application* (RIA) standard is more than just a marketing ploy. It's really just a matter of letting developers see what's possible. This section examines where Flash stands in comparison to its apparent competition.

Not Java

The one technology that's similar to Flash in both capability and penetration is Java. First, realize there's Java the language (used behind the scenes on the server) and then there's client-side Java (running in the browser). As a language, it's perfectly suited for many uses. On the client side, however, it's lacking. Although Java can achieve great tasks, its significance is hindered by its limits. Problems include the fact it can take an enormous amount of work to build a client-side Java app, it takes a long time to get up and running when a user loads a Java app, it can quickly use up your computer's resources, and it often behaves differently on different operating systems. Hey, I don't mean to bury client-side Java, but the fact is that Flash has delivered on promises that Java never could. (Flash is easy to build, lightweight, relatively fast performing, and consistent.)

Not Director

Macromedia has a confusingly similar product to Flash called Director. Director has been around much longer, and therefore its roots are in producing applications that run on the desktop or CD-ROM. The Director browser plug-in is called Shockwave. In many ways, the capabilities of Flash and Director overlap. However, Director excels in several key areas: performance, media support, and features useful in applications made for the desktop. The fact that people's computers continue to improve reduces the significance of Director's performance advantage. Also, the new Flash Players continue to get faster.

In the area of media support, Director can display (at runtime) nearly any native media format. Flash can display only JPG and play only MP3 audio or FLV video. In addition, Director can display true 3D graphics while tapping into a computer's 3D video acceleration. That is, not only can you display 3D models and animations, but you also can use script to change camera angles, object placement, or even lighting.

Finally, Director is made for desktop applications. Director includes several built-in features and ways you can extend Director native functionality through third-party xtras. Pretty much anything any application can do, Director can too. For instance, I've made applications that print high-resolution catalogs or automatically update themselves via the Internet.

That said, Flash does have some advantages over Director, including the following:

- Support to both read and write XML (whereas Director can only read it).
- A younger and more streamlined language. (Although the Director Lingo language is perfectly capable, it is hindered by a patchwork of changes.)
- The Flash plug-in is at about 98 percent of market, whereas Director Shockwave is at roughly 63 percent.

The thing is, you can embed Flash SWFs inside Director and effectively get the best of both tools. Unfortunately, Director MX currently only supports Flash Player 6 SWFs.

You can find more comparisons between Flash and Director at www.macromedia.com/software/director/resources/understanding.

Not HTML or JavaScript

Obviously, Flash isn't HTML. There's no point comparing Flash applications to static HTML (that is, individual HMTL pages coded by hand). However, as you'll learn in Chapter 3, "Technology Overview," an application server can dynamically generate HTML on-the-fly. That is, based on user input or timely data, the application server will produce a custom-looking HTML file in a fraction of a second. To users, it looks like a page created just for them. In many ways, this is a Flash application's real competition.

Nearly all Internet applications use an application server behind the scenes (that is, on the server side). When you investigate flight schedules, purchase a book, or bid at an auction, chances are good your request is being sent to an application server, which then triggers a follow-up action and generates a response in the form of a new page that you view. It can be a bit complicated to build, but the worst part (in which Flash may be able help) is that the user experience may be lacking. For example, you might fill in a form with 10 different options and click Submit only to find that nothing matches your request. You then go back to make another try—each time sending a request to an application server, which then generates a complete HTML page that must download.

Although Flash has the reputation of being a bandwidth hog, when you design an effective application, it's actually possible to make Flash more bandwidth friendly than HTML! For example, it's easy to send requests to an application directly from Flash. When the response arrives, Flash needs only to redraw the appropriate parts of the screen. It doesn't need to reload the whole page (meaning a less-disruptive experience and less bandwidth).

JavaScript can prove quite effective. However, don't try to make full-fledged applications entirely in JavaScript. Basically, JavaScript is a client-side scripting language because it downloads with your HTML. Flash also runs on the client side, but Flash can reach out to download additional media or data. In the case of JavaScript, the language is nearly identical to Flash ActionScript—so it's quite powerful. However, the capabilities of JavaScript are limited to affecting the browser. As for Flash, it can do "Flash" things such as animate, play sounds, and so on. For the most part, Flash can do anything JavaScript can, but better. The notable exception is directly controlling the browser. With JavaScript, for instance, it's easy to open a new window with no browser buttons. For these situations, you'll want to mix Flash and JavaScript. That is, Flash can easily trigger functions you've defined in your JavaScript by using `getURL`. (Chapter 2 touches on JavaScript.)

Flash's Coming of Age

When Flash 5 came out, programmers went wild with the new full-fledged scripting language ActionScript. Then Flash MX came out, exceeding everyone's expectations as to how many features could get crammed into a single upgrade. Now Flash 2004 introduces so many advances it boggles the mind. If nothing else, this progression proves that Macromedia is targeting application developers. I don't think there's any intent to alienate graphic designers and animators, but because they've already adopted Flash there's less potential growth in that area. In any event, Flash 2004 and the Flash Player 7 are an application developer's dream.

What's New?

The inclusion of ActionScript 2 will surely attract hard-core programmers (although, I should note, it's not covered in detail in this book). Other features especially geared toward application development include the following:

- Forced text aliasing, which enables you, by turning off antialiasing, to ensure that smaller text looks crisp.

- Version 2 components that sport the new Halo skin, as well as offer improved performance and additional features. This all means you don't have to spend time developing common interface elements—they're already built. Countless other improvements are covered in detail in Chapter 12, "Using Components."

- Cascading Style Sheets (CSS) support means you have greater text layout control using a standard format (as discussed in Chapter 6, "Basic Data Exchange").
- Improved array sorting speed and features that help you manage large quantities of data.
- The ability to customize the context menu (right-click) and to trap changes in the mouse wheel to give the user just one more way to interact.
- The ability to respond to the user's mouse wheel. For example, you can scroll a display when they scroll their mouse wheel.
- Text metrics, giving you more information about where text appears.
- A MovieClip Loader object that simplifies the process of displaying external media.
- The addition of the `<img>` tag to embed images or SWFs within your text displays.
- Native support for Flash Video files (FLV) and the ability to produce video using nearly any video editor (if you buy Flash Pro).
- Plus countless other features that, although cool, may not apply directly to applications.

Where Flash Fits In

In a simplified way, Flash is the pretty face you can put on any data. To be a little more respectful, I should say Flash can make complex data more digestible. Giving users access to advanced features and infinite sets of data is fine, but it must be presented in a way that makes it easy for them to find what they want. This is where Flash fits in.

Flash is appropriate for any application where images, sounds, or animation can support and enhance a message. Again, it's not as though you're spicing up something that's otherwise boring. In fact, if a piece of multimedia is not supplementing a message, it is most certainly distracting from it. Chapter 2 looks at many such considerations. If a media element can help a message, however, you should include it. Flash is great at supporting media such as audio, video, animation, and text.

I think an overly simple definition of a Flash application is when Flash appears by itself in its own window. It's actually possible to integrate Flash into HTML frames or tables. That is, Flash doesn't have to take up the whole screen. This approach can be a bit more work, and, frankly, there are fewer and fewer reasons to consider it.

Nearly every previously justifiable reason to avoid Flash has been addressed. For example, HTML will automatically "flow" as you change your margins. Although Flash can be set to scale, it's not terribly useful as text gets tiny when the window shrinks. People tend to design their Flash apps to a fixed window size (which is certainly easiest). However, Flash has an onResize event for which you can write code that rearranges the screen—effectively behaving like HTML. Other show-stopper limits of Flash have been addressed, such as making content accessible to people with a variety of disabilities (covered briefly in Chapter 2). My point here is that before you avoid Flash for a specific reason, make sure the issue hasn't been addressed.

Finally, one of the most subtle solutions Flash can deliver is putting content in a branded display. If all you want to display is a video clip, for example, you can choose from a variety of solutions. However, only Flash makes it possible to completely control the look and feel of the interface. (You could argue this is bad because the user would have to "learn" your interface—but only if you do something unorthodox or unintuitive.) Actually, users will always see "About Macromedia Flash Player" if they right-click—but that's it. Every other attribute of the viewing experience can include your branded look. Branding is an almost subconscious way to emphasize a message.

One last note about where Flash fits in. There's a new home for your Flash applications called Macromedia Central. In a nutshell, Central is a browser that just plays Flash movies. There are additional features and capabilities that you don't get in browser-based Flash movies when they run in the Central desktop player. Additional features are supported, such as background tasks (for instance, check a stock price even when the user isn't actively using your app) and the ability to deliver a compelling experience even while offline. Finally, Central provides an easy way for you to distribute your applications (and charge for them if you want). Central pops up in several places throughout this book, but not in its own chapter. The reason is that a Central app is really just a Flash app that was designed for and deployed using Central. Anyway, check it out—I guarantee it will be the next big thing provided someone makes a killer app for it.

Glossary

Generally glossaries go in the *back* of a book so that you only have to look up definitions to words you don't know. However, I've already used words that I think need some explanation. It's not that I think you haven't heard "scalable," but people use that word for several different meanings. This mini-glossary will help you talk the talk, and it can help you understand me. I'm just trying to relay information in this book, and the more you understand my terms the better. Plus, I can poke fun at a few catchphrases.

Places or Times

Client side Code that executes on the user's machine. Flash SWFs and JavaScript both run on the client side.

Server side Code that executes on your web server computer. Application server code (such as ColdFusion) is server side, as is the Flash Communication Server.

Author time or **design time** Edits you make while building an application.

Runtime When an app is running for the user.

Things

Killer app A piece of software so useful that it attracts people to adopt the underlying system needed to run it.

Rich media Audio, video, or graphics. Really just the new word for *multimedia*.

IDE (Integrated Development Environment) A software tool that gives you complete access to create and edit source files. Basically, the Flash authoring tool.

API (Application Programming Interface) The set of commands and functions that, through programming, give you access to an underlying system. For example, Flash has a Drawing API that lets you draw lines, curves, and fills, effectively giving you complete access to the drawing tools built into Flash.

SDK (Software Development Kit) The documentation, samples, and needed tools that get you started using a system. For example, you can download and study the SDK for Macromedia Central.

Technologies

Application server Software that runs on the server side that can produce custom HTML on-the-fly. Also, application servers can access local or remote databases.

Plug-ins Add-on software tools that extend the functionality of your browser.

Shockwave Director's plug-in technology. The .swf extension in Flash movies used to stand for **S**hockwave **F**lash, but now it officially stands for **s**mall **w**eb **f**ormat.

Thin client The client-side component required to run Flash movies (that is, the player). It's "thin" in that it's small enough to download quickly.

Hot Words

Scalable Two meanings. A graphic can scale to different dimensions. Also, if you plan for your application to grow, it will be considered scalable if it can handle more and more users (without collapsing).

Parse The way you can go through a set of data and extract just the elements that match the objective for which you're looking. I probably overuse this term to also mean the process of translating a set of data to some other format. For instance, going through and capitalizing each word involves a parsing process.

Collaboration Often used to describe how an application can help a group of people work together.

Legacy An existing system. Usually companies expect your new app to work with their legacy systems.

Mission critical Overused term to mean "really really—no I mean *really*—important." The idea is that if you fail to deliver the mission-critical objective, the project is doomed.

Populate Used as a verb to mean "fill in."

Some of these terms I like to make fun of, but they're still important because it's nice to have an idea what someone means when you hear the term used.

Makeovers

You don't have to just take my word for it that Flash can deliver RIAs; I'll show you it can. The following section walks you through a few examples of rich Internet apps and point out both where they succeeded and where they leave a bit to be desired.

Broadmoor Hotel

This example gets a lot of airtime from Macromedia even though it's not exactly state of the art. (It came out in 2001.) In any event, it's useful as an example of an RIA because, for one thing, people can identify with the problem it solves—namely, making a hotel reservation efficiently. If you visit www.broadmoor.com and follow links to make a reservation, you'll see a single-screen reservation tool, as shown in Figure 1.3.

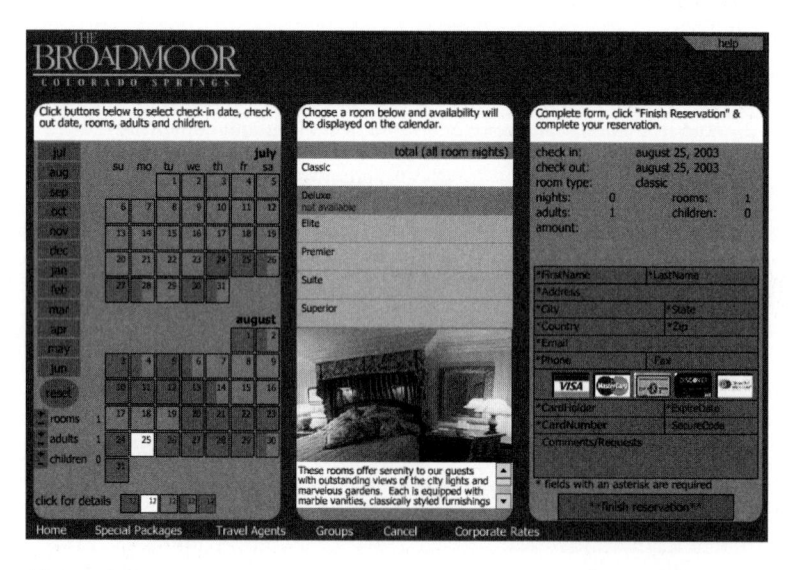

Figure 1.3 *In one screen, you can book a room at the Broadmoor Hotel.*

One key feature is that you'll never make a request only to find out the dates aren't available, because everything is updated while you make selections. When you click Date Ranges in the calendar on the left, for example, any room types unavailable for those dates are immediately removed from the list in the center. Similarly, when you select a room type, the dates for which that room is unavailable are removed from the calendar. Another cool feature is that you're given a photo of the room right inside this interface. The icons provide another subtle, but useful visual clue (statuses such as available, unavailable, or available for a checkout date only). Finally, you can pay for the room and complete the reservation from the column on the right. Unlike some particularly frustrating sites, you won't fill in a form only to be told you're missing key information (and then have to fill it in again). You never leave this "oneScreen" interface (as it's called by the developer iHotelier.com).

Although this example doesn't include a "before and after," if you've ever made any sort of reservation online, I'm sure you can appreciate some of the advantages of this interface. Note, however, a legitimate criticism of the Broadmoor example: The text is hard to read. If they would have only had the Flash 2004 Alias text option, I think it would have looked a lot better.

XML News Aggregator

Macromedia has been great at deploying useful Internet apps (using Flash) for their own needs. The registration form to their MAX conference provides an excellent example. So does the DevNet Exchange, where you can search and display a variety of extensions to Macromedia products. The only problem with these examples is that rarely are non-RIA versions available for comparison.

The XML News Aggregator is a good example to study, too, because it has both an HTML and Flash version. These two versions of the same tool gather headlines from a variety of Macromedia-related weblogs (also called *blogs*). This app enables you to scan just the headlines, with various icons identifying attributes of the story, and to link to read more (see Figure 1.4).

You can check out the HTML version yourself at www.markme.com/mxna. This version is perfectly useful. In fact, the text display can be easier to read and more transferable if you try copying. In this example, however, the HTML version can't be customized very much. About all you can do is limit the list to articles in a single category.

The Flash version drops the "Macromedia" because you can actually customize it to import and display feeds from anyone's blog (provided the blogger has an RDF syndicated version and uses standard tags—more about RDF in Chapter 6). Figure 1.5 shows what the Flash version looks like.

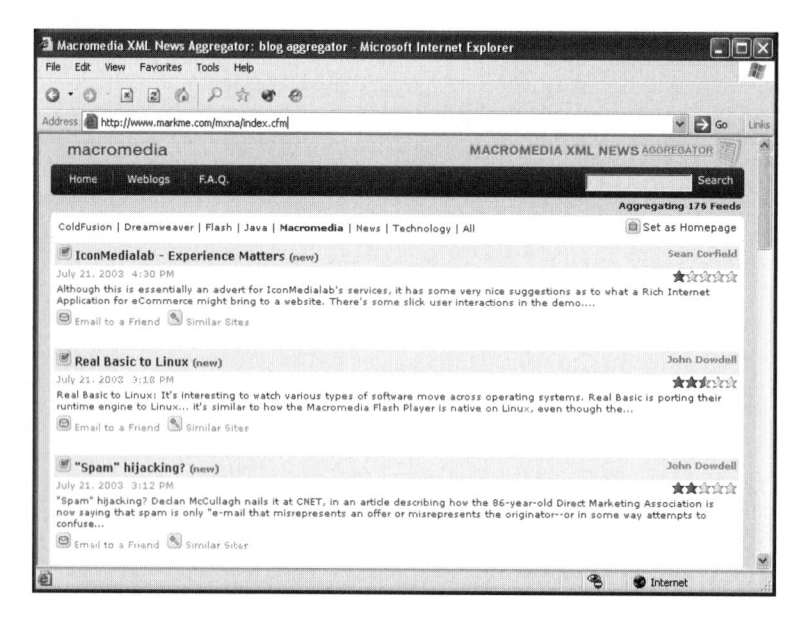

Figure 1.4 *The HTML version of Macromedia XML News Aggregator is nice, but it lacks the features found in its Flash counterpart.*

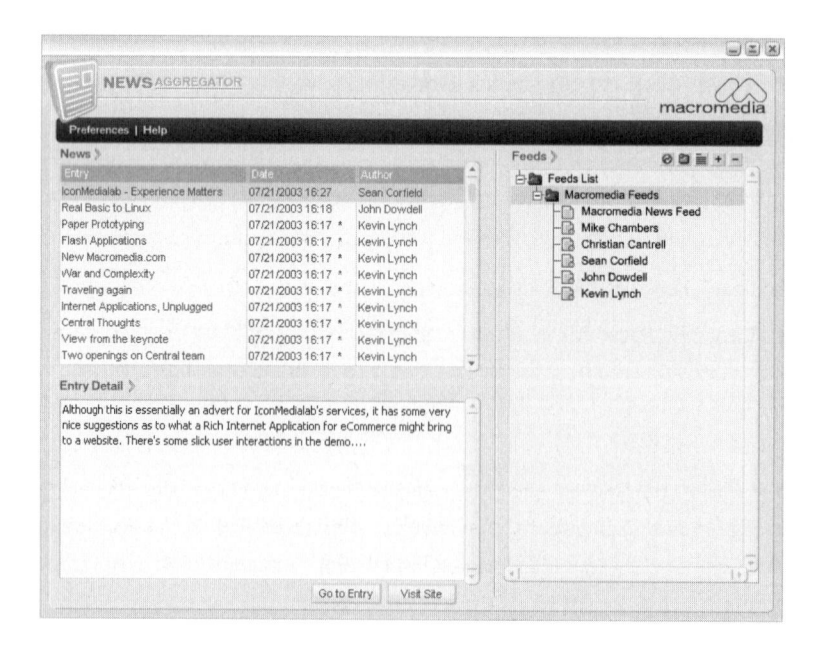

Figure 1.5 *The all-Flash News Aggregator enables you to customize which blogs to monitor.*

This version doesn't really include much "rich" media. However, a few attributes do stick out. First, several animated icons appear while the app is busy downloading. Just seeing the animation tells you the app is working. Also, the entire display's colors, fonts, and layout are presented exactly as the designer wanted. For example, there were no restrictions on what typeface to use like there is when using HTML. On top of this, the layout will look the *same* on any machine using Flash. Finally, the Tree component was used represent a hierarchy of nested folders in a space-efficient manner.

Overall, the Flash version uses space more efficiently. If they had gone further, they would have let users arrange and resize the different panes. Keep in mind, however, that you can actually pick through the code for this application because it's included in Macromedia DRK 3 (Developer Resource Kit—a quarterly CD-ROM available by subscription or individual purchase). Finally, realize that this app is the real thing: I can use it to monitor several blogs that follow without actually surfing anywhere.

Stampede Cattle

The following example highlights an application I built to extend an existing HTML-based cattle auction site with a real-time auction component. That is, they had and still have an "eBay-like" auction site where buyers can explore the catalog of available cattle. Buyers can place bids in advance and, eventually, the cows will go to the highest bidder. Naturally, this can take several days. My client had planned the real-time auction long before the Flash Communication Server (FCS) was available. It was like a product made for their application. What I built with the server-side developer was a Flash app that serves as a virtual sales ring. You're welcome to attend a live auction at www.stampedecattle.com (see Figure 1.6).

Bidders still place bids in advance using the existing HTML site (and the highest pre-bid shows up during the live auction). Then on the day of an auction, you can enter the Flash interface and see each lot go up for sale. The auctioneer makes a few last-minute announcements and JPGs of the cattle show up in the ring. Then the clock starts ticking. Buyers can place bids, and everyone sees the state from which the bid arrives. It *feels* like a real auction because you'll often see a buyer from one state trying to outbid another. There are a bunch of other features, including an auditing feature that archives every auction. In addition, the auctioneer has a different view of the application—one with more details, such as a list of connected buyers. It's a kick to watch (which you're welcome to do by logging on as a spectator). To me, the most amazing part is the sheer volume of cattle involved. Each sale that lasts about 1 hour involves about $3 million in cattle!

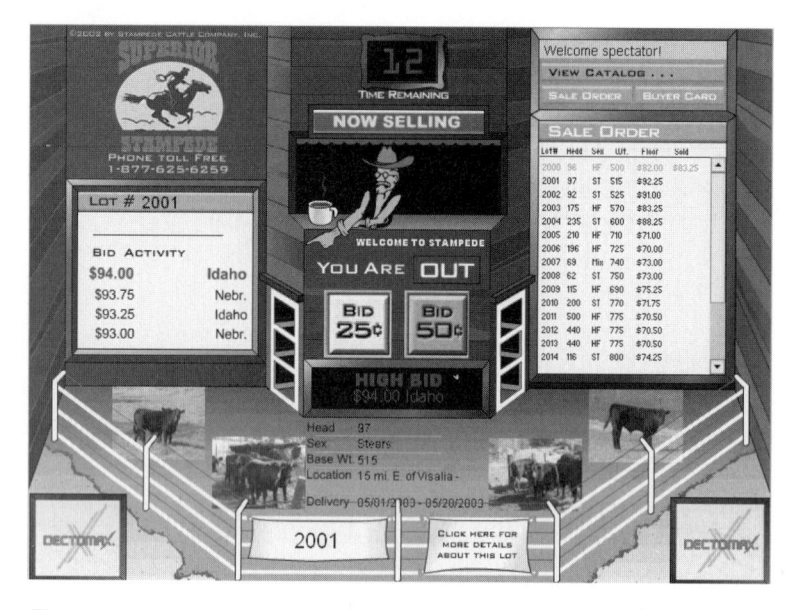

Figure 1.6 *While keeping the look and excitement of a real auction, Stampede Cattle can move $3 million worth of cattle in a matter of hours (without getting their hands dirty).*

I wanted to point out this example because it's not a case where we tried to replace an existing site. This app is integrated with what they already had. We used Flash where it could do something unique—specifically, enable bidders to connect to the same set of data and to be notified of changes in real time. There was a fair bit of audio and animation, too. Although these may seem gratuitous, in fact the goal is to engage the user. It's no secret the objective is to encourage bids. A live auction has a lot of emotion, so by adding a sense of urgency with sound effects and timing we made this app effective.

Summary

I hope you enjoyed this tour demonstrating why RIAs, why now, and why this book. I realize that I don't have to convince many of you that it's going to be cool building all these rich apps with Flash. I take it that reading this book is your commitment to that end. However, it's also useful to consider these issues because you may be called on to convince someone else—or even justify your existence in a project. The next chapter discusses specific consideration when designing an application. Just remember, however, that you can still learn a lot from a subject that may not apply directly to your current project.

{Chapter 2}

Designing Flash Applications

You probably already have some ideas for the rich Internet applications you plan to build. (Even if you don't, you'll get lots of ideas throughout this book.) Obviously, a lot steps are required between an idea and a finished app. Many people have great ideas, but only some can turn those into reality. For example, it's not surprising when someone says, "Oh, that invention! I thought of that years ago." Well, it's the person who goes and does it who succeeds. In any event, this book may not turn you into a go-getter, but it should definitely help map the way to your destination. And this chapter in particular will help you clarify your goal and confirm that it's valid, attainable, and has a high likelihood of success.

The guidelines and considerations you find in this chapter should be addressed at the start of designing any rich media application. This chapter covers the following topics:

- Learn to identify and evaluate the benefits you expect your app will provide.
- Learn to select the right tool for the job.
- Address all kinds of fundamental usability issues, including accessibility by people with various disabilities.
- Consider different deployment alternatives, including targeting so-called occasionally connected computers (OCCs) with Macromedia Central.

It's not so much that this chapter answers the question "do I really have a good idea?" (although it can). Instead, it answers "what can I do to ensure success?"

Identifying the User Benefit

Your application must justify itself by providing a specific benefit. This is often called the *value proposition*—that is, exactly what value it proposes to provide. It's fine to make a Macromedia Flash movie that "looks cool"—it just wouldn't be an "application." Justifying an app using the return on investment (ROI) approach is often easiest, but not all viable applications have a direct or measurable economic value. For example, some of the best email applications are free. Anyway, all this talk about value does tend to overlook what *should* be your primary focus: the user benefit.

Identifying what the user who experiences your application will gain is really key. Naturally, although you still need to justify your investment in building an application, if you forget to start with the user, your application will surely suffer. This section considers some of the ways to evaluate your application idea while keeping focused on the user.

Objectives

An easy way to formalize how your application will benefit the user is just to list the objectives you intend to solve. Here are just a few ideas of worthy objectives:

- The app will give users a faster way to select a restaurant for dinner.
- The app will enable our salespeople to create a customized catalog for their customers instead of making one catalog for everyone.
- The app will sell used furniture to the highest bidder in a realistic and engaging auction atmosphere that becomes more popular than our brick-and-mortar auctions.

Naturally, when you get to the nitty-gritty specifications of your application, you must include more detail. These are more general.

An interesting way to phrase these objectives is in such a way that they answer a follow-up question: compared to what? That is, "A quicker way to select a restaurant…compared to what? Quicker than picking via the Yellow Pages? The web? Faster than playing rock-scissor-paper? The first objective could be expanded to "a more efficient way to select a restaurant than reading menus posted on their front windows." This example also changes the meaning of the objective. As you put your objectives to the test, you'll find that you not only clarify them, but also change them sometimes, too.

In the case of objectives, you don't want ambiguous goals or empty promises. For example, this objective is too vague: My app will make it fun to go to the dentist. It doesn't say *how*. Here's one that exhibits a classic fallacy called a *bogus claim*: My app will help travelers identify the best restaurant in town. First, there's no way to measure what's "best," and, second, it's vague. Although these bad examples are fun to consider, just remember to avoid tricks and fallacies. By following the advice in this section, you can eliminate uncertainty and phrase objectives in such a way that they help you consider alternatives to your app (discussed later in this section).

Measuring Success

The more time you spend identifying objectives, the more time you will save when it comes to deciding how to measure success. After all, you measure success by seeing how close you got to your objectives. If your objective is to reduce printing costs, for example, you measure success by taking the difference between the original costs and post-application costs. Usually it isn't quite as easy as "take original costs minus new costs," so that's why you clarify.

Even though you won't actually measure success until after you deliver, it's important to have a plan in place before you start. For one thing, it serves as a guide as you build. You can periodically return to what you consider a success and see whether you think you're going in the right direction. It's not as though you can plan a project and then just do it—you'll need to make adjustments as you go (at least that's my experience). A set of objectives and measuring tools serve as a compass keeping you pointed in the right direction. Having said this, you don't want to blindly follow your objectives despite information revealed as you're building. However, you can get pretty bogged down by trying to solve every problem you encounter. Even if such problems are worthy of resolution, sometimes it's best to put them aside. During a tight production, for instance, it may make perfect sense to say, "We're not going to address that issue. Although it might be nice, it's not a stated goal for our app." This isn't a cop-out; instead, it is a realistic way to ensure projects get finished.

Another reason you need a plan in effect before you start is that you want a baseline measurement to which you can compare. If you're trying to see costs go down, you had better have a record of the current costs. You might say "no duh"—but remember this point if you need to convince others that it's important to identify your plan ahead of time.

Success doesn't have to be totally monetary. For example, a goal might be to reduce calls to your company's support staff. You could measure success by counting calls or even timing the duration of each call. Here I'm just trying to give you ideas on ways to measure success. The thing is, it really just depends on your application. And, ultimately, there are some things you just can't measure, such as how "good" you application is. If your goal is to make a better user experience, it can be difficult to measure (but just as important as anything). Keeping a practical eye on measuring success, however, is always a good idea.

Considering Alternatives

As great as your idea may be, alternatives always exist. Alternatives include competitive applications, variations of the solution you have in mind, and even nothing. (I love the "status quo" alternative because I'm already done!) Seriously, you want to make sure your solution offers something the alternatives don't. Notice I didn't say "you want your app to be the best alternative." Although being the best is nice, there's also a place for the fastest, the cheapest, or even the most popular. You just want to make sure your app has a marked benefit in some area.

A good place to start considering alternatives is to look at the status quo. No doubt your user is already doing something related to what your app will do. I think it's quite likely your solution will be different. Keep in mind that even if you know your app will be better, users will have to switch *from* whatever they're doing. Often applications are intended to be used on a regular basis. It becomes doubly hard to get potential users to switch from whatever they're doing because they have to invest some learning. Also, you might be asking them to change a routine, and habits are hard to break. By the way, don't think your app is immune from this requirement if "the boss" is just going to order employees to use the new app. That really isn't enough if you want it to be successful—they have to *want* to use it.

It sounds bad, but you can often draw people to your app by identifying something they dislike in the existing solution. This is not unlike how negative campaigning works (for better or worse) in politics. Here it's not so personal when you say "don't you hate the way you have to do all this stuff in the existing app?" They say necessity is the mother of invention; well, so is dissatisfaction.

Some applications have more than just the status quo to worry about. Public applications have to compete on the open market. In fact, this is the main reason why custom applications are easier to justify. If you have visions of becoming rich delivering the next killer app, you must carefully consider the alternatives. Keep in mind, however, that you can succeed in many different ways, including popularity or availability. The history of technology is littered with countless "better" ideas that failed because of poor distribution. I'm not suggesting that your app can be lacking in a major way if you just compensate by being popular. More to the point: Your app can succeed for a variety of reasons. It's best to identify what makes yours different from the competition.

Considering we're talking about rich *Internet* applications (RIAs), you can best discover your competitors on the web. Without this sounding too much like a pep talk, I do want to encourage you to still consider your project even if you find something that appears to offer the same thing your app does. If I didn't follow that advice when writing this book, for example, I would have stopped long ago when I heard of others on the same topic. The thing is, I don't necessarily think that *this* book is better than any of the competition. I do know it's different, however, because it offers my perspective. In the case of your app, study the competition. Don't fool yourself into thinking that anything they do, you can do better. But clearly identify what makes your app different. If you really do find a duplicate to your idea, then, yes, move on to something else (or even consider teaming up with them). Luckily, we're not yet at the stage where software is a commodity—there's plenty of room for everyone's personal variations.

Finally, one advantage we have when comparing to alternatives is that most existing applications don't use Flash. That makes our apps easy to differentiate. However, it also brings out the question as to whether there are more appropriate alternative technologies. (This chapter covers other available tools and technologies, in case you think Flash may not be the best solution for your application.) Also, most likely, your competition isn't Flash. Not that you can't find poorly implemented Flash examples, but there are even more using standard technologies (mainly HTML). Hopefully, your app will offer more than just a spiced-up version of something else. That said, the following section covers how to rationalize the spice you do decide to add.

Rationalizing "Rich Media"

Within the term *rich Internet applications*, *rich* refers to rich media such as graphics, sounds, animation, and video. The cost of such media runs deep. Although intuitively this means RIAs take longer to download, you can actually make the opposite argument. A well-built Flash interface can both cover up such downloads (making them unnoticeable) and reduce refreshes (and download less media than a conventional application that keeps reloading content into the browser—for example, when updating the price of a product you're configuring). Although such arguments are indeed valid, there does come a point where rich media does mean longer downloads (and higher costs from your Internet service provider host).

If the question were only a matter of file size, this discussion could just move on to how to compress and stream media. In fact, other costs apply. For one, the production cost for rich media is almost always greater than traditional alternatives. Actually, because there's not really an "alternative" to video, the alternative costs nothing. In any event, illustrations, graphics, photographs, video, audio—they all cost money to produce. And if you're thinking of using clip art, just remember there's not only a cost of licensing the material, but you have to search for the appropriate clip. (Of course, you might find a free clip, but it might not perfectly match your message or it might look cliché when people recognize an overused image.) I don't mean to sound like Scrooge, however; I do recognize the value of rich media. Make sure your cost analysis includes both the price and the value. Luckily the most valuable asset in most RIAs is data—presumably data you either own or intend to offer in a new or unique form.

Finally, the last cost I want to mention is how the app affects the user experience. For example, does the world really need a text editor that makes a different sound effect for every key press? Gratuitous special effects can be cute the first time, but they become really tiresome over time. For every video, sound, and even every pixel in the interface, you really ought to ask whether it's really necessary and whether it adds or distracts from your message. I'm not joking about every pixel. The information design guru Edward Tufte developed the term *chart junk* to refer to superfluous graphics added to graphs. This term is even more appropriate for computer screens because screens have so little room for data. (For example, a 1024×768 screen has less resolution than a wallet-sized photo.) The point is, because we live in a finite world, justify every item you add to it.

I wish I had more specific rules for you to follow when you identify the user benefit. Just keep in mind that it's good to question the validity of every item in your app—perhaps more so during the initial stages because you have more opportunity to fix it. It's not like you're being cheap. If it helps, think of yourself as an advocate for the user.

Selecting Technologies

The tremendous variety of new technologies related to Flash apps are very exciting. To keep current, you have to casually study everything but nothing in depth until you're ready to use it. The reason not to study everything in depth is that you'd never finish (or by the time you did, the technology would be supplanted). This section looks at ways to approach the current state of the art as well as how to keep an eye on the future.

When analyzing a new tool or technology, it's important to think about positioning. That is, how would it fit into your project? How could it have helped you in a past project? Or, perhaps, how would someone using it actually use it. Consider the new CSS style sheet support in Macromedia Flash MX 2004, for instance. I can sum up that feature in two words: text formatting. The point is that although the description doesn't really do it justice, it's enough for now. It's sort of like you want to pigeonhole the technology and move on. Then, if later a need arises, you should be able to remember the appropriate technology. Ideally the order is that you first have a need, and then select a tool. However, you won't really know what tools are available unless they're familiar.

It's easy to fall into the trap of designing a project around the available tools. Although Flash MX 2004 includes a "loading" progress bar component, for instance, please don't add some huge media file just to use it. That's backward. It's fine to say I want this huge media file (for whatever justifiable reason) and then recall a new progress bar is available. That is, instead of grabbing a hammer and looking for a nail, it's fine to recall hammers are available if you happen to come across a nail. I already mentioned the issue of justifying every piece of media, and that advice applies here, too.

The following three sections cover the state of the art in an attempt to pigeonhole everything. Don't worry if the descriptions seem terse; the next chapter—Chapter 3, "Technology Overview"—is dedicated to getting into the details of the technologies covered in this book. Right now, however, the focus is on placement.

Tools

The Flash family needs a minivan. It's not just "Macromedia Flash" anymore. There's Flash MX 2004, Flash MX 2004 Professional, Flash Remoting, Flash Communication Server, and Macromedia Central. Then there's Breeze and even Breeze Live. And that's just the Flash family. Check it out. The following table lays it all out, albeit with few details.

Flash MX 2004	The upgrade to Flash MX. It's the tool used to create Flash animations and applications. (Lots of great additions over Flash MX.)
Flash MX 2004 Professional	The same as Flash 2004 except additional features, including external Flash Video creation, the project panel for workgroups, a standalone script editor, additional data integration components, and screens (forms/slides) that basically enable you to author without the timeline visible.
Flash Remoting	A way to send data to and from application servers over an optimized binary protocol called AMF (Action Message Format). In addition, data is automatically parsed so that, for example, database queries arrive as a Flash object. (Flash, by itself, can exchange HTTP data and Flash Pro can handle the SOAP format.)
Flash Communication Server	A standalone server to which your Flash-created SWFs can make persistent connections (allowing real-time interaction with others) that are optimized to both record and transmit live or recorded audio/video streams. Probably Macromedia's coolest product ever.
Macromedia Central	Almost like a replacement to the browser but designed to only display Flash movies and web data. Features unavailable in browsers include special on/offline features for occasionally connected users, support for collaborative data sharing (between different apps), and direct support for outside web services. Depending on how many people jump on this, it may become Macromedia's coolest product ever.
Breeze	Both a tool and a service. The tool converts a Microsoft PowerPoint presentation into a Flash movie and enables you to add audio and chapter delineations. Users can watch your Breeze presentation online (on a hosted or dedicated server). Additional navigation tools enable users to pause, play, and jump to different chapters in the presentation.

Breeze Live	A turnkey application built with Flash Communication Server to enable rich online meetings. It's a very well-thought-out application with tons of useful features. If nothing else, it proves what's possible with Flash Communication Server.
Dreamweaver	A text editor. Sounds funny, but that's all it produces! Granted, there are a million related features that make editing, previewing, and deploying powerful web pages easier.
Fireworks	A raster graphics editor. Although Fireworks uses a native format of PNG (to include additional data such as layers), it can export any common raster graphic, including JPG, GIF, and BMP. In addition, it has lots of web-centric tools, such as JavaScript rollovers, and features to integrate well with other Macromedia products. (It competes with Adobe Photoshop, although they're different tools.)
Freehand	A vector graphics program. Freehand has its roots in print, where it directly competes with Adobe Illustrator. Although Flash will import graphics from either tool, it's usually better to re-create the artwork in Flash. This can be an extra investment of time but can also reduce file size.
Application Server (including ColdFusion)	A web server (configured and connected so that people can browse to it) that delivers customized pages based on a programming language. Instead of creating static pages by hand, an application server can dynamically create pages on-the-fly.
JavaScript	A client-side scripting language because it interacts with the user's browser. JavaScript is appropriate for triggering pop-up windows and a couple other tasks that Flash can't do on its own. The good news is JavaScript is nearly identical to Flash's ActionScript.
Java	Basically, just a programming language. When it runs on the client side, it's unduly complex, intrusive, and—frankly—no better than Flash. When running on an application server, however, it can be transparent to the user and as powerful as the programmer makes it. Like ColdFusion, it can process client requests and then return customized pages on-the-fly. Any backend technology (including Java) can include Flash on the front end. (Backend being the web server, and front end being the user's browser.)

It turns out this table mainly covers stuff considered in this book. (Well, we won't really get into Java and the backend stuff—only how Flash ties in.) Obviously, other solutions compete with Flash. Nothing is truly equivalent, however, so just understand what Flash can do and you'll be able to appropriately compare.

Media Formats

Assuming you've rationalized all the costs of adding a particular media element (as discussed earlier), you still have to make a decision as to exactly what format to use. The decision you make affects your production approach, the deployment mechanism, and—most importantly—the user experience. The following three tables cover considerations when making a media selection for graphics, video, and audio, respectively.

Raster Graphics

Generally, these are appropriate when the nature of the image cannot be drawn using vector tools (like in Flash); for example, product images or photographs. On the same note, they tend to be larger than vector graphics, so only use them when appropriate.

Graphics Format	Production Concerns	Delivery Concerns	User Experience
GIF, PCT, BMG, PNG	Use library properties to compress during export (JPG) or leave lossless (PNG/GIF).	File size is inversely proportional to quality.	Only PNG supports transparency.
JPG (imported)	Select Library Properties, use imported data, or you'll recompress.	File size is inversely proportional to quality (but JPG is usually the most efficient).	Effective compression for continuous-tone images.
JPG (external)	Can't view until you test. FLAs remain small, and you can replace images any time without using Flash.	Modularity means the download is distributed over time.	Timely downloads mean delays are spread out, although forcing a long initial download is sometimes desirable.

Audio

Music and sound effects can add a dimension of realism (especially when subtle). Sound also tends to trigger emotional responses. Start with the highest quality possible and don't fall for the fallacy that lower quality is acceptable for voice. If the content is naturally occurring (like a human voice), users have a clear idea how it *should* sound, so they'll more likely notice when it sounds bad. In any case, there's only one tool to judge audio quality: your ear.

Audio Format	Production Concerns	Delivery Concerns	User Experience
WAV, AIF	No significant differences; however, you should *always* import the highest quality possible and let Flash do the compression.	Only use the Library property Raw for high-quality desktop applications; otherwise, use MP3 or voice based on experimentation.	Only timeline sounds will be progressively downloaded. (A sound object requires everything to be downloaded first.)
MP3 (imported)	Ideally the MP3 compression is done effectively, because you don't want to recompress in Flash.	Like JPG, be sure to always use imported MP3 quality (instead of recompressing).	Only timeline sounds will be progressively downloaded. (A sound object requires everything to be downloaded first.)
MP3 (external)	Nice because your FLA files remain small and you can swap out audio files later.	The `loadSound()` option for stream means sounds will progressively download.	Even better than external JPGs; you can hear a sound while it downloads.
MP3 (streamed)	Requires Flash Communication Server for both testing and delivery.	Can't distribute as standalone app unless you're sure of the Internet connection (and you open your server to outside connections).	Even better than regular MP3 streaming because it's *true* streaming (not just progressive), meaning you can seek and experience much better performance.
MIDI (external)	Requires a proxy sound because you won't hear the real MIDI until you deliver.	Only works on hand-held devices such as PocketPC.	MIDI is tiny, but PocketPCs may not fit in your pocket protector.

Video

There's nothing like video. When you want to demonstrate how an expert performs a task, only video will do. Also, live video interaction is unique. Do ask yourself, however, whether the content really warrants video—because not only does it mean more bandwidth, but also more constant attention from the user.

Video Format	Production Concerns	Delivery Concerns	User Experience
MOV, AVI, MPG (imported)	Besides occasional compatibility issues, pretty straightforward.	Files are large, so you might consider importing into separate files to become SWFs you load via `loadMovie()`.	Quality isn't quite as good as FLV and can only progressively download.
FLV (imported)	Requires you to produce the FLV outside Flash, meaning that you need a third-party tool as well as the video encoder that ships with Flash Pro or, for the best quality, use Sorenson Squeeze. In fact, you can record local streams from your webcam to make FLVs using the free production version of Flash Communication Server, but this isn't appropriate for content such as movies.	Same as imported MOV, AVI, MPG.	Can expect better quality.
FLV (streamed)	Requires you to produce the FLV outside Flash (either with a third-party tool or Flash Communication Server).	Must be streamed from Flash Communication Server.	More important than quality (which can be great); you can truly stream the video (as opposed to progressively download).

Chapters 9, "Advanced Communication Server," and 10, "Production Techniques," cover the Flash Communication Server (which is the only way to stream media into Flash). Notice that the preceding discussion didn't include general media elements such as animation or text. Countless books have been written about how to employ these—here the focus is on the "rich media."

Deployment

It is impossible to discuss the topic of media selection without mentioning deployment. Depending on how you're planning to delivery your project, certain issues may become more or less important. If you're delivering on a CD-ROM, for instance, you probably don't care so much whether a video is 100MB. On the web, however, that would take upward of an hour to download even on the fastest connections.

This section briefly covers the common delivery options. Although this book doesn't cover all of these topics in detail, you definitely want to think about where you're headed as you design your app. For example, I had a client who wanted to convert a 50MB CD-ROM project to run on the web. It wasn't impossible, but my task would certainly have been easier had I known this objective early on.

In an ideal world, the deployment stage can be equivalent to licking an envelope and stamping it. That is, a well-planned and well-built app can be quickly converted from the production and testing format to the final delivery format. It *should* be a painless process.

Here is a series of questions regarding deployment that can help you both design an application and help you see options not previously considered.

Will the App Be Run in the Browser or as a Standalone Projector?

If in a browser...

What version of Flash will you require?

What window size do you plan to use (and required user screen resolution), or do you want your app to be resizable?

If standalone...

Do you want it to work on both Mac and Windows?

What platform-specific features do you plan to use (for example, printing, writing preferences, copying files, and standard dialog boxes are all unique to the operating system)?

Will it have connected features? (That is, does it require an Internet connection?)

Will the connection need to be persistent, or will you only need to connect periodically (say, to download updates)?

These are just the sorts of questions you can ask as you design your app. You can ask more. And it's not like you're being pushy; after all, they have to be answered eventually. When asked something such as whether they want it to work on Mac or Windows, most clients answer "both." That's fine, but no matter how you answer, it will affect your design and production plan.

The preceding questions aren't really loaded—there's no right answer. For any question that's a "yes," however, consider the addition suggestions in the following sections.

Building for the Browser

If your app isn't restricted to the browser, you're given more privileges to make changes to the user's computer. Although this means a malicious developer could do harm (making a wary user less likely to run it), it usually just means you're given more latitude to do things, such as display data downloaded from any web site. In a browser, Flash can only tap into data residing on the same domain. Additional restrictions are lifted when you deploy a standalone projector. One big disadvantage of standalone apps, however, is that the user must download the EXE. (You'll learn how Macromedia Central solves this issue later in this chapter.)

An in-browser application can either pop up to a preset size (via the JavaScript `window.open()` command) or just reside in whatever-size window the user's browser is set to. When popping up, you have the option to prevent the user from resizing (by setting `Resize` to `0`). What this all comes down to is the question of screen size. When laying out your application, it's easiest to just pick a screen size and stick with it (carefully considering what screen size your users can accommodate). I recommend against making a Flash app that's taller than the HTML page, one that requires the user to scroll to view all the content (see Figure 2.1). Instead, if you need more vertical space, create a scrolling mechanism inside Flash. Incidentally, you can only ensure no scrollbars appear if you're doing a pop-up window (and you don't pop open a window taller than the user's screen height).

Figure 2.1 *If you make your app taller than the HTML window, users may not know to scroll down for more content.*

{ Note }

Pop-Up Script For your reference—or in case JavaScript isn't your bailiwick—here's script you can use in one HTML file (say the home page of your site) that can pop open a fixed-size window in the center of the minimum screen resolution of 800×600:

```
1   <html><head><title>your title</title>
2   <script language="javascript">
3   <!--
4   function launch(){
5     if(screen.height>=600){
6       popup(450,550,"app.html");
7     }else{
8       alert("You need to be running 800x600 or greater.");
9     }
10  }
```

continues

```
11  function popup(width, height, filename){
12      var left = (screen.width - width) / 2;
13      var top = (screen.height - height) / 2;
14      var attributes= "left=" + left    +
15                     ", top=" + top     +
16                     ", width=" + width +
17                     ", height=" + height +",";
18      attributes+="toolbar=0,location=0,directories=0,";
19      attributes+="status=0,menubar=0,scrollbars=0,";
20      attributes+="resizable=0";
21      window.open(filename,"appwindow",attributes);
22  }
23  //-->
24  </script>
25  </head>
26  <body>
27  <a href="#" onClick="launch()"> launch </a>
28  </body></html>
```

The idea is your main app is app.html, but first you want to check whether users are running 800×600 or greater (line 5). Then, you just figure out the center of the screen and pop open a window (line 21) with nearly every attribute set to 0 (lines 14–20). The trigger is a hyperlink on line 25. This code is just a start; you can modify it for additional features.

By the way, you also can let your Flash app open other windows directly. Just include the popup() function in the JavaScript portion of the file that houses your Flash app (say, app.html). Then, inside your Flash movie use a variation of this code:

```
getURL("javascript:popup('300', '300', 'somefile.html')");
```

Finally, it's possible to let the user resize the screen and make your adapt on-the-fly. I'm not talking about having Flash scale, because that makes small text illegible (although letting it scale is easier than what I show next). Basically, there's an event triggered called onResize(), and you just write code to respond accordingly. The idea is easy: When the user resizes, your code rearranges things onscreen. Doing it well can be quite involved, depending on what you are displaying. Here's a quick example: Suppose that when the user resizes the browser, you want your content to remain at 100 percent except for four graphic borders that should always fill the browser (as shown in Figure 2.2).

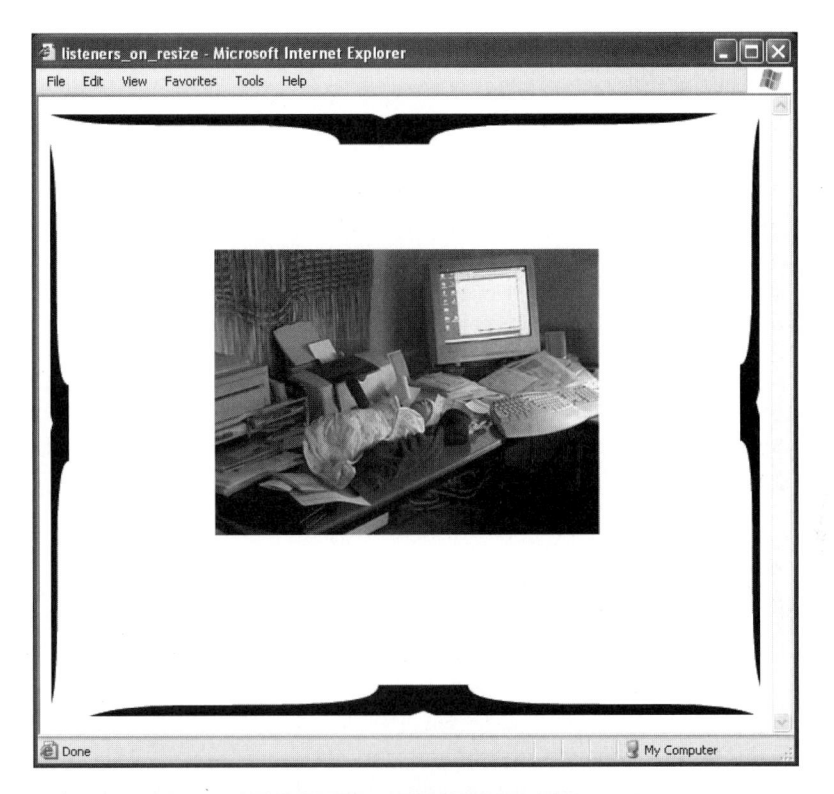

Figure 2.2 *Trapping* onResize() *means your app can change layouts as the user resizes the browser.*

First, you need to use the No Scale setting either in your HTML Publish settings or with this line of code:

```
Stage.scaleMode="noScale";
```

Then you set up a listener, as follows:

```
myListener = new Object();
myListener.onResize = reDisplay;
Stage.addListener(myListener);
```

My `reDisplay()` function is defined here. Notice that I use `Stage.height` and `Stage.width` to display the borders. (Stage properties are only accurate when you are using noScale.)

```
startWidth=400;
startHeight=400;
function reDisplay(){
  left_mc._height=Stage.height;
  left_mc._x=(startWidth-Stage.width)/2;
  right_mc._height=Stage.height;
  right_mc._x=(startWidth+Stage.width)/2;
  top_mc._width=Stage.width;
  top_mc._y=(startHeight-Stage.height)/2;
  bottom_mc._width=Stage.width;
  bottom_mc._y=(startHeight+Stage.height)/2;
}
```

The two keys to redisplaying your screen are setting up a listener that knows when the user resizes and accessing the `Stage.width` and `Stage.height` properties to ascertain the new size. With this information, you can do complex rearranging such as having a button bar that adapts to the width or even changes from vertical to horizontal as appropriate.

Distributing Standalone Applications

If you think you've got a lot of deployment questions to answer when building for the browser, you're right! In many ways, standalone applications are easier because you rarely worry about file size or browser incompatibility. However, the mere number of options available is a bit overwhelming. You know every EXE ever built? Well, you can pretty much do anything they can. This discussion covers the options in a general manner, instead of taking a detailed look at every possibility.

The basic way to distribute an application as a projector is just to embed the Flash Player into your SWF. It's done automatically from an option in the Publish settings. The only funky part is that creating a Mac projector on Windows compresses it as BinHex (HQX), whereas making a Windows projector from Mac zips (ZIP) it. This makes file transfers to and from the different operating systems possible—although you'll want to uncompress it on the target platform for final delivery.

The two significant "extra" features you can include when distributing a Flash projector are the ability to go full screen and a quit feature (not applicable in the browser). To make your app go full screen, just use this code:

```
fscommand("fullscreen", true);
```

This is great if you build a presentation in Flash, because it hides the desktop and taskbar. In addition, if you want it to go full screen but not to scale (that is, just mask out the desktop), you can add the following command:

```
fscommand("allowscale", false);
```

If you're not the only one running this app (that is, if you're distributing it), you probably want to include something that executes `fscommand("fullscreen", false)`, because using the standard "un-full screen" key (pressing Esc) isn't intuitive. Alternatively, you can add a quit button as explained next.

To close your Flash projector, use `fscommand("quit")`. Obviously, you don't want this to execute in the first frame (wait until the user clicks the quit button instead).

Unfortunately there's not much else a Flash projector can do. However, several third-party companies have produced tools that extend what's possible with Flash projectors. These tools all involve building your app in Flash, but then, at the last stage, you build the projector using their tool. At that time, you can add additional features to your app. They also have ways for you to write ActionScript that taps into even greater capabilities. For example, I built an app that enabled users to download Acrobat files to disk. In my Flash app, users could select PDF files, and then I triggered code that presented the user with a standard Save As dialog box. Then I used still more custom code to copy the files from a CD to the specified location. With these tools, you really do have nearly limitless options available.

I've included a list of tools with which I'm familiar and have had some experience using. These are probably the most popular tools. They're all variations on the same idea, although each has its respective advantages.

- **SWF Studio** (www.northcode.com). The first in this field, SWF Studio just recently released the only Mac projector tool of its kind, called flashthing. Also, Northcode provides prompt email support.
- **Screenweaver** (www.screenweaver.com). If nothing else, the Screenweaver app itself is a model RIA—built in Flash! It really is impressive. Of course, it also has hundreds of script triggers available and some really fancy support for nonsquare or transparent applications.
- **Flash Studio Pro** (www.multidmedia.com). Similar to these other tools, except its price for personal usage is very good: free.

This book would probably spin out of control if I were to attempt to document these and the countless other third-party tools. For example, I haven't mentioned there are many tools for turning your Flash animations into screen savers. You can also find several obfuscation tools that turn your completed code into spaghetti so that others can't make sense of it if they attempt to hack into it. Finally, I also didn't mention perhaps the best projector maker with optimized performance and a complete programming language of its own: Macromedia Director MX! I guess the main point I wanted to make is that there are lots of options out there. And, RIAs definitely include desktop apps with greater richness and feature sets than in-browser apps.

If standalone apps are so great, why don't we just go study those? Mainly because of distribution. First you have to get the user to download your EXE and trust you enough to install it. Then you have to invest an effort to ensure users are using the most up-to-date revision of your product. This isn't impossible, but more traditional web apps (and Flash RIAs) avoid most of these challenges. There is one tool that blurs the delineation I've spent the last section defining, and that's Macromedia Central.

Using Macromedia Central to Target Occasionally Connected Computers (OCCs)

Macromedia Central is basically a standalone projector that gets installed on the user's machine, but with several unique properties. First, the installer is entirely contained inside the newer Flash players (version 6,0,65 or later); so, the first time a user visits a site containing a Central app, the 1MB Central projector gets installed automatically. That is, you still create your app as a Flash SWF, but it runs inside the Central projector, which is easily installed. This removes the need for users to trust your site. Also, after users download the main Central projector, they can download and install additional Central apps by just downloading the SWF. Central manages all your installed apps. Figure 2.3 shows how I can launch any of the six apps I have installed.

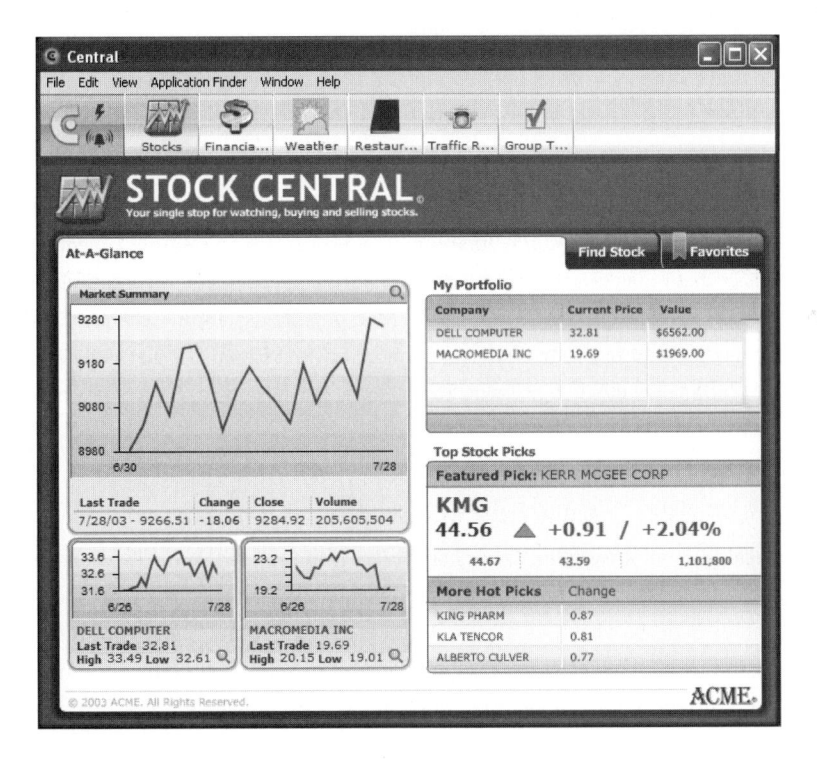

Figure 2.3 *Macromedia Central includes a button bar for quick access to any installed app.*

One of the cool ideas with Central is that a single app can have several components. For example, "pods" are like mini-apps that are small enough for users to leave visible at all times. Also, "agents" are code that runs in the background. Because Central apps can easily reach out and grab data on the Internet, a pod and agent combination can monitor a stock price (to take an overused example) and even alert you when a price reaches a certain level.

Once installed, your app lives in the company of all other installed Central apps on the user's machine. Therefore, your app should "play nice" by ensuring messages sent between agent and pod don't cross wires with other app's agents or pods. On the positive side, Central set up a vehicle that enables users to select data collected by one app (say a stock price) and send it to another app (maybe a graphing tool). Such collaborative apps offer a future where there aren't any "killer do-everything apps" (and instead just app modules that users can snap together to make their own killer app)!

Central really does offer some cool possibilities. Although it's only in its first edition now, its future will be determined by the supply of great apps. After all, Central is only a container. If developers make cool apps that everyone wants, Central will take off.

A couple more details can help you gain a perspective on Central. I mentioned earlier that projectors are given additional privileges that could certainly mean a risk to security. In the case of Central, Macromedia has enforced the same security model used in Flash. One exception is that you can also load media or data from domains outside your own. However, an app I write can't see or modify data saved by your app—unless the user consciously decides to share it. Basically, Central is Flash Player 6 (with a couple extras). So, Central is equivalent to Flash in both what it can and can't do.

Because Central is on the user's hard drive, it can run when the user is not online. Your app downloads and then, presumably, connects to the Internet. Users who've indicated they're offline will be sending an event to your app so that it doesn't bother connecting to the Internet. You can certainly do plenty of useful things if you plan your app with this in mind. A user could work on his workgroup calendar, for instance, and your app could then make updates to the data online during a synchronization process the next time he's connected.

Although there are only a few technical on/offline issues to consider, the real work is in designing your app to be interesting both on- and offline. The concept of such on/offline users is being called OCC (for occasionally connected computer). Realize that although this includes jet-set business persons with their fancy wireless Intel Centrino laptop, you can also include modem users who are occasionally connected. This increases both your potential audience and suggests new ideas for applications.

Incidentally, the vehicle to send data between separate components of your application is Flash's local connection object. Chapter 6 "Basic Data Exchange," covers this in detail. Saving preferences between sessions is handled through the local shared object (also covered in Chapter 6). The good news with these technologies and any other supported in Central is that they're basically all Flash. You can leverage your Flash skills to build Central apps.

Finally, if you do want to make a publicly available app and make money selling it, you're welcome to use Central's built-in merchant features. There's a try/buy mechanism that you can use to get people hooked during, say, a 30-day trial period. The user can pay through Central, and Macromedia will send you the money directly (after taking their cut). You don't have to use this feature, but it offers more than just a way to make money. Your app immediately has the credibility of Macromedia.com behind it (instead of the fly-by-night impression from somewhere such as phillipkerman.com). Additionally, you can register your product so that it automatically appears in Central's Application Finder tool. This way users don't have to stumble across your web site—they'll see your app listed as in Figure 2.4.

I really think Central is neat. It fits well into this book's topic—but it's only part or the RIA picture. For this reason, you won't find a separate chapter dedicated to Central. However, throughout the book I mention how Central fits in where appropriate. Here, it fits into design insofar as you need to know what's possible to design an app that's useful.

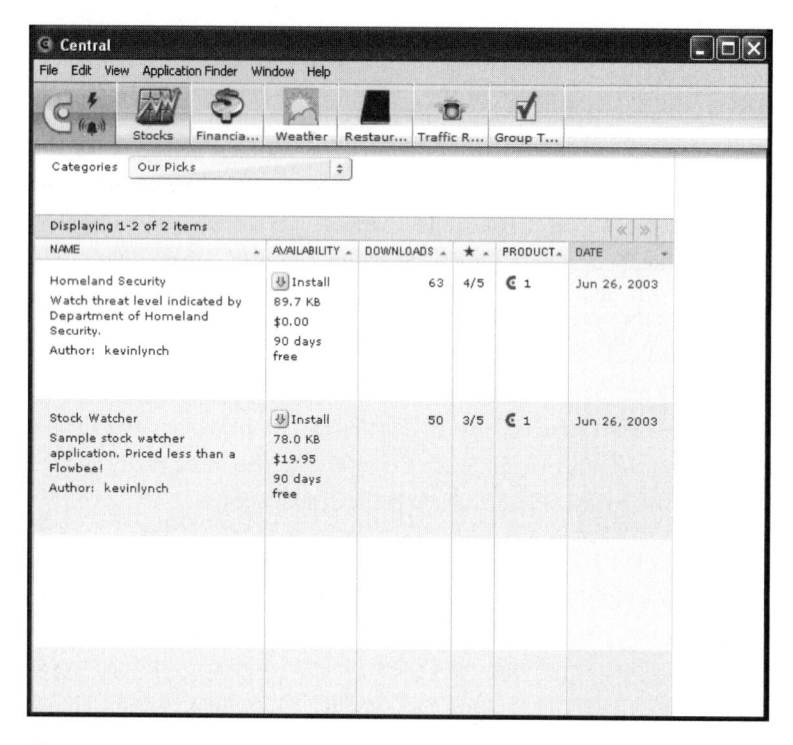

Figure 2.4 *Central's Application Finder means users have a single place they can browse for applications.*

Designing for Accessibility

Unfortunately, designing for users with reduced abilities in such areas as motor skills, vision, and hearing is considered only as an afterthought. The best time to address accessibility is early and often—that is, when you plan as well as while you're building. This section points to issues you should address while building and discusses how best to address them.

General Issues

By the way, access is not an all-or-none situation. For example, vision disabilities range from blindness to low vision to color blindness. And sometimes people are only temporarily disabled. It all boils down to the, perhaps surprising, fact that making your app more accessible will also make it more usable.

The primary limits are vision (including clarity in colors and detail), motor skills (such as using a mouse, which some people can't), and reduced hearing. The easy way to approach all of these is to recognize and avoid times when critical content is only available through one sense. If you play an audio message "click the spacebar when you're done," for example, you should repeat it with onscreen text. Most likely, however, you'll find countless cases where you only use visual clues including text for important information. Ultimately, these folks need the text read to them and images described. Luckily you don't have to provide all that audio yourself. Instead, you can just make the text and descriptions available to devices that support Microsoft Active Accessibility (MSAA)—otherwise known as screen readers.

Vision

I guess the good news is that Flash automatically provides text descriptions to screen readers of your buttons, clips, dynamic text, and input text. It also exposes your static text so that it too is readable. Unfortunately, if you've moved a movie clip off stage, you probably don't want the screen reader to describe it to the user. Ultimately you'll want to take the initiative to describe your own clips, hide specific ones, and turn on and off the descriptions using ActionScript when necessary.

Here's a quick overview. In the Accessibility panel, you can select buttons, clips, and dynamic or input text and modify their respective accessibility settings. In fact, if you have nothing selected, the panel reflects your movie's accessibility settings (see Figure 2.5). The two primary ways to use the panel is to either exclude an item from being exposed (by unchecking Make Accessible) or to override the automatic naming feature by specifying a name or description. In addition, because buttons, clips, and input text are interactive, you can have their tab index set here as well as a shortcut defined (such as Ctrl+1). (You need to write additional ActionScript to respond to the keyboard shortcuts you specify— all you're doing here is telling the users how they're supposed to access the field or button.)

Manually selecting and setting every object onstage is not the only way to override the automatic naming features. You can do it all with script. Naturally, every object you intend to affect needs an instance name, but from there you can set name, description, and tab index properties using _accProps (as described next). Also, you can take control of tabbing and selections through the Key listeners and the Selection object. Here are the basics. During runtime, you can effectively make changes to the Accessibility panel's settings using script.

54   Part I   Development

You create an _accProps object, set a few properties, and then use `Accessibility.updateProperties()` to invoke the changes. Inside the _accProps object, there are expected property names that match the Accessibility panel's fields. Here's an example of how you can re-create the manual settings shown in Figure 2.6, but by using the following script.

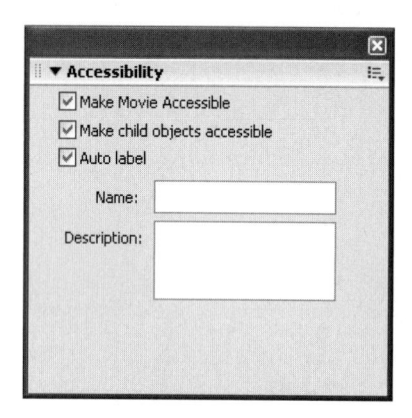

Figure 2.5 *Global Accessibility settings are visible when nothing is selected.*

Figure 2.6 *Making settings in the Accessibility panel is manual, but a script can do it automatically.*

```
myButton._accProps=new Object();
myButton._accProps.silent = false;
myButton._accProps.name = "the name";
myButton._accProps.description = "the description";
myButton._accProps.shortcut = "Ctrl+1";
myButton._accProps.tabIndex = 1;
Accessibility.updateProperties();
```

You can easily match the properties to the corresponding options in the figure—but notice Silent is the opposite of Make Accessible. In this case, we need a button with the instance name `myButton`. Had we been addressing a movie clip instance (or the main movie itself—by leaving off `myButton`), the additional property `forceSimple` could be set to `false` in place of Make Child Objects Accessible (an option only available for clips).

Although the details of how to technically expose names to persons with limited visibility may seem involved, the *real* work is thinking of clear names. Incidentally, the `name` property should always be very short. The `description` is equivalent to the HTML `longdesc` property. Here you can write in explicit detail—although do try to keep it concise.

Motor Skills

Ideally, users can use your app without much mousing around. Seriously, a mouse can be very difficult to operate, and there are several ways to design your app to account for this. First, avoid tiny buttons! If nothing else, make the hit state as large as possible, even if that means expanding beyond the button's borders. Also, if you find while testing that you click the wrong button or something, take it as a sign that you need to make it bigger. Sometimes it's even more than just the button's size that's a problem. Consider, for instance, a slider control like that in Figure 2.7. You can increase the hit state so that more than just the tiny box is clickable. But what happens when the user clicks the line—not the box? It would be nice if the box jumped to where the user clicked and automatically started dragging. The point here is that even if you're requiring a mouse, it doesn't mean you have to require the precision of a surgeon.

Consider, too, that blind folks won't be able to use the mouse. So, although I've included the following discussion under motor skills, realize it applies to low vision, too. Taking control of the tab order (as opposed to letting Flash do it automatically) involves several related mechanisms. The first step is to set the `tabIndex` property of any particular object. The only catch is that in Flash Player 7 each movie clip has its own tab sequence. That is, two clips could both have fields with indexes 1, 2, and 3. While one clip was focused, you'd just cycle through its three fields; then when the other clip was focused, you'd cycle through its fields. To make a particular field receive focus (say, when tabbing out of the last field in one clip), you can use `Selection.setFocus(clip.field)` (replacing `clip` and `field` with the actual clip and field instance names). In addition, if you're using just one of the new UI components in your movie, the new

Focus Manager steps in. Basically, this means you'll see a green glow on the currently focused object—which includes text, buttons, and any interactive component such as radio buttons, combo boxes, and so on.

Figure 2.7 *Tiny sliders are fine so long as you don't make them difficult to select.*

Although setting focus is fairly simple, the hard part is figuring out *when* you want to set it. That is, trapping the event you want to use to trigger the change is a bit trickier. Generally, you want to look at Listeners for the Key object and the Selection object.

By the way, to test any keyboard controls you add, be sure to select Disable Keyboard Shortcuts from the Control menu (when you're doing a test movie). Otherwise Flash's built-in keyboard commands will override yours.

Hearing

The fact that some people may not be able to hear your app means that to make it more accessible you should provide captions. This not only means the entire transcript of narration needs to be available in readable form, but also a description of what's shown onscreen. This normally applies to video. Keep in mind that this means you need to describe anything onscreen for those visually impaired, too. I suppose a lot of RIAs have more to do with data than video presentations, but it can still come up.

When you need to caption a piece of timed content (such as a video), realize that you need to figure out the sync points "offline." That is, during production you might build a mini-app that enables you to watch the video and click a button every time the next line of text should appear. You need to record those clicks and use that time information during playback. For a video inside a movie clip, it's easy to tie the sync points to frame numbers in the clip. If you're playing external FLVs, you'll want to check out the `send()` method (covered in Chapter 8, "Foundation Communication Server"), because it embeds events right into a video. Finally, straight audio has a `position` property that you can use with the Sound object.

Throughout this section on accessibility, you might have thought terms such as *low vision* were some attempt to be politically correct. Although I do think it's important to be sensitive, there are all sorts of disabilities that range from mild to extreme. In fact, provided you live long enough, you *will* experience some limits. In any event, the best way to approach accessibility is to make your app more usable.

{ Note }

Third-Party Accessibility Tools If you do plan to create a fully accessible app or even just need to do a lot of captioning of audio or video, you should check out two products made for Flash MX 2004. HiSoftware has two products that plug in to Flash. HiCaption includes both a production tool for adding captions and the code needed to play back those captions inside your Flash app. The other product, AccVerify/AccRepair, is a test bed application that you run on your Flash app. It scans your Flash document and will report instances such as places where you haven't provided text equivalents or you've created a funky tab order. Check out both products at www.hisoftware.com/macromedia/.

Summary

For a chapter that didn't get into nitty-gritty technical details, a lot of details were covered—everything from ensuring that your app fills a need, that it doesn't attempt to replace a better alternative, and that it uses the technology wisely, to ensuring that it gets deployed in the most sensible way. This chapter also briefly discussed Macromedia Central as a possible delivery mechanism. The chapter ended with issues related to accessibility (issues related to which are best kept in mind early in a project). Because this is the last chapter in the "Development" part of this book, you can get ready for more technical details and chances to apply this knowledge.

{ Part II }

Technology

3 Technology Overview   61
4 Working with Complex Data   91
5 Presenting Data   115
6 Basic Data Exchange   135
7 Exchanging Data with Outside Services   187
8 Foundation Communication Server   227
9 Advanced Communication Server   275

{Chapter 3}

Technology Overview

As you saw in the preceding chapter, designing an application involves mixing user needs with a functional design. You also must use the appropriate technology. This chapter concentrates on the technology available to Macromedia Flash MX 2004 applications. I think it's important to start with a need and then look for a solution. The converse, starting with a hammer and then looking for a nail, will nearly always fail the test of usefulness. This technical chapter is based on the premise that you've already established a need that Flash can solve.

As the first technology chapter, this chapter introduces nearly every concept that appears in the book. This chapter is as detailed as possible without getting into practical exercises. Instead of showing you *how*, this chapter shows you *why*. The main goal is to show you a bit of *everything* so that you can see how things fit together. Don't worry if a topic seems to be glossed over here—it will almost certainly appear later. Sometimes it's best to get the big picture and then come back for details. Although this approach may appear redundant, it will help you synthesize. In any event, think of this chapter as a detailed tour of what follows.

This chapter covers the following topics:

- A technical and visual map to the rest of this book—almost like an index of what follows
- An introduction to key approaches, including code-data separation, data management and presentation, and modularization
- Notes about configuring your work environment so that you can follow the exercises that appear in upcoming chapters

If you could buy this book in Cliff Notes form, it would be this chapter. Maybe that's not totally accurate because you *will* find several gems here that don't appear later.

Data Handling

A key element to any application is data. Data can download from an outside source or be input by the user. Putting the data in order and making sense of it is the developer's job. If users wanted raw data, they'd read a dictionary or page through reams of database records. Although users may want options as to what data is presented, they expect the computer to process that data for them. Chapter 4, "Working with Complex Data," discusses many ways to arrange and structure data to make processing easy and efficient for you, the developer. Chapter 5, "Presenting Data," covers ways to present the data in a lucent manner for the user to digest.

Separating Code and Data

When handling any data, it's best to carefully keep your programming code and presentation graphics separate from the raw data. Ideally, you will be able to modify the data without touching the code. If nothing else, your programming must adapt to expected changes to the data. If you build a tool to search an employee database, for example, it should continue to work even when new employees get hired. It's like you know employees will be added, so you need to plan for that. Also, you'll often have to start programming before the final content is available. Keeping code separate from the particular content means you can swap content without breaking your code. Figure 3.1 shows the folder structure I used for a project. We stored language-specific images in their own folders.

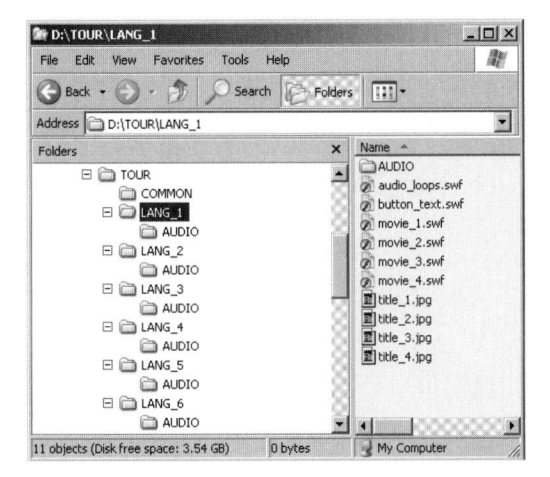

Figure 3.1 *By keeping language-specific content in separate folders, the same code was used for each of the six language translations.*

Code data separation also applies to presentation style and content. A word processing program would be pretty lame if you got different words by just changing a font style. If your application is easily skinned, you'll be able to change the colors and layout without affecting the underlying code (or particular content). Having said this, I think the nature of your content should be linked to how it's presented. In fact, changing fonts *can* affect the way a message is perceived. In such cases, I'd just say the "content" includes style attributes—so they can't really be separate. In any event, it's best to attempt to keep presentation attributes independent of code.

It's a bit of a fantasy to expect to recycle your code from one project to another, but not entirely impossible. Instead of investing undue stress to write the ultimate piece of code that never goes out of date, it may be more efficient to concentrate on your core objectives. I recycle *pieces* of code all the time. So, the more you can modularize and make code that's separate from your specific application's data, the better. In any event, I've yet to develop an app that can be skinned for a different client with absolutely no touch-ups required. Aspiring to this goal is worthy nevertheless.

Figure 3.2 shows two similar-looking projects side by side—one for a winter greeting card, one for a baby congratulations. Even in the nearly duplicate process, however, a fair bit of tweaking was necessary. (You can see a version of this app at www.phillipkerman.com/card.)

Figure 3.2 *I've used the same underlying code for several similar products, shown here as a baby congratulations and as a greeting card.*

Structuring Data

Regardless of how the user ultimately views the data presented by your app, the way that data is organized is entirely up to you. What goes on behind the scenes is unimportant to the user. It's like a bouquet of mixed flowers. The recipient doesn't care whether the flowers are grown in rows and columns inside a boring greenhouse (in dirt no less!). It's the final presentation that users care about. In Figure 3.3, you can see data organized in a way only a programmer could love—but, then again, the programmer is the only person who ever sees it.

```
questions=[];
questions.push({topic:"Gender",    question: "What is your current gender?",
                                   options: ["Male", "Female"]});

questions.push({topic:"Geography", question: "Where are you from?",
                                   options: ["Portland Metro",
                                             "Another area of Oregon",
                                             "Washington",
                                             "California",
                                             "None of these"]});

questions.push({topic:"Age",       question: "How old are you?",
                                   options: ["less than 25",
                                             "25 - 34",
                                             "35 - 44",
                                             "45 - 54",
                                             "55 or over"]});
```

Figure 3.3 *Code organized in a way that only a programmer would call pretty.*

As a developer, you can structure the data however you want. In simple terms, structuring data is deciding whether you're going to have 10 rows of 3 columns each or 3 rows of 10 columns. Obviously it's more than an arbitrary decision. However, it's a common mistake to squeeze data into the narrow view the user will ultimately see. For one thing, you'll often need to maintain data the user never sees (say, a list of passwords). You can actually think of it as bad code data separation to match the underlying structure to how the user eventually sees the data presented.

One notable exception to this "developers preference" rule is when working with an existing legacy data source. Even when you must work with a fixed data source, however, you can process the data to reorganize it in whichever way you want—either after it arrives via Flash or even by some outside tool such as a database that imports the data, processes it, and then exports. The key is that because you're the one who has to get a handle on the data, it should be formatted to your liking.

Another consideration is network efficiency. You don't want to download the entire Oxford English Dictionary just because you think it might be useful. However, you may find situations where keeping a cache of related data can actually reduce network requests. The topic of structuring data to reduce bandwidth comes up when using the Flash Communication Server (covered in Chapter 8, "Foundation Communication Server," and Chapter 9, "Advanced Communication Server").

I keep saying organize the data how you prefer, not necessarily how the user will see it. The flip side of this is you don't want your data structure to influence the layout. Organizing information for processing has a different set of objectives than how the data is presented. Even if programmers are doing the layout, they should think about user needs first.

Presenting Data

Originally, I had a single chapter for both organizing and presenting data, but there was just so much to say! Chapter 4 actually covers a lot more than just structuring data. Namely, you'll see many ways to process and sort data. But it's not until Chapter 5, that you'll actually visually present the data. It's sort of like how the typesetting stage culminates months of prework organizing and writing a manuscript. Provided the groundwork is in place, presenting data can be pretty easy. That's not to say, however, that it's just a matter of putting a pretty face on the data.

Presenting data involves all kinds of visual vehicles. Naturally, text is the primary way to display data. However, you also can use simple graphics to represent data. For example, a graph can often consolidate an enormous amount of data into a small space. Graphs also enable you literally to see things you could never derive from numbers and text.

It's actually possible to analyze data and present the results in subtle or nonvisual ways. For example, you could have a sound effect with its volume matched to some data. Or, you could change the rate an animation plays to match a number. In this book, you won't do these specific tasks, but when your data is available in an organized form, it's not tough to extract just the parts you need.

Before turning to getting data into and out of Flash, let me say it's not like you're lying when you show your user only a small snippet of all the data. It's more like you're editorializing. Again, if users wanted the raw data, they wouldn't need your app. When you maintain data both behind the scenes and onscreen for presentation, it's like you're purposely filtering information for the user. This isn't a bad thing. Naturally, you probably want to give users a way to drill down for more detail, but being concise is a challenge.

Data Exchanging

It's quite possible that your application gathers data, processes it, and then presents it—all based on information the user supplies. You'll take a giant leap, however, when you can make your app reach out and read data from an outside source. Another step in sophistication is when your app can then send data out for others to access or just to a repository for safekeeping. Chapters 6, "Basic Data Exchange," and 7, "Exchanging Data with Outside Services," discuss a wide range of ways Flash can consume or publish data. In this section, you'll learn why this is so cool.

Loading

It's sort of a chicken and the egg question as to which comes first: reading data or writing it. In fact, all data in your app can originate in the user's brain and get typed in. However, even in the most simple cases, loading *some* data from an outside source is useful because—if nothing else—you can separate the code (in your Flash movie) from the data (data you load from outside, for instance). It can be as simple as creating a text file with data and storing it adjacent to your Flash movie. Keeping data separate pays off when, for example, you can make updates for your client by just changing a couple values in a text file. Figure 3.4 shows the code for a matching game where I can change the values for "name" and "star" to create a whole new game. Naturally, planning for such changes is what makes changes easy. However, just externalizing data you expect to change is only one reason you need to load data.

```
name1=Jason Alexander
&star1=Jay Greenspan
&name2=Kirstie Alley
&star2=Gladys Leeman
&name3=Lucille Ball
&star3=Dianne Belmont
&name4=Dyan Cannon
&star4=Samille Friesen
&name5=Bill Clinton
&star5=William Blythe
&name6=Joan Crawford
&star6=Lucille LeSueur
```

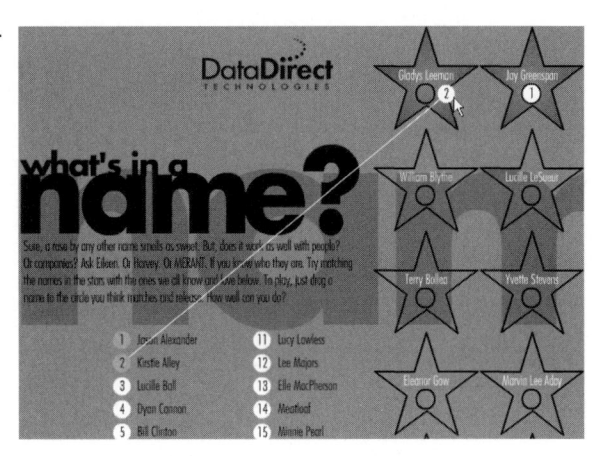

Figure 3.4 *The actual names used for this matching game are kept external (shown on the left).*

Often you'll want to present timely data inside your app. In such cases, the data *must* load from outside Flash. In fact this means that Flash needs to get the data from a database (either at your location or remotely). The point is, you can't present the current temperature by reading in a flat text file (unless you're constantly resaving that file with new data). Imagine manually typing a number into a text file every time the temperature changes—you'd get pretty exhausted. The point is, Flash can tap an application server for this data.

There's an upcoming section on application servers that shows how they can produce timely data for Flash to consume. However, we can first consider how that data is formatted. Here's a list of the possible ways data can arrive into Flash:

- **URL encoded.** This form always contains pairs of names with matching values—for example, "first=phillip last=kerman." It's almost like how variables are assigned in Flash. The actual format looks like what was shown in Figure 3.4. There are other details regarding how this must be formatted, but the key limitation is the values always arrive as string. Even if the data were to contain "age=38," the value for age would be "38" not 38. This can mean a lot of parsing and cleaning up after the data arrives.

- **XML.** This is similar to URL encoded in that all values are strings. However, XML is nicer in a couple of ways. First, you can structure the data contained in XML so that context is given to parts of the data. For example, you can effectively say "here is a list of cities where we have offices," and then proceed to list them. In this way, values are given context by appearing in categories. The second advantage is that XML is extensible, meaning you can add values to particular categories (called *nodes*). When you load XML, it's easy to ascertain both the values and how many values are contained.

- **AMF packet.** The Action Message Format (AMF) is a protocol used with Flash Remoting. You need Flash, an application server (such as ColdFusion MX), and Remoting installed. When Flash requests data, your application server prepares a packet and sends it back to Flash via AMF. Although there is a bit of work on the application server side, when the data arrives in Flash it's always in a single variable. That variable can be a number, a string, or even an array or generic object that contains even more values. The great part is you don't have to convert strings to numbers, or any other data types for that matter. (You'll learn more about data types in Chapter 4; for now just consider how a number is fundamentally different from a string of characters.) Besides making your life easy by eliminating the need to parse data types, AMF is a binary format that puts data in small packets that travel over the Internet efficiently.

- **SOAP packets.** Simple Object Access Protocol (SOAP) is based in XML but contains standardized elements that describe what's contained inside the file. XML can include some context of what's contained; a requirement of SOAP is that it *must* contain a description of both what's contained as well as documentation of the rules for the particular file. Luckily, we don't have to produce SOAP-formatted data. SOAP happens to be the format by which all web services transmit data. You'll see web services later in this chapter, but basically it's just a way for other companies to open access to some of their databases in a standardized form. Anyway, Flash now supports SOAP/web services (although you still have to go through an application server to reach outside your domain). It's comparable to AMF in that the data can contain any data type. However, it's better than AMF because you don't have to buy Flash Remoting (although, to be fair, Remoting comes free with ColdFusion). On the downside, SOAP isn't as lightweight and efficient as AMF. Having said all this, I don't think you need to be clairvoyant to see web services (therefore SOAP) is the direction of lots of tools, including Flash.

Although it may seem the ways of loading data all climax with SOAP being the best, note that there are uses for all of these. For one thing, both URL-encoded text and XML will work with plain-text files that you create manually—sort of a low-tech approach, but quick and dirty for many uses. As you'll see in the

"Writing" section, you do need an application server to send any data out of Flash. That is, you can't just write text files with Flash.

The data exchange chapters of this book concentrate primarily on the mechanics of getting the data into and out of Flash. The first step is always making sure the data is in the right format. One misplaced character can render a set of data useless. Another mechanical issue is ensuring the data fully loads before you begin to process it. That is, you can't just say "find out temperature in Portland, Oregon and display it in this text field." Instead, you must first define how to display that data onscreen (when it finally arrives), and then make a request to load. The sequence matters. The issue is that requests to load outside data are not immediately answered. You'll soon read the details of all of this, but it does help to understand the process before you plan something that's impossible.

Parsing

Although I said AMF (Remoting) and SOAP (web services) can send you any data type and thus alleviate you from needing to parse it, you'll still spend a fair bit of time parsing. Parsing can also mean extracting small portions. In the case of getting the temperature, you may find a web service that can give you the temperature, barometric pressure, and the dew point. If you just want to display the temperature, you must parse that from the data you receive. (If you can figure a way to *just* load the temperature, this might reduce bandwidth—but receiving a few extra details probably isn't that big of a deal.)

Other words come to mind when thinking of this topic: collating, pruning, formatting, extrapolating, plotting. I'm just going to generalize and call it all parsing. When you parse data, you step through line by line or sometimes letter by letter. Obviously, you can write loops that do this automatically, but the point I want to make here is that you shouldn't worry too much about preformatting the data before it arrives in Flash. It would be nice if data always arrived custom fitted to your needs, but you don't want a single project to dictate that your remote functions are less generic. It's really not a big deal to do a bit of parsing; in addition, it's really common.

Writing

Reading data from outside sources connects your application to the world. But sending data from Flash connects your users to the outside world. There are many ways Flash lets you write data. Generally, it's just a matter of changing the direction of flow in the four "reading" methods described earlier. The only catch is when sending data out of Flash you'll usually need someone listening on the other end—not so much a person, but rather an application server that can take the data and insert it into a database, for example.

This discussion doesn't cover all the ways your application server can process data. Instead, this discussion just covers how to get it out of Flash. In fact, Flash Pro ships with several data components that automate this process. It's pretty cool because they can even send just the portion of data that changes in order to reduce bandwidth. The thing is, you don't *need* Flash Pro to write data to a database, but the alternatives are so much more cumbersome that I think it would be a disservice to cover anything except the best way possible.

Keep in mind there are other reasons to write data in addition just to dumping information into a database. Perhaps you want to let the user fire off an email to a friend with a link to the greeting card the user just produced (with your app). In this case, you have to get the data out of Flash, but it doesn't need to go any further than an email that gets sent out. My point is it's really up to you what you do with the data after it leaves Flash. This discussion focuses on the mechanics of preparing the data and then sending it.

In addition to writing data in "traditional" ways, you'll spend a fair bit of time in Chapter 6 using SharedObject Local and the local connection objects. The SharedObject Local enables you to save data on the user's hard drive, so that when the user returns you can pick up where he left off or recall other data he saved locally. The local connection object enables you to send message data to other movies running on the user's machine. This makes multiwindow applications possible in browsers as well as in Macromedia Central (discussed later this chapter).

Synchronizing

The concept of synchronization involves ensuring everyone is looking at the right data. If you're talking about a live application where multiple people are connected simultaneously, you'll likely want to make sure they're all in sync. In more traditional applications, the user may be making adjustments to data, but you don't necessarily want to send an updates over the Internet for every tiny change. For example, as users edit a text field, you probably don't need to send an update for every character they type—waiting until they click submit is fine.

Selecting a logical time to send updates is just a matter of analyzing your application. The challenge arises, however, when you must resolve a conflict. If any user is allowed to change the title of a shared document, for example, and two people both try to change it, you've got to handle the situation gracefully. Being aware of the potential is half the work. Addressing this issue is really just a matter of letting users "request" to make a change, and then, if there's a conflict, giving them the information that their attempt failed. You'll see the technical issues with this approach in Chapters 8 and 9 during the coverage of the Flash Communication Server. But like I say, being aware is half the work—so you'll be able to apply the same concept to any application. The general tip I'll give you now is to try to identify areas of possible conflict and think of ways to address these cases (functionally, not technically).

Ensuring Successful Data Exchange

Any time you read or write data, there's a chance it will fail. If the user loses her Internet connection, for example, obviously data can't transmit. It's really easy to build an app without considering such possibilities. Try to resist that temptation.

There are two general problems for which you should account: A known error is encountered, or such a long delay persists that you should cancel the operation. Both Flash and most outside tools have a set of known possible errors for which they'll notify you. If you attempt to load a JPG file that doesn't exist, for instance, an error displays in the output window. (There's actually a new feature in Flash MX 2004—coincidentally called the Error object—that enables you to write your own runtime error messages, along with the code that reacts to it.) The two sides to dealing with error messages are, first, the operation must have a built-in set of error codes, and, second, you need to write code that follows up when such errors occur.

As for timeouts, many operations have a built-in timeout error. If you attempt to connect to the Flash Communication Server and the server was turned off, for example, Flash generates its own error message after about 10 seconds. Quite often, however, if the Internet connection is down or you attempt to read data that just doesn't exist, Flash just quietly waits, and waits, and waits. Because such operations are asynchronous, your movie will, thankfully, continue to run while it waits. However, you really ought to account for the possibility that an operation will fail.

Ensuring data is exchanged comes down to the following general approach:

1. Define the script that receives data when successful.
2. Define the scripts that react to possible errors.
3. If you're using an outside application server, make sure the scripts you are calling always return either an error, the data you were seeking, or just a "success" notification (if no data was supposed to get sent back).
4. Start a timer that will trigger after some acceptable timeout period (and scripts 1 and 2 above clear that timeout, because it won't be needed if either of those trigger).
5. Finally, attempt to send or request data.

Like I say, it's easier to just do steps 1 and 5. In fact, that's all you need—when everything is working. Suppose you prefer to make your app "silently fail" and just continue like nothing happened. If users click login and nothing happens, for example, they'll probably attempt again. Although you could certainly improve this experience by giving users more information, there are definitely times when no error trapping is necessary. Having said that, you really ought to try to account for every potential failure.

Web Services

I've mentioned web services already because they're so darn useful, but I think it makes sense to define them here. Consider how a company might make a web site that gives you access to its data. Building such a site requires more than just structuring the data; the presentation must be designed. For users to access the data, they must visit the site and interact with the given interface. That's fine, but web services make that general task (accessing information) possible without the visual interface.

The way it works is a company can make available any or all of its data via a web service. This involves a definition file (WSDL, for Web Service Definition Language) that defines how an outside developer can make requests for data. This file mainly defines the methods, the parameters they accept, and the sorts of data that get returned. Then a developer can make a SOAP request (over standard HTTP), and the data will be returned. Without getting into more details, consider what this means. Through web services, I can track my UPS package and I can search Amazon's book collection. Of course I can do all that through the respective companies' web sites, too. If I use Flash as the user interface and a web service behind the scenes, however, I can take the data returned and present it however I choose inside Flash. For a company that makes its data available, it means that data may reach more people than would otherwise be possible through its main web site. In fact, many web services are free, but many require that you first register for an ID number (called a key or token) so that they can track your activity—or, where you agree, charge you accordingly.

Generally, I think companies correctly see web services as a way to give their data more reach—not so much a direct moneymaker. This may change. For now, however, web services make it possible for you to put a "Flash face" on any data available. Visit www.xmethods.net to see just some the available web services. A memorable moment for me was building a quick Flash app (while sitting in my rocking chair) that let me type a message and my own phone number, which then rang and a computer voice read my message. Maybe I'm a geek, but I thought this was sort of profound.

One quick note: Using Macromedia Central you can build an app that connects *directly* with an outside web service. Users need to first acknowledge the operation (or set a preference not to ask again). In Flash you always need to go through your own application server to reach out to other web services. (Actually, exceptions to that restriction are when you test movies and when users run a Flash projector or SWF on their desktop.)

Application Servers

Unfortunately I'm not certified to, nor is this book able to, fully explain how to operate an application server. For one thing, there are tons from which to choose. Luckily, the way Flash interacts with any application server is basically the same. Here I want to define what makes a web server an application server and give you an idea what it means to integrate an application server with your app.

Basics

A *web server* is just software running on a computer and optionally connected to the Internet. When the web server is configured properly, any user can type http:// followed by the IP address associated with the web server's Internet connection. Provided you've registered a domain name, users can alternatively type in that domain name and it will redirect to the associated IP address.

For performance reasons, you probably don't want to use the computer running a web server as your main work machine. However, it's not as though users visiting the web site will get full access to your machine. When configuring your server, you need to define a default root directory (that is, the default location to which users are sent when they type in your home web address). The common name for this folder is wwwroot. Inside that folder, you'll put your HTML documents, embedded images, and SWF files. You can structure subfolders, too. Inside my wwwroot, for example, I have a folder called clients, which you can reach by typing **http://www.phillipkerman.com/clients**. Naturally, you can set up rules for passwords and thus protect certain folders and so on.

An application server runs in place of or on top of your web server. The way it differs is that when a user requests a specific page instead of just sending the user a document that's been prepared ahead of time, you can make the application server software first run a script, which then, effectively, creates a file and then sends that. Usually it doesn't produce an actual file but just sends contents of a file the same as it would if it were sending a copy of an actual file. The idea is that you can define a basic template that includes dynamic elements that don't get populated until the user requests a page. It's almost as though there is a monkey inside the machine that sees a visitor is attempting to receive a page, and that monkey opens up Dreamweaver and creates an HTML page that he saves and then sends to the visitor (all in a fraction of a second).

Listing 3.1 shows a simple ColdFusion template.

Listing 3.1   Simple ColdFusion Template

```
1    <html>
2    <head> <title>roster</title> </head>
3    <body>
4    <B>All the people in the database:</B> <BR>
5    <table>
6    <cfquery name = "myPeople" datasource = "people">
7                    SELECT *
8                    FROM PEOPLE
9    </cfquery>
10   <cfoutput query="myPeople">
11     <tr>
12        <td width="200"><b>#first#</b></td>
13        <td width="200">#last#</td>
14     </tr>
15   </cfoutput>
16   </table>
17   </body></html>
```

The user never sees this actual page; instead, lines 6 through 15 get replaced with the results of the SQL `"SELECT * FROM PEOPLE"`. That is, the "people" data source (basically an Access database file that you've identified as a data source) has a table called people from which all records are drawn. What actually appears in the web page is each first name (in bold) followed by each last name (followed by a line break `<BR>`). Figure 3.5 shows that output.

```
All the people in the database:
George          Bush
Laura           Bush
Phillip         Kerman
Max             Kerman
John            Smith
Sally           Smith
```

Figure 3.5 *A ColdFusion template displays this excerpt from a database.*

What's wild is that if the user does selects View, Source in his browser, he'll see what appears to be a manually created HTML page (see Figure 3.6).

```html
<head> <title>roster</title> </head>
  <body>
    <B>All the people in the database:</B>
    <BR>
    <table>
        <tr>
            <td width="200"><b>George</b></td>
            <td width="200">Bush</td>
        </tr>

        <tr>
            <td width="200"><b>Laura</b></td>
            <td width="200">Bush</td>
        </tr>

        <tr>
            <td width="200"><b>Phillip</b></td>
            <td width="200">Kerman</td>
        </tr>

        <tr>
            <td width="200"><b>Max</b></td>
            <td width="200">Kerman</td>
        </tr>

        <tr>
            <td width="200"><b>John</b></td>
            <td width="200">Smith</td>
        </tr>

        <tr>
            <td width="200"><b>Sally</b></td>
            <td width="200">Smith</td>
        </tr>

    </table>
</body></html>
```

Figure 3.6 *The actual HTML produced by ColdFusion looks as though it could have been typed by hand.*

So the idea is you write code that gets processed the moment the user requests a page. In the case of displaying all records in a database, if the user comes back later and that database has been updated, he'll see the new results. I really think the image of a monkey taking orders and producing HTML pages by hand is the best one to understand how application servers work.

Concepts

There are just a few more concepts to make sure you understand servers generally. First, application servers operate on the standard procedure of request and response. That is, a user makes a request, and the server responds with the answer (usually a web page generated on-the-fly). There are ways to fake it so that users believe they are spontaneously receiving notice when changes occur. This usually involves a polling technique where a script in the client's page (written in JavaScript, for example) will periodically re-request a new web page. In this way, you might see sports scores update as they happen. In fact, you're still probably following the request and response model.

One exception is when a persistent connection is established. Although several technologies can make persistent connections, you'll learn how to do so here only using Flash Communication Server. The thing is, you can do quite a lot with request and response.

I described how a ColdFusion template can populate itself and then send out a standard HTML page to the user. In fact, you don't have to bury your code right into a single template. You may find it useful to recycle the code that grabs all records from a database and use that in several different pages. Most application servers should have a mechanism for you to do this. In the case of ColdFusion, there's CFCs, or ColdFusion Components. These are pure code files that can run scripts upon request from any template in the web site. The reason I point this out is that when it comes to Flash accessing the power of an application server, there are no need to generate an HTML page. That is, Flash just wants the raw data from the database—it doesn't need the records formatted with bold text. In the case of the preceding ColdFusion example, Flash just wants the results from the SQL query and can handle displaying itself.

Application servers can do many things, but—by far—the most common thing is accessing databases. You can either look through a database to get records that match your query or you can send values that get inserted into the database. I suppose you can do other things, such as create or modify tables in the database.

Generally, however, you either grab data or send data (or do both, such as add a record and then find out the new total number of records). Writing to a database involves little more than packing up the variables to send, invoking a remote method (on an app server), and expecting that method to take the variables it received and put them into the database.

When requesting data from a database, you can follow a couple of approaches. You can just grab everything from a table in a database and then worry about parsing through it once inside Flash. Of course, this can mean a long initial download of data, but it also means searching for information within that data will be very quick because it's done entirely inside Flash. You need to consider how large a block of data is appropriate. One benefit of making repeated requests for data from a database is that the data will always be as current as your last request. It's really sort of subjective, and you just have to look at the nature of the data—how large it is, and how timely, for instance.

The process of extracting just records that match your need is called *making a query*. A query is basically a matching expression such as "all records in the students table with a last name of smith." Queries return an array full of records. Each record is a generic object with property names that match the columns (or field names) in the database. Your application server can build queries in several ways. For a concise book on using SQL (a common query language), check out *Sams Teach Yourself SQL in 10 Minutes* (Sams, 2001).

Besides accessing databases, an application server can act as your gateway to web services. Because the Flash Player is restricted from directly accessing a web service residing on a separate domain, you need to go through your application server. It's called making your server act as a proxy because all it does is forward your request and channels the response back to Flash. You can find simple starter files for most common application servers in the Macromedia TechNotes 16520 and 14213. (Just type those numbers into the Search field at www.macromedia.com). All you do is install the files on your application server as directed, and then Flash movies (residing on your server) can use your application server as a proxy, which then makes calls to outside web services.

Finally, application servers include several other unique features that may prove useful. For example, it's usually really easy to trigger a script that sends out an email. In addition, an application server usually has logging capabilities. Also, various approaches to authentic connections are usually available. I guess I just want to point out application servers can do more than just access databases and web services.

Integrating Flash

It was tough to explain application server concepts without mentioning how Flash integrates. For the most part, separating Flash from the application server is similar to basic code data separation. The Flash movie is the presentation of data, whereas the methods on the application server are the code. Although we can't keep things totally separate, the model fits. If for no other reason, you should strive to keep things modular and separate so that you have less to maintain.

Integrating Flash with the power of your application server is mostly an issue of configuring your work environment. That is, you need a way to test locally while working but then seamlessly migrate your application to the real server when you're ready for the public. Your work environment is discussed later in this chapter; for now just realize that Flash has a different set of restrictions when on a web server than when running locally (which includes when you "test movie"). That is, on a server, a Flash movie can only access data residing on the same domain. Actually, with the Flash Player 7 there's a new restriction that the domain name has to match *exactly* (for example, http://phillipkerman.com is considered different from http://www.phillipkerman.com). If an existing Flash 6 movie makes such a cross-domain attempt and the user is using the Flash Player 7, the user will see the dialog box shown in Figure 3.7.

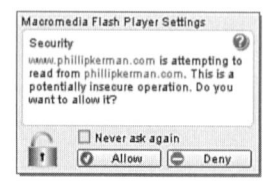

Figure 3.7 *This Security dialog box appears when users visit old content that doesn't abide by the new "exact domain matching" rules.*

To bypass this (so that the user doesn't even see that dialog box), just set up a policy file. The idea is you can place policy files on any server (for which you control) and specify the other domains that are allowed to access your server. For example, my publisher can post SWFs on their domain that attempt to access phillipkerman.com. Provided I placed a policy file on phillipkerman.com that effectively says "it's okay to accept connections from www.newriders.com," it'll work.

The deceptive part is that you could build a huge application that successfully reaches out to application servers and web services on other domains—but only while you're testing. You can even successfully test the SWFs in a browser.

But not until you put the SWFs on an actual web server (say in the wwwroot folder locally) will you see it doesn't work!

I realize these are somewhat esoteric details, but you really need to know the potential and limits before you build an application.

Components

Components are ready-made movie clips containing all the code needed for a specific task. For example, you can use a blank List component and make it appear with a list of options from which the user can select. Figure 3.8 shows the interface from a movie voting application you'll build in Chapter 8.

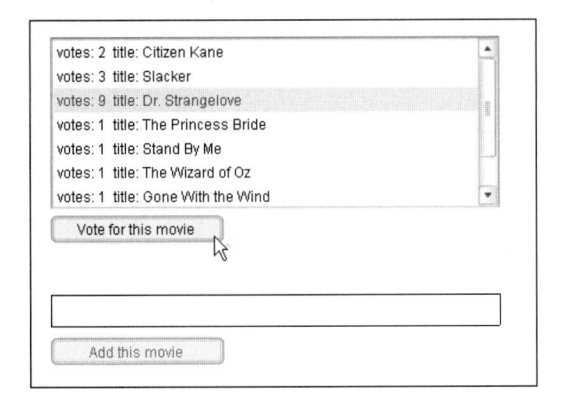

Figure 3.8 *The interface portion of this movie voting app (built in Chapter 8) uses several new components.*

This particular example includes a List and two Button components. Changing the contents of a list or enabling and disabling a button are just two simple tasks you can achieve with these components. Flash ships with a variety of "version 2" (V2) components that not only reflect an updated graphic look (called *Halo*) but also function differently. There's a whole chapter on components, but they'll pop up during many exercises before that because they're so useful.

Using Components

At first I thought components would stifle creativity, but in fact, they relieve you from the mundane task of designing and programming common interface elements. (I should note, I'm talking about the user interface [UI] components; there are others that solve more specific needs.) The only downside is that they require a bit of investment to learn. Worse yet, there have been many changes to the way they work over the old "V1" components. There are two shards of good news in this: You can use V2 components and deliver to Flash Player 6, and the investment of learning V2 components is paid back in time saved using them.

> **{ Note }**
>
> **Primary Differences in V2 Components** The best improvement is that most contained properties are now accessible directly, like any clip property. For example, in the past if you had a ListBox component with an instance name `my_lb`, you could find the currently selected index using `result=my_lb.getSelectedIndex()` or set the index using `my_lb.setSelectedIndex(1)`. Now, if you have a list named `my_list` you can do the same thing but using `result=my_list.selectedIndex` and `my_list.selectedIndex=1`. After you figure out the property names, this is so much better.
>
> Another big difference is the way you make the components trigger code in your movie. In the past, you would use `setClickHandler()` or `setChangeHandler()` to specify a homemade function you wanted to trigger. Now you use `addEventListener()` and specify both the event (`"click"`, `"change"`, or whatever applies to the particular component) and the function you want to trigger. For example:
>
> `my_list.addEventListener("change",doClickList);`
>
> Now, any time the `my_list` List component changes, the `doClickList()` gets triggered. The only trick here is to find the events available to the component type. (For example, buttons only have a `"click"` event, but not a `"change"` event.) The cool thing is that some components have several events you can trap.
>
> Finally, a subtle difference that seems worth mentioning too is that the automatic parameter that arrives in any function call is not a reference to the component instance any more. It's a custom generic object that contains several properties. For you to get a handle on the instance that triggered your code, look for the `target` property. Check out the following "old vs. new" example that assumes you have some buttons associated with the `doClick()` function (either through `setClickHandler()` or `addEventListener()`).
>
> Old way:
>
> ```
> function doClick(b){
>    trace("a reference to button clicked: " + b)
> }
> ```

> **New way:**
> ```
> function doClick(b){
>    trace("a reference to button clicked: " + b.target)
> }
> ```
> The idea is that instead of each button having its own function, you can have several buttons that all trigger `doClick()`. Then you figure out who triggered it when you're inside the function.

I really didn't want to get so specific in this chapter, but these tips should help avoid some frustration. In addition, you will use components in several places before you get to Chapter 12, "Using Components"—so this should help.

Providing Data to Components

Generally speaking, you just populate your components and then let the user interact with the data presented. Often you'll change the contents of a component while the movie plays. For example, the movie voting application we build lists how many votes each movie received. As you add votes, the display needs to change.

The wizards who designed the components realized this was a typical need, so they made some components "data aware." These support the concept of data binding. There are a few ways to implement this. Basically you can link a data-aware component to your data so that any time the data changes the component automatically reflects the change. This is primarily an automatic data-synchronization feature. I mention this feature because we won't fully exploit it until Chapter 12.

Data Components

Flash MX Professional 2004 ships with a several data components that are arguably worth the price difference over Flash MX 2004. These components are a bit different because they include no visual interface. They're just used to connect to outside data sources. In addition, the DataSet and DataHolder components help you manage data maintained inside your Flash movie. It's just a bit confusing because these are different from the "data-aware" components discussed in the preceding section.

How Flash Communication Server Works

I like to say the Flash Communication Server (FCS) is one of Macromedia's coolest products ever. I've crammed nearly everything I know about it into Chapters 8 and 9, but you can certainly learn more. The primary goal of its inclusion in this book is to get you actually playing with it—to learn the capabilities and to understand the way to approach a project using FCS. Here I want to give you just an overview of what it can do.

FCS is software that runs adjacent to your web server. You still place SWFs and HTML files in your standard web server, but inside your Flash movies you can include a script to connect to FCS. When a connection is made, users remain connected until they leave or you boot them off. This means not only can they send data directly to the FCS server, but the FCS server can send data to the users without the users first requesting it. This is true "push" technology as opposed to the standard "request and response" model. This persistent connection makes possible all kinds of applications, chat being the easiest to understand. One connected client can send a text message to the server, and it can relay that message to all connected users. In addition, if there's a user identified as Spanish, FCS could first translate that text to Spanish (via a web service) and *then* send it to that user, as Figure 3.9 shows. (And this is just a simple example.)

Figure 3.9 *This real-time translating chat app was up and running in just over an hour.*

Maintaining multiple persistently connected users is pretty cool. A nice added fact is the FCS is really efficient. You can build an app that only sends out notices to connected users with the actual data that changes. It's possible to make very-low-bandwidth usage apps—lower than most any app, not just other Flash apps.

The feature that gets the most airplay is support for live and recorded streaming media. This means that not only can users interact by typing or moving their mouse, but they also can speak into their computer's microphone or wave at their webcam and the pictures and sound are uploaded to FCS. That video feed can be saved for later playback as well as shared with any other connected user live. Besides simple video chat, the applications for education and business meetings are really great. There are actually other video chat solutions, but what makes FCS so cool is that it's all in Flash. That is, while the video is going you can also have an immersive Flash experience. With just a little creativity, you can make some powerful applications.

Here are a couple applications I built with FCS. I made what could be the first Flash answering machine for my web site (see Figure 3.10). You can leave a text, audio, or video messages as well as look at other messages people have left. In addition, if you leave your message marked private, only you (the person recording the message) and I can view or delete the message. I also built a real-time cattle auction for `www.stampedecattle.com` (shown in Chapter 1, "Replacing Web Pages with Applications"). Every couple of weeks, bidders enter a Flash movie that connects to FCS. It looks like a traditional sale barn, but all animated. The auctioneer announces the cattle and you've got plenty of details and images onscreen. Finally, when the bidding starts you see a clock countdown and every bid (as well as the state from where they came). If you turn off the motor-mouth auctioneer, it actually works great on slow modems! It's definitely the most involved FCS project I've done yet, and in retrospect it wasn't really *that* hard.

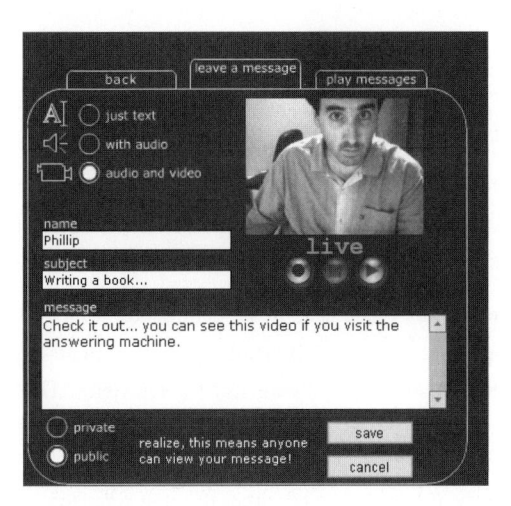

Figure 3.10 *The answering machine on my web site was the first Communication Server app I built (`www.phillipkerman.com/machine`).*

Technology Map

I produced Figure 3.11 as an attempt to represent all the different topics covered in this book. It's impossible to cover them all at once. The idea is that you'll be able to refer back to this "big picture" from any part in the book. At the start of each chapter, I include a version of this map with an indication of "you are here." Hopefully, this helps you keep your bearings and reduces the need to continually explain how things fit together.

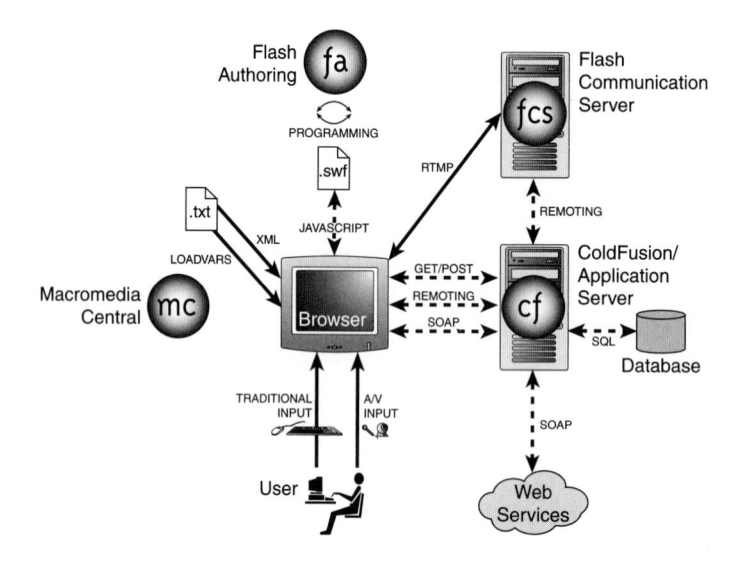

Figure 3.11 *This figure attempts to show nearly every technology discussed in this book.*

Let me walk you through this image. At the top center, you have Flash authoring where you basically create SWFs that play within the browser (directly below). The bottom center signifies how a user can interface using a mouse, keyboard, or webcam and mic. Any standard SWF can take user input and, through programming, perform operations inside the movie (shown right below Flash authoring).

Flash can also reach out. The simplest manner is by launching new windows or affecting the browser in other ways, but primarily using JavaScript. In addition, you can connect a SWF to the Flash Communication Server (top right). These connections are persistent, so every connected user can remain synchronized. Another way for Flash to reach out is to make requests to (and handle replies from) application servers (right). This is achieved either through standard GET/POST, Flash Remoting, or SOAP. I show ColdFusion, but nearly any application server will work. (Incidentally, Flash Communication Server can also use

Flash Remoting and thus reduce the total bandwidth, compared to having each client make requests.) The fact you can send and receive data from an application server means you've got access to the whole world—both local databases and remote web services.

Finally, on the far left you have Macromedia Central. In many ways, this is really just a customized browser that plays Flash movies. Because you have additional privileges to bypass certain security limits as well as control over what gets cached for offline access, however, I think it's worth representing. I really think Macromedia Central is cool, but it's not like there are many additional technical concerns. The biggest issues involve application design—that is, what sort of features can you incorporate in Central that you can't in other places? For this book, I periodically mention how Central fits into a particular topic, but this isn't a Central book *per se*.

Configuring Your Work Environment

This section is less an overview of technology as much as it is a reminder that you're about to start producing applications. Before you start, there are a few steps worth taking.

Configuration Folders

Flash and other Macromedia software will all get installed within a Macromedia folder (inside Program Files by default on Windows or Applications on Mac). Within the Flash MX 2004 program folder, you'll find a folder called "en" (for English). Within *that* folder, you should see several folders including First Run and Configuration (see Figure 3.12).

First Run is the most interesting. This folder contains various configuration files that affect the Flash workspace (things such as the contents of the Actions panel and the Help panel). The interesting part is that this folder serves as a template. Its contents will get copied into another location every time you launch Flash. On my machine, that location is: C:\Documents and Settings\Phillip\Local Settings\Application Data\Macromedia\Flash 2004\en\Configuration. Notice the path will be similar on your machine, but you'll need to replace Phillip with the login you use on your computer. The idea is that personalized settings will be saved in the Local Settings version of the Configuration folder. If you don't have such a folder, the First Run folder gets renamed Configuration and is copied to that location.

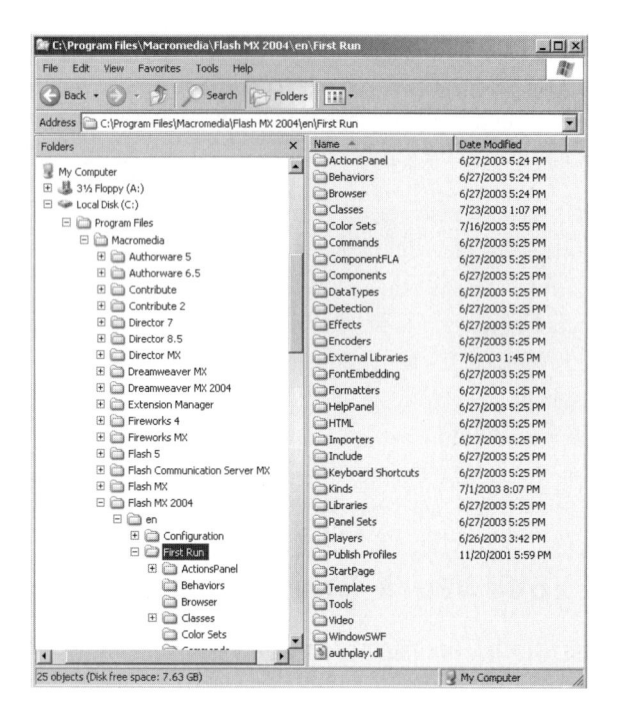

Figure 3.12 *You'll find several configuration folders in the First Run folder.*

The configuration folders have several elements. Just remember that changes to either usually require you to relaunch Flash to see the changes. I'm not going to document every subfolder; just remember that they come up many times later, so you should be familiar with how to find those folders. Personally, I've added shortcuts to both (the one adjacent to Flash and the personal copy inside Local Settings) to my Favorites for quick access.

While on the subject of configuration folders, it's important to note that you can navigate to Documents and Settings\Your Name\Application Data\Macromedia (notice Application Data is the folder not Local Settings) There you'll find a few other interesting folders. The two you may find that are of particular interest are Flash Player and Central. (You won't see Central unless you've installed at least one Central app.) Inside the Flash Player, you will find a folder for each domain you've visited that uses SharedObject Local. These are like JavaScript cookies that let web sites save a little bit of data on your computer so that it's easy to pick up where you left off at the time you return. You'll learn how these work in detail in Chapter 6.

The Central folder is similar to the Flash Player folder except you'll find actual SWF movies (as well as JPGs and MP3s). This makes it possible for Central apps to run even when you're not online. What's sort of weird is that SharedObject Local files created by any Central app actually appear in the Flash Player folder exactly as they would had they been written by those domain's web pages. It's not super complex, but it is worth snooping through these files and folders to familiarize yourself. In production situations, you'll find it's often easiest to just keep this folder open and delete or create files manually.

Players

There are countless versions of the Flash Player. When you do Test Movie, (that is, Control, Test Movie) you use the authplay.dll version (or, on Mac the AuthPlayLib version). If you double-click a SWF, you'll be running the SAFlashPlayer (SA for standalone). Finally, if you publish and view the movie in the browser, you'll be using the Flash Player (either the ActiveX control for Internet Explorer or the plug-in for Netscape and others). On top of all this, there are both "release" and "debug" versions of the player. Multiply all that by the different revisions of the Flash Player, and you'll reach a pretty big number.

I don't mean to confuse matters. After all, you don't have to test everything you build with each player, but it's a good idea to get a handle on how to access each player. First, adjacent to your installed version of Flash 2004 you should find a folder called Players. It contains the standalone players as well installers for the web players. The version used when you do a test movie is named authplay.dll, and it appears in the First Run folder. Unfortunately, all these players will become out of date as soon as a new minor revision of the Flash Player is released.

I can recommend two TechNotes at Macromedia that cover how to remove and install the players: 12727 and 14157. (Just type either number into the Search field at www.macromedia.com). If you're really into archiving all the minor revisions, you'll want to back up any files before you install newer versions. Finally, you also can check out the TechNote 14266 for links to nearly all the old versions of the Flash Player.

My main point here is "know the players and where they are." The other huge tip I can give you is this: Files with the extension .swf (or .fla for that matter) will automatically get re-associated with whatever application last launched it. If you drag a SWF on top of an old Flash 4 standalone player you downloaded from

88 Part II Technology

Macromedia, for example, next time you double-click a SWF it'll run that stand-alone player. I find it easiest to maintain as few Flash Players as possible—and keep them all in a central location. I also keep a SWF on my desktop that contains a text field (named version_txt) and this simple script in the first frame: `version_txt.text=$version`. That way, I can quickly check what version of the Flash Player I'm running. Also, you can find the authplay.dll version by either accessing its file properties or just opening Flash and selecting Control, Debug Movie. You'll see the Flash Player version listed under _level0, as shown in Figure 3.13.

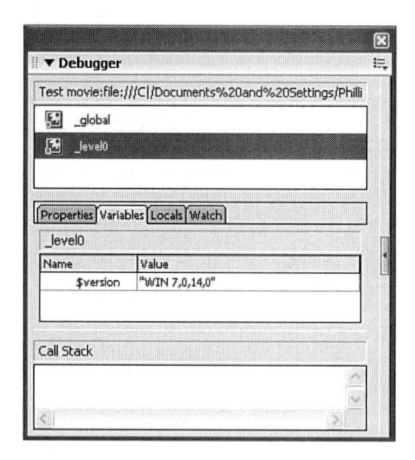

Figure 3.13 *You can quickly determine player version used when testing by selecting Control, Debug Movie.*

Understanding *localhost*

You can run countless free web server software programs locally on your computer. (For example, Macromedia has a free developer version of ColdFusion that includes a web server.) Installing a local web server is quite useful because you can test your applications without actually uploading to a public web site. As mentioned previously, the root will commonly be a folder named wwwroot. However, running a file in your local web server takes more than just opening a SWF or HTML file inside the wwwroot folder. You'll want to be sure the URL appearing in the browser begins with `http://` and nothing else. To reach that wwwroot folder, you should be able to type one of the following addresses:

```
http://localhost/
http://192.168.1.1/
```

Don't ask me why, but sometimes the second option works when `localhost` fails, even though they should be the same.

There are lots more details, such as port numbers and configuring a router to forward HTTP request to a particular computer on your network. Systems vary greatly, and this topic is easily researched elsewhere. In any event, you'll want to make sure your setup is doing what you expect.

Publishing

If you've figured out where your configuration folders, Flash Player versions, and local web server are located, surely you can move a few SWF files to the correct location. Personally, while I'm testing I often do things manually. For example, "test movie" and then move the SWF by hand to the right location, open the browser, and point to that file—making sure to begin **http://localhost**. When you consider all the other folders you have to deal with, it gets really tiring really fast.

A few features attempt to "do the thinking for you," which is why I initially avoided them. Things such as Dreamweaver's Site panel, Flash's Publish command, and the new Project panel in Flash Pro. Without fully documenting these, let me just say this: Take the time to figure them out. They can save a lot of time. Having said this, please don't use anything you don't fully understand. It's not like you're going to cause the Internet to collapse, but instead you can be lulled into thinking everything's working. If you don't know why, however, it can be excessively difficult to troubleshoot when something does go wrong. In addition, you might end up doing something that appears to work but you're just fooling yourself. I don't want to sound too elite on this matter—the tools aren't that tough to figure out.

Here's a rundown of some of the cool things you can do now:

- Flash Pro's Project panel can export several related SWFs and even upload the files to an external FTP site.
- Dreamweaver's Site panel can do all of that except the SWF export.
- Flash MX 2004's new Publish profiles mean you can save every last detail in your Publish settings and load those settings when you start a new project. (Just remember to select Import/Export, and then Export to save a profile to disk or Import to load one you've previously exported.)

In fact, I've yet to really exploit all of these features in a real live project. However, one thing that saves a ton of time is the folder icon that now appears under the Formats tab of the Publish Settings dialog box. It simply lets you browse to a folder where you want files to export. It's a tiny feature, but it shows you how you'll likely discover more little things that can save time.

Finally, if there's one manual process that puts undue stress on me, it's the way I have to clear my browser's cache. That is, if I test an application in the browser and then make an update to the files, I can retest but I might be viewing the old file! That is so frustrating. A lot of people set their browser to not cache, but I don't. Because I know the steps to clear the cache, I can practically follow them in my sleep. I often put a version number right onscreen and confirm I'm looking at the latest revision when I test.

I could go on with little tips, but you'll see more where appropriate throughout this book. In addition, there's a whole chapter on productivity later in this book. Being efficient isn't part of some personal goal to become more like a machine. Instead, being productive means you'll have more time for other interests, including relaxation.

Summary

In many ways this chapter was inadequate. I covered everything but nothing in enough detail to really go use it. That's okay because the goal was an overview. Ideally your interest is sparked and you want to dig in deeper. Also, we can go off in various specific directions now, but you shouldn't get lost because topics can be put in perspective.

This chapter introduced the following:

- How data considerations can be quite involved.
- The three data exchange formats Flash supports (text, AMF, and SOAP).
- Many reasons why data exchanges involve error checks and synchronization issues.
- How application servers work.
- Some basics about the V2 components.
- The graphic map that appears as a guide in subsequent chapters. Be sure to refer back to this figure.

{Chapter 4}

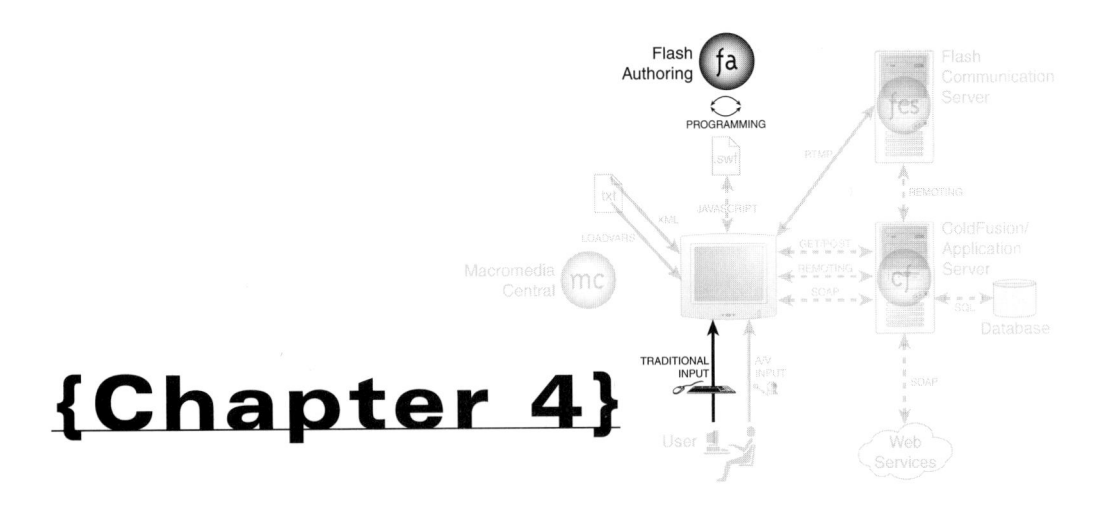

Working with Complex Data

Although computers are great at gathering, manipulating, and calculating raw data, humans prefer their data presented in an orderly fashion. The same way all the world events can be organized into a newspaper by editors, rich Internet applications (RIAs) should present just the important data. If you're buying a house in a new town, for instance, you don't need to know all the prices ever paid for houses, but you may want to know the median price paid in the past 90 days. Unfortunately, as the programmer, you have to sift through all the data gathered to extract just the important parts—and present it in a visually interesting way.

This chapter covers different ways to store, manipulate, and generally manage data. You'll see how storing all data in an easily accessible way makes your job easier when it comes to extracting and presenting just the meaningful parts. The orderly data you gather in this chapter leads straight into Chapter 5, "Presenting Data," where you'll see ways to present the data.

I keep saying "all this data" as if all the world's information is at your disposal. (Actually it is, as you'll see during the discussion about linking to web services in Chapter 7, "Exchanging Data with Outside Services.") But from where does the data come? In fact, the really cool applications you build will involve importing data from outside sources and then presenting that data inside Macromedia Flash MX 2004. There are lots of sources for outside data, including databases, web services, and other connected users. This chapter concentrates on working with data after it's inside Flash. Realize the simplest source of data is from you, the author—just type it in. For this chapter's apps, that's the source of the data.

Of course, everything you learn in this chapter also applies to manipulating data gathered from outside sources. This apparent non sequitur of learning to manipulate data before you learn how to gather it actually makes sense. You'll be better equipped to decide how the data should be gathered after you can clarify your preference for how it's organized inside Flash. For example, only after you measure and decide which windows to dress can you order the curtains. In any event, there's lots of interesting information about manipulating data inside Flash.

Specifically, this chapter covers the following topics:

- Identifying the appropriate data type for variables
- Comparing homemade (or "generic") objects to arrays
- Sorting arrays and parse objects
- Structuring data for easy access and manipulation

Structuring Data

You can't control the weather, but if you're gathering weather information, you can certainly control how the data is organized. That's what this section is about: deciding how data is stored so that it's easy to access just the parts you need. You'll see that structuring data is totally up to you. The goal is to make the data organization easier for later when you analyze and display the data.

This section first examines selecting the data's form (its data type), then compares two particularly useful data types (arrays and objects), and then—finally—shows you how to figure out how to get at the specific values contained.

{ Note }

Comparing Arrays and Objects Both arrays and objects are discussed as comparable ways to store data (each with its respective benefits). In fact, arrays are a type of object. As such, objects offer much more than arrays, so I don't want you to see arrays as an equal. When it comes to how you structure data, however, they are definitely comparable.

Data Types

Variables are nothing more than containers for data. You make up a variable name, set its value, and then you can access the data contained. The *type* of data is up to you. Strings, numbers, arrays, and objects are all examples of data types. Only if your variable contains a number can you do "number things" to it—such as mathematical operations like divide and subtract. If your variable contains a string, you can do "string things" such as capitalize or extract specific characters. How you treat or what you store in a variable depends on its data type.

{ Note }

Flash MX 2004's Strong Data Typing ActionScript 1 is an "untyped" language, which means you can store one data type in a particular variable (say, a string) and then later store a different data type (say, a number) in that same variable and the contents will always be treated appropriately. You can still do that. If you use ActionScript 2.0 (AS2), however—a Publish Setting option—you can take advantage of *strong data typing*. This just means that for the first use of any named variable, you can specify it will always be treated as a particular data type—say, String. Then, later, if you mistakenly use that variable where a number is required, or otherwise treat it as anything but a string, your movie will not compile. That is, you'll see a Type Mismatch error in the Output panel when you test or publish the movie. The advantage is that Flash can perform slightly faster because it doesn't have to constantly check what data type a particular variable contains. Additionally, it can help make your code clearer. Perhaps the best side effect is that because Flash will know what data type your variable contains, it will trigger code hints when you later type the variable name followed by a period. The downside is if you don't follow the rules, it becomes a real hassle because your code won't compile.

The way you cast a variable as a particular data type is with the casting operator (:). After a variable's first declaration, type : followed by the data type you want to use. It looks like this:

```
var myName:String="Phillip"
```

Notice that :String gets inserted into an otherwise perfectly legitimate line of code. Also, you may see casting for parameters. For example, the following code says the myFunction() accepts a number only:

```
function myFunction (someParam:Number){}
```

continues

> Use this when you feel ready. In the meantime, just realize what the colon is used for, because you'll likely see strong typing in example files (but not much in this book).

Although there are many data types, they are always treated one of two ways: as primitive (also called *value*) and by reference. The difference arises when you copy a variable. Primitive variables (which include numbers and strings) are copied "by value," whereas reference types (including arrays, objects, and clip instances) are copied "by reference." Copying a primitive variable really copies the variable's current value, whereas copying a reference variable just creates a pointer to the original variable. This can mess you up if you copy a variable and then change the original and see that the copy also changes. Take this example:

```
1    myOriginal=[1,2,3];
2    myCopy=myOriginal;
3    myOriginal[0]="one";
4    trace(myCopy);
```

Line 3 changes the myOriginal array, but that also changes myCopy because it isn't a copy of the value; instead, it's just a reference to the original.

The way you can copy just the *contents* of the myOriginal array is by replacing line 2 with this code:

```
myCopy=myOriginal.slice();
```

The slice() method can also copy a portion of your array; when you forgo any parameters, however, it copies each element. Note that this solution only works when the array is one level deep (that is, when you don't have any nested arrays).

A great analogy is how copying a file on your computer is like copying by value, whereas making a shortcut (or alias) to that file is copying by reference. If you change the original reference variable type, all references to it change as well.

The following list categorizes typical data types as primitive or reference.

Primitive (or Value)	Reference
`Number`	`array`
`String`	`object`
`Boolean`	`function`
`Undefined`	`movieclip`
`null`	

By the way, you can always see the type of a particular variable by doing `trace(typeof someVariable);`. Just replace `someVariable` with the variable in question. In addition, there's an operator called `instanceof`. With this, you can check whether a variable contains a particular data type. For example, `trace(_root instanceof MovieClip);` should display true in the Output window.

The difference between primitive and reference type variables is important, but above all you need to keep track of the data type you're storing in each variable. By following a logical and consistent way of naming each variable, you're making a good start. Also, documenting how each variable is used when commenting is another good habit. Actually, using AS2's strict data type casting is a way to force you. However you do it, know what type of data is contained in a variable before you go accessing them.

Homemade Objects Versus Arrays

If you ever felt limited by the idea that each named variable can contain only one value at a time, surely you've discovered arrays. I like the analogy that an array is like a line-ruled sheet of paper where you can write something different on each line (or row). A sheet of graph paper is like a multidimensional array because you can store different values in each cell, based on row and column. The many benefits of arrays come down to convenience and expandability. It's more convenient to store a bunch of phone numbers in a single named array variable instead of coming up with a new name for each one. Also, an array is expandable if, say, you want to let users add as many contacts as they want to an address book. You'll see how easy arrays are managed in the "Sorting Data" section later in this chapter.

Making Generic Objects

In a similar way, generic objects enable you to store lots of values in a single variable (also called *associative arrays*, or *short objects*, or just *objects*). The major benefit generic objects offer is that each value in the object has a name. You should think of the values as properties because that's how they're accessed. Just like how a clip has an _x property and an _alpha property, your generic objects can have any properties you name. To reference the phone property, you could use myObject.phone, provided your object name is myObject.

> { Note }
>
> **Associative Arrays Aren't Arrays** Personally, I don't like the term *associative array* because generic objects don't support any of the cool array methods such as sorting.

What follows is a quick rundown on how you formulate your own generic objects.

Use new Object() to initialize:

```
myObject=new Object();
```

Then, start creating and populating properties using standard dot syntax:

```
myObject.someProperty="a value";
myObject.anotherProperty="another value";
```

Alternatively, you can create and populate in one line (in what's called a literal way) by surrounding with curly braces, placing properties followed by a colon and its value, and separating properties with commas, as follows:

```
myObject={someProp:"a value", otherProp:"val 2"};
```

I generally prefer the first approach (creating the object and then adding properties). However, the literal one-line way is convenient because when you don't really need a variable, you're passing just the value of an object.

In either case, to access an object's various properties' values, use the standard dot syntax:

```
trace("someProperty is "+myObject.someProperty);
```

(As discussed later in this chapter, you also can access properties using a string inside brackets, with no dot: myObject["someProperty"].)

> **{ Note }**
>
> **Nesting Data Types** Arrays and objects break the concept of name/value pairs. Whereas a plain variable containing a string does just have a name and a value, an array has one name and several values. In the case of an object, the object has a name, but contained within the objects' value is a collection of named properties—each with its own value. When you start nesting data types, it can get even more complex. For example, you could have an array full of objects. Or, the value of one property in an object could be an object itself. Keep in mind that you can usually design the data structure to fit your needs so that instead of "deciphering," you'll just be drilling down to access the data you need.

This discussion would be rather academic without application examples. Remember, you decide how to structure the data. Your data structure is completely subjective, but you should strive to make things easy for yourself—easy to access and change data as well as easy to adapt to unforeseen changes. Consider a contact management application—a rolodex if you will. Listing 4.1 shows one way to structure the data:

Listing 4.1   Array of Contact Objects

```
1  contacts=[];
2  contact1=new Object();
3  contact1.first="Phillip";
4  contact1.last="Kerman";
5  contact1.phone="503-555-1212";
6  contacts.push(contact1);
7  contacts.push({first:"George",
8                 last:"Bush",
9                 phone:"800-555-1212"});
```

In the end, the `contacts` array has a generic object in each slot (or *index*). Each object represents a different person and contains the three properties `first`, `last`, and `phone`. Lines 7 through 9 demonstrate how you can create a literal object (in this case, immediately pushing it into the array); lines 2 through 6 do effectively the same thing, but create an unnecessary variable (`contact1`).

Although creating the `contacts` array in the preceding example may seem like a bit of a chore, the benefits of this structure are apparent when you begin accessing the data. For example, you can reference the phone number of the first contact with the expression `contacts[0].phone`. Only because you happen to have the variable `contact1` can you similarly say `contact1.phone`—but you don't have to. The expression `contacts[0]` returns the entire object in the first slot; so if you just add `.phone`, you'll be grabbing the phone property of the object in the array.

Listing 4.2 provides a quick example of the sorts of gymnastics possible with the data structure for `contacts`:

Listing 4.2 Extracting Contact Object Data

```
1   myField_txt.text="";
2   for(var i=0;i<contacts.length;i++){
3       var thisOne=contacts[i];
4       myField_txt.text+= Number(i+1)+": ";
5       myField_txt.text+= thisOne.first + " ";
6       myField_txt.text+= thisOne.last + ", ";
7       myField_txt.text+= thisOne.phone + "\r";
8   }
```

The loop started in line 2 repeats while the variable `i` is less than the length of the `contacts` array. For each iteration, line 3 conveniently stores an entire object (in the current index). It turns out the difference in saying `thisOne` or `contacts[i]` isn't much—but when you need to dig even deeper into an array or object, such temporary variables prove really helpful—if for nothing else, to reduce your typing. Anyway, lines 4 through 7 continue to add formatted text to the `myField_txt`'s `text` property. Notice that to control the output, at the end of each line I concatenate a colon, space, comma, or return character (`"\r"`).

> **{ Note }**
>
> **Start Counting at Zero** Remember, in Flash arrays (and strings) start counting with zero for the first index. Just to make things interesting, ColdFusion starts counting with one.

The output looks like this:

```
1: Phillip Kerman, 503-555-1212
2: George Bush, 800-555-1212
```

Benefits of Arrays

The beauty of this structure is that you can add as many contacts as you want. Finally, remember that this is just one way to structure the data. Another design might involve an array full of arrays. So where you were pushing an object before, you could push an array instead:

```
contacts.push(["Phillip", "Kerman", "503-555-1212"]);
```

The one downside to this structure is that you must remember "first name is first, last name is second, and phone number comes third." I can think of two reasons why a generic object is better in this case:

- The data for each person is known. (That is, you always need those three attributes.)
- Giving names to those three properties makes them easier to access (as opposed to memorizing the order). This also puts your data in context, which can help you later or others reading your code.

Generally, try to use generic objects if the data has much more meaning when named and use arrays if the quantity of data is unknown or you expect it to grow and shrink. The following sorts of data are best suited for an array or for object:

- **Arrays**

    Several values to be used in statistical analysis, such as test score averages

    A collection of bookmarks the user saves

    A variety of color values to be selected randomly

- **Objects**

    User profiles such as name, rank, number

    Current user preferences such as music on or off, background color, and language

    An individual bookmark—which can be saved in an array with other bookmarks, but the individual bookmark can have properties for page number and the given name for the page

To drill home the idea that you can nest arrays and objects as deeply as you want, here's one more variation to the `contacts` array (presumably to make things more convenient, not just convoluted). Suppose you want to include each contact's children's names. You could start over and take the approach in Listing 4.3.

Listing 4.3 Objects Containing Arrays Nested in an Array

```
1    contacts=[];
2    contacts.push({first:"Phillip",
3                   last:"Kerman",
4                   phone:"503-555-1212",
5                   kids:["Savannah"]});
6    contacts.push({first:"George",
7                   last:"Bush",
8                   phone:"800-555-1212",
9                   kids:["Jenna", "Barbara"]});
```

Notice in lines 5 and 9 that way down inside the `kids` property of each nested object is an array (containing one or more strings).

This way, you could later determine how many children a contact had by using the following:

```
contacts[i].kids.length;
```

Notice that this example uses an array as the value for each contact's `kids` property. This makes sense because you don't know how many children someone may have, and there's really no need to identify each child with property names such as `child1`, `child2`, and so on.

By now you should be getting a better sense how arrays and objects differ in their usefulness. Keep in mind that the general rule (that arrays are better for unlimited and unclassified data) can be broken. And, you can always change your mind later. However, designing the data structure is an architectural decision best suited for early in a production.

Using Objects Like Arrays

The biggest limit of objects is they lack all the cool array methods (such as `sort()`, `push()`, and `pop()` to name a few). You'll learn how to manipulate arrays using methods in the next section. For now, however, you need to understand that although the standard for-loop (as used earlier) won't let you loop through properties in an object, the for-in loop will! Listing 4.4 provides a template that you can use with any generic object.

Listing 4.4   Looping Through an Object

```
1    myObject={prop:"val",prop2:"val2"};
2    for (p in myObject){
3        var thisProperty=p;
4        var thisValue= myObject[p];
5        trace(thisProperty+":"+thisValue);
6    }
```

Basically, the for-in loop (when used with an object) will set the iterant variable (p in this case) to a string version of the actual property name. Notice in line 4 that you can ascertain the value of the property by placing the string property name inside brackets (instead of following a period in as in the standard dot syntax).

Dynamically Referencing Properties

The fact you can grab properties' values by using either `object.property` or `object["property"]` may seem insignificant, but this brings out a very important point. Using the "string in brackets" access is the only possible way when you fashion a property name dynamically. This can certainly happen if you use an object for data that might have been more convenient as an array. Consider this simple object:

`dogs={dog_1:"max", dog_2:"hank", dog_3:"skippy"};`

Suppose you have another variable `currentDog` and its value is 2. To access `"hank"`, you could use the following expression:

`dogs["dog_"+currentDog];`

That is, `"dog_"+currentDog` equals `"dog_2"`; but because that's a string, you need to surround it with brackets. I promise this technique will come up time and again. You also should know this technique works with clip instance names. That's because movie clip instance names are like properties of the timeline where they reside. The syntax looks the same as `object.property` after all:

`_root.box_1._x=100;`

Following the same rule of string names in brackets, you could use the following:

`_root["box_"+1]._x=100;`

Naturally, the 1 could be a variable. Notice that after _root there's no dot. Notice, too, that although you can normally leave off _root (as in `box_1._x=100`) when using this bracket reference, you must precede it with the path to the movie clip.

If this section wasn't totally clear, consider rereading it because you'll see many instances of nested values referenced this way.

Associating Functions with Event Properties

It's actually possible to store references to functions inside properties of an object. And as it turns out, I can't think of many times when it's anything more than a convenience. (Perhaps you plan to trigger one of several different functions and decide to store which one inside an object.) The reason I mentioned this, however, is that so many advanced features use that model. Consider this example:

`my_btn.onPress=function(){play();};`

It looks like the my_btn button instance has a property called onPress into which a literal function is stored. That's exactly what it is! The only thing special is that onPress is built in…and Flash knows when to trigger it. You can store functions in a ton of other expected property names, and they'll trigger at the appropriate times. You'll learn all the important properties that work this way in time, but for now look at these example fragments in Listing 4.5 to see how familiar they are knowing what you know now.

Listing 4.5 Examples of Storing Functions in Properties That Match Flash Events

```
1   my_sound.onComplete=function(){ trace("sound done");};
2   myResponder.onData=function(data){
3     trace("the data " + data + "was received");
4   }
5   my_connection.onStatus=function(info){
6     if(info.code=="NetConnection.Connect.Success"){
7       play();
8     }
9   }
```

The basic idea here is associating functions with known Flash events (in the form of properties). Line 1 defines a `trace()` command when the `my_sound` instance of the Sound object completes playing a sound. Line 2 differs slightly because the `onData` event (triggered when outside data is received) includes an argument (called `data` in this case) that contains the actual data received. Finally, Line 5 shows that when the `onStatus` event triggers, the argument received is actually an object itself that may contain a property called `code`. Receiving an object as the argument is a convenient way to stuff lots of named data (as properties) instead of having multiple arguments—and it happens to be the standard way a lot of the advanced events work. (Incidentally, `onStatus` is the event triggered when data returns from the server. You'll see it when using the Flash Communication Server (in Chapter 8, "Foundation Communication Server," and Chapter 9, "Advanced Communication Server"), although it also pops up a few other places.

Generic objects are more than just a great way to store complex data (although, that's the main reason you're studying them now). The investment learning is paid back time and again throughout ActionScript. In addition to how many events are triggered (as you just saw), Flash functions commonly return or accept single-object parameters chocked full of named properties. This way, a ton of data can be compacted into a single variable name. Here are just a few methods that accept or return generic objects: `setTransform()`, `getBounds()`, `getTextExtent()`.

For an example that's new to Flash MX 2004, check out all the details you can find out about how text will display using `getTextExtent()`. The properties `height`, `width`, `ascent`, `descent`, and `textFieldRequiredHeight` are all crammed into one generic object. Here's an example:

```
my_fmt=new TextFormat();
my_fmt.font="Arial";
my_fmt.size=32;
details=my_fmt.getTextExtent("Phillip");

trace("height is "+details.height);
trace("width is "+details.width);
trace("ascent is "+details.ascent);
trace("descent is "+details.descent);
```

You'll learn about the TextFormat object (the first 3 lines) in the next couple of chapters. For now, notice that `getTextExtent()` returns, into the variable `details`, an object with several properties that you can then display in the Output window. You may not need everything in that `details` variable, but there's only one method—it just returns several values inside the properties of a generic object.

The bulk of work managing complex data involves first designing the structure, then importing it (or populating inside Flash), and then accessing individual elements as needed. To filter out just the parts you need, often you'll want to leave the original data untouched as you copy elements. However, there are plenty of times when the original data isn't so sacred—you'll want it permanently modified. This chapter deals with actually changing the data, whereas the next chapter on presenting data covers how to filter.

Comparison to DataProvider Object

Despite having said the data structure is up to you, the developer, I have been gravitating toward arrays containing generic objects. This just happens to match the format of columns and rows (rows being the slots of the array, and columns being the names of properties contained in each object). So, it's a good format to use when appropriate.

On top of the good reasons to use this format, it just so happens it matches the general structure of the DataProvider object. (Yes, *another* object type.) It's so cool how DataProviders work with components that if I try to explain it here, the book may catch fire. It's covered in detail in Chapter 12. If you just want to see something cool, drag a List component on stage (or—better yet—if you have Flash Pro, drag a DataGrid) and name the instance **my_component**. Copy the code from Listing 4.3, where the `contacts` array was populated, and add the following code after it:

```
my_component.dataProvider=contacts;
```

Test the movie and you'll see that the component automatically fills with the data (see Figure 4.1). What's really wild is that if the `contacts` array changes later (using the DataProvider's `addItem()` method in place of how you might expect to use `push()`), the component will update and stay in sync. I know that we're not really talking about presenting data yet, and certainly not covering components yet, but this was so cool I had to mention it. The good news is that DataProviders are like arrays full of generic objects but more.

first	last	phone	kids
Phillip	Kerman	503-555-1212	Savannah
George	Bush	800-555-1212	Jenna,Barbara

Figure 4.1 *You can link your data to a component by assigning a DataProvider.*

Sorting Data

One of the best ways to help users analyze complex data is to sort it in some logical manner. Consider the `contacts` array from earlier in this chapter: a user could quickly find a particular contact if the array were sorted alphabetically; or, maybe, the user wants to list all the phone numbers from a particular area code. By sorting, you simplify large quantities of complex data.

Using the *sort()* Method

The good news/bad news is that Flash has several built-in sorting routines, but they often don't work the way you expect or need. Consider this simple array:

```
prices=[230,345,179,365,300,159];
```

Suppose these are house prices (in thousands of dollars, naturally) and you plan to plot them on a graph. This is a perfect case for the Array object's `sort()` method. The array will actually change order when you execute the following code:

```
prices.sort();
```

Note that unlike some methods that just return a value, `sort()` permanently changes the array.

I don't know whether it was evil of me to show this example first, because it was almost too easy. Now try this one:

```
people=["van Hoff", "Smith", "Adams", "Zwebber"];
people.sort();
trace(people);
//outputs: Adams,Smith,Zwebber,van Hoff
```

The problem is that although Flash can sort numbers fine, it considers all uppercase letters to come before any lowercase. Naturally, it's totally conceivable to force everyone's name to start with an uppercase letter, but that's not ideal. It turns out that Flash MX 2004 adds a few useful sorting options that can help you avoid difficult workarounds. For example, you can sort without regard to case using myArray.sort(Array.CASEINSENSITIVE). (Just type **Array.** and you'll see a code hint with the rest of the sort variations.) Finally, you can combine sort options by separating them with |. Suppose you want to sort descending and not case sensitive—just pass Array.CASEINSENSITIVE | Array.DESCENDING.

Here's an adjusted version of the preceding example:

```
people=["van Hoff", "Smith", "Adams", "Zwebber"];
people.sort(Array.CASEINSENSITIVE);
trace(people);
//outputs: Adams,Smith,van Hoff,Zwebber
```

Using the *sortOn()* Method

The sort() method definitely only works on arrays. Even when your arrays contain generic objects in each slot, however, you can take control of the sorting. The sortOn() method is especially designed for sorting arrays full of objects. Listing 4.6 some starter data that is used for the next few examples:

Listing 4.6 *songs* Array Containing Objects

```
songs=[];
songs.push({artist:"Fugazi",
            songtitle:"Waiting Room",
            time:"02:53"});
songs.push({artist:"Beastie Boys",
            songtitle:"Alive",
            time:"04:48"});
songs.push({artist:"Radiohead",
            songtitle:"Creep",
            time:"03:56"});
```

Even a moderately complex array (such as this one that contains objects) requires a different tack when sorting.

At this point, you can't use `songs.sort()` because Flash can't put objects in order. Because you also can't do `trace(songs)` (try it if you want), I've come up with the following function in Listing 4.7 for testing purposes.

Listing 4.7 Utility Function to Display the *songs* Arrays Contents

```
1   function traceAll(theArray) {
2     var total = theArray.length;
3     for (var i = 0; i<total; i++) {
4       for (var p in theArray[i]) {
5         trace(p+"="+ theArray[i][p]);
6       }
7       trace("----");
9     }
9   }
```

Most of this should be a review, but do notice the temporary variable `total`. Line 2 stores the `length` of the array so that line 3 doesn't repeatedly (on every loop) recalculate the array's `length`. This gets around a slight quirk in Flash's efficiency.

To use this function, just pass an array. Keep in mind that this only goes one level deep into the array's contained objects. You can download a loop that will dig as deep as necessary from www.phillipkerman.com/rias.

At this point, you can use `sortOn()` to specify any property name on which to perform a sort. For example, you can sort by artist name:

```
1   trace("before:");
2   traceAll(songs);
3   songs.sortOn("artist");
4   trace("after:");
5   traceAll(songs);
```

Basically, line 3 is the only one doing any work; the rest is to see the results. The `sortOn()` method just accepts a string name for the property on which you want to sort the array's objects.

This data can be sorted by "artist", "title", or "time", and it works in all cases. However, sortOn() has the same limits as sort(). Namely, to sort without regard to case (or any other variation), you need to either write your own compare function or use one of the built-in sorting options (such as Array.CASEINSENSTIVE). (For example, try changing "Beastie Boys" to "beastie boys" and sortOn() renders unfavorable results.) It's pretty simple: Just pass your compare function or built-in option as the second parameter in sortOn(). Say, songs.sortOn("artist",Array.CASEINSENSITIVE).

Finally, you can pass an *array* of property names and sortOn() will have a logic to follow when there are matches. For example, you want to sort by artist, but if you have a bunch of Beastie Boys you want those sorted by song title. Just use songs.sortOn(["artist", "songtitle"]). (Notice, that's one array in the first parameter—you can still use the second parameter for a sorting rule.)

Sorting is one way to change an array's contents, if only the order of its contents. When it comes to displaying the contents of an array, having it sorted can certainly help the user. (Do realize, however, that displaying a portion of or a sorted view of an array doesn't require that you physically change the data.) Just remember that sorting permanently changes an array. Also, after you do add to an array, it will need to be re-sorted to stay in order. The next example shows how the user can populate an array as the movie plays—so the order is determined by the user and doesn't need to change.

Building a Slide-Show Maker

This discussion moves to presenting data next chapter, but first consider the following example, which will give you a good idea how to build something the user gets to populate. That is, you're spending a lot of time structuring and presenting relatively static data that the user accepts because it's interesting. Here you'll see the user creating the data as he adds pictures to create his own slide show.

You need to first structure the data despite the fact you don't know the exact images the user will select. Basically, you need to make a place to hold the data. In the end, you need an array full of slides. An array is a good choice because the total number is unknown. Into each slot of the array, you can have the picture's title and, perhaps, the frame number where it resides. But an array may not be enough for all the data. It may be nice to have room for a few more variables that track general information such as a name for the particular show and the date created. There's no rule against maintaining separate variables: one for the array of slides, one for the show name, and one for date saved—but I still say we stuff *all* this data into one generic object. Later, when you actually save this show you'll see why one variable is useful.

To look mainly at code and the Flash stage, consider this bare-bones collection of interface elements and their respective instance names (shown in Figure 4.2):

- **Button components**

  add_pb, delete_pb, next_pb, previous_pb, save_pb

- **Input text fields**

  title_txt, show_txt

- **List component**

  show_lb

In addition to the items listed above, you need a movie clip with the instance name content. Inside this clip, select the first several frames, press F6 to make keyframes, and then put a different picture on each frame.

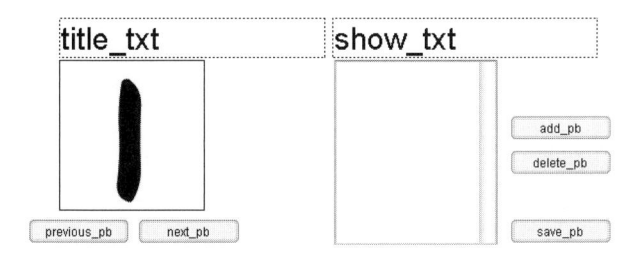

Figure 4.2 *The slide-show example includes several components, some text, and a movie clip. Note that the button labels shown match the instance names.*

Glance at all this code in Listing 4.8, and then read the explanation that follows about the important lines.

Listing 4.8 Complete Slide-Show Code

```
1    //===========
2    // SET UP BUTTONS
3    add_pb.setLabel("add");
4    add_pb.addEventListener("click", doAdd);
5    delete_pb.setLabel("delete");
6    delete_pb.addEventListener("click", doDelete);
7    delete_pb.enabled=false;
8    save_pb.setLabel("save");
9    save_pb.addEventListener("click", doSave);
10   save_pb.enabled=false;
11   next_pb.setLabel("Next");
12   next_pb.addEventListener("click", doPager);
13   previous_pb.setLabel("Previous");
14   previous_pb.addEventListener("click", doPager);
15   previous_pb.enabled=false;
16   //===========
17   // BUILD DEFAULT TITLES ARRAY
18   titles = [];
19   titles.push("page one");
20   titles.push("page two");
21   titles.push("page three");
22   titles.push("page four");
23   titles.push("page five");
24   titles.push("page six");
25   //===========
26   // STOP THINGS ON PAGE 1
27   content.stop();
28   title_txt.text = titles[content._currentframe-1];
29   show_txt.text="";
30   //===========
31   // INTIALIZE THE LIST BOX
32   show_lb.removeAll();
33   show_lb.addEventListener("change", clickLine);
34   // INTIALIZE THE SHOW OBJECT
35   // show.pages will contain an array of objects:
36   // {title:"string", frame:1 }
37   // show.time is the last date saved
38   // show.showname is the title for the whole show
39   //===========
40   show ={pages:[],
41          time:new Date(),
42          showname:show_txt.text};
```

```
43   //==========
44   // DO PAGER (next_pb's and previous_pb's click handler)
45   function doPager(whoSaid) {
46     //figure out direction
47     var direction;
48     switch (whoSaid.target) {
49     case next_pb :
50       direction = 1;
51       break;
52     case previous_pb :
53       direction = -1;
54       break;
55     }
56     //jump to new frame
57     content.gotoAndStop(content._currentframe+direction);
58     //set title text
59     title_txt.text = titles[content._currentframe-1];
60     //check buttons
61     next_pb.enabled=true;
62     previous_pb.enabled=true;
63     if (content._currentframe == content._totalframes) {
64       next_pb.enabled=false;
65     }
66     if (content._currentframe == 1) {
67       previous_pb.enabled=false;
68     }
69   }
70   //==========
71   // DO ADD (add_pb's click handler)
72   function doAdd() {
73     //push both their title, and the current page
74     show.pages.push({title:title_txt.text,
75                     frame:content._currentframe});
76     show.time=new Date();
77     show.title=show_txt.text;
78     refreshList();
79   }
80   //==========
81   // DO DELETE (delete_pb's click handler)
82   function doDelete() {
83     var currentLine = show_lb.getSelectedIndex();
84     oldShow = show.pages;
85     total = show.pages.length;
```

continues

Listing 4.8 Complete Slide-Show Code (Continued)

```
 86     show.pages = [];
 87     for (var i = 0; i<total; i++) {
 88       if (i != currentLine) {
 89         show.pages.push(oldShow[i]);
 90       }
 91     }
 92     refreshList();
 93     show_lb.selectedIndex=Math.min(currentLine,
 94                         show.pages.length-1);
 95     delete_pb.enabled=(show.pages.length>0);
 96   }
 97   //===========
 98   // CLICK LINE (show_lb's change handler)
 99   function clickLine() {
100     content.gotoAndStop(show_lb.selectedItem.data);
101     title_txt.text =show_lb.selectedItem.label;
102     delete_pb.enabled=(show.pages.length>0);
103   }
104   //===========
105   // REFRESH LIST (utility function)
106   function refreshList() {
107     show_lb.removeAll();
108     var total = show.pages.length;
109     for (var i = 0; i<total; i++) {
110       show_lb.addItem(show.pages[i].title,
111                       show.pages[i].frame);
112     }
113   }
```

More than half this code just monitors and maintains the interface state. Lines 1 through 15 set the labels, click handlers, and enable properties of the buttons. Notice that on lines 34 through 42, I document and create the show object. The comments include how you can access the different elements (such as show.pages for the array of saved pages).

Check out the doAdd function (lines 71 through 79) where I set the three properties of the show object. In the case of the pages property, I actually push a generic object (with properties title and frame) onto the end of the array. If you ever need to jump to a page already saved, you can extract a single item in the array and use its title property (for display text) and frame property (in a gotoAndStop() command). It turns out

I didn't quite do it that way. When adding items to a List component, you may include both a value for the label and a value for the data. Only the label is visible to the user, but the Flash programmer can access either the `label` or `data` property for a given item in the list. On line 100, I just use the `data` of the selected item in the list. And on line 101, I use the `label` property. When adding items to the list, I added both `title` and `frame` properties as `label` and `data` respectively—shown in lines 110 and 111.

Although you'll learn more in Chapter 12, there's one more feature I want to highlight. The `doPager` function on line 45 is sneaky because either button (`next_pb` or `previous_pb`) can trigger this function—I'm just taking advantage of the fact that most components pass as the only parameter an object full of details about itself, so the switch case that follows uses the `target` property received to figure out in which direction to move.

Although this example shows a completed project, you can adapt several concepts to other applications. For example, you can make a "back button" or history feature for your application by automatically adding each visited frame to an array. Also, the natural next step to this slide-show maker is to make a slide-show *player* mode. That is, a modified interface that only lets the user step through previously saved slides. Actually, in Chapter 6, "Basic Data Exchange," you'll see how to use the local shared object to save the slide shows you create.

It was difficult to study how to manipulate and change data without displaying it too, because that's the easiest way to judge the results. In any event, presenting data is covered next. Just remember that the data is yours to fashion as needed.

Summary

No matter how well you structure your data, you can always find a better way. In this chapter, you saw several ways to use arrays and generic objects together and by themselves. You also saw several ways to loop through all the contents so that you can present just the information you want. Making an adaptable structure means that you can make changes to the presentation without affecting the underlying code.

You learned the following main skills in this chapter:

- How to analyze and design a structure for data using arrays or objects or arrays full of objects (really how to structure data any way you like it)
- How to parse through or sort the data

- The start to a slide-show app that lets the user build a list that you maintain using arrays, objects, and even presenting it onscreen

Having a good handle on organizing your data will make the next chapter on presenting data much easier for you. In this chapter, you rarely "saw" anything unless you popped open the debugger or did a `trace()`. The next chapter takes your data and look at ways to present it to the user.

Project Ideas

Here are a few project ideas based on managing complex data:

- **Photo sorter**

    Create an image viewer to preview and sort an archive of digital photographs. The only manual part would be getting a list of filenames (which you could do with an application server such as ColdFusion). It would be cool to give users a way to associate keywords with any individual photo. Then, they could create lists (well, arrays) of photos that match a particular query. Naturally, users will want to save any settings between sessions—so you need to apply skills covered in the next chapter regarding the local shared object. Macromedia actually produced a sample app like this called My Photo included in the Developer Resource Kit Volume 2, but I'd like to see something that enables users to add the keywords and do searches.

- **Tic-tac-toe**

    Alright, so you probably won't make your first million doing this game, but it's a good exercise. You can store the state of the game board in a nested array. Make a mode to play against the computer for an added challenge. Another good game to try is Concentration. You'll want to find an array-shuffling routine to randomize the board.

- **Graphing application**

    Take any data source to which you have access, think about how best to visually represent the data, and create a graph. You may want to check out the various drawing methods (listed as "Drawing Methods" under the Movie Clip object references). It really depends on how you want to create the graph. You can actually do quite a lot by placing clips onstage (like we did with the library and Olympic medal examples earlier). Ideally, you should make your code as adaptable as possible. For example, a nice challenge is to make it calculate a scale factor based on the range (from low and high) of values you happen to collect. Check out the Flash Charting components (available at www.macromedia.com/exchange) for a great model. (Naturally, you should strive to find better/different ways of making graphs.)

{Chapter 5}

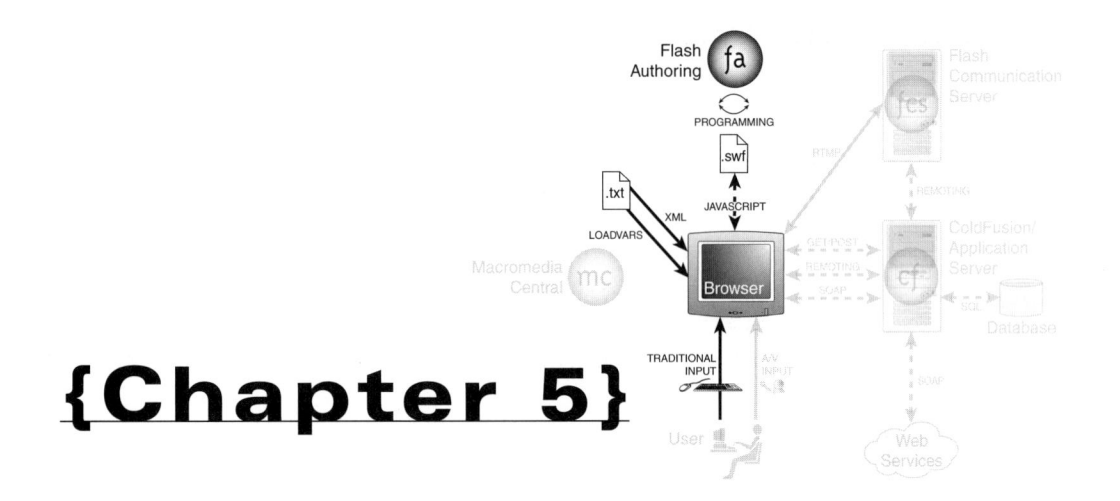

Presenting Data

If your data is structured well, you will find it's easy to present it however you want. In Chapter 4, "Working with Complex Data," a lot of time was spent designing data structures so that the data was easy to access. In this chapter, you'll see how that work pays off. I think it makes perfect sense that Chapter 4 discussed only how to design and structure data, and this chapter deals with data presentation. That's because a key concept you'll learn is that keeping the formatting separate from the actual content makes your code more transferable. You should be able to modify and change either the content or the layout without one affecting the other.

{ Note }

Parsing The idea of going through a large set of data and only extracting the pieces you need is called *parsing*. Parsing can include restructuring data from one format to another (for example, taking a long string of words and making it an array with each word in a different index). I don't use the word parsing much in this chapter, but feel free to throw it around when discussing the topic with others—it's a common term.

This chapter begins where Chapter 4 ended. That is, each example here starts with nicely structured data. Then, it's necessary to figure out ways to turn that raw data into something presentable for the user. Primarily, the examples focus on displaying text; however, you'll also learn how to use movie clips and dynamically drawn shapes to make visual presentations. Specifically, this chapter covers the following topics:

- How to display text, images, and hyperlinks using standard Hypertext Markup Language (HTML)
- How to use the new Cascading Style Sheets (CSS) support in Macromedia Flash MX 2004
- How Flash's built-in TextFormat and TextField objects fit into this picture
- Other options, including runtime drawing and clip creation

At the end of the chapter, you'll see the code for an example that combines nearly everything covered in this chapter.

Formatting Text

Although Flash MX 2004 supports only a few HTML styles, you can do quite a lot with text colors, fonts, and even hyperlinks. In addition, Flash MX 2004 now supports most styles from Cascading Style Sheets (CSS). Finally, there's also an *under*documented feature to make your hyperlinks trigger Flash functions. This chapter covers all of these.

Using HTML Text

To populate a dynamic or input text field, you just set that field's `text` property as in `fieldInstance_txt.text="some string"`. (Notice that to trigger the code-completion hints, I named the instance with the suffix "`_txt`"—that's part of the name, not some property.) Confusingly, field instances have both a `text` and an `htmlText` property. To use `htmlText`, the field must have its `html` property set to `true` (either with code, `fieldInstance_txt.html=true`, or by physically clicking the Render as HTML option in the Properties panel as Figure 5.1 shows).

The new TextArea and TextInput components offer a nearly identical interface (that is, the way you access and set data) plus a few additional features. The killer detail is that whereas regular text fields have both a `text` and an `htmlText` property, the components have only a `text` property. In either case, you'll want to set the `html` property to `true` if you plan to display formatted text.

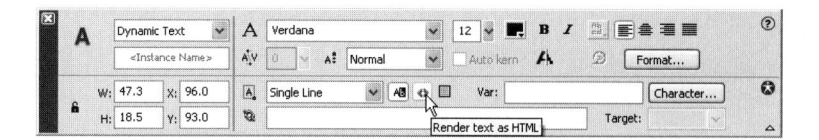

Figure 5.1 *The Properties panel has an option for HTML, although you can effectively click this button with the code* `htmlText=true`.

It's best to keep your content free from any HTML formatting and just format at the time the text is presented onstage. That is, you want to keep separate the content from the display. Listings 5.1 and 5.2 start with the following unformatted data and then formatting is added when it gets displayed.

Listing 5.1 Cookie Recipe Raw Data

```
1   recipe=new Object();
2   recipe.title="Cookies";
3   recipe.ingredients=["2 cups flour", "1 egg",
4           "1 stick of butter", "1 cup sugar"];
5   recipe.directions="Beat egg, sugar, and butter\r";
6   recipe.directions+="Mix into flour\r";
7   recipe.directions+="Cook at 375 for 10 minutes";
```

There's really no particular reason that I put each separate ingredient in an array where each direction is a long string separated by return characters (`"\r"`—which, could have just as easily been the constant `newline` outside the quotes). You can certainly reformat ingredients as a long string with `join()` or directions as an array with `split()`.

After you have the recipe object populated, you can use the following code (along with an onscreen dynamic text field named `my_txt`—with nice tall and wide margins).

Listing 5.2 Displaying the Recipe in HTML Format

```
1   var theObj=recipe;
2   var theField=my_txt;
3   theField.html=true;
4   theField.htmlText="<font size='24'>"+
5                     theObj.title+
6                     "</font><br>";
7   var total=theObj.ingredients.length;
```

continues

Listing 5.2 Displaying the Recipe in HTML Format (Continued)

```
8     for (var i=0;i<total;i++){
9       theField.htmlText+="* <i>"+
10                          theObj.ingredients[i]+"</i>";
11    }
12    theField.htmlText+="<br>";
13    theField.htmlText+=theObj.directions;
```

The first two lines stuff the specific object and specific text field instance into the local variables `theObj` and `theField`. This occurs so that later the code can be more useful (and generic) as a function that accepts those two arguments. Anyway, line 3 ensures the field will accept HTML. Line 4 builds a string by wrapping `<font>` tags around the `title` property. Because the font size value (the string `'24'`) is effectively a string within a string, I used single quotation marks, which is covered again later. The loop on lines 8 through 11 goes through the ingredients, placing an asterisk and then italic formatted text. Finally, the directions are dumped in at the end (line 13). Figure 5.2 shows the output.

By the way, if you instead use a TextArea component, the same code will work if you change each instance of `htmlText` to read `text`.

Cookies

* 2 cups flour
* 1 egg
* 1 stick of butter
* 1 cup sugar

Beat egg, sugar, and butter
Mix into flour
Cook at 375 for 10 minutes

Figure 5.2 *A recipe formatted using HTML.*

You can actually do much more with HTML formatting, but the idea of putting text within tags is always the same. In line 4 of Listing 5.2, you may have noticed that I nested single quotation marks (`'`) within a string that, itself, was surrounded by regular quotation marks (`"`). Sometimes you need to embed a regular quote mark within a string. All you need to know is that the backslash (`\`) is called an escape character, meaning the character that immediately follows should be taken literally. For example, `"This book is \"cool\"."` results in: `This book is "cool"`. Just remember if you want a backslash to show up, you need two—the first one escapes the second one.

Another interesting oddity is that although Flash identifies hexadecimal values (for instance, for colors) with `0x`—as in `0xFFFFFF` for white—HTML and CSS use `#` (as in `#FFFFFF`). The following example shows how you can color a portion of text:

```
my_txt.htmlText="I'm <font color=\"#FF0000\">mad</font>";
```

By the way, I could have used single quotes around the hex value.

{ Note }

Managing Escaped Quotations Because such escaped text can be difficult to manage, I often store complex strings in variables, something like this:

```
redText="<font color=\"#FF0000\">";
postText="</font>";
my_txt.htmlText="I'm "+redText+"mad"+postText;
```

Using the *img src* Tag

A new feature supported in HTML text is the `img src` tag for embedding images or SWFs. Like regular HTML web pages, this means images and text flow around each other as shown in Figure 5.3.

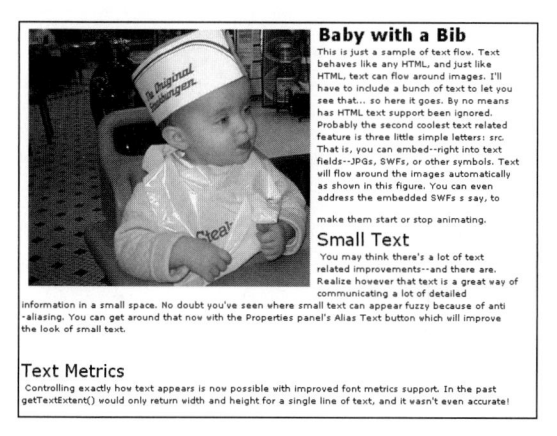

Figure 5.3 *Text fields can now display HTML with embedded images—and text will flow around the image.*

This feature is pretty easy: Just stick this form inside your html:
`<img src="some_image.jpg">` or `<img src="some_movie.swf">`. In addition, a few tags such as `width` and `height` work just like HTML. In addition, you can use the `id` tag to give the image or SWF an instance name. You can then address that clip as if it were nested in your text field. Here's an example:

```
my_txt.html=true;
my_txt.htmlText="<i>My movie:</i>";
my_txt.htmlText+="<img src='movie.swf' id='myClip'>";
```

Then, to address the clip, say to set its alpha, use the following:

```
my_txt.myClip._alpha=50;
```

Although simple, the inclusion of `img src` is a really great way to present visuals along with your text.

Hyperlinks to Flash Functions (*asfunction*)

You may be familiar with the HTML code `a href` used to create hyperlinks. This is supported in Flash as well. For example:

```
my_txt.htmlText="Click <a href='http://phillipkerman.com'>here</a>";
```

Although this is cool and all, it's really no different from Flash's `getURL()` command. And that only enables you to navigate to a new web page. You also can use `a href` to invoke Flash functions (either built-in functions or homemade functions). This means you can trigger any homemade script—not just web navigation—from what behaves like a regular-text hyperlink. It's called as function, and here's an example:

```
my_txt.htmlText="Click <a href='asfunction:doFunction'>here</a>";
```

Assuming you have a function declared called `doFunction()`, the preceding link will trigger it (when the user clicks). You'll see in the "Processing and Displaying" listing at the end of the chapter that we use `asfunction` to trigger code that sorts and displays the results. Notice the parentheses you might expect in a function trigger don't appear in the `htmlText` (just `doFunction` not `doFunction()`). This leads to the point that follows regarding passing parameters.

To pass parameters, you separate the function call (and any additional parameters) with commas:

```
my_txt.htmlText="Click
➥<a href='asfunction:doFunction,param'>here</a>"
```

In the preceding example, the string `"param"` is passed. If you want to pass a variable's value, you need to take it out from within the string:

```
my_txt.htmlText="Click
➥<a href='asfunction:doFunction,"+myVar+"'>here</a>"
```

(Again, because these concatenated strings can get pretty hairy, you'll definitely want to try to create variables to hold such involved strings.)

The asfunction technique is a great way to embed lots of clickable items into a block of text. Figure 5.4 shows an example from the real-time cattle auction site that I worked on.

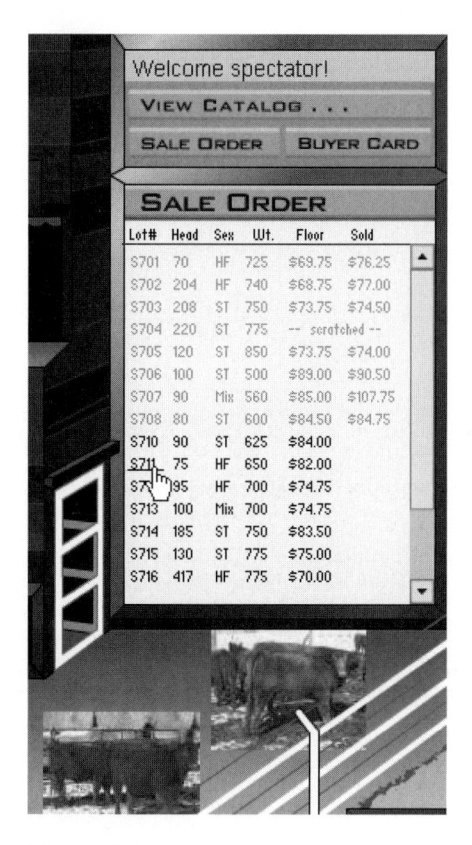

Figure 5.4 *Clicking lot numbers triggers a function that displays detailed information about cattle.*

Using CSS (Cascading Style Sheets)

The new support for CSS formatting is sort of a cross between HTML formatting (discussed previously) and the TextFormat object (coming next). It depends on whether you load an actual CSS file into Flash or you do all the formatting by hand inside Flash. I find it makes more sense to load CSS files and use `htmlText` because the formatting uses an existing standard (CSS and HTML). Because doing the formatting inside Flash (via the TextObject) offers more dynamic control, however, this chapter covers that as well.

Importing CSS Definitions

The coolest part about CSS support is that you can use your existing style sheets, provided the style is supported (because, like Flash's HTML support, not all properties are supported). However, the format of your CSS file matches the CSS standard of which you may be familiar. Here is a simple declaration that you can save in a file called my_styles.css:

```
.headline {
  font-family: "Arial", "Arial";
  font-size: 28px;
  color: #003399;
}
.main {
  font-family: "Arial", "Arial";
  font-size: 12px;
  color: #000000;
}
```

Without turning this into a CSS book, let me explain that the preceding code defines the styles `.headline` and `.main`. (Notice that the period is part of the name as a matter of convention so that I don't accidentally overwrite a built-in function.)

Now all you need to do is load those definitions into your app and start formatting text by tagging with `.headline` and `.main`. That's two steps: Load, and then apply the format. As you'll learn in the next two chapters, when loading external data you can't expect to start using it immediately after requesting to load it—that is, you have to wait for it to fully load. The form is "define what to do once it loads, then start loading." Listing 5.3 shows how you can import and then apply the CSS styles previously defined to a text field instance `my_txt`.

Listing 5.3   Importing and Displaying CSS Styles

```
var my_css = new TextField.StyleSheet();
my_css.onLoad = function(success) {
  if (success) {
    displayText();
  } else {
    trace("error loading");
  }
}
my_css.load("my_styles.css");

function displayText () {
  my_txt.styleSheet = my_css;
  my_txt.htmlText    = "<.headline>This is a headline</.headline><br>";
  my_txt.htmlText   += "<.main>this is the main style</.main>";
}
```

First I create the `my_css` variable into which I put an instance of the TextField StyleSheet object. That object has its `onLoad` event defined (to react when data is loaded), and then I commence loading (using `load()`). Notice when the data does finally load, I trigger my function `displayText()`, which goes and assigns the `styleSheet` property of the text field, which finally gets populated in the last couple of lines.

So, CSS is pretty cool. You can even define a:hover for when the user rolls over a hyperlink. Check this out:

```
//added to your my_styles.css file:
a:hover{
   font-family: "Arial", "Arial";
   font-size: 12px;
   text-decoration: underline;
   color: #0000FF;
}
//then put this inside the displayText() function above:
my_txt.htmlText+="<.main>click this <a href='#'>hyperlink</a>!</.main>";
```

Just replace # with an URL or `asfunction` if you want it to really do something. Also, if you set the `my_txt`'s `selectable` property to `false`, the cursor won't flicker between an I-beam and finger. Keep in mind your a:hover tag should use the same font family size as text has normally. Now the <a> tag makes sense, and you can perhaps more fully understand how you can use CSS to mark up a lot of text in Flash.

Formatting CSS Inside Flash

Whereas I definitely like keeping CSS styles in an external file, there are a couple reasons to define the format inside Flash. First, it makes it easy to make modifications to text and styles while the movie plays. If you want to give users the power to select their font size (to take a simple example), there's no reason to define a bunch of variations of your style. Second, CSS style definitions within Flash use a convention that's nearly identical to the TextFormat object. You could argue this is both an advantage and disadvantage, because although you're not leveraging the CSS standards you are recycling Flash skills.

Whether you define the CSS inside Flash or in a CSS file, the last step is always the same: You set a text field's `styleSheet` property and then use your custom tag as with any HTML. It's the stage where you define the CSS that differs. Here's what it looks like first in CSS, and then in Flash:

```
//inside a css file:
.myTag {
  font-family: "Arial", "Arial";
  font-size: 12px;
  color: #000000;
}
```

```
1   //the equivalent but entirely inside Flash:
2   var styles = new TextField.StyleSheet();
3   styles.setStyle(".myTag",
4      {fontFamily: 'Arial',
5       fontSize: '12px',
6       color: '#000000'}
7   );
8   my_txt.htmlText="<.myTag>here it is!</.myTag>"
```

Basically, you just make an instance of the TextField.StyleSheet() object. Then, you just define each style using the `setStyle()` method. Notice this method accepts two parameters: the name you'll use (as a string) and the properties you want to set in the form of a generic Flash object. Just like how your CSS file can have more tags, you can continue to execute the `setStyle()` method as many times as you want. Finally, line 8 just shows how you apply the style the same way you would using a CSS file.

At this point, the only advantage of defining the tags inside Flash is that you don't need to wait for a CSS file to fully load. However, earlier I said defining the style inside Flash makes it easier to reformat on-the-fly. What's cool is that after you assign a style to a text field's `styleSheet` property, any subsequent changes to the style are immediately reflected in the text! Here's an example that's exciting if only for the potential it offers:

```
_root.onMouseDown = function() {
  styles.setStyle(".myTag",
    {fontFamily:'Arial', fontSize:'22px', color:'#000000'});
};
```

Obviously, you'll probably only want to change styles at key moments. For example, maybe the user presses a button and all the important words highlight. Creative and subtle use of this feature can prove really powerful.

Deciding whether to store your CSS inside Flash or as a separate CSS file is entirely up to you. To help decide which approach makes sense, consider these points:

- External CSS files remain in their native format. Therefore not only are you using a standard format, you also can recycle and use the same files elsewhere in your site.

- External CSS files must fully load before you use them, so there's an additional step you must follow.

- Internal (Flash-defined) styles are more closely aligned with ActionScript syntax. This includes the TextFormat object, which is discussed next.

- Internal styles also enable you to make changes at runtime. Although you could load two separate styles (using external CSS) and then reformat the text when you want to make a change, it's a little easier with internal styles.

Using the TextFormat Object

The good news about using the TextFormat object is that the process is nearly identical to using homemade generic objects. You create an instance and then start setting property values. However, you can only select from properties available to the TextFormat object. That is, you don't make up formatting properties at will (only set properties listed in Figure 5.5). The only thing that's weird is that after you create a TextFormat instance, nothing is seen until you *apply* the format to a particular field onscreen. So, the process is make a TextFormat object, set its properties, and then apply it to an onscreen text field.

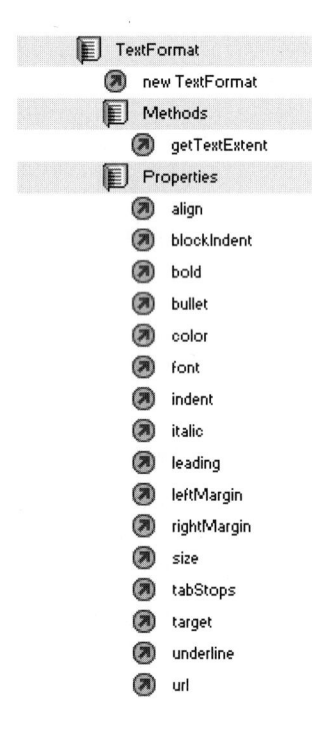

```
TextFormat
    new TextFormat
    Methods
        getTextExtent
    Properties
        align
        blockIndent
        bold
        bullet
        color
        font
        indent
        italic
        leading
        leftMargin
        rightMargin
        size
        tabStops
        target
        underline
        url
```

Figure 5.5 *The TextFormat object's properties should look familiar because most are common formatting terms.*

Here's a quick example:

```
my_fmt=new TextFormat();
my_fmt.font="Arial";
my_fmt.bold=true;
```

At this point, the `my_fmt` instance is just floating around in memory. Not until you apply it to a text field onscreen will you see anything. Here's how you might do that:

`my_txt.setTextFormat(my_fmt);`

As long as there's a field onscreen called `my_txt`, this will change its format.

Often developers get messed up when they misuse `setTextFormat()` and `setNewTextFormat()`. That is, remember "new" will affect only the new text appearing in a field, whereas the regular `setTextFormat` affects what's already present in the field. Also, both methods accept *up to* three parameters. It's weird because no matter how many parameters you use, the last parameter is always the TextFormat object. If you want to format just a single character, you can pass an integer and then the format, as follows:

`my_txt.setTextFormat(2,my_fmt);`

Realize this changes just the third character because it starts counting with 0 (0, 1, 2, and so on). If you want to format a range of characters, you can pass two integers followed by the format, as follows:

`my_txt.setTextFormat(2,7,my_fmt);`

This formats the third through the eighth character.

So that's the TextFormat object in a nutshell! It's comparable to using `htmlText` as shown in the preceding section. Personally, I find the TextFormat a bit unwieldy when I'm trying to format individual characters. Surely, it can be done, but I find it easier to think in "begin tag/end tag" terms. TextFormat objects are a more convenient way to store all the properties of a format. That is, I recommended storing gnarly HTML tags in variables…but even then, you'll end up with a lot of variables. You can store every attribute for a format in a single variable.

Listing 5.4 is a modified version of the code used earlier—but this example uses the TextFormat object rather than `htmlText` (assume the `recipe` object variable is already populated—as was done earlier):

Listing 5.4 Displaying the Recipe Using TextFormat Objects

```
1   breakPts=[];
2
3   theField.text="";
4   theField.text+=recipe.title+"\r";
5   breakPts.push({begin:0,
6                  end:theField.length-1});
7
8   total=recipe.ingredients.length;
9   for (var i=0;i<total;i++){
10      theField.text+=recipe.ingredients[i]+"\r";
11  }
12  breakPts.push({begin: breakPts[breakPts.length-1].end,
13                 end:theField.length-1});
14
15  theField.text+=recipe.directions;
16  breakPts.push({begin: breakPts[breakPts.length-1].end,
17                 end:theField.length-1});
18
19 title_fmt=new TextFormat();
20 title_fmt.size=44;
21
22  ingredient_fmt=new TextFormat();
23  ingredient_fmt.italic=true;
24  ingredient_fmt.bullet=true;
25
26  plain_fmt=new TextFormat();
27
28  theField.setTextFormat(breakPts[0].begin,
29                         breakPts[0].end,
30                         title_fmt);
31  theField.setTextFormat(breakPts[1].begin,
32                         breakPts[1].end,
33                         ingredient_fmt);
34  theField.setTextFormat(breakPts[2].begin,
35                         breakPts[2].end,
36                         plain_fmt);
```

The first 18 lines are nearly the same as the earlier example that used `htmlText`. However, I made an array called `breakPts` that gets populated with generic objects—each with a `begin` and `end` property. You see on lines 5, 12, and 16 I store where the most recent block of text begins and ends. To figure the beginning point, I reach into the array and find the previous object's end value (except for the first one, which I figure starts at index 0). The endpoints are always the current length of the field minus 1 (remember we start counting at 0). Finally, I create the three TextFormat objects on lines 19 through 26. I really didn't need line 26 (or 34 for that matter) because the `plain_fmt` is left at all the default values. Anyway, I end it all with the three `setTextFormat()` lines that each reach into the array and grab `begin` and `end` properties as needed. Figure 5.6 shows the result.

Cookies
- 2 cups flour
- 1 egg
- 1 stick of butter
- 1 cup sugar

Beat egg, sugar, and butter
Mix into flour
Cook at 375 for 10 minutes

Figure 5.6 *The TextFormat object produces results that are equivalent to HTML, although the bullets are unique.*

You can see the most challenging part of using the TextFormat object is specifying which characters to affect. Also, I had to rearrange the code in the preceding example because it wouldn't work if I tried formatting the text before I was finished adding text. I just waited until I was done populating the text to format it, but I think it's worth mentioning that this sort of workaround is sometimes necessary.

Additional Layout Options

Ideas can be communicated many ways—text is just one. Not only are movie clips containers inside of which you can display media and text placed manually, but—on-the-fly—you can embed other clips, create text fields, and draw primitive shapes. The last few features explored in this chapter all enable you to create clips, text, or drawings on-the-fly:

- `attachMovie()` enables you to dynamically create clips (drag them from the library by using code). That is, you'll attach (think "put") one clip inside another. (Even if you're attaching a clip to the _root timeline—that's still a clip.)

- `createTextField()` enables you to create dynamic or input text fields on-the-fly.
- `createEmptyMovieClip()` enables you to create completely empty clips in which you draw or place other clips or text.
- The MovieClip object's drawing methods enable you to draw lines, curves, and filled shapes.

All four of these clip-, text-, and shape-generating features are methods of the MovieClip object, meaning you always precede with `"someClipInstance."`. Also, when using `attachMovie()` to grab clips out of the library, you need to set the linkage setting for that item in the library.

I want to walk through an example that uses all of these dynamic "media-generating" methods. Squeezing in the topic of Flash's drawing methods potentially makes this topic appear unimportant. It's one thing to say you can draw lines, curves, and optionally fill shapes with color—which is true. It's entirely different, however, to see when this can be useful. The idea of drawing graphs comes to mind immediately, and this is a great application for drawing. Figure 5.7 shows a plotting application that displayed student scores. In this case, I used code to draw all the lines (even the grid because that was dynamic). However, because the graphics on the endpoints were somewhat unique (appearing in four different variations), I used `attachMovie()` to pull those from the library. Finally, I used `createTextField()` for every label appearing on the graph.

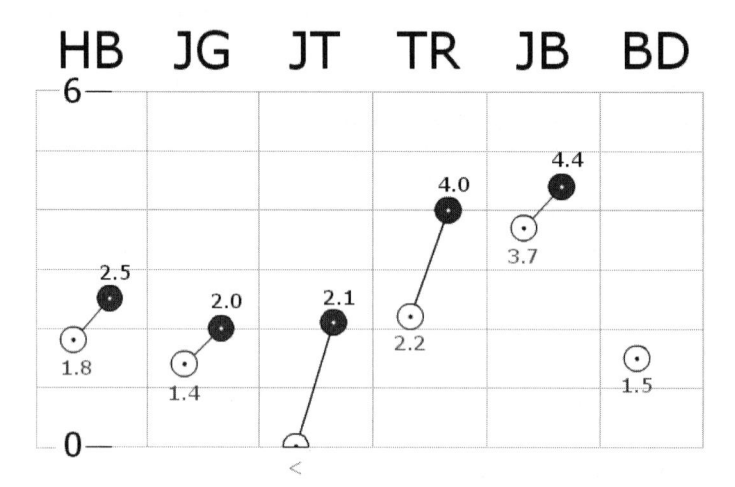

Figure 5.7 *Drawing methods and* `attachMovie()` *were used to create these dynamic graphs.*

Although drawing graphs is interesting and can be challenging, you can build dynamic displays for the user in so many other situations. The following (arguably contrived) example exploits many of these dynamic layout controls to both explore them and to apply some of the skills developed over the previous few chapters. The following code dynamically draws a table that behaves similarly to the DataGrid component. This table displays text and column lines based on data in an array. Figure 5.8 shows the results.

Figure 5.8 *Although it's not the same as the DataGrid component, we'll create these columns that the user can sort.*

The code is listed here in two parts (the initialization in Listing 5.5, and then the processing and display in Listing 5.6). I'll walk through the code just to explain my approach. The main idea is not to step through each line, but to see all the pieces working together in an applied example.

Listing 5.5 Populating the Data

```
1   content = [];
2   content.push({avail:true,  name:"Apples",  price:"0.70" });
3   content.push({avail:true,  name:"Oranges", price:"0.60" });
4   content.push({avail:false, name:"Mangos",  price:"1.50" });
5
6   var propCount = 0;
7   for (var c in content[0]) {
8      propCount++;
9   }
10  cHeight = 10;
11  totalWidth = 200;
12  cWidth = totalWidth/propCount;
13
14  my_style = new TextField.StyleSheet();
```

continues

Listing 5.5 Populating the Data (Continued)

```
15   my_style.setStyle(".h",   {fontFamily:'Arial', fontSize:'14px',
16                              fontWeight:'plain', color:'#000000'});
17   my_style.setStyle(".hb",  {fontFamily:'Arial', fontSize:'14px',
18                              fontWeight:'bold', color:'#000000'});
19   my_style.setStyle(".r",   {fontFamily:'Arial', fontSize:'12px',
20                              fontWeight:'plain', color:'#333333'});
21   my_style.setStyle(".rb",  {fontFamily:'Arial', fontSize:'12px',
22                              fontWeight:'bold', color:'#333333'});
23   my_style.setStyle("a:hover", {textDecoration:'underline'});
```

The content array should look familiar—just an array full of objects. Then in lines 10 and 11, I define homemade variables cHeight (for column height) and totalWidth. To figure the cWidth (line 12), I first have to count how many properties are in each object. Lines 6 through 9 count the properties in the first slot of the array (which should match each item in the array). Then, I just define some styles: h for headline, hb for headline bold, r for regular, and rb for regular bold—normally I wouldn't be so cryptic, but I'm just trying to keep the rest of the code concise.

Listing 5.6 Processing and Displaying

```
24   owner = this;//handle on main timeline
25   function doDisplay(sortOrder) {
26     //sort it:
27     content.sortOn(sortOrder,Array.CASEINSENSITIVE);
28     //local vars:
29     var c;//current column name
30     var cNum;//current column num
31     var r; //row num
32     var nl; //next level
33     var this_txt;//temp holder to address text
34   
35     owner.the_mc.removeMovieClip();
36     nl = owner.getNextHighestDepth();
37     owner.createEmptyMovieClip("the_mc",nl);
38     owner.the_mc.lineStyle(2,0x000000,100);
39     cNum = 0;
40     for (c in content[0]) {
41       owner.the_mc.moveTo(cNum *cWidth,0);
42       nl=owner.the_mc.getNextHighestDepth();
43       owner.the_mc.createTextField("c_txt"+cNum, nl, (cNum*cWidth), 0,
44                                    cWidth, cHeight);
```

```
45      this_txt = owner.the_mc["c_txt"+cNum];
46      this_txt.styleSheet = my_style;
47      this_txt.selectable = false;
48      this_txt.autoSize = "center";
49      this_txt.html = true;
50      if (sortOrder == c) {
51         this_txt.htmlText = "<a href='asfunction:doDisplay,"+c+"'>"+
52                             "<.hb>"+c+"</.hb></a>";
53      } else {
54         this_txt.htmlText = "<a href='asfunction:doDisplay,"+c+"'>"+
55                             "<.h>"+c+"</.h></a>";
56      }
57      for (r=0; r<content.length; r++) {
58         nl=owner.the_mc.getNextHighestDepth();
59         owner.the_mc.createTextField(c+r,nl,
60                                      cNum*cWidth,(r+1)*cHeight,
61                                      cWidth,cHeight);
62         thisOne=owner.the_mc[c+r];
63         thisOne.styleSheet = my_style;
64         thisOne.selectable=false;
65         thisOne.autoSize = "center";
66         thisOne.html=true;
67         if (sortOrder == c) {
68            thisOne.htmlText="<.rb>"+content[r][c]+"</.rb>";
69         }else{
70            thisOne.htmlText="<.r>"+content[r][c]+"</.r>";
71         }
72      }
73      owner.the_mc.lineTo(cNum*cWidth,(content.length+1)*cHeight);
74      cNum++;
75   }
76   owner.the_mc.moveTo(cNum*cWidth,0);
77   owner.the_mc.lineTo(cNum*cWidth,(content.length+1)*cHeight);
78   owner.the_mc.doDisplay = owner.doDisplay;
79 }
80 doDisplay("avail");
```

There's just one function, doDisplay(). It gets triggered once initially (line 80) and then whenever the user clicks a column head. That is, the column heads are formatted in lines 51 through 55 and include the asfunction. The variable c contains the actual column name text and it's used both as the parameter for the doDisplay() calls as well as the text being formatted (in either the <.hb> or <.h> style—depending on whether the column name matches the sortOrder in line 50).

continues

To understand the loops, it helps to know what all gets created. Everything is created *inside* the clip `the_mc` created in line 37. Actually, line 35 removes it (provided it's already onstage from a previous sort). The point is additional text instances and lines get created inside this clip. Instead of tracking all these lines and text instances (to ensure they get removed), I just destroy `the_mc` which also destroys all the contained lines and text instances. Notice the extensive use of Flash MX 2004's new `getNextHighestDepth()` method (lines 36, 42, and 58). In the past you had to keep track of all level numbers with your own variables.

Line 40 sets up a loop that—for as many items that `content` contains—draws the lines, creates the text blocks, and formats all text.

Finally, bracket reference is used in lines 45 and 62 because we're specifying clip names by dynamically building a string. This technique requires you to precede with the path to the object (`_root` in this case). But that's hard-wired! Unfortunately, you can't just use the relative reference `this` because that would point to the `doDisplay()` function. So, a great solution is to set a variable to `this` somewhere outside any function (for instance, `owner=this`), and then replace each instance of `_root` in the code with `owner`. (The use of `owner` in this way is common among Flash programmers.)

I wish we could continue with more examples of these layout options. I do think this last listing has been a good summary, however.

Remember that the drawing methods can do more than just create primitive shapes and lines. Even complex images are made up of lines and shapes. You may be interested to know that many of the new user interface components use drawing methods to create nearly everything you see onscreen. When you do venture into complex drawings, realize you can create building blocks of drawing functions. For example, you could make a function that accepts parameters for width, height, x and y, and then draws a rectangle. You just have to think from the inside out. Whether you're drawing shapes or creating text and clips, you have to take one step at a time.

Summary

Now you've seen there are nearly countless ways to present data. Ideally, the presentation stage is as fluid as possible. That is, concentrate on having well-organized data first. If the values in your data are easily accessible through script, you'll have no trouble presenting it visually.

{Chapter 6}

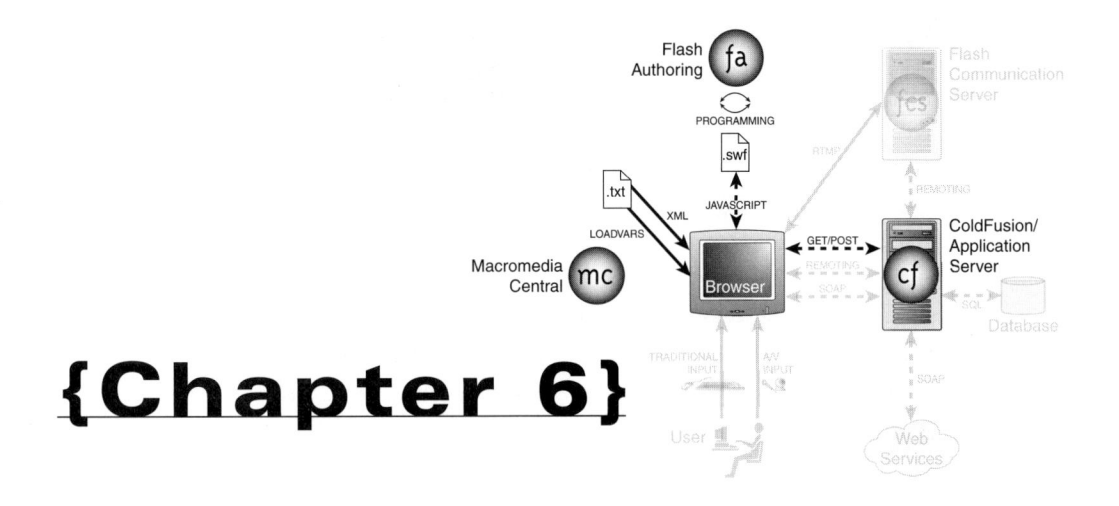

Basic Data Exchange

In the preceding chapter, you learned ways to structure, manage, process, and manipulate complex data. This chapter covers basic ways to both import and export data. Chapters up to this point have covered how to deal with data after it's inside Macromedia Flash MX 2004. But from where does the data originate? For example, you may want to import up-to-the-minute news from an outside source such as another web site. Actually, the data source need not be on the other side of the world. You can import data stored in a simple text file, thus eliminating the need to open Flash for every minor change. (Just edit the text file.)

Another way to exchange data is to save it. Sometimes you'll change data after it arrives inside Flash (for instance, the user adds to an array), in which case you may want to save those changes. If a user changes data, it needs to be exported from the Flash file so that you can import it again next time the app runs (perhaps to let the user pick up where he left off). (Remember, variables will naturally vanish if you don't export them for safekeeping.)

It turns out there are many different *protocols* for importing and exporting data. This chapter covers data exchange methods that require no more than Flash, a browser, and a simple text-editing program. (In later chapters, you'll learn ways to incorporate application servers, databases, web services, and the Flash Communication Server.)

> **{ Note }**
>
> **Protocol** A protocol is more than a way of sending and receiving data. It's the entire process of how the data is formatted, how it travels, and how it's processed when received—all necessary to ensure successful data exchange. For example, think of the protocol for sending a package: It's the entire process of wrapping it, attaching a label, paying for land or air stamps, getting the recipient's signature, and, finally, the opening of the package with a box cutter.

Specifically, this chapter covers the following topics:

- The local shared object, which enables you to write variables to the user's disk and then later read the values
- The local connection object for letting one app trigger events in another app
- The LoadVars object to import and export data in flat URL-encoded form, including text files and conventional application servers
- The XML object to import and export structured data

You'll see that many of the objects covered in this chapter are variations of the same thing. However, each is suited for a particular task. For creating files on the users' machine so that you can read them back the next time they visit your app, use local shared objects. For sending messages between more than one Flash app, use local connection. Both LoadVars and the XML object are similar in that they can read data (from disk or an application server) and write data (to an application server). They differ in the format of that data. The simple name/value pairs supported by LoadVars is fine for certain data, but when your data is more complex you will want to use the XML format.

Ultimately, these are all basic ways to exchange data. Don't let that discount the fact they're all very useful. We just don't cover Flash Remoting, data components, and the new support for the Simple Object Access Protocol (SOAP) until next chapter. Also, realize the foundation skills you learn using the *local* shared object and *local* connection objects will apply directly to learning how to use their *remote* counterparts in Chapter 8, "Foundation Communication Server," and Chapter 9, "Advanced Communication Server."

Saving Data with the Local Shared Object

The local shared object enables you to save variables in a file on the user's hard drive. This way, you can restore any variables saved during previous visits to your application. Local shared object files (LSOs, or SOLs as their file extension is .sol) are nearly identical to cookies, but offer one big advantage: Variables containing any Flash data type get restored to the same data type. Because cookies only support string data, storing other data types involves a "to string" conversion when saving and then a "from string" process when restoring—what a drag! If the variables in your LSO file contain arrays full of objects with nested strings (or anything really), they get restored just as you saved them. Another advantage LSOs have over cookies is your movie doesn't have to be playing in a browser to work—Flash projectors can effectively read and write data to disk.

{Note}

Remote Versus Local Later you'll see how the Flash Communication Server supports remote shared object files (RSOs). Not only do RSOs remain on your sever, you also can share the contained variables with multiple simultaneous users. Really, however, the two differ in purpose: LSOs are for permanent storage between sessions, and RSOs immediately notify each user when another user makes a change to a variable. The good news, however, is they share similar syntax and data structures—so you'll be able to apply what you learn in this chapter to other topics.

The applications for LSOs storing data for later retrieval are wide reaching. Basically, the idea is to give the users a break by not making them do anything more than once. For example, once they see an intro animation, they shouldn't be forced to see watch it again. Or suppose they enter their name once; the next time they visit you shouldn't ask again. And just like standard HTML, you can display previously visited links in gray. This chapter provides examples such as these, and hopefully you'll think of other scenarios where it would be convenient to store a variable so that it can be read back in later.

Before looking at creative solutions to practical challenges, let's first look at the technical details.

Using the Local Shared Object

The basic syntax for LSOs involves first creating a variable instance and identifying the LSO's filename, and then setting variables (contained in the `data` property of the variable instance). Listing 6.1 shows the skeleton form.

Listing 6.1 Local Shared Object Skeleton

```
1   my_so=SharedObject.getLocal("filename");
2   my_so.data.someVariableName="a value";
```

The first line does two things: creates an instance of the shared object in the variable `my_so` *and* identifies the LSO file that gets saved to. If you're familiar with most objects (for instance, the Sound object or Color object), line 1 breaks the expected form that uses the constructor `new` (as in `my_color=new Color()`). Another weird thing is that if the file `"filename"` doesn't exist (and it won't the very first time this code is run), it gets created as soon as data is flushed to disk (specifically, when you close the Flash movie or implicitly call the `flush()` method). (More about where the LSO gets saved in a minute.) After you have the variable (called `my_so` here), you can set as many variable's values by storing them as named properties inside the built-in `data` property. For example:

```
my_so.data.oneVar="a";
my_so.data.otherVar="b";
//...and so on
```

{ Note }

Code Analogy to Shared Objects   Because the shared object's structure is just an object inside an object, it might help to visualize how you'd have to build it if you had to do it by hand:

```
my_so={data: {} }
//or:
my_so=new Object();
my_so.data=new Object();
```

From this point you can access properties inside `data` (such as `my_so.data.someProp`).

The confusing part is that shared objects handle all of this for you, so you don't actually do it this way.

Seeing Whether a Shared Object Is Populated

Before moving on to more details, note that all users will either be returning or they'll be first-time users. For returning users, you may want to restore their settings; for new users, you may want to take them through some initialization process. Shared objects for return users have a `data` property full of named properties containing values, but a new user's shared object will actually have the `data` property but without any properties. That is, when checking whether the user is returning or new, you can't just check whether the `data` property is `undefined`. This *won't* do it:

```
1   my_so=SharedObject.getLocal("userdata");
2   if(my_so.data==undefined){
3      //do initialization stuff
4   }else{
5      //check values
6   }
```

The point is, as soon as you create the shared object variable (`my_so`), it will in fact have a `data` property. A corrected version of line 2 must involve a specific property name that you set, and therefore a property you expect to find in the shared object of a returning user. This property name will be `undefined` for new users (`if(my_so.data.expectedVariableName==undefined){` and so on). You'll see this issue arise in all the examples that treat new and returning users differently.

Storing Shared Objects on the User's Machine

The seemingly esoteric topic of exactly where shared object files get saved is worth discussing now. There's an optional second parameter in the `getLocal()` method—namely, a way to specify where the physical file will get saved and hence a way to override the default location. You can't just store SOL files anywhere on a user's hard drive. You're given a folder that matches your domain name, which resides inside a special Flash Player folder (which appears in slightly different locations depending on your operating system). By default, SOL files appear in subfolders that exactly match your web site's folder structure, and then inside folders that match the SWF filename, and finally in SOL files that match the name provided in the first parameter in `getLocal()`. Figure 6.1 shows this visually: `id.sol` is created by my code `getLocal("id")` when you visit the `machine.swf` file at www.phillipkerman.com/machine/.

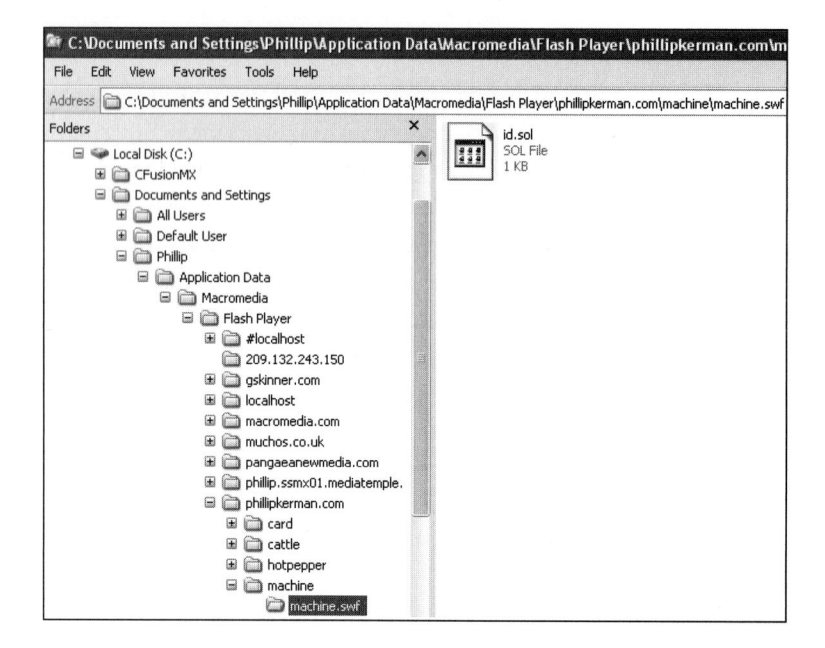

Figure 6.1 *In the Flash Player folder on the user's hard drive, SOL files appear in a specific folder structure.*

The default structure seems convenient enough—and it's certainly clear who created each file. But what if you want access to the variables in a shared object when visiting a different part of a web site? For example, maybe I want to read that ID data (in `id.sol`) when a user visits my main web site as well as the machine subfolder. Anyway, all that explanation is to say that to point to an SOL in a location other than the default, just provide a second parameter beginning with the standard HTML conventions for root: `/`. For example, both of the calls in Listing 6.2 access the same file.

Listing 6.2 Sharing Shared Objects Throughout a Site

```
//in phillipkerman.com/machine/machine.swf
id_so=SharedObject.getLocal("id","/");

//in phillipkerman.com/site.swf
id_so=SharedObject.getLocal("id","/");
```

Alternatively, you can specify subfolders (such as `"/all_sos"`) into which the SOL files get saved. This folder structure doesn't need to match your web site's structure because you're just specifying how the folders get structured on the user's machine.

Flushing Data to Disk

One more tiny technical detail before delving into the examples: The updated values for a shared object are automatically written to disk (that is, "flushed") when the user leaves the particular page. Although waiting until this moment makes me nervous, it actually works fine even if they close the browser. If you plan to store a ton of data (well, anything more than the default 100K per domain), however, the user must first okay it through the Settings dialog box, Local Storage tab (see Figure 6.2).

Figure 6.2 *Through the Local Storage tab in the Settings dialog box, users can control how much disk space is given to a shared object file.*

The System Settings dialog box automatically appears (open to the Local Storage tab) the instant Flash tries to flush data that exceeds the user's limit. When using `flush()`, Flash checks only the current size of the LSO. If you expect the LSO to grow in size and want to reserve enough space (so that Flash doesn't wait), you can pass the number of bytes you expect to use. It makes sense to check that the user will accept using the disk space, before the user spends time setting a ton of variables.

To reserve 500K, for instance, which is really a lot, you can use the following:

`my_so.flush(500000);`

But it's not that easy. Although the two possible outcomes are simple (success, because they accepted it; or failure, because they didn't), you need to give the users who see the dialog box enough time to answer…and then check their answer. Listing 6.3 provides a universal code sample that does it all.

Listing 6.3 Disk Space Checker

```
1   my_so = SharedObject.getLocal("myFile");
2   my_so.onStatus = function(info) {
3     if (info.code == "SharedObject.Flush.Failed") {
4       enoughSpace = false;
5       //and trigger failure code
6     }
7     if (info.code == "SharedObject.Flush.Success") {
8       enoughSpace = true;
9       //proceed with application
10    }
11  };
12  var result=my_so.flush(500000);
13  if (result) {
14    enoughSpace = true;
15    //proceed with application
16  }
17
```

Because you have no idea how long the user will take to answer the dialog, you structure a callback for the onStatus event (that gets triggered when the user finally does answer). In line 2, the argument is named info, and we're looking for one of two explicit strings based on the value of the code property inside that parameter. Line 12 initiates the attempt to reserve space. Notice, flush() will return a value (either true or "pending"). If there's already enough space allotted, line 13 sees result is true and proceeds without incident. If not, the only two ways back into the code are accounted for in lines 3 and 7. Realize that if you put any code in line 17, it would execute right away. That is, the flush() won't just hang out and wait for the user to answer the dialog—that's what onStatus is for.

You might think the info object in onStatus is unnecessarily complex. Granted, it'd be way easier if onStatus just passed back true or false (based on success)—but that's not how it works. Macromedia instead passes an object with properties so that they can easily expand it later. Basically, it's just a convenient way to stuff a ton of values in a single argument (the same reason anyone uses objects).

> **{ Note }**
>
> **Displaying System Settings** You can force the dialog box to appear by using System.showSettings(). In addition, you can optionally pass 0, 1, 2, or 3 to cause one of the four tabs in the dialog box to appear (Privacy, Local Storage, Microphone, or Camera respectively). Basically, any time that dialog box needs to appear, it will do so automatically—but now you know how to do it manually.

Practical Examples Involving Local Shared Objects

Now that you understand nearly every detail of local shared object files, you should find the following examples not only useful, but also easy to figure out.

Making a Skip-Intro (Forever) Feature

Without getting into whether you should have an intro animation, quite often you do need to show the user something once (teach them, if you will) but not twice. Check out the simple solution in Listing 6.4.

Listing 6.4   Skip Intro

```
1   intro_so=SharedObject.getLocal("intro");
2   if(intro_so.data.seenIntro){
3      gotoAndStop("postIntroFrame");
4   }else{
5      intro_so.data.seenIntro=true;
6      gotoAndPlay("beginIntro");
7   }
```

Pretty simple, isn't it? Line 2 checks whether the seenIntro value is true. If so, the user jumps to frame "postIntroFrame". Otherwise, the seenIntro property is set to true and the user goes to the frame where the intro begins. If you want to give the user an option to view the intro (for instance, a See Intro Again button), you can't just jump back to this frame—it will take the user directly to "postIntroFrame". I suppose you could first set intro_so.data.seenIntro to false and then jump back, but I was thinking to replay the intro you just take them back to play the "beginIntro" frame.

Getting a Username Once

Perhaps the most common use for cookies is to save a username. Instead of making users type in their name every time, just store the data on their computer and it will appear as if your site remembers them. We'll start with a simple version in Listing 6.5, and then look at something a bit richer.

Listing 6.5 Saving a Username (Simple)

```
1    username_so=SharedObject.getLocal("username");
2    username_txt.text=username_so.data.username;
3
4    username_so.onChanged=function(){
5      username_so.data.username=username_txt.text;
6    };
```

Notice that instead of checking whether the LSO had a username property in line 2, I just populated the input text field `username_txt`. It just doesn't seem to be a problem to populate a field with `undefined`. Finally, line 5 is the one that resets the value for the username property (inside the `data` of `username_so`, naturally). Notice how convenient the text field's `onChanged` event is. Without it, I'd have to come up with some logical time to go and set the shared object's value (perhaps when the user clicks OK or something). This technique is foolproof, even though it's slightly inefficient how it resets the value after every keystroke the user makes. (By the way, I could have used the `onChanged` listener variation.)

Refining the Login App

Listing 6.6 adds a password option to the preceding example. The following code won't do any validation on the password. (This is something that needs to be handled on the server side anyway.) All you need is two input text fields (instance names `username_txt` and `password_txt`), a CheckBox component (`remember_ch`), and a Button component (`proceed_pb`), as shown in Figure 6.3.

Chapter 6 Basic Data Exchange 145

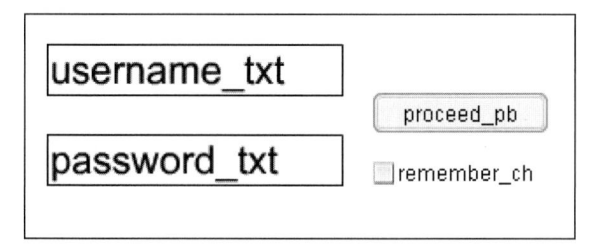

Figure 6.3 *A couple of input text fields and two components are all you need to save a username and password.*

Listing 6.6 Saving a Username and Password

```
1   userinfo_so = SharedObject.getLocal("userdata");
2   if(userinfo_so.data.username==undefined){
3      username_txt.text = "";
4   }else{
5      username_txt.text = userinfo_so.data.username;
6   }
7   password_txt.text = "";
8   //if remembering...
9   if (userinfo_so.data.remember) {
10     remember_ch.value=true;
11     password_txt.text = userinfo_so.data.password;
12     setRememberMode();
13  }
14  //always save username
15  username_txt.onChanged = function() {
16     userinfo_so.data.username = username_txt.text;
17  };
18  //remember checkbox
19  remember_ch.addEventListener("click",setRememberMode);
20  function setRememberMode() {
21     //get and save their preference
22     var whichWay=remember_ch.value;
23     userinfo_so.data.remember=whichWay;
24     if (whichWay == true) {
25       //set password and start monitoring
26       userinfo_so.data.password = password_txt.text;
27       password_txt.onChanged = function() {
28          userinfo_so.data.password = password_txt.text;
29       };
30     } else {
```

continues

Listing 6.6 Saving a Username and Password (Continued)

```
31        //clear password, and stop monitoring
32        userinfo_so.data.password=null;
33        password_txt.onChanged=null;
34      }
35    }
36    //proceed push button
37    proceed_pb.addEventListener("click", proceed);
38    function proceed(){
39      trace("username "+username_txt.text);
40      trace("password "+password_txt.text);
41    }
42    //optional:
43    password_txt.password=true;
```

The code probably looks worse than it is. Initially, the username_txt field is either cleared (the first time when username is undefined or is filled with the value of username (line 5). By default, the password_txt field is cleared (line 7); if the LSO's remember property is true, however, line 10 sets CheckBox's value to true, line 11 populates the field, and then line 12 triggers the setRememberMode() function (which is mostly redundant here except for lines 27 through 29, where monitoring of password changes commences). Lines 14 through 17 are from the previous code listing. Line 19 triggers the function setRememberMode() any time the user clicks the remember_ch CheckBox. Inside setRememberMode(), line 22 ascertains their preference, and then line 23 sets their preference in the LSO. Finally, provided the user wants to save the password, line 26 sets the password property to the current value in the field and lines 27 through 29 set up the onChanged callback (so it gets resaved as the user types). Notice that lines 32 and 33 both clear the variable and stop the monitoring of the onChanged event.

Finally, starting on line 37 I show how the push button can just trace the user's input username and password. Of course, you must pass those to some authentication routine. (Here I just wanted to show that you cannot just pass the local shared object's password property, because it will have no value when the remember property is false.) Notice, too, that line 43 will make the password_txt field show asterisks no matter what is typed (but makes it harder to test while developing).

{ Note }

Doing What You Say You're Doing It's interesting to note that it would have been easier to go ahead and save the user's password in the LSO, but just not reveal it unless the user opted to "remember." That's not too cool because the LSO file can be hacked like any cookie (by someone with access to the user's computer). The implication that unchecking the Remember Me option will destroy any record of the password is important enough to abide by it.

{ Tip }

Saving Multiple Usernames For a challenge, try expanding this feature so that several people can log on via the same computer. That is, save more than one person's username and password, make the usernames appear in a ComboBox component, or automatically fill in the password when a user types a username that matches one saved previously. You can download my solution from www.phillipkerman.com/rias.

Save Feature for the Slide-Show Maker

In Chapter 4, "Working with Complex Data," we built a slide-show maker. It was mainly an exercise in structuring an array full of objects the user could populate. At the time, we included a Save button but didn't program it. Now you'll see in Listing 6.7 how to save all the data (no matter how complex) into an LSO. Refer to the file created in Listing 4.8, "Complete Slide-Show Code" (or download it).

Listing 6.7 Adding a Save Feature to the Slide-Show Maker

Start with Listing 4.8. To enable the Save button, comment out line 10 to read as follows:

```
//save_pb.enabled=false;
Cut lines 40-43 and in their place type this code:
40  show_so=SharedObject.getLocal("show");
41  if(show_so.data.show==undefined){
42     show ={pages:[],
43            time:new Date(),
44            showname:show_txt.text};
45  }else{
46     show=show_so.data.show;
47     refreshList();
```

continues

Listing 6.7   Adding a Save Feature to the Slide-Show Maker (Continued)

```
48        show_lb.selectedIndex=0;
49        clickLine();
50        show_txt.text=show.showname;
51    }
52    function doSave(){
53        show.showname=show_txt.text;
54        show_so.data.show=show;
55    }
```

Basically, if the LSO's `show` property is `undefined` (line 41), the `show` variable initializes just as before (lines 42 through 44). Otherwise, line 46 stuffs the `show` property into the `show` variable. Incidentally, you could have replaced every instance of `show` with `show_so.data.show`, but that would have been more typing. Lines 47 through 49 restore things by triggering old code. Line 50 restores the title of the saved show.

Finally, `doSave()` (which is the Save button's `"clickHandler"`) saves the title and then stuffs the whole `show` variable back into the LSO.

In the online version of this application, you'll see that I threw in a few enhancements. For one thing, the preceding code just saves one slide show. You'll find that the code to save multiple shows really isn't too much more work—mainly you just have to add interface elements to let users name their shows and the means to select one to load. In addition to the "edit show" mode that you've seen so far, I also added a "play show" feature that removes everything except the content and fancy forward and back buttons. It really is fun adding useful features when you have a good foundation.

The main thing to take away from this exercise is just that any variable can be saved in an LSO no matter how complex.

Limitations of the Local Shared Object

Before moving on to other data exchange mechanisms, you need to understand when LSOs aren't appropriate. The fact that all the data is saved locally means users who log in from different computers will effectively find their data is lost (if they're not at their same computer). For this reason, you want to consider storing just a minimum of data locally and store most of the data remotely (on the host server). Okay, so you may be thinking that I just finished showing you all the cool ways to store a ton of data locally and now I tell you not to. Not really, just realize that other strategies may make more sense than keeping everything local.

LSOs are great for standalone projectors (for example, to store user bookmarks or other preferences). The default location for these SOL files is within a folder called localhost, and then inside a folder structure that matches the hard drive where the projector is run. This means that if you move the projector, a new `SOL` is created. Just remember you can always provide a second parameter when performing the `getLocal()` command to override where the SOLs appear. Although the fact new SOL files are created may appear as nothing more than an annoyance to overcome, you can, in fact, take advantage of this. It's a quick-and-dirty way to maintain separate values. For example, just run the slide-show maker from two different locations, and you'll have two independent LSOs.

Finally, you can't *really* store any data type in an LSO. People have tried without success to store a Sound object or a MovieClip object. It just doesn't work. It would be kind of cool, I suppose, to create an image with the MovieClip's Drawing application programming interface (API) and save the clip containing the image, but it just doesn't work that way. You could, however, very easily store the data necessary to redraw the image when the user returns to the file.

I guess that because the local shared object is so convenient, I thought I'd point out some of the limits for balance.

Sharing Data Using the Local Connection Object

The local connection lets two or more Flash movies send messages to each other. Although the movies can be in different parts of the same browser page or in pop-up windows, the communication takes place only on the local machine (hence the name "local connection"). When you build Macromedia Central apps, this feature is used extensively. That is, you're main app can trigger events in your pods (mini versions of your app).

Sending messages to Flash movies playing on other people's machines would be really powerful—and you'll get to see how in Chapters 8 and 9. Even still, applications for the local connection object are pretty wide. For example, you could create an optional pop-up help window that could effectively take control of the main window. Also, you can save download time by loading audio or other media into a separate Flash movie and then letting several other movies play the music. The best part about learning how the local connection object works is that the syntax is consistent with its remote connection counterpart (called NetConnection).

Local Connection Fundamentals

A "basic" local connection script always has at least two parts. That is, because one movie is triggering a function in another, you need two separate movies. For the following skeleton, think of two movies: one called receiver.fla and the other sender.fla. Listing 6.8 shows the two pieces of code, which are then followed by an explanation.

Listing 6.8 Local Connection Skeleton

```
1    //receiver.fla
2    my_lc = new LocalConnection();
3    my_lc.onMyMethod = function(param) {
4      trace("my method received: "+param);
5    };
6    my_lc.connect("myConnection");

1    //sender.fla
2    my_lc = new LocalConnection();
3    _root.onMouseDown=function(){
4      my_lc.send("myConnection", "onMyMethod", "hello");
5    };
```

In line 2 of both, an instance of the local connection object is stored into the variable my_lc. (Don't get thrown by the fact that both files use the same variable name—they could be different, and being the same is not in conflict because the variables are in two different movies.) In the receiver file, lines 3 through 5 define how to handle the onMyMethod event (which is, obviously, my own made-up name). Finally, in line 6 we connect the instance of my_lc to a connection named "myConnection". Think of this name as the common gateway name over which all communication will take place.

The sender file is a bit simpler. After you have an instance of the local connection (line 1), you can trigger remote methods using send(). Just include the connection name (in this case "myConnection"), the method name as a string ("onMyMethod" here), and any parameters separated by commas.

Incidentally, the only reason it's a bit unconventional looking (triggering a method using a string name, for example) is just a matter of how send() works. You would expect to see something more like this:

```
my_lc.onMyMethod("hi");
```

It turns out that this will work...but just inside the receiver file.

Because this example only executes a `trace()` you need to create a SWF from sender.fla, and then test the movie receiver.fla, and finally go back and launch the sender.swf from your file system (or browser).

There's really not much more than what's shown in the preceding skeleton. From here, you just need to get creative finding useful applications for the local connection object. That's what we'll do in the next few sections.

Creating a Guided Tour Help Feature

Here's a fairly simple example that is both powerful and extensible. Suppose your existing application is not totally clear to new users. You *could* make a complete standalone tour based on the real app, but that could become out-of-date if the app ever changed; in addition, it's much easier to show how something works by showing the real thing. This example launches a separate window that will highlight and control parts of the main app. It'll be an optional feature for users and it will automatically adjust to reflect the current state of the main app. To concentrate on just the local connection aspects, the rest of the code is fairly simple.

For Listing 6.9a, you'll create two files: main.fla and helper.fla. In main, place three PushButton components onstage and a MovieClip component containing an outline about the same size or bigger than the buttons. Give the highlight an instance name highlight and name the three buttons home_pb, contact_pb, and projects_pb.

Listing 6.9a Guided Tour: Main File

```
1   stop();
2   frameList=["Home", "Contact", "Projects"];
3   buttonList=[home_pb, contact_pb,projects_pb];
4   var total=buttonList.length;
5   for(var i=0;i<total;i++){
6       var thisButton=buttonList[i];
7       thisButton.setLabel(frameList[i]);
8       thisButton.setClickHandler("navigate");
9       thisButton.section=i;
10  }
11
12  function navigate(componentRef){
13      currentSectionNum=componentRef.section;
14      gotoAndStop(frameList[currentSectionNum]);
```

continues

Listing 6.9a Guided Tour: Main File (Continued)

```
15     highlight._x=-1000;
16   }
17   //navigate to the first section initially
18   navigate(buttonList[0])
19
20   //LC STUFF
21   help_lc=new LocalConnection();
22
23   help_lc.onShow=function(whichOne){ //just highlight
24     var thisButton=buttonList[whichOne];
25     highlight._x=thisButton._x;
26     highlight._y=thisButton._y;
27   }
28   help_lc.onGo=function(whichOne){ //really navigate
29     navigate(buttonList[whichOne])
30   }
31   help_lc.onGetSection=function(){ //"return" section
32     help_lc.send("helper","onSetSection",currentSectionNum);
33   }
34   help_lc.connect("help");
```

Although the local connection object doesn't show up until line 21, I do have a couple notes on the first part. I maintain two arrays: `frameList` containing frame labels and `buttonList` containing references to (not names of) the buttons. The loop in line 5 labels each button (line 7), sets the click handler (line 8), and finally creates a home-made property called `section`. Realize that components trigger their `"clickHandler"` by passing just a reference to themselves. In line 13, I extract that value and store it in `currentSectionNum`—for use both immediately in line 14 and much later in line 32. (That's why `currentSectionNum` is not a local variable.)

The local connection object code looks much like the skeleton for a receiver. Notice that when the local connection instance is created (line 21), all methods are defined before the `connect()` method is executed (in line 34). The methods `onShow`, `onGo`, and `onGetSection` will all get triggered from the other file (using `send("help"`, `"methodName"`, `parameter)`). Finally, line 34 makes a connection to `"help"`. Although I want to cover lines 31 through 33 later, notice for now that in line 32 we're doing a `send()` *from* this movie *to* the other movie over the connection named `"helper"`. That's because you can have only one receiver per connection name.

Chapter 6 Basic Data Exchange 153

This code will make more sense when you see the helper pop-up file's code. All you need is six standard Flash buttons (show_1_btn, show_2_btn, show_3_btn, go_1_btn, go_2_btn, go_3_btn) and a dynamic text field (prompt_txt). The code in Listing 6.9b goes in a separate file called "helper.fla".

Listing 6.9b Guided Tour: Helper File

```
1   helpText = [];
2   helpText.push("All about the home section");
3   helpText.push("This is the contact section");
4   helpText.push("What you need to know about projects");
5
6   show_1_btn.onPress = function() {show(0);};
7   show_2_btn.onPress = function() {show(1);};
8   show_3_btn.onPress = function() {show(2);};
9   go_1_btn.onPress = function() {go(0);};
10  go_2_btn.onPress = function() {go(1);};
11  go_3_btn.onPress = function() {go(2);};
12
13  my_lc = new LocalConnection();
14  function go(which) {
15    prompt_txt.text = helpText[which];
16    my_lc.send("help", "onGo", which);
17  }
18  function show(which) {
19    prompt_txt.text = helpText[which];
20    my_lc.send("help", "onShow", which);
21  }
22  my_lc.onSetSection = function(toWhat) {
23    show(toWhat);
24  };
25  my_lc.connect("helper");
26  my_lc.send("help", "onGetSection");
```

The idea is this help file has three "show" and three "go" buttons. (You could clean it up quite a bit—perhaps even make an autorun mode to automatically trigger the buttons.) Anyway, the two main functions (show() and go()) change the prompt_txt and then invoke a send() to trigger onShow or onGo in the other file. Lines 22 through 26 are a bit more complex. As a "sender" file, this local connection instance doesn't need to connect(). (It effectively connects when it does the send() method.) In line 25, however, we connect to the name "helper" (not "help" as the other file did). That's

continues

154   Part II   Technology

Listing 6.9b   Guided Tour: Helper File (Continued)

because the other file is given access to trigger the `onSetSection` method (line 22). See, when this movie first loads, line 26 triggers the `onGetSection` method (way up in line 31 of the other file) and that, in turn, triggers `onSetSection` in this file. The idea is that I want the help file to immediately get in sync with the other file—that is, ascertain the value of `currentSectionNum`.

To test this file, open the main file, and then launch the helper. If you want to let the users launch the helper upon request, it just takes a bit of JavaScript. First publish both files (so you get a couple HTML files), and then add a button in the main file that triggers this code:

```
getURL("javascript:openHelp()");
```

Then, in the HTML for the main file, add this code in the head of the file (above `</HEAD>`):

```
<script language="JavaScript">
function openHelp(){
  window.open( "helper.html", "","width=300, height=300");
}
</script>
```

I'll admit that I didn't just add this helper feature to an existing file. That is, I had the local connection object in mind when building the main file. However, this sort of thing really isn't difficult to add later. (For example, months after I built my main web site, it took less than 3 hours to add the video guided tour.) You want your code to be as centralized as possible…using common functions for multiple buttons and arrays that contain content or button references, for example.

Downloading Media into a Single Window

Now you'll see how all the sounds for an entire site can load into a single window and even a way to enable users to use their Back button within your all-Flash site. The next two examples require an HTML frameset. The user visits a single page that points to two other HTML pages: one that occupies 100 percent of the height and the other whatever's left over (nothing). The second frame is effectively invisible, as Figure 6.4 shows.

We'll add a bit more HTML than you see in Figure 6.4, but the basic structure should be clear. In the following example, one large SWF containing all the sounds will load into bottom.html and the main application will load into main.html. The main movie will trigger sounds (via a local connection object). I can think of two immediate benefits of keeping things separate: Music can continue to play uninterrupted when navigating to other pages; and, the main movie can load (visually) while the sounds download at their own pace.

This project involves more than two files: First you create the frameset (Listing 6.10), then the sounds movie, and finally two main movies (between which you'll navigate to confirm the sound doesn't hiccup). The following steps explain the process and show the code:

```
index.html:
<frameset rows="100%,*">
  <frame src="main.html"      name="main">
  <frame src="bottom.html" name="bottom">
</frameset>
```

```
main.html: embed src="main.swf"
100% of browser

bottom.html: embed src="other.swf"
```

Figure 6.4 *Visiting index.html will fill the browser with the file main.html, although bottom.html (and its SWF) also gets loaded in an invisible frame.*

Listing 6.10 Playing Sounds in a Separate Frame

1. The first step is to create the frameset with this code in a file named index.html.

```
<html>
<head>
<title>Playing Sounds</title>
</head>

<frameset rows="100%,*" frameborder="NO" border="0" framespacing="0">
  <frame src="main.html" name="main">
  <frame src="bottom.html" name="bottom">
</frameset>
<noframes><body>you need a new browser</body></noframes>
</html>
```

continues

Listing 6.10 Playing Sounds in a Separate Frame (Continued)

Anyone who knows HTML will realize I'm leaving out standard document information at the top—but this code will work with most modern browsers.

2. To create the sounds movie, import one sound loop and two incidental sound effects. Give each sound a linkage identifier name—I used: `"monotonousLoop"`, `"sorry"`, and `"laugh"`. (To set a sound's identifier, select it in the library, choose Linkage from the library's menu, select Export for ActionScript, and fill in the Identifier field.) Nothing goes onstage! Just, this code in the first keyframe:

```
1   my_lc=new LocalConnection();
2   my_lc.onSFX=function(whichSound){
3       sfx=new Sound();
4       sfx.attachSound(whichSound);
5       sfx.start();
6   };
7
8   my_lc.onMusic=function(way){
9       if(way){
10          backMusic.start(0,99999999);
11      }else{
12          backMusic.stop();
13      }
14  };
15
16  backMusic=new Sound();
17  backMusic.attachSound("monotonousLoop");
18
19  my_lc.connect("music");
20
21  my_lc.onMusic(true);
```

Basically, the two events (onSFX and onMusic) run code related to Sound objects. onMusic accepts `true` or `false` as a parameter in order to start or stop a sound. (Notice that we trigger `my_lc.onMusic(true)` in the last line to get the music started initially.) Finally, line 19 connects to `"music"`.

Before proceeding, save this file in the same folder as index.html and name it **bottom.fla**. Finally, select File, Publish to produce bottom.swf and bottom.html.

3. In a new file, place onstage four homemade buttons with the following instance names: on_btn, off_btn, sfx_btn, navigate_btn. Label the buttons with text to identify them. Here's all the code for this file:

```
1   my_lc = new LocalConnection();
2   on_btn.onPress = function() {
3       my_lc.send("music", "onMusic", true);
4   };
```

```
5    off_btn.onPress = function() {
6       my_lc.send("music", "onMusic", false);
7    };
8    sfx_btn.onPress = function() {
9       my_lc.send("music", "onSFX", "laugh");
10   };
12   navigate_btn.onPress = function() { getURL("main2.html");};
```

Three buttons execute send() three different ways (to trigger methods in the bottom.swf). The last line just navigates to another page that we'll create called main2.html.

To finish, save this file next to the others, name it **main1.fla**, and publish it (to make main1.swf and main1.html). Finally, select File, Save As, and name it **main2.fla**. Before publishing again, however, change the "laugh" in line 9 to read "sorry" and "main2.html" in line 12 to read "main1.html". Then publish. The idea is that main1.html and main2.html can jump back and forth.

In addition to the source FLA files, you should have the following files all in one folder:

```
index.html
bottom.html
bottom.swf
main1.html
main1.swf
main2.html
main2.swf
```

Launch index.html in your browser, and even though you can only see main1.html (and main1.swf), you will hear music from bottom.swf. You can even navigate to main2.html and the music won't skip a beat.

The old invisible frameset trick… actually, it's very useful. This particular example has one downside: The users will invariably see the main movie before the sounds fully download. This means they may not hear anything if they click to play a sound too early. There's actually an error-checking event, onStatus, that reports when a send() command fails to be received.

You can use a modified version of the following code in both main files:

```
my_lc.onStatus = function(info) {
  if (info.level == "error") {
    //display an error message
  }
};
```

I believe the only possible value for the `info` parameter is `{level:"error"}`. In the chapters on Flash Remoting and the Flash Communication Server, you'll see that such info objects can contain much more information. Here, you either get that error or you get nothing at all.

{ Note }

Eliminating the Need for Error Checks   I figure it's always better to avoid the "damage control" approach (error messages) by preventing their need entirely. In the preceding example, a better solution is to hide the buttons until it is safe to click them. However, just having the sounds movie send a signal (via the local connection object) isn't enough because it's possible for sounds to load first; or—even more likely—the sounds could be fully loaded, but when the user leaves and comes back there won't be a new signal from sounds (if it never refreshes). Anyway, this solution is definitely workable—you'll need main to both "ask" sounds if it's already done loading and require sounds to broadcast that it's done loading even if main doesn't ask. Basically, my point is "an ounce of prevention is worth a pound of cure." If you can prevent users from ever pressing the buttons before it's time, you won't need to give them a message when they click too early.

A Better Back Button

Flash movies have the notorious problem of not supporting the browser's Back button. If after making a few selections within your movie, users decide to go back by pressing the browser's Back button, they go back all right—all the way to the previous site! And then if they press the Forward button, they start all over at the beginning of your Flash app. Even worse than the Back button failing, users can't bookmark sections within the Flash app. We'll fix all that in this next exercise, which nicely follows the preceding exercise because we'll use a frameset and the local connection object.

Chapter 6 Basic Data Exchange   159

> **{ Note }**
>
> **What Back Button Problem?** The solution you're about to see is really cool. However, you may be familiar with how Flash supports "named anchors." These integrate into HTML like standard anchors but only resume Flash movies to specific frames in the main timeline. Not only does this restrict how you structure your app, you also can't increase the level of granularity (think "bookmark-ability") any greater than with keyframes.
>
> Ultimately, however, I believe many applications rightfully challenge the Back button's value. For example, you can open your app in a window without buttons and use the local shared object to save the interface state so that users who leave will resume exactly where they left off. Unfortunately, eliminating people's expectation for a Back button is probably harder than just working within a metaphor that may not be ideal.

Here's the strategy we'll use: As in the previous sounds example, the main page will fill the screen and the hidden frame will contain another SWF. Unlike the sounds example, however, the main page will never refresh. Instead, the hidden frame reloads (in a slightly different way) each time we navigate within the main page. Clicking Back just reloads the hidden frame. The job of the SWF in the hidden frame is to tell the main SWF the values of all pertinent variables. The really wild part is the main movie doesn't control itself! Check out the visualization in Figure 6.5 as you follow the sequence outlined here.

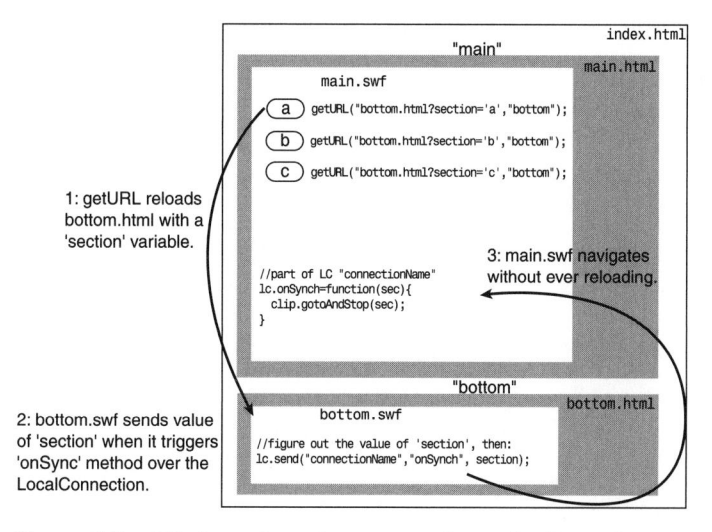

Figure 6.5 *This figure shows the sequence of pages loading and messages passing that make a better Back button.*

Here's the sequence of events when a user navigates (for instance, by pressing a button in the main movie):

1. A `getURL()` triggers to replace just the hidden frame (and passes an additional parameter).
2. The movie in the hidden frame loads and checks the values of the parameters received.
3. The hidden movie issues a `send()` to trigger a method in the main movie.
4. The main movie's method changes the onscreen content.

Although this may seem like a circuitous way to navigate inside a single file, think about what happens when the user clicks the Back button (or for that matter, when the user returns to this page having bookmarked it). Basically, the user picks up at Step 2. That is, the hidden frame at which the user is arriving contains all the old parameters, so it can proceed to issue the `send()` and the main movie will restore itself.

Using *FlashVars* in HTML

The Back button solution includes a couple of HTML-related topics that may be new to you. First, to provide the bottom movie with unique parameters each time the user navigates, we'll use JavaScript and perform the `document.write()` method. Basically, we create a dynamic string that becomes the HTML the instant the page loads. Within the Flash object/embed tag we can pass variables to the Flash movie through the `FlashVars` tag. That is, the main movie says "load the bottom frame with these variables," so we need to pass those variables to Flash. You'll see all of this plus more JavaScript in the code in Listing 6.11, so I thought a quick warning was in order.

Listing 6.11   A Better Back Button

1. Create the frameset file (named index.html) with the same code used in the preceding example:

```
1  <html>
2  <head>
3  <title>Back Button</title>
4  </head>
5
6  <frameset rows="100%,*" frameborder="NO" border="0" framespacing="0">
7    <frame src="main.html" name="main">
```

```
8      <frame src="bottom.html" name="bottom">
9    </frameset>
10   <noframes><body>you need a new browser</body></noframes>
11   </html>
```

You're welcome to change `bottom.html` and `bottom` to something else, just remember the name of the frame I'm using is `"bottom"`.

   2. Create a simple main movie. Use three homemade buttons (red_btn, green_btn, blue_btn). Also make a MovieClip component and put, into its first frame, a `stop()` and label it `"home"`. Then put colored splotches in three later keyframes labeled `"red"`, `"green"`, `"blue"`. Give the clip an instance name content. (Look familiar? Yeah, this is my standard test file.) Put this code in the frame of the movie:

```
1    frameLabels=["home","red", "green", "blue"];
2
3    red_btn.onPress=function(){ navTo(1); };
4    green_btn.onPress=function(){ navTo(2); };
5    blue_btn.onPress=function(){ navTo(3); };
6
7    function navTo(where){
8      var theString="bottom.html?section="+where;
9      getURL(theString, "bottom");
10     //content.gotoAndStop(frameLabels[where]);
11   }
12
13   my_lc=new LocalConnection()
14
15   my_lc.onSynchronize=function(where){
16     content.gotoAndStop(frameLabels[where]);
17   };
18
19   my_lc.connect("history");
```

First notice the commented line 10. Basically, if this movie didn't send all navigation requests through the outside movie, that's all we would need inside the `navTo()` function. Click a button, go to a frame label: simple. But here we're not actually going to navigate until the other file triggers the `onSynchronize` event (line 15). The way it works is `navTo()` fashions a string in line 8 and uses that for the first parameter of the `getURL()` command. Basically, we're always navigating to `"bottom.html"` but by adding `?section=1` (when the `where` parameter is 1) we're passing a parameter that can be parsed by the bottom movie and used when it issues a `send()` command (as you'll see in a minute). Finally, notice that `getURL()`'s second parameter means only the frame called `"bottom"` gets replaced.

continues

Listing 6.11 A Better Back Button (Continued)

Save this file adjacent to the index.html, name it **main.fla**, and publish it (to create main.html).

   3. Next we'll create bottom.html, which hosts the bottom movie (that we'll create later). The following HTML only appears hairy because it's hard to format in a book (hence, you should just download the source instead of typing it in). Here it is:

```
1    <html>
2    <head>
3    <title>Controller</title>
4
5    <script language="JavaScript">
6      var_string="currentSection="+window.location.search;
7    </script>
8
9    </head>
10
11   <body>
12     <SCRIPT language="JavaScript">
13       document.write(
           '<OBJECT classid="clsid:D27CDB6E-AE6D-11cf-96B8-444553540000"
           codebase="http://download.macromedia.com
           /pub/shockwave/cabs/flash/swflash.cab#version=6,0,0,0"
           WIDTH="100" HEIGHT="100" id="bottom" ALIGN="">');
14
15       document.write(
           '<PARAM NAME=movie VALUE="bottom.swf">
15a        <PARAM NAME=FlashVars VALUE="' + var_string + '">
           <PARAM NAME=bgcolor VALUE=#000000>');
16
17       document.write(
           '<EMBED src="bottom.swf" bgcolor=#000000
           WIDTH="100" HEIGHT="100"
17a        FlashVars="' + var_string + '"
           NAME="bottom" ALIGN="" TYPE="application/x-shockwave-flash"
           PLUGINSPAGE="http://www.macromedia.com/go/getflashplayer">
           </EMBED>');
18
19       document.write('</OBJECT>');
20
21     </SCRIPT>
22
23   </body>
24   </html>
```

Notice that the four document.write() lines of code (13, 15, 17, and 19) should each appear on one line. They effectively create the same basic code you'll see in any Flash published movie (for example, main.html). But this technique enables us to produce the HTML dynamically (whereas if you just typed it in, it'd be hard wired). Namely in lines 15a and 17a, we slip in the variable var_string as the value for the FlashVars tag. FlashVars enables you to set initial values for any variables using the URL-encoded form. For example, the value "oneVariable=value&otherVariable=otherValue" is interpreted as if you put the following code in the first keyframe of the movie:

```
oneVariable="value";
otherVariable="otherValue";
```

It's a bit of a drag because you can only pass string values—but because we know what to expect, our Flash movie can parse it out. Way up on line 6, we create the var_string variable setting it equal to "currentSection=" plus the search property in the URL (for example "?section=1"). The result is that the bottom movie initially executes the following line of code:

```
currentSection="?section=1";
```

We just need to parse the value of currentSection and extract the 1 at end.

4. Finally, we can make the bottom movie. Just remember not to ever publish this movie—you'll be making the SWF, which is fine, but you don't want to overwrite the beautiful bottom.html file you just created! Anyway, bottom.fla has nothing but this code in the first frame:

```
1  currentSection=
    ↪currentSection.substring(currentSection.indexOf("=")+1);
2
3  if(currentSection==""){
4    currentSection=0;
5  }
6
7  my_lc=new LocalConnection();
8  my_lc.send("history", "onSynchronize",currentSection);
```

Because currentSection will have a value that looks like "?section=1", we can reset currentSection using substring() and indexOf() and extract just the part after the equals sign. In case it has no value, line 4 will set it to 0. Finally, line 8 triggers onSynchronize and passes the value of currentSection.

I'll be the first to admit this parsing routine is not particularly extensible—but we only need that one number to send with the onSynchronize method. For an example that passes and parses much more complex data, check out the following discussion of how Macromedia's PetMarket sample application does it:

www.macromedia.com/devnet/mx/blueprint/articles/back_button.html.

continues

Listing 6.11 A Better Back Button (Continued)

Remember to save the movie as **bottom.fla**, and then test it (don't publish it!) to create bottom.swf.

To test this application, you need to run index.html on a web server. (You can't just double-click it.) If you have ColdFusion MX or IIS installed, you can move the files to its wwwroot folder and run it with an URL starting with `http://localhost`. You could also upload it to web space at your service provider.

By the way, if you change the bottom.html file's `document.title`, the browser will display a more meaningful title when going back (as in Figure 6.6). Here's a quick-and-dirty line of code you can place under where `var_string` is assigned in bottom.html:

```
document.title="sec "+window.location.search.substring(9);
```

This code is a bit hard wired (extracting all the characters beginning with the ninth). An HTML guru can surely come up with something more dynamic.

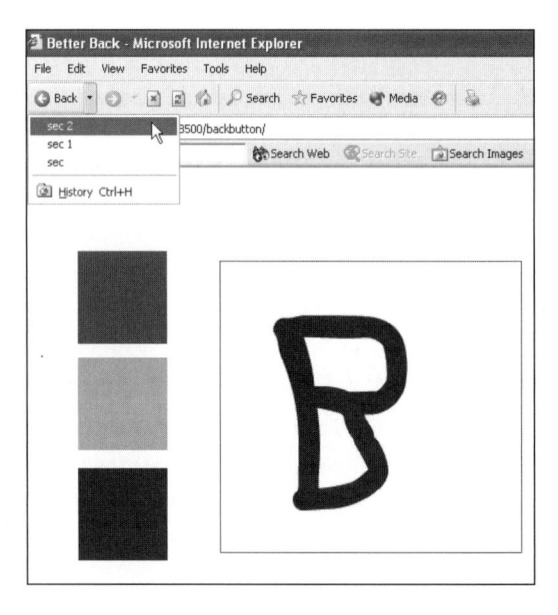

Figure 6.6 *That Back button will display a more meaningful title when you set the* `document.title`.

Of course, the main file in the preceding example wasn't particularly exciting. However, to expand this feature to a complex application, you need to take some time to consider granularity—that is, how frequently do you need to navigate in this manner (that is, using getURL() and then writing HTML and sending commands via the local connection)? I suggest you let most buttons trigger functions directly with the main movie. Only use this technique for instances when the "state" of the interface changes—big changes, if you will. You can let the Back button track every little movement, but that will be more work and a bigger pain for when users want to go way back (because they'll have to click several times). Anyway, you just have to plan out this issue.

When I first learned about the local connection object, I made an application that let the user drag an object in one window and see another object move in parallel motion in the other. Hopefully, after seeing the practical examples here, you agree that the local connection object can do more than just this "phantom" effect. Remember, too, that the underlying syntax and core theory of the local connection object also applies to the NetConnection object that is covered in the Flash Communication Server chapters.

One last thing to remember: Although we were passing simple strings and numbers, the local connection object will enable you to pass *any* data type as parameters when you issue a send(). You saw more of this sort of thing when we saved arrays full of generic objects in local shared object files. With the local connection object, you also can pass such complex data.

Flat Data

Despite the dull sound of "flat data," this topic isn't boring. *Flat data* is made up of names and corresponding values (often called *name-value pairs*). Just think of a series of variables each being assigned a single value, and you have the idea. I guess the opposite of flat data is structured data (such as XML in the next section) or perhaps relational data (like most databases support). In this section you'll see how to import flat data from a text file (or application server), parse it, and then, optionally, send it back to a server.

> **{ Note }**
> **Loading Variables by Any Other Name, Surely the Same** Although there are actually a few different ways to do—basically—the same thing, we'll only look at the LoadVars object (even though the `loadVariables()` method and `getURL()` can also be used in similar ways).

Keeping variables and their values in an external source (for instance, a text file) means you can change them without opening Flash. For example, you can display the day's news in your app. To update the news, you just edit the contents of the text file.

Formatting

It turns out that when the data is formatted correctly, it makes little difference whether you import it from file or a server. Flat data must be formatted as an URL-encoded string. This means an ampersand (&) separates each pair, and a single pair is divided by an equals sign (=).

> **{ Note }**
> **Unicode Support** Flash now supports Unicode-encoded text both within the authoring environment and when importing flat data. This means characters from other languages can be displayed (provided the user's computer can display that language's text).

In addition, specific characters need to be escaped (that is, they need to replaced by alternatives—for example, what if you want an ampersand as a value?). Some people have the list of off-limits characters memorized, but for the rest of us here's a quick way to use Flash to URL-encode your text by hand:

```
myText="this is an ampersand &"
trace("Before: "+myText);
myText=escape(myText);
trace("After: "+myText);

//output:
Before: this is an ampersand &
After: this%20is%20an%20ampersand%20%26
```

The function `escape()` will return an URL-encoded string. (Incidentally `unescape()` will covert text back). Notice that even spaces should be replaced with the code `%20` and ampersands with `%26`. Luckily, importing from text files doesn't require such a strict adherence to URL-encoding rules. Here's an example of a suitably formatted text file we'll import:

```
title=Sugar%26Spice&subtitle=ain't that nice
```

Notice the only visible ampersand separates the two name-value pairs. By the way, there's a great formatting trick that keeps text in a legitimate form while making it easier to read. Here's an example:

```
title=Sugar%26Spice&
&subtitle=ain't that nice&
```

By putting an ampersand at the end of the first line, I'm ensuring the subsequent return character (and possible line feed) is not part of the first `title`'s value. Having two ampersands (separated only by a return) should be against some rule—it works great. You can effectively place each name-value pair on its own line as long as you start and end each line with an ampersand. (The first line is fine without an ampersand, but you're welcome to put one there for consistency.)

Importing

After you have your data formatted, you can create a LoadVars instance and use `instanceName.load()`. Once loaded, the variables become named properties of the instance you created. One of the reasons I'm only showing LoadVars is that by supporting the `getBytesLoaded()` and `getBytesTotal()` methods, it enables you to monitor progress as the data loads (which is important when loading a ton of data).

Before you start loading, you need to first define how the data should be handled after it does load. That is, the sequence is "here's what to do when it loads, now go load it." It actually makes sense to define it in this order because you don't know how long it will take to load.

LoadVars Object Fundamentals

Here are the basics. For the following examples to have something to load, create a text file named `filename.txt` saved adjacent to your Flash file with the following content (Listing 6.12):

```
title=Sugar%26Spice&
&subtitle=ain't that nice&
```

Listing 6.12 Skeleton for *LoadVars.load()*

```
my_vars=new LoadVars();

my_vars.onLoad=function(success){
  if(!success){
    trace("problem);
    return;
  }
  trace("title is: " + this.title);
  trace("subtitle is: " + this.subtitle);
}

_root.my_vars.load("filename.txt");
```

The first step is to create an instance of the LoadVars object (in the variable my_vars). Inside the onLoad event I'm being extra careful by confirming the parameter received (called success here) is true. If everything's okay (that is, success *is* true), I'm accessing the title's value with this.title. If later you want access it, use the my_vars instance name (my_vars.title).

Advanced LoadVars Examples

Naturally, the preceding skeleton code doesn't fully exploit all the benefits of the LoadVars object. You can get a lot of mileage out of getBytesLoaded() and getBytesTotal(), plus LoadVars instances also have a loaded property that turns from false to true. Let's look at an example that monitors the progress.

Displaying Download Progress

The only problem with testing the following example in Listing 6.13 is you'll either need a really slow Internet connection or a lot of data (to slow things down enough to see the progress bar). You'll need a text file (name it **data.txt**) with a bunch of text in it. When I was testing it, I just pasted all the text from this chapter into data.txt. Sure, it's not in the right format, but for this example we're just showing the download progress. In addition to the data.txt file, you need a wide rectangle-shaped movie clip onstage with the instance name bar. Draw a wide rectangle shape onstage, select it, and then choose Insert, Convert to Symbol (or F8), and select the middle left registration option (as Figure 6.7 shows). This way when we increase the clip's _xscale, it will appear to grow to the right.

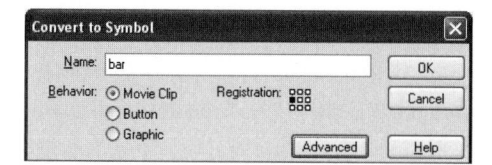

Figure 6.7 *Using the left-center registration option means increasing _xscale will grow the rectangle to the right.*

Listing 6.13   Showing a Progress Bar When Loading Text

```
1   bar._xscale=0;
2
3   myVars=new LoadVars();
4
5   myVars.onLoad=function(){
6     clearInterval(progressInterval);
7     bar._xscale=100;
8     trace("done");
9   }
10
11  progressInterval=setInterval(function(){
12    bar._xscale=myVars.getBytesLoaded()/myVars.getBytesTotal()*100;},
13    50);
14
15  myVars.load("data.txt");
```

This code mixes two basic tasks: scaling the bar clip and loading the data. Right before we begin loading, we use setInterval() to declare a function that will trigger every 1/20 of a second (that is, every 50 milliseconds, as shown in line 13). The first parameter of setInterval() is an inline function that just sets the bar clip's _xscale to what percentage of myVars has loaded. That is, in line 12, _xscale becomes getBytesLoaded() divided by getBytesTotal() times 100. (If both Loaded and Total are equal, the fraction will be 1, and that times 100 is 100—and the bar will be stretched.) When the onLoad event triggers (line 5), we clear the interval and then make the bar fully extended (because it's likely the last time we set _xscale the data hadn't fully loaded). In place of trace() in line 8, you could use alternative code that jumps to a new frame or whatever you want to do when the data is fully loaded. The point is that you can't do anything with the data until you get to line 8.

Parsing Imported Data into an Array

Probably the biggest limit with importing flat data is that you need to have a good idea of what you expect to find in the file. Because you're probably defining exactly what variables are in the file, it's really not a huge deal. But what if you want to make something more dynamic? Suppose for example, that you want questions for a quiz, but you want the code to adapt to as many questions as you happen to have contained in the file. Your text file will not only need variables for each question's content but also variables to describe how many questions are contained. Instead of walking through how to build a quiz, this discussion concentrates just on how to convert one built in Flash to one that imports questions from a flat file. The challenge is in the fact the quiz was already dynamic, in that it would automatically adapt to however many questions were present. (By the way, you can download both the "before" and "after" versions of this quiz.)

Here's the code from the inside Flash file (that is, the part we want to externalize):

```
questions = [];
questions.push({q:"What's Oregon's capital?",
             a1:"Portland",
             a2:"Salem",
             a3:"Eugene",
             correct:2});
questions.push({q:"What's California's capital?",
             a1:"Sacramento",
             a2:"San Francisco",
             a3:"Los Angeles",
             correct:1});
```

Nothing too fancy here: The `questions` array will contain as many items as there are questions. Into each slot is a complete generic object: properties for the question, three answers, and the one that's correct. (For fun you might try building a dynamic quiz based on this structure.)

It actually makes sense to design the data structure this way before you work on loading it from a flat file. That is, we have a structure that's convenient for coding the project. Next consider how you can design a text file that's easy to generate. Here's what I came up with:

```
totalQuestions=2&
&q_1=What's Oregon's capital?&
&a1_1=Portland&
&a2_1=Salem&
```

```
            &a3_1=Eugene&
            &correct_1=2&
            &q_2=What's California's capital?&
            &a1_2=Sacramento&
            &a2_2=San Francisco&
            &a3_2=Los Angeles&
            &correct_2=1&
```

First, notice the `totalQuestions` variable. Because we'll have to look for expected variable names, we need to know for how many questions to look. That is, *every* variable needs to have a unique name. (Notice the questions are q_1 and q_2...if there were a third question, it would be q_3.). This clear naming convention (that is, the original property names plus an indicator for which question it goes with) is both a convenience and a necessity. When the data arrives inside Flash, I'm going to populate the `questions` array just like it was before. (I do not want a million unique variable names—the array full of objects was what I had and that's what I want to keep.) You'll see in the following code that we need to know how many questions so that we know how many to look for.

Listing 6.14 shows how we get it into Flash.

Listing 6.14 Importing Flat Data into an Array of Objects

```
1   myData=new LoadVars();
2   myData.onLoad=function(){
3     questions=[];
4     var total=Number(this.totalQuestions);
5
6     for(i=1;i<total+1;i++){
7       var thisObj=new Object();
8       thisObj.q=this["q_"+i];
9       thisObj.a1=this["a1_"+i];
10      thisObj.a2=this["a2_"+i];
11      thisObj.a3=this["a3_"+i];
12      thisObj.correct=Number(this["correct_"+i]);
13      questions.push(thisObj);
14    }
15  }
16  myData.load("questions.txt");
```

After the data loads, lines 3 through 13 do all the work to convert the flat data into an array. Line 3 dimensions the `questions` variable as an array. Notice that in line 4 I first calculate for how many questions we'll need to loop. Because all data will be strings,

continues

Listing 6.14 Importing Flat Data into an Array of Objects (Continued)

I make sure I use a number version of `totalQuestions`. (If you forgo the `Number()` function, the loop will go for 21 loops—see line 6 says `total+1`, which is `"21"` if `total` is a string.)

Inside the loop (on line 7), I first make a temporary generic object called `thisObj` onto which we'll assign properties before stuffing it in the array (on line 13). Lines 8 through 12 just set the values we need in `thisObj`.

The main thing I wanted to show in the preceding example is that you need to do some work to parse the flat data to structure it (in this case, as an array full of objects). And, no, you can't store arrays or objects in flat data files—only one string value per variable name. You can actually simulate an array in a string value by separating items with commas. There's even a string method called `split()` that will do some of the work for you. Inevitably, however, you'll need to do some parsing. Actually, in the preceding case, after the array is built we should probably delete the LoadVars object (`myData`) because it's not needed but continues to take up memory. Although a variable can't delete itself (for instance, as the last line in the `onData` event), you could instead place a `stop()` at the top of the code and a `play()` inside the `onData` event and finally use `delete(myData)` in the next frame.

Server Interaction

Loading text files that have to be created by hand really isn't a huge time saver. However, you can apply everything we've done so far loading text from files to loading data from a server. In addition, it's possible to send variables and their values from Flash to a server (which, in turn, can process it). Although I'm being a bit simplistic, it is as easy as what we've done so far.

Loading Data from a Server Script

Loading data from a remote web server can be as simple as changing the address of the text file. For example:

```
my_loadVars.load("http://www.phillipkerman.com/data.txt");
```

Where before we just expected the data.txt file to reside adjacent to the Flash movie, here we include an explicit path. What's cool, however, is there are server script languages that can perform a procedure (like a query on a database) and return the results when a user requests the file. That means your `load()` method could trigger a server script that generates an up-to-date file. Provided the file `script.cgi` generated and returned URL-encoded text, you could use:

```
my_loadVars.load("http://www.phillipkerman.com/script.cgi");
```

This way, the CGI script would provide values drawn from another source at the moment requested. Say, getting the latest traffic data, for example.

Without going into server script details, check out this quick example of loading variables from a script file on a ColdFusion server. Listing 6.15 shows the ActionScript.

Listing 6.15   Loading from a Dynamic Server Script

```
result_txt.text = "loading";
my_vars = new LoadVars();
my_vars.onLoad = function(data) {
  result_txt.text=this.returnedvar;
};
my_vars.load("my_script.cfm");
```

I'm expecting a variable named `returnedvar` and the script file is called my_script.cfm. Of course, you'll also need a text field with the instance name `result_txt`. The reason you can't test this with a simple `trace()` is that the file must run from a browser on a web server (which renders `trace()` useless).

Here's the content of the my_script.cfm file:

```
<cfoutput>returnedvar=#CGI.SERVER_NAME#</cfoutput>
```

I think of the ColdFusion tag `cfouput` as similar to the JavaScript `document.write()` seen earlier. When this page is requested, only what is inside that `cfoutput` tag displays. The dynamic part is `#CGI.SERVER_NAME#`. Variables are surrounded by pound symbols (#) and, in this case, the `SERVER_NAME` is just a property of the `CGI` environment variable (think "built-in object").

What's interesting about this example is that if you were to visit the `my_script.cfm` page in a browser, you would see only `returnedvar=localhost`. Check it out; that's what our text file looked like. So, the real lesson here is not "how do you write ColdFusion code" (because, really, this is just a taste—and it's probably incomplete besides), but rather if you get your application working with a hard-wired text file, you can use that as a model when building a dynamic server script.

Sending Data to a Server Script

Enough getting—it's time to give back. You would want to send variables from Flash to your server for two general reasons: You either just want to send the variables (maybe for safekeeping or for some kind of follow-up action) or you want to send variables to further specify what kind of results you want. Compare both these situations to sending parameters to a function. However, some functions include a line starting with `return`, where you can send data back (most likely based on the parameter received). That is, you can either send, or send and get.

It turns out just sending variables should be straightforward. Just change `load()` to `send()` and all the named properties in your LoadVars instance get passed. That's according to theory. In fact, I've seen `send()` fail, so I suggest using `sendAndLoad()` even if you only *need* to send. In this case, create the instance, set some property values, and then do the `sendAndLoad()`. That's a bit different from the `load()` examples where we just processed the received variables. We never *set* any properties in the LoadVars instance. Here's what it might look like:

```
user_vars=new LoadVars();
user_vars.username="phillip";
user_vars.score=100;
user_vars.sendAndLoad("process_scores.cfm", user_vars);
```

Notice we're setting both the username and score properties in the user_vars instance, and then issuing `sendAndLoad()`. All the properties inside the user_vars variable are sent. The second parameter identifies which object will be receiving the data getting returned, although—in this case—we only care to send, so it's not being used. (You'll see in the next section how this works when you do need data returned.) By default, Flash sends these variables using form "POST". You can specify "GET" by supplying that as the third parameter:

```
user_vars.sendAndLoad("process_scores.cfm", user_vars, "GET");
```

By the way, this example using GET with the user_vars instance is effectively the same as typing this address into a browser:

```
process_scores.cfm?score=100&username=phillip
```

It's nice that GET shows you values right in the URL (when testing manually like this). However, POST has the advantage of posing no limit on the length of the values you're passing. Also POST doesn't expose the variables the way GET does.

Although there are other subtle differences between GET and POST, the biggest difference in your code applies to how you access variables after you're on the server side. Here's an example of what that process_scores.cfm page might look like when using GET:

```
<cfset subject="test results for " & #URL.username#>
<cfmail to = "boss@phillipkerman.com"
        from = "reporter@phillipkerman.com"
        subject = #subject#
        server="mail.phillipkerman.com">
#URL.username#'s score was: #URL.score#
</cfmail>
```

The idea is that when Flash issues the sendAndLoad(), the two variables (username and score) are used to generate a customized email. If you use POST rather than GET, just change each URL in the preceding code to FORM—which is how ColdFusion accesses parameters received this way.

> **{ Note }**
>
> **Sending Email from ColdFusion** To send email from ColdFusion, you need to set up the mail server (under Server Settings in the ColdFusion Administrator interface).

Getting Data Back from a Server Script

Server-side scripts can do more than just accept parameters and run. They can return values. When using LoadVars for such an exchange, you need two instances: an outgoing LoadVars (onto which you attach variables and send them) and an incoming LoadVars (that brings with it variables when triggering the onLoad event). Listing 6.16 uses the instance names incoming and outgoing to help keep things straight.

Listing 6.16 Exchanging Variables Using *LoadVars.sendAndLoad()*

```
1   result_txt.text = "loading"
2   outgoing = new LoadVars();
3   incoming = new LoadVars();
4   incoming.onLoad = function() {
5     result_txt.text = this.value_returned;
6   };
7
```

continues

Listing 6.16 Exchanging Variables Using *LoadVars.sendAndLoad()* (Continued)

```
8    outgoing.value_sending="does this work?";
9    outgoing.sendAndLoad("sayhello.cfm",incoming,"GET");
```

This example is a typical use of sendAndLoad(). The instance outgoing has a property value_sending tacked on, and then outgoing is used with the sendAndLoad() method. Notice the second parameter passed is the incoming instance. That's because incoming is the one with an onLoad event defined. The third parameter is optional (but because it uses the POST method by default, I need to specify). The server script sayhello.cfm just needs to assign a value to value_returned for line 5 to work as expected.

Here's the content of sayhello.cfm:

```
<cfoutput>value_returned=
➥#urlEncodedFormat("you said :" & URL.value_sending)#</cfoutput>
```

Notice that because we're using the GET method, ColdFusion finds the parameters it expects as properties inside URL (where POST uses FORM). Also, I tried at first to omit the urlEncodedFormat() function like this:

```
<cfoutput>value_returned=you said : & URL.value_sending#</cfoutput>
```

However, the spaces around the colon aren't in the right form. ColdFusion will return the string in the correct form using the original code (with the urlEncodedFormat() function).

I told you it would get more interesting. Although loading flat data from a text file is nice, loading (and optionally sending) data from and to server scripts is more exciting because they can perform dynamic procedures. That is, data is up-to-date if it's fashioned the instant a Flash movie requests it. In addition, you can send data outside Flash, to a server script, which can then process it for safekeeping—in these examples, sent out in an email, but it could just as easily have been stuffed in a database.

Alas, all variables sent or received using LoadVars are in string form. You really have to know which variables are expected and which ones must be treated as numbers. And, as for passing arrays and objects, there's no direct way. You have to parse it on the way out and on the way in. It's really not that bad (not until you compare it to Flash Remoting). Just remember that externalizing data by putting it in a text file requires no other tools other than Flash. And, loading or sending/loading data to server scripts can be free, too, if you use a server-side language such as PHP.

XML Structured Data

Entire books have been written on XML (eXtensible Markup Language) but, for our purposes, it really doesn't have to be terribly complex. Simply put, XML is a way to store string data in a structured form. That means not only can you store names and values of variables (like URL-encoded text), you also can ascertain descriptive properties of what's contained. That is, you can find out how many of a particular type of variable is contained. If your XML file contains data for a quiz, for instance, you can structure it so that—once imported—Flash can immediately know how many questions are contained. In addition, Flash can see that one question has three possible answers and another has four. When we were loading URL-encoded text, we pretty much needed to know the structure or use an additional variable for that information. With XML you get a picture of the data as well as the values in the data.

> **{ Note }**
>
> **Flash and DTDs** There's actually more information that XML files can include in the form of a document type description (DTD). These are sort of like a table of contents for what follows. Flash can read the `"DOCTYPE"` declaration through the `XMLDocTypeDecl` property, but it can't parse though all the DTD data. Fortunately, the natural hierarchy structure of XML files will be enough to make our lives easier.

The hierarchical structure of an XML file is tags inside of tags (although you'd call them "children" inside "nodes"). In addition, any tag can include named attributes (like properties). It doesn't matter whether you store values inside of tags or as attributes of tags. However, because tags can nest multiple tags inside of themselves, grabbing the value of a tag can return an array full of subtags. Grabbing an attribute's value always returns a single value.

Here's an example from which you can learn a few terms:

```
1    <quiz>
2        <question q="What is the capital of Oregon?">
3            <answers correct="2">
4                <possible>Portland</possible>
5                <possible>Salem</possible>
6                <possible>Eugene</possible>
7            </answers>
8        </question>
```

```
 9      <question q="2+2 is 4">
10        <answers correct="1">
11          <possible>true</possible>
12          <possible>false</possible>
13        </answers>
14      </question>
15  </quiz>
```

Without knowing any XML, you can probably agree with the following statements:

- Within quiz there are two questions.
- The first question's q is "What is the capital of Oregon?".
- Inside the answers tag for the first question you can see the correct is "2".
- There are a total of three possibilities inside the answers of the first question.
- Finally, the second question has two possible answers.

Notice these statements include references to values as well as structure (for example, how the second question has two possible answers). Does the file say "2 possible answers" anywhere? No, we just counted them. This is the same as how an array's length property provides structural information.

Loading XML

Loading data contained in an XML file is virtually identical to loading text. However, you create an instance of the XML object rather than the LoadVars object (see Listing 6.17).

Listing 6.17 Skeleton *XML.load()* Code

```
 1  my_xml = new XML();
 2  my_xml.ignoreWhite=true;
 3
 4  my_xml.onLoad = function(success) {
 5      if (!success) {
 6         trace("problem");
 7      } else {
 8         trace("okay");
 9      }
10  };
```

```
11
12  my_xml.load("quiz.xml");
```

The only new thing, really, is line 2. Basically, by ignoring white space you're free to put spaces and hard returns into your XML file.

I wish that at this point I could say that you now know everything about XML. In fact, after running the preceding skeleton code you can get information and grab values from the my_xml instance. However, digging deep into a structured XML file requires a bit of parsing.

Parsing XML

After you've successfully loaded XML data, you can access data contained in one of three general ways: Just grab specific expected values inside the instance as needed; parse through the expected structure and store values inside other variables (such as arrays or generic objects); or run a generic parser that automatically moves the values into arrays and objects. People have written several automatic parsers that dive into any legitimate XML data and churn out easily accessible Flash variables. (You'll find one at my site for this book: www.phillipkerman.com/rias.)

I find that it's usually easier to deal with the data restructured into Flash variables. If you plan to import data, change it, and then send it back to a server (as the XML object supports sendAndLoad() like LoadVars), however, you may want to keep the data as XML. That way you can make changes and just send it back when you have finished.

To make your own parser or to grab individual values, you need to get a good handle on the object's structure. Listing 6.18 shows just a few one-line expressions to grab either information or values from the my_xml instance (after it loads the quiz.xml data shown earlier). They look a bit gnarly, but I'll explain what I derived from them next.

Listing 6.18 Practice Expressions

```
my_xml.onLoad=function(){

trace("total questions: "+
this.firstChild.childNodes.length);

trace("question 1: "+
this.firstChild.firstChild.attributes.q);

trace("correct one: "+
this.firstChild.firstChild.firstChild.attributes.correct);

trace("total possible: "+
this.firstChild.firstChild.firstChild.childNodes.length);

trace("first possible: "+
this.firstChild.firstChild.firstChild.
     ↪childNodes[0].firstChild.nodeValue);

trace("second possible: "+
this.firstChild.firstChild.firstChild.
     ↪childNodes[1].firstChild.nodeValue);

trace("third possible: "+
this.firstChild.firstChild.firstChild.
     ↪childNodes[2].firstChild.nodeValue);
}
```

First, notice this is all within the `onLoad` event, because I don't want to execute any of it until the data is fully loaded. (It also means `this` is effectively `my_xml`.) Without going through each line, let me summarize by saying you can grab the following:

- Nodes (which return an array of nodes)
- A single node (which returns an XML object)
- Attributes of node (which return generic objects)
- Values of nodes or attributes (which return strings)

From there, you just have to figure out how far down the hierarchy to dive. Note that even though the `quiz` node appears to be at the root of the file, it's actually the first child (either `this.firstChild` or `this.childNodes[0]`). Therefore, `this.childNodes[0].childNodes[0]` grabs the first entire `question` node. The `attributes` property returns a generic object full of all the named attributes in a particular node. Finally, `nodeValue` will return the text between the tags of a particular node. The part that messes me up all the time is that when you dig down and find the node, you have to get the `nodeValue` of its first child—not just the node's `nodeValue`! For example, the third `possible` is shown here (`nodeName` returns `"possible"`):

`this.childNodes[0].childNodes[0].childNodes[0].childNodes[2].nodeName;`

However, to get the value of a node, you can't just change `nodeName` to `nodeValue`. You must use `firstChild.nodeValue`.

It makes sense to begin any parsing effort by writing a few expressions as I did in the preceding listing. Those are the handles I'll need to extract any data contained. However, deriving those expressions often involves a lot of hunting and pecking. Here's an easy way: Just get the skeleton code that imports the XML data and do a Debug Movie. For example, Figure 6.8 shows how I found the first question.

Figure 6.8 *Digging into an XML object is easiest with the Debugger.*

I just selected the `my_xml` variable, clicked firstChild (`my_xml.firstChild`) where I saw `"quiz"` for the `nodeName`, and then clicked firstChild again (`my_xml.firstChild.firstChild`), and I saw `"question"` for the nodeName. And, finally, I clicked attributes (`my_xml.firstChild.firstChild.attributes`), where I saw both the q property and its value `"What's the..."`. Hopefully, diving in this way makes an otherwise unwieldy expression such as the one in the following `trace()` clearer:

```
trace("first q "+my_xml.firstChild.firstChild.attributes.q);
```

You'll still probably need to do a bit of pecking when parsing through an XML object, but I've found the Debugger invaluable.

For a good exercise, try to re-create the entire quiz example from earlier in this chapter using XML the way I structured here. You can find my solution within the downloadable files for this chapter.

Browsing Amazon Through Flash

The quiz is cool and all, but here's an example that is not only practical, it's also really cool. Online retailer Amazon.com has a version of their web service that returns XML structured data. In Listing 6.19, I create a LoadVars instance but pass it an XML object when performing a `sendAndLoad()`. (Remember, one instance is to fashion the data you're sending and one is to carry the data getting returned.) The only thing you'll need to make this work is the Amazon Web Services Kit (downloadable from Amazon.com; just search for "web services"). Download the kit and apply for a "token" (an ID). Amazon controls access to their data.

Listing 6.19 Importing Amazon Product Details

```
1   in_xml=new XML();
2   in_xml.ignoreWhite=true;
3   in_xml.onLoad=function(){
4     trace("first author is :"+
      ➥this.childNodes[0].childNodes[0].childNodes[3].
      ➥childNodes[0].childNodes[0].nodeValue)
5   }
6
7   out_vars=new LoadVars();
8   out_vars.ignoreWhite=true;
9   out_vars.t="webservices-20";
```

```
10    out_vars["dev-t"]="YOUR_TOKEN_GOES_HERE";
11    out_vars.AsinSearch="0735712956";//or any ISBN
12    out_vars.type="heavy";
13    out_vars.f="xml";
14
15    out_vars.sendAndLoad("http://xml.amazon.com/onca/xml2",
16                                            in_xml,"GET");
```

Not too bad eh? One thing to notice is that Flash doesn't like the dash in the developer token property (`dev-t`) on line 10, so I just set it using the string/bracket reference technique. Remember to replace `"YOUR_TOKEN_GOES_HERE"` with the token provided when you sign up. And, you can try other book ISBNs, too. Of course, the `trace()` statement in line 4 is a bit long—but that's just where the author name was hiding. Again, I used the Debugger to figure it out (see Figure 6.9).

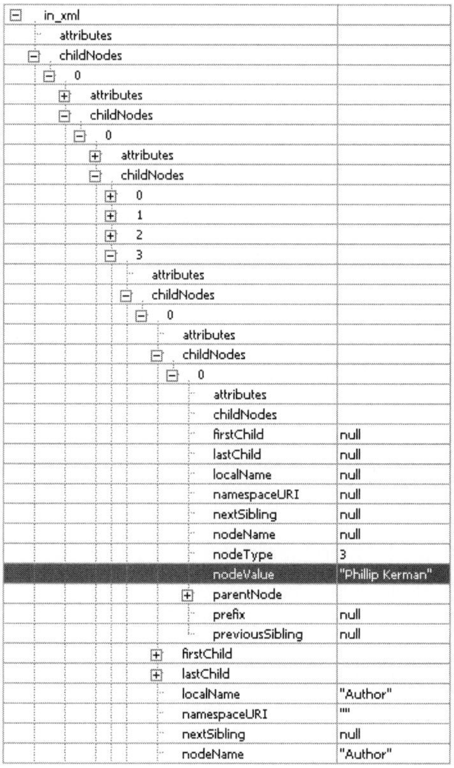

Figure 6.9 *You can find all kinds of data in the XML object returned from Amazon.*

> **{ Note }**
>
> **Loading Data from Outside Your Domain**   Before you get *too* excited about loading XML, realize that this example won't work after you publish it and post it on a web server. That's because the Flash player is restricted from accessing data on other domains (unless your domain is on the list of approved domains in the policy file on the other domain—in this case Amazon.com). There are a few ways around this: Place a policy file on the domain that you want to access, but load XML from your same domain, or place a script on your domain that fetches the outside data and returns it to Flash. This last solution is called a proxy script, which you can find in Macromedia TechNote 16520.
>
> The steps to make the Amazon example work with a proxy script on ColdFusion are as follows:
>
> 1. Download the template proxy.cfm (from Macromedia's 16520 TechNote).
>
> 2. Change the second line to read:
>
> ```
> <cfset dataURL="http://xml.amazon.com/onca/xml2?"&CGI.QUERY_STRING/>
> ```
>
>   (CGI.QUERY_STRING adds the parameters sent from Flash.)
>
> 3. Change line 15 (in Listing 6.19) to point to the installed proxy.cfm file:
>
> ```
> out_vars.sendAndLoad("http://localhost/proxy.cfm", in_xml,"GET");
> ```
>
> This solution means Flash only accesses your domain. It's just that your domain can go get data from outside and send it back to Flash. If you think this is a dumb rule that app servers can break but Flash can't, please realize that only the Flash SWF actually downloads and runs as a script on the user's machine. App servers execute scripts *on the server* and then return plain HTML (or other text values). You definitely wouldn't want a malicious SWF snooping around your local network or local domains.

You can certainly expand this to allow the user to type in various book titles. You'll find all kinds of additional properties that you can send when making the sendAndLoad() request. It's actually possible to entirely re-create the Amazon web site, with searching and shopping carts, all with a Flash interface. You'll see other cool applications like this when we look at Remoting and the Data Management components in Chapter 7, "Exchanging Data with Outside

Services," but this example is particularly cool because it doesn't require any middleware.

Summary

This chapter showed you nearly all the ways to get data in and out of Flash short of outside tools such as application servers. To summarize, here are the main skills you have now:

- Saving any data you want and reading it back from local shared objects
- Triggering events in other Flash apps through a local connection instance
- Reading and writing flat data with the LoadVars object
- Reading and writing structured data with the XML object

Hopefully, too, you have a clear idea how all these options compare so that you can select the right tool for the job.

{Chapter 7}

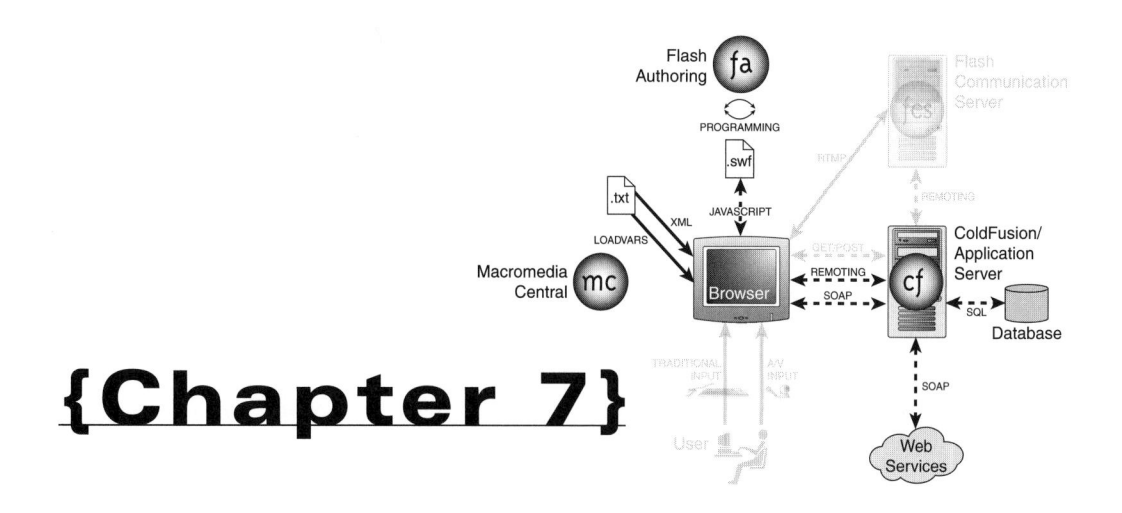

Exchanging Data with Outside Services

This chapter covers advanced ways to exchange data with application servers and web services. In Chapter 6, "Basic Data Exchange," you actually saw two ways to import and export data (using the LoadVars object and standard XML). The primary limit with both of those approaches is that data must always travel as strings. That is, when you import a number, it arrives in Macromedia Flash MX 2004 as a string. If you send a number out to an application server, it turns to a string. This is a real pain when you consider the work involved in parsing arrays and generic objects that you pass back and forth. This chapter shows two ways to exchange data that requires no parsing. Namely, Flash Remoting's protocol (Action Messaging Format or AMF) and web services (Simple Object Access Protocol or SOAP). Additional benefits include AMF's efficiency and performance features and SOAP's common data format.

In addition to a better way to exchange data, this chapter covers the new data management components that ship with Flash MX Professional 2004. These offer direct access to web services without the need for Flash Remoting. In addition, the data management components include powerful yet simple ways of binding imported data to visual displays (such as onscreen text) and even tracking changes so that you can send updates back to a database efficiently.

This chapter covers the following topics:

- How to pass data between application servers and Flash using Flash Remoting
- How to use the data components found in Flash MX Professional 2004
- How to use the Component Inspector to define schemas and set up bindings
- How Flash Remoting compares to Flash's native SOAP support

{ Note }

What Do You Need? This chapter covers tools that you may need to install or purchase separately. Specifically, Flash Remoting can be installed on several different application servers—although it comes free with ColdFusion MX. The 30-day trial of ColdFusion is perfectly suitable because after the trial period you can continue to use it in a limited manner as the "production version."

Flash MX Professional 2004 is required to use the data management components. This gives you direct access to web services as well as data binding. Actually, any time you see the Component Inspector's Bindings or Schema tab, you'll know you're looking at the pro version.

Realize that even if you only have the standard edition of Flash, this chapter can give you a clear idea of what the pro version offers. If your app needs to perform the sorts of tasks demonstrated here, you owe it to yourself to get the pro version. That said, you can still do lots of things with just the standard version, too.

Flash Remoting

Flash Remoting isn't so much a product as it is a feature supported in Flash. Remoting is a way that Flash apps can directly invoke methods residing on your application server. This means, anything your server can do, Flash can do. If your application server has a method (that is, a function) that searches a database and returns the results, Flash can trigger it and get the data back into your Flash app. You can think of Remoting as a channel over which Flash connects to methods residing on the application server.

To set up Remoting, follow these three steps:

1. Install and enable Remoting on your server. (It's built in to ColdFusion MX.)
2. Install the free Remoting components for Flash (basically a library of AS files).
3. Write methods for your application server and write scripts in your Flash apps to trigger those methods.

Of course, when you deploy your app it will also need access to a Remoting-enabled server. Most likely this means your web server has an application server running adjacent to it. If you don't already have a deployment plan, install ColdFusion MX 6.1 as well as the Remoting components for Flash (both available at www.macromedia.com).

How It Works

Figure 7.1 shows the sequence of events for a Flash app accessing a remote method (that is, a method on your server).

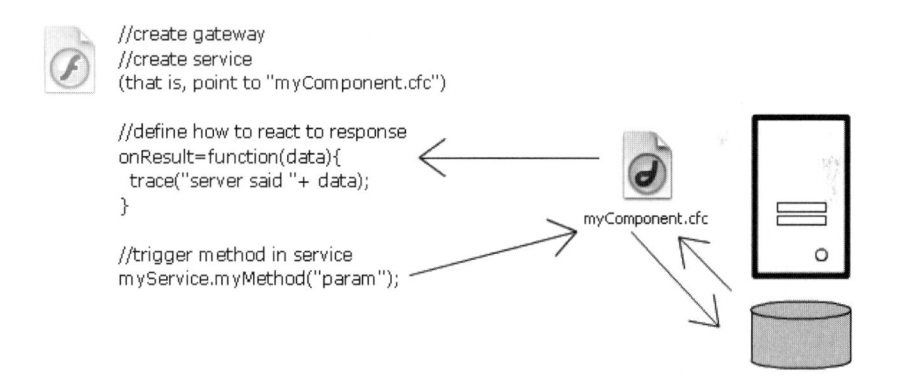

```
//create gateway
//create service
(that is, point to "myComponent.cfc")

    //define how to react to response
    onResult=function(data){
      trace("server said "+ data);
    }

    //trigger method in service
    myService.myMethod("param");
```

myComponent.cfc

Figure 7.1 *The sequence Flash Remoting follows.*

It all starts and ends with Flash. Flash makes a request and sends optional parameters to the remote method; the method processes the request by either triggering subsequent actions (maybe sending an email or adding a record to a database); finally, an optional message containing data is sent back to Flash, which you can process as you want. Because this is asynchronous (meaning Flash won't just freeze while it waits for a reply), you'll first define how you want Flash to handle the response and then trigger the method. The entire process is similar to how you can trigger functions within a Flash movie.

One part of this description that I left out is about preparing and processing data. That is, I didn't explain how Flash must first prepare the data it sends as a parameter, how that data arrives at the remote method, how the remote method prepares data it's going to send back, or how that data arrives back inside Flash. I didn't explain it because it doesn't matter! Primarily, this is just part of your design decisions. If you want to send a generic object containing properties for name, age, and telephone and expect the remote method to extract values for each property and insert them into a database, for example, it's up to you. The great part is that you can pass any data type you want. Although the ColdFusion language doesn't include generic objects, it does have the struct data format, which is basically the same thing. The syntax varies, but your application server and Flash don't need to translate anything. It's almost as though the two sides can speak their own (different) language and it gets translated over the Remoting channel.

Later in this chapter you'll see how you can forgo Remoting and access remote functions that are built as web services. The reason to consider Remoting, however, is that the AMF protocol used is way more efficient than SOAP (the protocol used by web services). SOAP is just a particular form of XML. As such it includes additional tags that all add up to a larger file (roughly four times as large). In the case of AMF, it's an optimized binary format. They both travel over HTTP, but the same data as AMF will always be smaller than SOAP. In addition, AMF can do tricks such as paging so that huge data sets effectively stream in bite-size packets.

The only legitimate gripe against Remoting is that it costs money (at least for non-ColdFusion servers) and it uses the proprietary AMF protocol. When you make the effort to expose your server-side method as a web service, you're producing something that can be used with anything else supporting SOAP. Making a server-side component that works with AMF limits it to Flash Remoting. It's not quite that bad with ColdFusion because the same code used for Remoting can be used by your regular ColdFusion pages. Ultimately SOAP is more universal. Although web services (that is, SOAP) are all the rage, you can't ignore the fact this standard is necessarily wordy.

Basic Remoting

There are always two sides to a Remoting call—Flash and the method on your application server. Flash has to set up the gateway over which data will travel, make a request, and define how to respond when an answer is received. The server-side method is like any function: It has a name, it specifies expected parameters, and it includes code to carry out the intended effect, including preparing and sending back a return value.

I use the starter script in Listing 7.1 for any Remoting application.

Listing 7.1 Basic Remoting Script

```
1   #include "NetServices.as"
2   #include "NetDebug.as"
3   myResponder=function(){
4     this.onResult=function(data){
5       trace("data returned is " + data);
6     }
7     this.onStatus=function(info){
8       trace("status is :" + info.description);
9     }
10  }
11  if (inited == null){
12    inited = true;
13    NetServices.setDefaultGatewayUrl(
14    "http://localhost:8500/flashservices/gateway/");
15    myGateway = NetServices.createGatewayConnection();
16    myService = myGateway.getService("path.to.cfc");
17  }
18  //trigger:
19  myService.doMyFunction(new myResponder(),"param");
```

The first line loads the NetServices library of ActionScript. The second line loads code for when using the NetConnection Debugger (available from Window, Other Panels). Then the "responder" object is defined. This handles all responses from the remote method. Inside you can see two event handlers. On line 4 `onResult` triggers when data is returned as expected. I happen to call the parameter `data`, although what's important is that all data is returned as a single parameter. Line 7 shows `onStatus`, which only triggers when an error occurs. Notice the parameter received is a generic object with a `description` property. That parameter includes other properties (`level`, `code`, and `details`), but `description` is the most digestible.

Finally, lines 13 through 16 only need to execute once (so I'm just using `inited` as a flag). Line 13 specifies the URL where Flash Remoting is installed. It's not like there's really a folder that matches—it's just always specified as flashservices/gateway (under your web site's root directory). Line 15 creates a gateway and stores it in the homemade `myGateway` variable. Then, line 16 uses `getService()` to point to the actual server-side method and stores this reference in the `myService` variable. In this case, there really is a file. The syntax uses dots rather than slashes, so `path.to.cfc` means that inside the root web site there's a file called `cfc` inside the `to` folder, which is inside `path`. That file contains the server-side method.

After everything has been set up (that is, we have a responder and a service), you can trigger a remote method (as shown in line 18). This example points to a function named `doMyFunction()` and passes `"param"` as the first parameter. Well, actually, it shows up in the second slot because Flash wants the responder object in the first slot. If the `doMyFunction()` were in the Flash file, we would just say `_root.doMyFunction("param")`. Because the function is remote, however, I use the previously defined `myService` and sneak an instance of the responder object in the first parameter slot.

That's the Flash side of Remoting in a nutshell. It really is pretty easy. Let me make a few additional notes before we look at some samples. I said the data returned (the parameter `data` on line 4) contains everything returned from the remote method. That is, if the method returns an array, `data` is an array. If the method returns a string, it's a string. In the case of query results, you get an array full of generic objects, each with matching property names. It just depends how the remote method is designed.

The same data type issue applies to the data you send. In the example, line 19 shows I'm passing a string (`"param"`). I could just as easily pass an array or object or number.

Finally, line 19 triggers the remote call. You might not want to do this right at the start of your app. Perhaps you want users to type in their name, and then you'll pass their name back to the remote method. You can put that trigger anywhere you want. In addition, you can even trigger the same function repeatedly—or before the results from the first call arrive back. Because it's asynchronous, you need a way to associate returned data with the right trigger. Maybe I have a remote method that can look up only one product's price at a time, but I still want to give the user a way to request several in one move. To solve this, you could change the responder to expect and track a parameter:

```
myResponder=function(id){
    this.id=id;
    this.onResult=function(data){
```

Chapter 7 Exchanging Data with Outside Services   193

```
      trace("data for "+ this.id + " is " + data);
  }
}
```

Then, pass a unique ID for each trigger:

```
myService.doMyFunction(new myResponder("request 1"),"param");
myService.doMyFunction(new myResponder("request 2"),"param");
```

Remoting Example

Here's a simple example that relies on a sample server-side method `convert()` that gets installed with ColdFusion. It's sort of cheating to show you this because you just have to believe the server-side method performs as described. (You'll see the server side in a minute.)

I have a button (`my_btn`), a text field (`result_txt`), and an input text field (`input_txt`), as well as this code in the first frame:

```
1   myResponder=function(){
2      this.onResult=function(data){
3         result_txt.text=data;
4      }
5   }
6
7   my_btn.onPress=function(){
8      myService.convert(new myResponder(), "F", input_txt.text);
9   }
10
11  NetServices.setDefaultGatewayUrl(
12       "http://localhost:8500/flashservices/gateway/");
13  myGateway = NetServices.createGatewayConnection();
14  myGateway.getService("cfdocs.exampleapps.cfc.tempconverter");
```

After installing ColdFusion, I found a server-side method called `tempconverter.cfc` (inside `wwwroot/cfdocs/exampleapps/cfc`)—hence the parameter in line 14. Notice that you don't include the .cfc file extension and that this particular method happens to be in a folder called cfc.

Take my word that the tempconverter file contains a method called `convert()` that accepts two parameters: the scale (`"F"` or `"C"`) and the temperature you want to convert. Line 8 is where I trigger that function and pass two parameters. I should disclose that I included the `onStatus()` event while troubleshooting this code.

Writing the Remote Method

The temperature conversion example just mentioned used a sample file, so I didn't have to first create a remote method. Obviously, you need a remote method before you can call it. We'll look at a quick ColdFusion example (and, in fact, you're welcome to check out the tempconverter.cfc file). However, it makes sense to keep Flash and the server side separate. In fact, I completed an entire project using Remoting where I stayed in Flash and the ColdFusion expert stayed in ColdFusion. It's a perfect separation of duties. We just communicated details including the method names, what parameters they expect to receive, and what data types they returned. I'm not just saying this to avoid covering the server side, but rather to point out this separation is what Remoting is all about. You get access to remote methods, but you don't have to know how they were built.

Here's an absolute minimum ColdFusion component (CFC):

```
1    <cfcomponent>
2      <cffunction name="sayHello" access="remote" >
3        <cfreturn "hi there">
4      </cffunction>
5    </cfcomponent>
```

If you know how to make a CFC, you'll notice two things. First, the preceding example avoids many optional tags that provide extra information. Second, the tag access="remote" is the one element that applies only to Flash (and it's required for Remoting). You can see the whole thing is a cfcomponent and there's one nested cffunction. A single component file can have additional functions. The method Flash would trigger in this example is sayHello(). Notice cfreturn is where the value "hi there" gets sent back to Flash.

There's a lot more you can do in CFCs. You can accept parameters, perform more elaborate procedures (such as querying or writing to a database), and return more complex data types such as arrays and structs (equivalent to Flash generic objects). The best example file I can recommend is Macromedia's free noteboard example available at www.macromedia.com/devnet/ria/note_board/ and shown in Figure 7.2. It comes with the Flash source files, the CFCs, and an accompanying article.

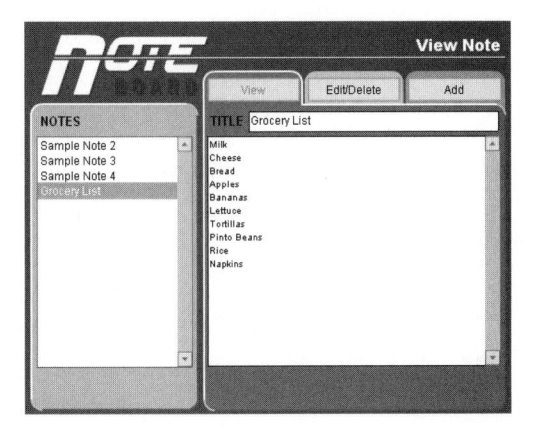

Figure 7.2 *The noteboard sample is a working application that uses Flash Remoting to edit a database.*

Remoting Tips

Although Remoting is very simple, the potential is much greater. However, you do need to be aware of a few details, covered in the following sections, as you embark on using Remoting in your app.

Complex Data

As mentioned previously, any data type can pass over Flash Remoting. This includes generic objects and arrays. It also includes arrays full of objects. Interestingly, when your remote method returns the results of a query (that is, all the records in a database table that match a particular criteria), it arrives in Flash as a generic object with several additional properties. It's called a recordset. The structure may not seem particularly logical, although you can easily dig in and extract the parts you need. Figure 7.3 shows both original database structure as well as the data returned to Flash (when the query returned all records).

Notice the array of objects that appear under the `items` property. The structure of a recordset is important for a few reasons. First, you commonly need to receive a set of records. Also, you may want to parse through the results. Finally, recordsets are really easy to use with components because—although a recordset doesn't fit the formal definition of a `dataProvider`—you can use it as a `dataProvider` and it works out great. For example, I could place a List component onstage (`myList`) and use `myList.dataProvider=data` inside the `myResponder`'s `onResult` event. Finally, check out the available methods for the recordset. There are fancy features such as the DataGlue object for rearranging columns. Check out the methods available under Flash Remoting in your Actions panel.

The other data types such as arrays and generic objects are more straightforward.

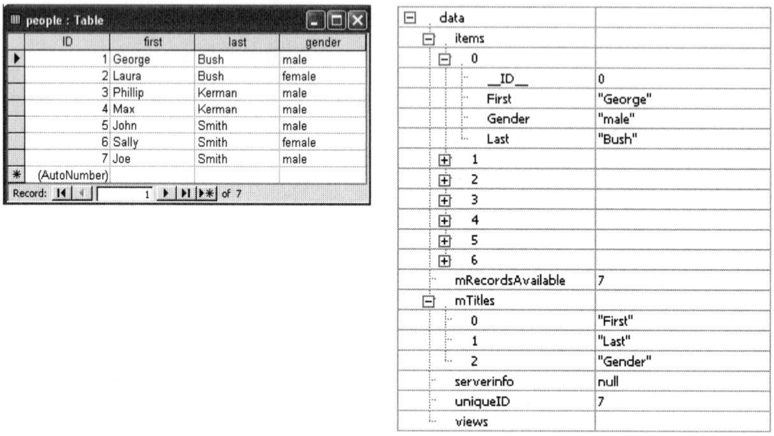

Figure 7.3 *The original data in Access (left) arrives in Flash via a query as a recordset with several additional properties.*

When to Use Remoting

Designing an app that uses Remoting is nearly the same as designing a utility function. That is, you have to decide which parameters the function will accept, what the function will do, and which values it returns—if any. But the decision whether to use Remoting is high on many people's list.

The reason to reach for Remoting is simply when you want access to something outside Flash. Most often this is a database. Application servers include methods to access and modify databases.

Another reason to use Remoting is because you want to get the data *out* of Flash. After a user completes a survey, for example, you can send all that data to the application server and have it store the data for safekeeping. Of course, this could mean writing it to a database, but it could also just forward the results in an email to someone.

Finally, a great reason to use Remoting is to recycle or mirror existing code. Suppose, for instance, that you're already using an application server to produce a sophisticated HTML-based app. If the code is modular enough, you should have little trouble converting it to work with Flash Remoting calls. This way you can convert your HTML front to a Flash front without rewriting all the code. In addition, if you want to run both an HTML and a Flash version of your app, you can do it with the underlying code.

Many of these "reasons to use remoting" are also "reasons to use web services/SOAP." Remoting does have a distinct performance advantage. In addition, it's free with ColdFusion. Also, you don't need Flash Pro. The only downside is that it's not a standard format like SOAP.

Data Management Components

For me, the inclusion of the six so-called Data components is what justifies Flash MX Professional 2004. Unlike the user interface (UI) components, the Data components have no visual component. Instead, they only help you connect to outside data, manage complex data inside Flash, and gracefully track any subsequent changes to the data (while in Flash) so that updates sent back to the server can be kept to a minimum. Integral supplements to the Data components are the Bindings and Schema tabs in the Component Inspector. The rest of this chapter shows you both the concepts behind the Data components and a clear idea about how to use them.

The Data Component Concept

The six Data components include two each of three general types: connectors, managers, and resolvers (see Figure 7.4).

The XMLConnector and WebServiceConnector help you import and export XML data or SOAP data, respectively. The DataHolder and DataSet help you maintain and process data while in Flash. Finally, the RDBMSResolver and XUpdateResolver both track changes to your data and prepare "deltaPackets" containing details of just the aspects that change. The two resolvers are identical except that XUpdate uses a standard format, and RDMS uses format more in tune with relational databases. (RDMS stands for relational database management system, which includes such tools as Access or MySQL.)

```
□ 🎲 Data Components
    🗟 DataHolder
    ▦ DataSet
    🗃 RDBMSResolver
    🌐 WebServiceConnector
    🔖 XMLConnector
    🗃 XUpdateResolver
```

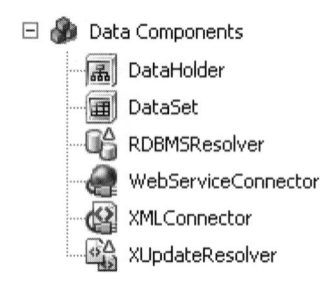

Figure 7.4 *These six Data components give you tons of control.*

Depending on your application, you'll drag one or more Data components onstage and effectively snap them together using the Component Inspector. You use this panel like the Parameters tab in the Properties panel—to populate and set properties of your component instances. In fact, the Component Inspector includes the standard Parameters tab, but adds two more: Bindings and Schema.

The Bindings and Schema tabs enable you to set even more properties because there are more details to specify. Bindings are how you link two or more components together. For example, you can bind the changing value in a numeric stepper to an array so that the user can select a single index in the array. Binding enables you to synchronize values so that when one changes, the other reflects the change. The Schema tab enables you to view and edit a visualization of the data structure. If your data is a generic object, for example, you can specify the contained properties (which later get bound to other components). Basically, you need a name for anything that gets bound and the Schema tab enables you to map out and name the data. An epiphany of understanding for me came when I realized *schema* is short for *schematic*.

The next few sections cover the details in sort of a chronological order based on how you might use the components. First you'll learn how connectors bring outside data into Flash. The first couple of examples actually require you to open the Bindings tab. Then you'll learn the details of binding data to visual components. You'll also need to understand schemas, because you can't bind data unless the schema is known. However, the schema often imports automatically, as in the case of a web service, because a description of its structure is included. In any event, the focus then shifts to the DataHolder and DataSet components because they help manage data as the app runs. Finally, the resolvers deal with tracking changes. Often the last step is figuring out what information you're going to send out of your app, and the resolvers help in this stage.

Even though I've organized this information linearly, when you build an app you'll approach all these topics simultaneously in a more integrated manner. This is comparable to how you might study the different parts of a car (steering wheel, brakes, gas pedal), but when you actually drive you use everything at once.

Connectors

The connectors (XMLConnector and WebServiceConnector) make reading and writing outside data a snap. In the case of reading XML, you just point to the file you plan to import (or the server that will supply it) and then "trigger" the component at runtime. It's the same with the WebServiceConnector: Point to the service, optionally include parameters (because many web services expect a parameter with your request), and then trigger the component. When the data arrives, it will immediately display in any visual components to which you've bound the data. For example, you can have a TextInput component into which the user types a three-letter airport code (say PDX for Portland), that value is bound to the outgoing parameter for a WebServiceConnector (which points to a web service that supplies weather information), and when the results arrive back that data is bound to a TextArea component that displays the current temperature. It's really easy to set up.

The only catch—particularly with the web services—is that a Flash app running in the browser is restricted from directly accessing a web service hosted on an outside domain. At the end of Chapter 6, you learned a technique that enables you to point to a simple script on your own application server that acts as a proxy for the real web service outside your domain. Just note that the following example will work only while you are authoring or running a SWF on the desktop. (It won't work in a browser unless you set up a proxy script.)

To try it out, place onstage a TextArea component (instance name `my_ta`) and a WebServiceConnector (named `my_ws`). Select the `my_ws` instance, open the Component Inspector, and select the Parameters tab. Type the following address into the WSDLURL field:

`http://live.capescience.com/wsdl/AirportWeather.wsdl`

(I found this public web service at `www.xmethods.com`—where you can find many more.)

After you enter the WSDL address, Flash attempts to parse the information contained. (Go ahead and type that same WSDL into your browser to see how the data is organized—basically it uses a common format to detail how the web service works.) When the parsing is complete (and provided it was successful), you can click in to the Operation field and see a drop-down list of all the methods available at that web service. Select getTemperature.

Select the Bindings tab and click the Plus button. This particular web service expects one argument. Click the row that reads arg0 : string (shown in Figure 7.5), and then click OK.

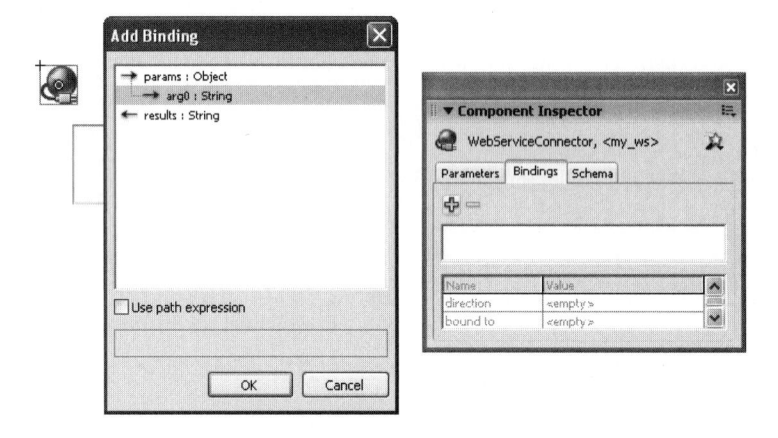

Figure 7.5 *We will bind a hard-wired value for this web service's parameter.*

Still in the Bindings tab, make sure the row params.arg0 is selected and click twice in the Value field for bound to. The Bound To dialog box appears, from which you can identify from where the value (for this parameter) will come. Check the box Use Constant Value and type **KPDX** into the field (the real airport code for Portland), and then click OK. Again, click the plus button in the Bindings tab. This time select Results. Now click twice in the Bound To field (for the row results), and we'll bind the value returned to our text area. In the Bound To dialog box, click TextArea <my_ta> on the left pane. The Schema Location pane shows text : String. In this case, the TextArea has only one property to which we can bind the data (otherwise you might see more in the right-side pane). Click OK. Notice that when you click the two rows now populated in the Bindings tab (params.arg0 and results) that params.arg0's direction is "in" and results is "out". That is, value KPDX comes into this component and the results go out (in this case, to the TextArea). Finally, to invoke the WebServiceConnector, place this script in frame 1 of the movie:
my_ws.trigger();.Test the movie and you'll see the temperature at my home.

Pretty cool. All we did was specify the address of the web service and the particular method we intended to trigger. Of course, we also had to specify a parameter and then bind the results to an onscreen TextArea. It turns out setting up the bindings is way more involved than getting the connector to work.

The XMLConnector is simpler in some ways because you can use it to just import data if you want. Here's a real quick example. Make a copy of the ActionsPanel.xml document that's inside the ActionsPanel folder inside the First Run folder adjacent to your installed version of Flash. Put the copy in a new folder. Make a new Flash document and save it in the same folder. In the Flash document, drag a Tree component (instance name my_tree) and an XMLConnector (instance name my_xc). Select the my_xc instance and select the Parameter tab. Set the value for URL to ActionsPanel.xml and set the direction to receive. (You can use send/receive for an application server providing data in XML, but here we're just reading a static file—you can't write to it.) Now select the Bindings tab and click the plus button. Select the row that reads results : XML and click OK. Click twice in the Bound to Value column, and then select Tree, <my_tree> in the pane on the left. Click OK. Finally, you need to trigger the connector. Type this code in the first frame of the document: `my_xc.trigger();`.

This XML example just takes the whole XML document and dumps it into the Tree component. This is not a typical need. More likely you'll want to import XML and then display only part at a time. For example, in Chapter 6 we imported the content for a quiz and displayed one question at a time. You can certainly do this with the XMLConnector, but it involves the Schema tab and much more binding. We'll look at those both next. So far you've mainly seen how the XML and web service connectors will import data from an outside source. Next you'll see more about what you can with the data after it arrives into Flash.

Bindings and Schema

Bindings are how you link a property in one component to a property in another. These properties can be visual (such as the text of a TextArea) or they can be variables contained in a complex data structure (say the firstname of the first record in a array full of generic objects). The schema is a map of data properties contained in a component. The TextArea maintains several properties (such as font color, _x, _width), but has just one data property (text), so its schema is very simple. For a web service that returns a query (array full of generic objects), the schema is a bit more involved. You always need a schema before you can start binding data values because those values have to have a name. The schema puts names on the data properties.

Here's an analogy. The red wagon my daughter got for her birthday included a set of directions. The schema, if you will, was a picture with the items labeled: 4 wheels, 8 long screws, 4 short screws, 2 axels, and 4 sides to the wagon. They could have called the axels "bars" for all that mattered, but when it came to the directions they just needed to use a name consistent with the original picture.

When you're designing an app that displays dynamic data, you won't know the exact values displayed but you need a handle on what sorts of values to expect. The schema puts structure and labels on that data. There are three primary ways to create a schema: automatically from a WSDL, automatically from a sample XML template, or manually. A web services WSDL file will provide the schema of both the values it expects you to send as well as the values it returns. You really can't modify these yourself. For XML, you can import a sample (either the actual XML or a file that contains the same structure of the actual XML). This technique involves a bit of developer intervention to make sure you do it correctly. But, again, you can't decide to change the schema inside Flash to something that doesn't match the actual XML. Finally, there are occasions when you'll want to define a schema by hand. Mainly this is to extend and add custom properties to components. This applies more to components that handle data once inside Flash—primarily the DataHolder, which you can structure however you want.

The schema definition is basically a copy of what you see when you added a binding. For example, Figure 7.6 shows the schema that was automatically generated for the weather web service example from earlier (using a WSDLURL of http://live.capescience.com/wsdl/AirportWeather.wsdl).

Notice that the main window of the Schema panel includes three "bindable" properties: params, params.arg0 (that is, arg0 nested in params), and results. This schema was produced automatically. When you select any one row, you'll see additional details below where you can modify things such as the names and data type. Because the web service often needs or returns specifically named properties, you probably don't want to change them here. (I'll come back to the settings for kind, formatter, and encoder later—but realize these let you further define how data is messaged on its way into or out of the component.)

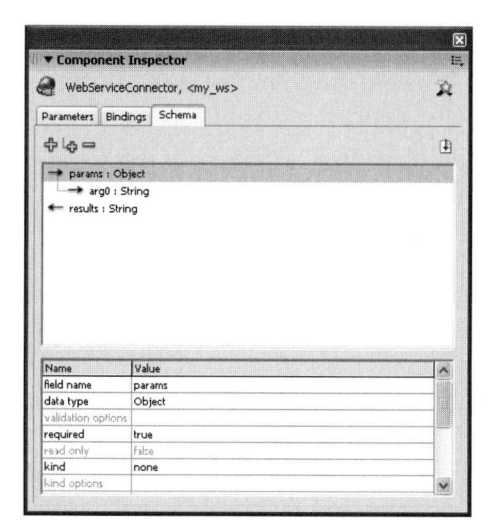

Chapter 7 Exchanging Data with Outside Services 203

Figure 7.6 *This relatively simple schema is created when Flash parses the WSDL.*

To see the power of a WSDL to declare its own schema, go back to the Parameters tab and change the operation to getSummary (another available method in the weather web service). Return to the Schema tab and notice the results now include seven separate properties (see Figure 7.7).

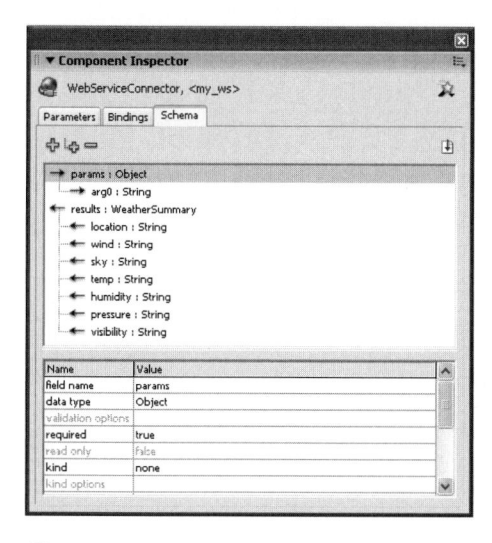

Figure 7.7 *Because the selected operation (that is, the method) is more complex, this schema displays all the subproperties that get returned in the results.*

At this point, you can bind just the humidity to the TextArea. Click the Bindings tab, select the row results, and then click the minus button. Click the plus button, and this time select Humidity (under Results, just like in the schema). Then click the Bound To field twice and point to the my_ta TextArea. We had to remove the old binding because you can only modify the settings in the bottom pane—not the bindings themselves. I find myself frequently removing bindings and adding new ones in this manner. Also, if you had removed the destination for that binding (the TextArea that is), the binding would have been removed automatically.

The second way you can define a schema is by loading a representative XML sample or the actual XML file. The point is, it's not the values in the XML but the names of the tags that matter. In the preceding example, we just dumped the entire ActionsPanel.xml data into the Tree component. If you'd rather display just part of the data, you need to bind specific properties from the schema.

Here's a slightly involved exercise using that same ActionsPanel.xml source file. Start a new file and drag onstage two TextArea components (with instance names title_ta and body_ta), one NumericStepper (instance name myns), and one XMLConnector (named my_xc) as shown in Figure 7.8. Save this file adjacent to your copy of the ActionsPanel.xml file. Select the my_xc instance and use the Parameters tab to set the URL to "ActionsPanel.xml" and the direction to receive.

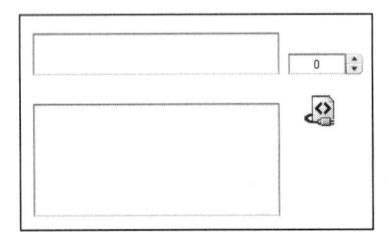

Figure 7.8 *This example steps through values in the ActionsPanel.xml with these four components.*

To import the XML schema, select the Schema tab and first make sure you select the row `results : XML`. That is, you want to describe the form of the data coming into the component, not the structure of the data going out. Then click the button Import Schema from a Sample XML File and point to the ActionsPanel.xml file. You may need to refresh by clicking the stage and then reselecting the my_xc instance, but ultimately you'll see a pretty gnarly schema that's only partially shown in Figure 7.9.

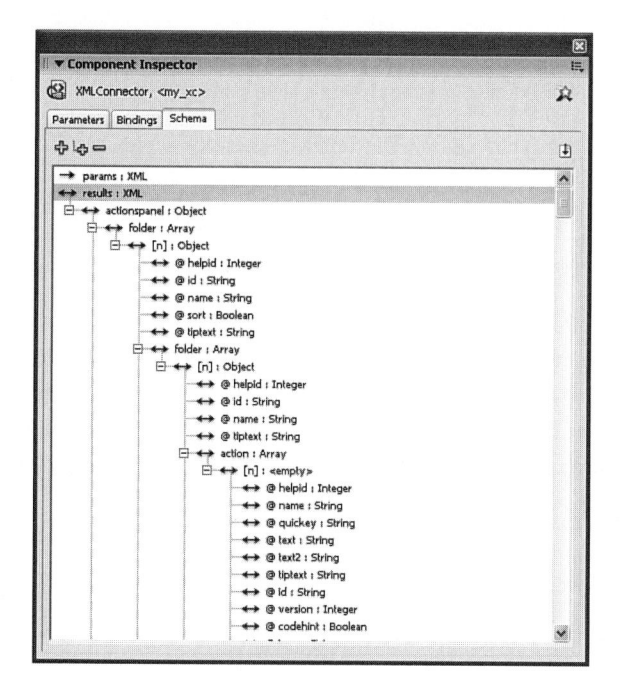

Figure 7.9 *Flash created this schema by parsing an XML file.*

If you had designed this structure, it would be easier to dig into. In this case, I suggest you start by collapsing the hierarchy (click the little box to the left of the first nesting under results). There are two nested properties: folder and a deprecate. Because folder is an array of objects, you see [n]:Object, under which you'll find six more properties (including one that is an array full of more stuff). For this example, give the user a way to step through each item in the top-level folder property and view the name and tiptext for each. All you have to do is bind those properties.

Select the Bindings tab and click the plus button. You'll see the same hierarchy you imported. Select the row @name:string (under the Object inside the folder property). Click OK. Set direction to out (because the value is going to go out of this component). Click twice on the Bound To value, and then bind to the title_ta TextArea component and click OK. Now, because the name property is nested inside an array, you'll notice the last row Index[0] defaults to 0. Instead of always displaying the 0 index, you can bind that value to the NumericStepper instance. Click twice on the value column for Index[0]. This time the Bound To dialog box is mostly grayed out—only because the default 0 is hard-wired as the constant value. Uncheck the Use Constant Value box and select the

`NumericStepper` instance listed on the left. Before you click OK, notice this component's schema has only one property (`value`), but this time its data type is `Number`. That makes sense, but it's the first one that's not a string.

Back at the Bindings tab, you can bind the `tiptext` property to the other TextArea (`body_ta`). Click the plus sign, pick `tiptext`, set `direction` to `out`, bound to the `body_ta` instance, and set the `Index[0]` to use your `NumericStepper`'s value. Finally, add this code to the first keyframe:

```
my_xc.trigger();
```

As you click the `NumericStepper`, you'll see a different excerpt of data from the entire XML file. The numeric stepper's default maximum value is 10, so with this data when you go past 7 you'll see `undefined` onscreen. The following script sets up an event listener that triggers when the XML is fully loaded, and then sets the ns instance's `maximum` property:

```
function resultsLoaded(me) {
ns.maximum=me.target.results.firstChild.firstChild.childNodes.length;
}
my_xc.addEventListener("result", resultsLoaded);
```

Sure, I had to dig to figure out how far down into child nodes I had to go. Just be sure to put this code *above* the trigger. Note that `result` is just one of the events for which you can listen.

{ Note }

Learning All the Component Event Listeners Here's a trick to learn which events a particular component can listen for. Select the component instance, open the Actions panel, and type `on(`. The code hints then appear listing all event names. Erase the code and then use the `addEventListener()` method as shown in the preceding code.

There are actually many more features of the Bindings and Schema tabs. You'll learn about additional ways to control the format and presentation of data in the "Formatting Data" section later in this chapter. For now you definitely have the basics. One potentially confusing issue is that for any binding you'll always have two sides: one property in one component bound to another property in another component. You'll see the two views of the *same* binding when you select either end. That is, you might select a WebServiceConnector and see how property from its results is bound to a TextArea component. In that case, you'll also be able to select the `TextArea` instance and see that it is bound to the WebServiceConnector. Editing either end will affect the other.

The tricky part is designing or studying the schema and then deciding how you're going to bind data.

DataHolder Component

The DataHolder is just a convenient way to store data while keeping it available for binding with any other components. In fact, any data-aware component includes properties to which you can bind other components' properties. Consider how the TextArea component has a `text` property that you can bind to. However, all components (except the DataHolder) are limited to a predetermined list of available properties, or in the case of the XMLConnector and WSDLConnector, limited to the properties contained in the remote source. The DataHolder is completely customizable. You can add properties as you see fit and structure the schema however you want.

I see the primary benefit for the DataHolder as sort of a repository where data from several different components can all be managed in one place. The only hassle with the DataHolder is that you must define the schema manually. Remember I said that in addition to importing an XML template or letting the WSDL define a schema, you could do it manually. The idea with the DataHolder is you can design the data however you want.

Instead of individually mapping several values returned from, say, a web service call, you can just copy the entire results to a DataHolder and pull out just the parts you need. Although the DataHolder is never absolutely necessary, it's often convenient as a sort of go-between. Complex data comes into Flash, gets sent to the DataHolder, and then the values appear in visual components.

Another primary benefit of a DataHolder is that you can access deeply nested data directly. Earlier the code to set the `NumericStepper`'s maximum value included this gem:

```
results.firstChild.firstChild.childNodes.length
```

It's possible to just map the entire node to a property in a DataHolder, say `records`, and then use the following:

```
myDataHolder.records.length
```

(This solution is shown in example files you can download for this chapter at `www.phillipkerman.com/rias`.)

Creating your own schema is like designing any data structure. It's up to you. By default, the structure for a DataHolder has one property, called `data`, that behaves as a generic object. Not only can you change this name, change it to another data type, or remove it entirely, you also can add more properties at either the same top level (`myDataHolder.someProperty`) or nested under other properties (`myDataHolder.data.someSubProperty`). How you design the structure is up to you. The Schema panel can take a little bit of practice (see Figure 7.10). Here are a few comments:

- Insert new top-level properties by clicking the leftmost plus button. That's how I added `topLevelProp` in the figure.

- Insert subproperties by first selecting the row under which you want the subproperty to appear and then pressing the second plus button. I added `subProp` by first selecting `topLevelProp`. You'll notice @ symbols in front of properties (which also have their `storage type` set to `attribute`).

- Some data types preclude you from adding subproperties. For example, an object can have a subproperty, but a string can't. Normally the buttons will disable accordingly, but you can still create illogical structures. Just don't approach it haphazardly.

- When structuring an array, the first subproperty should have the name `[n]`. Notice that's how the `myArray` is structured. The idea is that `myArray` is an array full of objects, each with a `first`, `last`, and `phone` property.

- When accessing property names in your code, they *are* case sensitive.

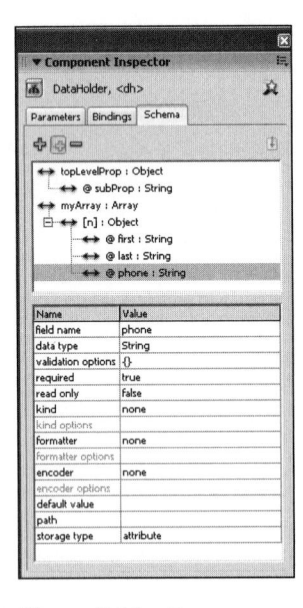

Figure 7.10 *For some components, you have to create your own schema manually.*

Chapter 7 Exchanging Data with Outside Services 209

In the following example, I use a DataHolder instance (named `dh`) configured as shown in Figure 7.10. Realize that the data that populates the DataHolder can come from anywhere. That is, you can bind to a DataHolder the results of a XML or web service connector, the data returned from a Remoting call, or data you type in manually. To simplify things, just use this code in the first keyframe:

```
contacts=[];
contacts.push( {first:"Phillip", last: "Kerman",phone:"503-555-1212"});
contacts.push( {first:"George", last: "Bush",phone:"800-555-1212"});
contacts.push( {first:"Bill", last: "Clinton",phone:"888-555-1212"});

dh.myArray=contacts;
```

That last line just populates the `myArray` property that was already structured in the `dh` instance. Now just add three Label components (`first_txt`, `last_txt`, and `phone_txt`), plus a NumericStepper (instance name `ns`). Back on the DataHolder, select the Bindings tab. Then click the plus button, select `first : String`, and then click the Bound To field and point to `first_txt`. Finally, click the value for `Index[0]` and point to the NumericStepper. Repeat this for all three properties so that the Bindings tab looks like Figure 7.11.

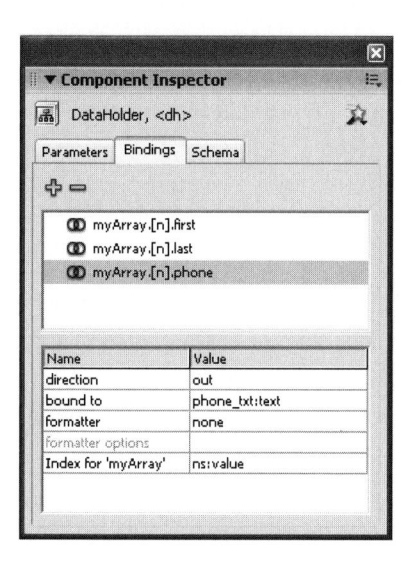

Figure 7.11 *The DataHolder should look like this after you've created the three similar bindings.*

Incidentally, you'll see in the Formatting Data section that instead of wiring up three bindings to three separate Label components, you can instead use Compose String to populate a single Label however you want.

One thing to take away from this exercise is that you can store your own variables in a DataHolder and then bind them to components. Had the data arrived from an XML or web service connector, however, there is no apparent reason why you would need to add the extra step of the DataHolder because you can bind directly from those connectors. In those cases, you still might want to use a DataHolder to, say, bind a deeply nested value to a property up toward the surface of a DataHolder. It's often easier to access data in your own customized structure you create for a DataHolder.

DataSet Component

The DataSet component is creepy the way it monitors every change to a set of data. Macromedia calls it a facade because it does its thing without really getting in the way. It's like the DataHolder because you can stick it between the source data and the presentation, but you don't need to create your own schema. The DataSet has a property called `items`, which is where you store an array of your data—also called the *collection*. (It has other properties, but inside of `items` is where you store your set of data.) Each slot of the `items` record contains what's called a *transfer object*. When the DataSet is involved, you can step through the data, index and search data, sort it, and even track changes, so it's easy to maintain updates.

Iterating Data

Although your DataSet's collection (that is `items` property) is an entire array, you can have only one selection at a time. In the simplest sense, you iterate through the data by changing the current selection. For the following examples, assume you have a DataSet instance named `ds` and this code is placed in the first keyframe:

```
contacts = [];
contacts.push({first:"Phillip", last:"Kerman", phone:"503-555-1212"});
contacts.push({first:"George", last:"Bush", phone:"800-555-1212"});
contacts.push({first:"Bill", last:"Clinton", phone:"888-555-1212"});
ds.items = contacts;
```

Again, you can bind any array to the DataSet instance's `items` property.

After this DataSet is populated, you can step the selection by using `ds.next()` and `ds.previous()`. At any time, you can grab the value of the current selection using `ds.currentItem`. For example, the following code could get triggered by a "next" button:

```
trace("old first name was " + ds.currentItem.first);
ds.next();
trace("current first name is "+ ds.currentItem.first);
```

Besides stepping through the transfer objects (that is, the data in your DataSet), you can modify or add more objects. For example:

```
ds.addItem({first:"George",last:"Washington",phone:"na"})
```

You might think you can just do `contacts.push()`. However, for the DataSet to track changes, you need to use `addItem()`. The same restriction applies to changing the contents of a component's DataProvider.

Sorting and Searching

Sorting and searching a DataSet collection is based on the array object's methods. However, DataSets use indexes to speed searches. For example, the first time you perform a particular sort (say, alphabetic by last name in descending order), all the items in the collection are given special tags that speed subsequent sorts. This is like how search engines can appear to search through every item on the Internet in a matter of milliseconds. The second search relies on information saved from the preceding search.

Apparently the way DataSets are sorted, searched, and indexed is based on Java standards. However, several details really threw me. Let me report the following about sorting (say, with a DataSet instance `ds`):

- You should give each sort that you perform a unique string name so that you don't keep redefining the same sort.
- Avoiding doubled sorts is so important that there's a method `ds.hasSort()` that will return `true` if a sort is found (matching the value you pass as a parameter).
- When you say `ds.addSort()`, not only will Flash add the details of the sort (and its given name) to your DataSet, it also will immediately perform the sort.
- To retrigger a sort, just use `useSort()` (and provide the name you gave originally as the parameter).

Here's a quick look at the syntax:

```
ds.addSort("mySortName", ["first"]);
```

The name for this sort will be `"mySortName"` and it will sort based on the field named `first`. Notice the second parameter is an array containing string versions of the field names. In this case, I just have one field, but it's still an array. In many ways, the `addSort()` method is similar to `sortOn()` (covered in Chapter 5, "Presenting Data"). You can even provide a third parameter such as `Array.CASEINSENSITIVE` or `Array.DESCENDING`. But do notice the first parameter is the name for this sort.

Later you can include code, such as the following, that ensures you're not performing the same sort twice:

```
if(ds.hasSort("mySortName")){
   ds.useSort("mySortName");
}else{
   ds.addSort("mySortName", ["first"]);
}
```

The idea is that you can create as many unique sorts as you want, but you just don't want to redefine the same sort twice. In addition, there's a `ds.removeSort()` if you know you won't be using the sort again, or you don't want to bother checking every time with `hasSort()`.

It makes sense that performing a sort will affect the current item. After all, items reorder when you perform a sort. The way it works with sorting is your `selectedIndex` doesn't change, just the value of the item in that index. In the case of searching, however, the index where the item is found becomes the `selectedIndex` value.

The detail about searching that freaks me out is that before searching for a matching value in a certain field, you must first perform a sort that includes that field. If you don't really want to change the entire DataSet's order, you just sort it anyway, do your search, and then sort it back the way it was.

When you perform a search (for example, `ds.find()`), the found object becomes the `currentItem`. Of course, you can use this to grab any property you want. You also can use `ds.getItemId()` to save a unique reference to transfer an object (that is, the item). The ID won't change even if the DataSet is sorted. Incidentally, the ID returned is a string. Realize you might quickly do a sort on one property (because you have to before searching), search for a specific value

Chapter 7 Exchanging Data with Outside Services 213

of that property, save off the found object or find its index, and then re-sort the data back to where it was. If there's a visual component onstage, the user won't see any change.

The code for a search can start to look pretty convoluted with all the extra sorting going on. You can definitely consolidate this code to something more generic (see Listing 7.2). To make this code work, you need that `contacts` array declared and associated with the `ds` instance's `items`. In addition, you need two buttons (`firstname_btn` and `lastname_btn`) plus a TextInput component (`input_txt`). If you want a visual, just add a DataGrid component. You'll need to manually bind the DataSet `items` to a DataGrid instance's `dataProvider` as well.

Listing 7.2 Searching for Transfer Objects in a DataSet's Collection

```
//put contacts declaration here
1   ds.addSort( "default", ["first"]);
2
3   firstname_btn.onPress=function(){
4     if (ds.hasSort("firstNameSort")) {
5        ds.useSort("firstNameSort");
6     } else {
7        ds.addSort( "firstNameSort", ["first"])
8     }
9     if(!ds.find([input_txt.text])){
10       trace("no find");
11    }else{
12       trace ("Found "+ds.currentItem.first + " " +
13                       ds.currentItem.last);
14       trace("Position in this sort "+ ds.selectedIndex);
15       trace("ID: "+ds.getItemId());
16    }
17    ds.useSort("default");
18  }
19
20  lastname_btn.onPress=function(){
21    if (ds.hasSort("lastNameSort")) {
22       ds.useSort("lastNameSort");
23    } else {
24       ds.addSort( "lastNameSort", ["last"])
25    }
26    if(!ds.find([input_txt.text])){
27       trace("no find");
```

continues

Listing 7.2 Searching for Transfer Objects in a DataSet's Collection (Continued)

```
28      }else{
29          trace ("Found "+ds.currentItem.first + " " +
30                          ds.currentItem.last);
31          trace("Position in this sort "+ ds.selectedIndex);
32          trace("ID: "+ds.getItemId());
33      }
34      ds.useSort("default");
35  }
```

Notice that I perform a sort initially (called `"default"`) just so that I can restore it after either search. Lines 4 through 8 just ensure the same sort isn't added twice. Then line 9 performs the `find()`. In fact, `find()` returns either `true` or `false`, so I use the `if` statement to see whether no match was found. When there is a match, just do some `trace()` gymnastics in lines 12 through 15 to show ways to access the found object. Finally, line 17 puts things back the way they were (with the default sort). Lines 20 through 35 are the same thing, but it sorts first by the `last` property (as in last name).

Like most of this chapter, if you see something that looks pretty cool, realize there's a lot more in the documentation. The idea here is to get a handle on what's possible.

Saving

You'll find the DataSet has several other useful features. It just takes a bit of digging. However, one is just too good not to cover here. The methods `saveToSharedObj()` and `loadFromSharedObj()` make saving and restoring a DataSet's entire collection super easy. The following simple example should blow you away.

We'll take the code for populating `contacts` array and assign it to the DataSet's `items`. Not only do you need to bind the DataSet's `items` to the DataGrid's `dataProvider`, but also set the DataGrid's `editable` to `true`, and then add two buttons(save_btn and restore_btn) plus this code:

```
//put contacts declaration here
save_btn.onPress=function(){
    ds.saveToSharedObj("testSO")
}
restore_btn.onPress=function(){
    ds.loadFromSharedObj("testSO")
}
```

Go ahead and make some edits to the fields in the DataGrid, and then click the Save button. Quit and come back later, and then click the Restore button. (By the way, there are manual methods to edit items in a DataSet—the DataGrid just makes it easy.) Please don't hate me for making you study local shared objects in Chapter 6. After all, now you really appreciate how useful this is. Remember there are many more methods in the DataSet documentation that I haven't covered.

Resolvers

The idea of resolvers is that you want to track changes to data, not the entire set of data. For example, the preceding example saved the whole DataSet to a LocalShared object. Even if you didn't make any changes or made very few, the whole set was saved. This is not an issue for LocalShared object files, but it adds unnecessarily to network traffic. If a user makes a few changes to some data that's downloaded, there's no need to upload the whole set of data again. You only need to send the bits the user changed (and what the user changed them to).

{ Note }

Resolvers Don't Actually Save Data Resolvers prepare data so that you can send it to your server where it can get processed. You'll see that resolvers just create an update packet containing a complete description of what has changed. But you still need to do some work on the server side to parse this data and then, presumably, update a database.

These two resolvers work in conjunction with the DataSet component to do just that. The XUpdateResolver uses a standard format to represent changes. It only applies to XML structured data, so you want to be careful not to make it try to resolve changes to arrays or generic objects. The benefit, however, is that it uses a standard language that several server-side databases support. The other, RDBMSResolver, is especially designed to describe changes to data in the form common to relational databases.

Both resolvers operate on the same principal. The DataSet actually tracks changes as they're made (either by the user interacting with an editable component that's bound to a value, or by any script that changes an object in the DataSet). Then, when you trigger the `ds.applyUpdates()`, a consolidated description of everything that changed gets packed up in a `deltaPacket`. The `deltaPacket` is bound to a resolver that uses the `deltaPacket` received to set its updatePacket property. The deltaPacket is an XML string that conforms to a known structure. The logical continuation is that you pass the deltaPacket back to your server. Because it's XML, you can bind the deltaPacket to an XMLConnector, which sends it to the server. Your server script will have to sort through the XML it receives and react accordingly (perhaps updating a database, for example). Finally, the server should send back an XML string that contains information as to whether the changes were successful. There are standard forms for this response. The results passed back to Flash can tie back into your resolver through its updateResults property. Believe it or not, this whole process not only makes the system much more efficient, but it can actually simplify things. Figure 7.12 shows a diagram of the entire sequence.

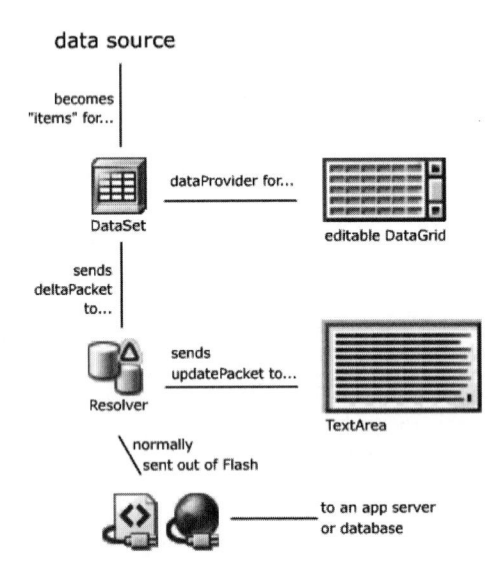

Figure 7.12 *Data is fed into the DataSet, which displays in the DataGrid. The DataSet also monitors changes and will send a deltaPacket to the Resolver which, in our examples, will just display in a TextArea (though normally sent out to your database through a Connector if you want).*

It's interesting to view the actual deltaPacket. Obviously, you'll have to study it further before you can write a server-side method that can parse through it. I should say, however, that it's not just some wacky homemade format that Macromedia came up with on a whim. There are volumes of information on the XUpdate standard and the corresponding XPath language, for example. In any event, it's easy to see the packets inside Flash as this quick exercise shows.

Take the `contacts` data script, `DataSet` instance, and editable DataGrid all used in the example from the "Saving" section earlier in this chapter. Add a button (update_btn), two TextArea components (x_txt and rd_txt), one XUpdateResolver (x), and one RDBMSResolver (rd). There's only a tiny bit of code to add; the main work is just setting a few bindings. First select the ds instance's Bindings tab and notice it should already be binding its dataProvider to the `DataGrid` instance. We'll add two more similar bindings—but to send the `deltaPacket` to the two resolvers. Click the plus sign, select `deltaPacket:Object`, click OK, click twice in the Bound To field, select the instance `XUpdateResolver` listed on the left, and make sure `deltaPacket` is selected in the pane on the right. Repeat these steps, but in the Bound To dialog box select RDBMSResolver.

Next you can bind the `updatePackets` to the two text fields. Select the `XUpdateResolver` instance and click the plus button in its Bindings tab. Select `xupdatePacket`, then OK. Click twice in the Bound To field and point to the x_txt TextArea, and then click OK. The encoder uses the XPath language to specify how the changed data will appear. For now select the x instance's Schema tab, click deltaPacket, find the encoder row, and select DatasetDeltaToXUpdateDelta. Finally, click the encoder options and type **items** in the "rowNodeKey" dialog box that appears.

The RDBMSResolver is a bit easier. Select the `rd` instance, press the plus sign, and select `updatePacket`. Click Bound To and point to the `rd_txt` TextArea. Talk about connecting the dots!

Finally, put this code in the first keyframe:

```
update_btn.onPress=function(){
  ds.applyUpdates();
}
```

Test the application and make just one simple edit through the DataGrid—maybe change `"Kerman"` to `"Kermanator"`. Press Enter to save it, and then click the Update button. The two TextArea components will fill with a bunch of details about what got changed (see Figure 7.13).

Notice that the XUpdateResolver's update packet shown in Figure 7.13 doesn't have enough detail to see exactly which row was edited—that record needs a unique identifier. For example, if you assume every record in the contacts array will have a unique phone number, you can use that as the identifier. If not, you need to add another field—perhaps `id`. To see what a legitimate XUpdate update packet should look like, go back and edit the encoder option for the x instance's deltaPacket (currently set to `items`) to read:

```
items[@phone='?phone']
```

The resulting update packets will always surround changes tags that identify the phone number. (For more on this format, research XPath expressions.) The point here is that the update packet we create must clearly identify what all has changed.

Note that we used both the XUpdate and RDBMS resolvers just to see how their update packets compared. You really only need one. Choosing one over the other has to do with several factors. XUpdate is a standard for XML. In fact, you only want to use XUpdate if the data is pure XML. Also because it's a standard, you will find server-side databases that support XUpdate directly. RDBMS is geared more for data in relational databases. Put simply, relational databases can include the same value in several places without actually making copies. If you designed the database, you should know whether it's relational.

```
<?xml version="1.0"?><xupdate:modifications version="1.0"
xmlns:xupdate="http://www.xmldb.org/xupdate"><xupdate:update select="[object
Object]">Kermanator</xupdate:update></xupdate:modifications>
```

```
<?xml version="1.0"?> <update_packet tableName="" nullValue="{_NULL_}"
transID="IID23998615937:Sun Aug 17 20:00:12 GMT-0700 2003"><update
id="IID70864849491"><field name="Last" type="String" oldValue="Kerman"
newValue="Kermanator" key="false" /></update></update_packet>
```

Figure 7.13 *The update packets for one simple change are shown here (XUpdate is on top and RDBMS below).*

Although update packets appear verbose and do require some parsing on the server side, they're actually very efficient. Consider that your DataSet may be much larger than this example. When you feel like packing up the changes made and sending it to the server, the `deltaPacket` creates the most condensed packet that also includes sufficient details for the server-side method to respond as necessary.

Formatting Data

So far, the only settings discussed for the attributes in the Schema tab have been field name and data type. Four options in particular—validation, kind, encoder, and formatter—control how the values for your properties are handled: how the values are treated when they arrive at the component, how they're passed on to other components, and how they're presented in visual components. Consider how clay comes from the earth, gets processed somehow into artist's clay, then artists shape it and harden it, and then its covered with glaze. The point is that the same exact raw material is treated and presented differently at the different stages.

Here's a quick rundown of the four options:

- **Validation** provides a way for you to check whether a particular value matches its designated data type. When it doesn't, an event is fired so that you can react accordingly. An interesting fact is that you'll find several unique data types such as `SocialSecurity` and `PhoneNumber`. In addition, you can even create your own data types to validate data.

- **Kind** is the raw data type at the core of the component. It's the form in which the data is stored inside the component (not how it's accessed by any ActionScript or other bound component). It's safe to say, you don't often need to modify this.

- **Encoding** is how data transforms. Encoding comes up when the original data isn't in the form that you need somewhere else—for instance, if you want to take a NumericStepper's value (a number) and send it to a TextArea. In that case, the encoding process effectively puts quotation marks around the number. Similarly, if the user is typing a string into a TextInput component and you've bound that value to a NumericStepper's number, the encoder also converts the string to a number (by effectively using the `Number()` function). The point is the data may get encoded in either direction. The two advanced encoders have to do with converting.

- **Formatters** are probably the most fun. They let you step in and perform any sort of manipulation before the data is presented. You'll see in the next section that this is how we can take a generic object with several properties and format it however we want for display in a TextArea.

We'll look at two formatter options (Compose String and Rearrange Fields) as well as some validation tricks.

Compose String

Instead of just binding a property's raw value directly to another component property's value, the Compose String formatter enables you to send any value you want by combining hard-wired strings with variables. Although it doesn't look like this, it's equivalent to something like this:

```
my_txt.text="The user's name is "+ item.first + item.last;
```

With the preceding code, I'm creating a string by combining some hard-wired words with the value of some properties. When using the Compose String option the syntax uses < and > to surround values like this:

```
The user's name is <first> <last>
```

A couple assumptions are made here. First, this string needs to be bound to another component (say a TextArea's `text`). Also, you need to have access to both the `first` and `last` properties. You should recall, however, that when setting up a binding you can pick one property (say `first` *or* `last`). However, in this case you need to pick a property that itself is an object with those two properties.

Here's a quick example. Way back when you first looked at the DataHolder component, I made you bind three properties to three separate Label components. It was a pain because not only did you have to do it three times, you also were grabbing the NumericStepper's value you had to bind. You could have used one Label. Just grab one TextArea (`composed_txt`), a NumericStepper (`ns`), and a DataHolder (`dh`). Put this familiar code in the first keyframe:

```
contacts=[];
contacts.push( {first:"Phillip", last: "Kerman",phone:"503-555-1212"});
contacts.push( {first:"George", last: "Bush",phone:"800-555-1212"});
contacts.push( {first:"Bill", last: "Clinton",phone:"888-555-1212"});
dh.myArray=contacts;
```

You also need to create the `dh` instance's schema (or use the earlier example). Figure 7.10 shows how it should be structured. (Remember the `[n]` for the name right inside the array.)

Finally, you can do one binding from the DataHolder to the TextArea. In the Bindings tab for the `dh` instance, click the plus button, select `[n]:Object` (not any deeper), and then click Bound To and point to the `composed_txt` instance. Set `direction` to `out`. Finally, change `formatter` to Compose String. Then, click in to the value for formatter options. Type the following text:

```
<first> <last> (phone <phone>)
```

You can test it now and see the formatted string `"Phillip Kerman ((503) 555-1212)"` in the TextArea.

Rearrange Fields

The Compose String example bound a property containing several subproperties to the text property of a TextArea. The composed string extracted just the elements needed and some hard-wired text. Rearrange Fields is a similar formatter because it takes a property (containing subproperties) and binds it to a component—but this time the destination property has one or more subproperties itself. The idea is that you say "this value from my originating property goes to that value in the destination." Rearrange Fields provides a way to map subproperties in the origin to subproperties in the destination.

It's probably easier than it sounds. However, the main requirement is that both components have subproperties. That is, you don't use Rearrange Fields when binding to a TextArea because a TextArea has just one property. Generally, it works great with any component that has a `dataProvider` or any for which the schema includes a property with subproperties.

This example populates a ComboBox with a customized presentation of the `contacts` data. You can use the same DataHolder and initial `contacts` array definition from the preceding example. Drag a ComboBox onstage and name it **cb**. Then select the Bindings tab in the DataHolder, and click `myArray : Array` (you don't want to go any deeper), and then click OK. Click `bound to` and point to the `cb` instance and make sure `dataProvider` is selected on the right side. Then click OK. Change the formatter to Rearrange Fields. Click the formatter `options` value and type the following:

```
label='<first> <last>'
```

This code says the `label` property in the destination should equal a string that combines two values. In a way, the right side of this expression is like the Compose String option because you can insert spaces or other hard-wired strings (outside the <>). When you test the movie, you should see the ComboBox populate with all the names (first and last).

Just to prove you can really rearrange fields, change the formatter options used to read as follows:

```
label='<first> <last>';data=.
```

This way the ComboBox will still display the same labels, but by using the period you've stuck the *entire object* (all three properties) into the ComboBox's `value` property.

Now, instead of extracting that value by using the ComboBox's `change` event, you can bind it to a Label component. Drag a Label component onstage and name it **currentPhone_txt**. Go to the ComboBox's Bindings tab and click the plus button, select `selectedItem`, click OK, click Bound To, and then select `currentPhone_txt`. (You can test it now and see [object Object] appear in the text field.) For fun, reselect the value binding and change the formatter to Compose String and use the following for the formatter options:

```
phone: <data.phone>
```

It's pretty cool when you get all the links working. I recommend approaching your projects by first designing how you want it to run in the end. Then work backward figuring out the data structures and the bindings.

Validation

Every property in your schema has a single expected data type. These include the standards (such as number, string, array, and object) but also additional ones such as social security number. Developers can even create their own data types, too.

> **{ Note }**
>
> **Custom Validate Scripts** The best way to learn how to write a custom validate script is by snooping through the ones used for the build in data types. In the First Run folder adjacent to Flash, find the files in the folder path `Classes\mx\data\types`. Chapter 13, "Building a Code Library," covers classes in general, but you can find a couple of example custom classes from my web site, too: www.phillipkerman.com/rias.
>
> To get you started, here are a few rules and a simple example. Your custom validation class must extend the class `mx.data.binding.CustomValidator`. Also, it needs to include a `validate()` method (which overrides the CustomValidator's method of the same name). Finally, when there's an error, you can trigger the CustomValidator's `validationError()`. Here's an example validation class that only considers "13" as valid:
>
> ```
> class Favorite extends mx.data.binding.CustomValidator {
>   function Favorite () {}
>   function validate (param){
>     if ( param!=13 ){
>       this.validationError ( "not favorite number" );
>     }
>   }
> }
> ```

You can set up an event handler to notify you any time a mismatch occurs. Actually, you need both a target component for which you'll ensure a valid value, and another component with a property bound to that target. Here's the code to trap either event (valid or not):

```
function validFunction() {
  trace('this is valid');
}
function invalidFunction() {
  trace('this is invalid');
}
```

```
my_txt.addEventListener('valid', validFunction);
my_txt.addEventListener('invalid', invalidFunction);
```

In Chapter 12, "Components," you'll learn more about this syntax. Now drag out a TextArea component (instance name `my_txt`) and you can add a value to it that will either be valid or invalid. Drag a NumericStepper and name it `ns`. From the NumericStepper's Bindings tab, click the plus button, select value, click OK, and then click Bound To and point to the `my_txt` instance's `text` property. Now, go to the Schema tab for the `my_txt` instance. Change the data type to Number, and then click the value for validation options. Enter **5** for Min and **8** for Max. (Incidentally, you can use XML to UI to create dialog boxes like this when you make a custom validate class.) Now when you test the movie, the Output window should fill with your two strings regarding validity. Obviously, you'll have to write your own code to respond to invalid numbers. Do notice that there's nothing wrong with having an invalid number in the `my_txt`. Flash triggers the invalid event, but it's up to you to respond appropriately.

Also, note that the previous code only works when the TextArea is bound to another component. If you just want a TextArea (and nothing else) you can always use a DataHolder and bind to the TextArea's `text` property.

Additional Details

Believe it or not, this chapter covers fewer topics than I had considered. I think it's enough to give you a great start. However, there are a few more comments that I just have to make.

Manual Scripts

You saw at the beginning of this chapter that Remoting requires you to send requests and handle results returned entirely in script. Don't forget that you can tie the results from a Remoting call to the DataHolder or DataSet components and you'll get all the advanced features such as binding. You just have to map data types appropriately.

Of course, you can replace both the XMLConnector and the WebServiceConnector using script, too. In Chapter 6, you saw how to both send and load using the LoadVars object and the XML object. For web services, you can use the following template (which should look similar to the Remoting code discussed earlier). Important note: To use the code in Listing 7.3, you must have a WebServiceConnector somewhere in your file (even if just in the library).

Listing 7.3 Web Services from ActionScipt

```
myWSDL= "http://www.domain.com/some.wsdl";
myService = new mx.services.WebService(myWSDL);
var myCallback = myService.myMethod("param1", "param2");

myCallback.onResult = function(data){
  trace("result is "+ data);
}

myCallback.onFault = function(fault) {
  trace("error " + fault);
}
```

This really is like Remoting. The benefits of doing this with the connector include that it's easier to handle errors and your results are immediately available to be bound. However, this relatively simple code is out in the open and you don't need to do all that mousing around setting up the components. Having said that, it's also possible to set up binding entirely in script. I suppose the main reason to point out the preceding code is to demonstrate how its similarity means you can leverage knowledge gathered in other places.

Debugging

One huge advantage of Flash Remoting is both the NetConnection Debugger and the Service Browser. The Debugger in particular is great because it will display every outgoing and incoming message. This can save a lot of time troubleshooting situations where the data is arriving but you're not using it properly. Just realize that if you installed the Remoting components, these two panels will show up under Window, Other Panels.

For Debugging the Data components, you can add the following code at the top of your script:

```
_global.__dataLogger=new mx.data.binding.Log();
```

With that in place, you'll see a ton of `trace` statements while the movie plays. To use script to stop the debugging, use `_global.__dataLogger=null;`. (Notice the double underscore in front of `dataLogger`.)

Proxy Script

There's good reason behind the Flash security restrictions. When you visit a web site, the SWF downloads to your machine and therefore is *inside* any firewall you might have. You don't want the Flash Player to let that SWF read and write to domains other than where it originated (namely, the domain inside your firewall). There are more details to this limit, but it's real easy to see how this prevents you from directly linking to outside web services.

{Note}

> **Macromedia Central Supports Web Services Directly** SWFs running in the Macromedia Central environment don't have the same restriction of reaching out to web services. They are effectively running on your desktop. Therefore, you can consume web services without any issue. Also, despite the fact that Central 1.0 supports Flash Player 6 features, it actually has a couple of extras—namely, direct support for SOAP. It uses practically the same syntax as shown in the "Manual Scripts" section earlier in this chapter.

While it makes sense that the Flash player can't reach out to other domains, it makes using public web services difficult. In fact, the weather examples in this chapter will work when you test the movie, but not in a browser. Basically, you need a proxy script—that is, a method on your server that you call as if it were the outside web service. This proxy script has one job: to channel your requests out to the other domain and relay the results.

It's relatively simple to write such a method. For example, you can take a ColdFusion component that invokes a web service call at a particular remote web service and just point to this CFC as a proxy. (In ColdFusion, if you just add "?WSDL" after the URL it will make the CFC behave as a web service.) This is just one solution. The bottom line is you need to go through your own application server to reach out to other domains. In Chapter 6, this was done to make the Amazon.com example work, using the Macromedia proxy script (which should be updated for Flash MX 2004 by the time you read this; check out TechNote 16520 by typing that number into the Search field at www.macromedia.com).

Summary

This chapter turned into a bit of a monster, but realize there's some really cool stuff here. After you map out your data structures, the Data components make some really powerful data management, display, and tracking features possible.

{Chapter 8}

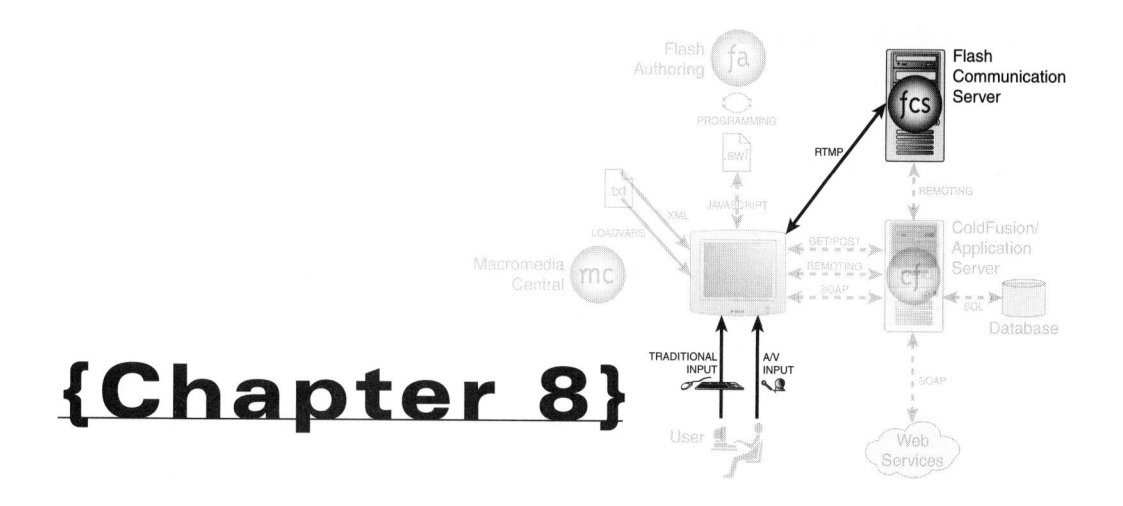

Foundation Communication Server

In my opinion, the Flash Communication Server (FCS) is the coolest product Macromedia has ever produced. Because it's not always clear what FCS offers over straight Macromedia Flash MX 2004, or when it's an appropriate solution, the primary goal of this chapter is to provide a technical foundation on which you can build while making pure FCS applications. Naturally, you'll be able to add FCS features to other applications, but the examples found here are pure FCS apps. The big step you'll have to take after reading this chapter is to first come up with a cool idea and then work out a solution. (I expect the skills acquired here will make that possible.)

Specifically, this chapter covers the following topics:

- How to configure and maintain your installed copy of Flash Communication Server
- How to use remote shared objects to share variables between connected users
- How to publish and play live or recorded streams (including MP3s)

Flash Communication Server runs parallel to your web server that hosts your SWFs. With a simple "connect" script in your SWF, however, you can set up a persistent connection to the FCS. This is different from the traditional "request and response" behavior of web pages and Flash movies. When users request a web page, they're sent that page (and embedded images and Flash movies), but then they effectively disconnect until they make another request. In the case of the FCS connection, it doesn't disconnect until the user quits or FCS says so. This way a connected movie can be immediately notified of any data as it changes. (An alternative way to keep current is called *polling*, where a SWF might repeatedly make requests such as "anything new?...anything new?...," which is obviously inefficient.) Macromedia developed a super-efficient means called Real Time Messaging Protocol (RTMP) for the data that travels over a persistent connection between FCS and a user's SWF movie. This is more efficient because data is only transmitted when necessary instead of continually polling to see whether anything's new.

After the connection has been made, you can send all sorts of "messages" to each SWF—simple data such as the value of variables, and live or recorded media such as video and audio. There's really a lot of possibilities, but I suggest we start at the ground and then move up.

{ Note }

The True Cost of Flash Communication Server My focus is to show you the capabilities of Flash Communication Server (FCS). When you see what's possible, you can determine whether it's worth the price. Note that you can learn and evaluate FCS by downloading the free developer version. For actual deployment, Macromedia offers several other versions supporting various bandwidth and total user limits. In addition, several web hosts have begun to offer FCS support. For example, adding the modest FCS support to my domain hosted at mediatemple.net costs only $15/month. My point is that it's easy to get sticker shock when you see the prices for FCS—just realize you have to balance the value and, also, there's lots of price options.

Configuration

Before you can deploy your first killer communication app, you need to first understand how FCS is configured. I recommend accepting all the default settings when installing the server so that the tutorials are easier to follow. In addition to deciding where the server gets installed, you have to select default port numbers, an admin name and password, and whether you plan to host files from a particular web server the installer finds on your machine. (Realize that FCS isn't a web server but rather a server that runs in conjunction with your web server.) Luckily, all the settings you make during installation can be adjusted later by editing the configuration files.

> **{ Note }**
>
> **Authoring Communication Apps on Macintosh** You can download and install the "authoring components" for Macintosh. However, you won't be able to run the server: It only works on Windows 2000/XP and Linux. The authoring components are just the communication components and the documentation. Authoring on the Mac involves having FCS running somewhere else. The main difference is that when your movie connects to FCS it must specify an absolute path to the server, whereas on Windows you can optionally use a relative path. Incidentally, these authoring components get installed on Windows when you install the server (provided you have already installed Flash).

Configuration Folders

A few basic concepts will help make sense of all the configuration settings. Notice adjacent to your installed version of FCS a folder called applications and one called conf. The applications folder enables you to maintain different FCS applications, and the conf folder enables you to change server configuration details. Both are discussed in more detail in the following sections.

Applications Folder

First understand that when you deliver your app, you'll still be producing SWF files hosted in HTML pages like normal. To make a SWF that connects to the FCS, however, it must point to a specific folder in the FCS's applications directory. (By default, that's inside C:\Program Files\Macromedia\Flash Communication Server MX\applications.) At an absolute minimum, you can just make an empty folder named my_app (inside the applications folder) and specify that name when connecting. The purpose of this folder is to store potentially sensitive files to which users won't have direct access, including script files (which can contain passwords), recorded video or audio streams, and shared objects (containing variables). You make a folder inside the applications folder and only the communication server will read and write files to that folder—not web site visitors. (You're welcome to change the default applications folder location, but you should *never* pick a folder that web visitors can access.)

When working on a particular app, you might spread files to three places: your app folder (inside FCS's applications folder) even if it's just an empty folder; your SWFs hosted by your web server (say, within the wwwroot folder); and your source FLAs that you keep while working. Take, for example, the sample application called tutorial_sharedball. After installing FCS, you'll find both the empty folder

```
C:\Program Files\Macromedia\Flash Communication Server MX\applications\tutorial_sharedball
```

and a folder full of the source file, SWF, and HTML inside your web server's wwwroot folder or, in my case, here:

```
C:\Inetpub\wwwroot\flashcom\samples\tutorial_sharedball
```

After you make a folder for each application, the only thing you put in that folder will be server-side scripts (covered in the next chapter) as well as prerecorded streams and MP3s (covered later this chapter). Although it may seem useless to have an empty folder, it provides FCS a place to both look for server-side scripts and write files (streams and shared objects) when necessary. (It turns out you can optionally place configuration XML files in the application directory for settings that apply to only that one application.) All this means is that for every application you make, you always want to begin by making an empty folder in the applications folder and then use that name when connecting.

Conf Folder

In addition to the applications folder, you'll find another folder adjacent to FCS called conf (short for configuration). All the configuration settings can be made through XML files contained inside conf. Although you can make many esoteric refinements, you will probably only edit a few settings here and there. Because there are several files, however, let me give you a quick rundown. (If you just want to jump right into building something, skip ahead to the section "Production Techniques" later in this chapter.)

Adaptors and Virtual Hosts

Even before understanding "adaptors" or "virtual hosts," remember that the hierarchy from the top down is server, adaptor, virtual host. Inside the server you can have several adaptors, and inside each adaptor you can have several virtual hosts (and, actually, each virtual host can have as many users as you want, too). A fresh FCS installation starts with the minimum: one virtual host (_defaultVHost_) inside the _defaultRoot_ adaptor inside the server. In a nutshell, this structure enables you to maintain multiple administrators, applications that use slightly different settings, and different web servers that all have access to your single copy of FCS. Figure 8.1 displays example hierarchy as seen through the administration console. Although you probably don't need all these options to start, the structure is built so that it's easy to expand. Think of how a new file cabinet needs to have drawers, file holders, and file folders even though you may only think you want store individual papers in it.

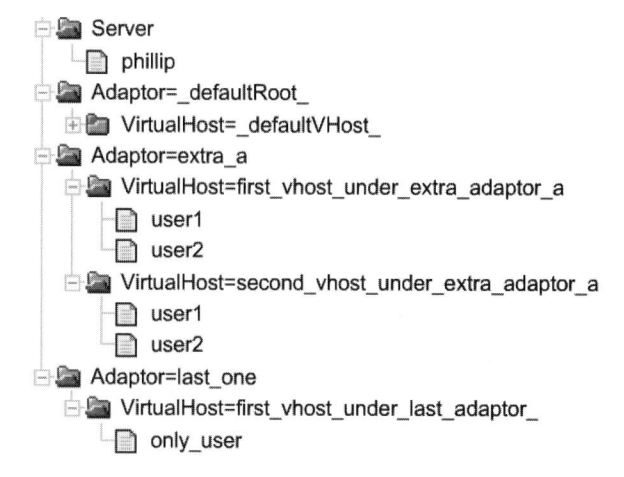

```
Server
    phillip
Adaptor=_defaultRoot_
    VirtualHost=_defaultVHost_
    Adaptor=extra_a
        VirtualHost=first_vhost_under_extra_adaptor_a
            user1
            user2
        VirtualHost=second_vhost_under_extra_adaptor_a
            user1
            user2
    Adaptor=last_one
        VirtualHost=first_vhost_under_last_adaptor_
            only_user
```

Figure 8.1 *Besides the default adaptor and virtual host (Vhost), notice two extra adaptors (extra_a and last_one). The first has two Vhosts (with two users each), and the second has one Vhost (and one user).*

Editing Configuration Files

Exactly how to edit the configuration files and how to create a new hierarchy of adaptors and virtual hosts is detailed both in the comments contained in the XML files as well as the FCS documentation. The basic approach I take is to copy and paste entire nodes (or tags) found in the XML files—for example, everything from `<Adaptor` to `/Adaptor>` or `<VirtualHost` to `/VirtualHost>`. As for what to change within the tags, let me detail just a few of the more common settings you may want to make.

You'll likely find a frequent need to edit Vhost.xml and Application.xml. They're inside the default virtual host (_defaultVhost_) inside the default adaptor (_defaultRoot_)—as such, copies also appear in additional virtual hosts you may add. Take a look inside Vhost.xml and notice the `<AppsDir>` tag. Here is where the location of your applications folder (discussed earlier) is designated.

Another interesting setting in the Vhost.xml file is the `<Streams>` tag within the `<VirtualDirectory>` tag. Normally, playing a recorded stream or MP3 requires that the file reside inside the particular application folder in use. However, you can change that behavior and specify a different directory in the `<Streams>` tag. This means several different apps can have access to the same library of MP3 files. Defining such virtual directories involves specifying an alias (that is, the short name you'll use when playing the stream) and the actual directory where the streams reside.

Without going through all the settings inside the Application.xml file, let me point out one interesting fact: Although the main Application.xml contains settings for all the applications within a particular virtual host, any individual application can have its own Application.xml file (stored in the application's folder). The settings in such a local copy override the global settings in the main Application.xml file.

> **{ Tip }**
> **Restart the Server** The big thing to remember, and something I'll repeat for emphasis, is that for changes to take effect you must restart the server.

Production Techniques

While programming and testing FCS apps, I find myself following and often forgetting to follow a certain set of procedures. You might think this section is more appropriate as a follow-up after you get the basics. However, if there's one thing that will frustrate you to no end, it's stupid mistakes. Hopefully, the following techniques will not only save you endless hours of rework, but also serve to introduce the basic mode of operation for a communication app programmer.

Restarting

Not only will you occasionally need to restart the Flash server (after making changes to the configuration files), you'll also need to restart your individual applications. What I didn't mention earlier is that although every app has an application folder, you also can run multiple instances of any single app. The best analogy to app instances is how a single chat application can have multiple "rooms." Just like movie clips or really any object, applications have instances.

Chapter 8 Foundation Communication Server

The first time a SWF connects to your app, an application instance is created. It remains in FCS's memory until you unload it, until you restart it (that is unload and then start again), or until it times out from inactivity. Even if you close all connections to FCS (that is, close the SWFs that are connected), the app instance and all application variables remain in memory until the instance unloads. Although you can always restart the entire FCS server, sometimes you only need to restart an individual app instance.

The Communication App Inspector is an invaluable tool that not only enables you to unload and restart app instances, it also contains other handy information about all apps currently running on your server. The App Inspector is available under Window, Other Panels (if installed in the WindowSWF folder) and through the HTML help files (to which you should have a link in your Start menu). To use the App Inspector, you need your admin name and password (specified at installation). Use `localhost` for the Host field when testing locally (as shown in Figure 8.2).

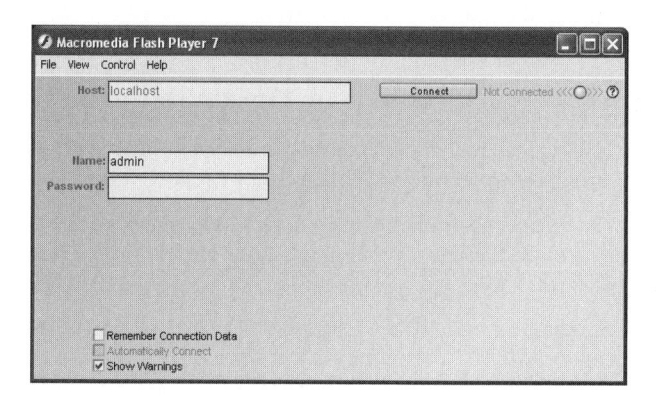

Figure 8.2 *Use* `localhost` *when logging in to the App Inspector locally.*

After you log in, the App Inspector lists all currently active application instances. You can select any line and either unload or click View Details for more controls (as shown in Figure 8.3).

The App Inspector is a pretty nice example of rich Internet application (RIA) programming itself, although it can take a bit of time to get comfortable with the interface. You can explore without much risk because critical maneuvers (such as restarting apps) include confirmation dialog boxes. Realize that when viewing details of a particular app, you can return to the previous screen by clicking Change App (effectively performing a "back" navigation).

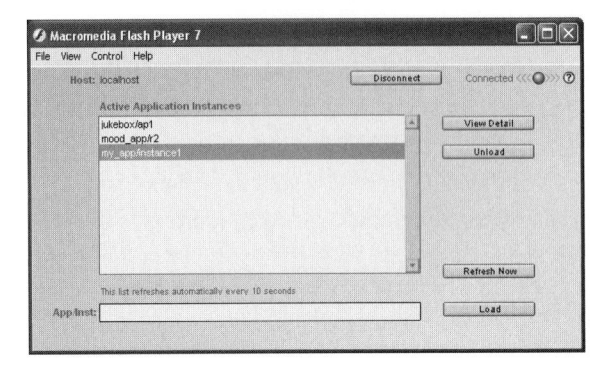

Figure 8.3 *Once logged in, you can access any active application.*

There's also a tool called the Administration Console (accessible from the HTML help files) that is similar to the App Inspector. Here you'll find more global settings such as additional virtual hosts and adaptors. You can actually load and unload app instances here as well as restart the entire server. However, I find it more effective to launch the Stop Server and Start Server batch files. (They're accessible from the Start menu or two .bat files inside FCS's tools folder.)

Here's a summary of how you can restart elements of FCS:

- View, load, and unload individual application instances through the App Inspector (as a Flash panel in the HTML help).
- View, edit configurations, load, and unload application instances as well as the server as a whole through the Administration Console (in the HTML help).
- Perform a hard stop or start of the FCS server through two batch files (in the Start menu or two .bat files in the tools folder).

Believe me, understanding how to restart will come in handy because you'll be doing it a lot!

Revisions

One of the purposes of the application folder is to give FCS a place to store streams and shared objects related to your application. In fact, such items get stored in subfolders that match your app instance. That is, inside your application folder you may find a folder called streams, inside of which you'll find a folder called myAppInstance, which contains the actual stream. It makes perfect sense to have a way to keep things straight. It's cool, too, that you can design an application and run multiple instances simultaneously.

The reason this discussion applies to production techniques is that while testing you'll likely try many ideas that don't pan out but that do leave discarded remnants that you don't need (such as unused streams or shared objects). In addition, application instances often remain in memory (hence, the fact you'll be restarting a lot). Another technique is to start with an application instance name such as test1. Then, if you ever need to start fresh, just start using the instance name test2, and everything related to test1 will clear out of your way. Finally, when you're ready to deliver the final product, you can change to a more meaningful instance name (although, I still recommend including a version numbering system to make later changes easy).

Remote Production

A Flash movie can connect to an FCS that resides on a different machine (say, at your Internet service provider or company's main web site). This means you can test movies on one machine that connect to FCS on another. Perhaps more important is that you can also use the App Inspector and Administration Console remotely, too. During a live auction, for example, I can monitor how many people are connected as well as do some casual debugging if necessary. There are just a few tricks that are worth covering when you need to perform such remote production.

You saw earlier that you can connect to a local copy of FCS by just listing `localhost` for Host in the App Inspector. If your server is installed remotely, you'll have to instead use the IP address to which FCS is bound. Actually, you can use the domain or IP and—to be more specific—you'll want to use the address of the adaptor. (See the HostPort setting in the Adaptor.xml file.)

{ Note }

Using a Subdomain When you go live, it's common (and easiest) to have FCS on a separate IP and domain than on your web server. Usually, this is just a matter of putting FCS on a subdomain of your web site's domain. For example, my service provider (mediatemple.net) hosts my domain phillipkerman.com, but they configured the shared FCS to use something like flashcom.phillipkerman.com. Regardless of whether you register a subdomain (the part that precedes your domain name), you'll always have a static IP address you can use.

236   Part II   Technology

You may need to work both locally and remotely (sometimes doing tests locally before uploading files), and that means you'll need to remember several host names, admin usernames, and passwords. Although the Remember Connection Data option in the various panels is nice, it only remembers the last set of data. Because that option uses the local shared object, however, you can just create multiple copies of the panel SWFs and each copy will remember its own set of data. For example, name one app-inspector_remote.swf and one app-inspector_local.swf. (Just search the FCS program folder for admin.swf and app_inspector.swf.)

I realize you probably want to get rolling with building cool apps, but I also know tracking bugs is easier when you're not wrestling with the tools. FCS adds additional levels of troubleshooting.

NetConnection

The first step in any Flash communication app is to connect to the server through the NetConnection object. Once connected, you can do all kinds of wild things (such as publish or play media streams plus send and receive messages to other connected users to name the two biggies). It always begins with a connection, however, and everything that follows is tied to that connection. Luckily it's pretty easy to confirm your connection gets established properly before preceding.

Basic Connecting

You can connect to an FCS app with just two lines of code; however, it's really best to set up a callback because it's an asynchronous operation. That is, you need to wait for the connection to complete before proceeding (and, confirm it was successful). Listing 8.1 is a nice starter skeleton on which to build.

Listing 8.1   Basic Connect Skeleton

```
1   my_nc = new NetConnection();
2   my_nc.onStatus = function(info) {
3     trace(info.code);
4     if (info.code == "NetConnection.Connect.Success") {
5       //proceed
6     }
7     if (info.code == "NetConnection.Connect.Closed") {
8       //say goodbye
9     }
10  };
11  my_nc.connect("rtmp:/my_app/my_instance1");
```

After you create a NetConnection object (line 1), you can connect (as in line 11). The string passed in the `connect()` method looks for an app called my_app (so it's imperative you create a folder in the applications folder called my_app). It looks as though my_instance1 is a subfolder, but it's actually an optional instance name. That is, you can have multiple copies of the my_app app running independently. If you forgo the instance name, _definst_ will be used (for default instance). In fact, you can use just lines 1 and 11, and it *should* work. The `onStatus` event, however, is useful to ensure your connection was successful (in which case the parameter that I'm calling `info` will have a property called `code` containing the specific string `"NetConnection.Connect.Successful"`). Naturally, you would want to replace lines 5 and 8 with your choice of code to react to a successful or failed connection, respectively. Realize that the `onStatus` event might trigger much later—for instance, if the server goes down. It also triggers when you purposely disconnect (by calling the NetConnection `close()` method). For this situation, you'll probably want to first set the `onStatus` event equal to `null` before you `close()` so that it doesn't run code you wrote to handle unintentional disconnects.

Although the preceding skeleton is suitable for many apps, there are more details worth discussing.

NetConnection Object Details

You just saw how the `connect()` method can optionally specify an instance name. There are actually more options, although they're not optional parameters; everything is tied to the first parameter (a string called a URI—for Universal Resource Identifier). You can vary the URI to connect absolutely to an FCS hosted elsewhere, to specify different ports, and to control how RTMP data can tunnel through HTTP connections. The following sections cover these three variations.

Absolute Connections

Listing 8.1 assumes a relative path to FCS—almost as if localhost was passed as the address. When your SWF is not running on the same host as the FCS, you need to make an absolute reference. To make an absolute connection to FCS, you just add the domain or IP address in front of the application name. For example, the following code hard-wires the my_domain.com domain:

```
my_nc.connect("rtmp://my_domain.com/my_app/my_instance");
```

The part that messes me up all the time is that you must precede a domain with double slashes (//), whereas your app follows a single slash (/). So, when you leave off the domain, you have just a single slash.

Ports and HTTP Tunneling

When the Flash Player encounters the `connect()` method, it attempts to connect to your FCS following a very specific pattern. It first attempts to connect over port 1935, then port 443, then port 80, and then it automatically attempts to tunnel through by sending RTMP data over HTTP (also called RTMPT). It turns out the automatic sequence of attempts is fine for many situations. However, you may find some users can't make a connection (well, the NetConnection can't) because their firewall blocks data from traveling through port 1935. If those users can visit any web sites, they can surely use the standard port 80. And even if their setup blocks RTMP data (another issue with some firewalls), they'll still be able to use RTMPT because that's really just plain HTTP. You might think the final attempt by the Flash Player (RTMPT on port 80) is the perfect failsafe. However, the problem is that if you are running your web server on the same machine that's running FCS, they can't both use port 80. A perfectly legitimate solution is to just use two computers: one for your web server (on port 80), and one for FCS (on port 1935, but with ports 443 and 80 open for when they're needed). Naturally, two computers probably means you'll need to specify the domain absolutely as you just saw.

Going out and buying two computers is not the only solution. In addition, relying on the Flash Player's sequence of port attempts is not ideal because connections take slightly longer as each attempt must time out before proceeding. Also, RTMPT only works with newer Flash Players (6,0,65 or later). In any event, you can override the default behavior with a little bit of scripting.

To force the Flash Player to try to connect through a specific port (that is, *not* follow it's normal sequence of 1935, 443, 80, and then 80 using HTTP), you need to take two steps. First, include a colon and then the port number in the `connect()` method. This is placed immediately before the application name. (That's after the host if you include it.) For instance, this example makes the SWF try just port 8080:

```
my_nc.connect("rtmp::8500/my_app/my_instance");
```

Notice that if you include the host domain, it appears between the two colons, as follows:

`my_nc.connect("rtmp://my_domain.com:8500/my_app/my_instance");`

Because the `connect()` method is inside your SWF, it just directs the Flash Player how to make a connection. Just saying "just try port 8500" isn't enough, however—your FCS has to be set up to listen to connect attempts coming in through that port. It's just a matter of adding any additional ports to the `<HostPort>` tag of your Adaptor.xml file. In summary, specifying ports requires you to edit both the `connect()` script and the Adaptor.xml. Also, forcing the SWF to connect through a particular port will tend to make connections complete more quickly because you don't have to wait for the player to keep trying ports.

Finally, the new HTTP tunneling feature is very cool because it means your RTMP data can travel over the innocuous HTTP protocol. As previously mentioned, RTMPT (that's RTMP over HTTP) is attempted on port 80 after all other attempts fail—provided you let the Flash Player follow its default (automatic) behavior. To override this and force RTMPT, you need to replace `rtmp` with `rtmpt` in your `connect()` method. For example, the following code uses RTMP over port 8080:

`my_nc.connect("rtmpt::8080/my_app/my_instance");`

Of course, you need to configure FCS to listen to port 8080.

{ Tip }

RTMPT Is Explicit Just remember that when you do specify RTMPT or port numbers, you're overriding the way the Flash Player naturally attempts different ports and protocols.

Before moving on to what you can do after you're connected, let me mention two other connection-related features we'll explore in the "Messaging" section of Chapter 9, "Advanced Communication Server." That is, you can pass additional parameters (after the URI), and those values are received on the server where they can be sorted out. For example, you can let people pass their username so that the server can track who all is connected. In addition, the server can accept or reject connections. Right now, provided you have that application folder, everyone is automatically accepted. If you've reached the capacity of users (say, 50 for FCS Personal), however, additional connects are rejected out of hand. Another thing you'll learn in the next chapter is how to send meaningful information back to the client when they get rejected (so that the SWF can take appropriate action). At this point, however, you have all you need to move on more exciting FCS features.

Remote Shared Objects

In Chapter 6, you learned about local shared objects (LSOs). With them, you could store values on the user's hard drive for later retrieval. Remote shared objects (RSOs) differ in many ways. The main idea of RSOs is that more than one user gets access to read and write values in an RSO. Also, when one user changes an RSO, all the users connected to the same app are immediately notified. This simple concept of letting multiple users see the same data in real time makes all kinds of applications possible—everything from text chats to shared whiteboard applications.

{ Note }

Remote Versus Local Shared Objects Although RSOs have an entirely different purpose than LSOs, they're similar in two ways: Variables are stored in the same data structure (that is, as properties inside the data property) and, when set to be persistent, their values get saved between sessions.

Setting and Accessing Data in Remote Shared Objects

You can access and set values in an RSO like in an LSO: Just create an instance that points to the shared object's name, and then set variables inside the instance's data property. Because RSOs are tied to a NetConnection, however, you need to wait for the connection to succeed. For this reason, I often just invoke a custom function to handle all RSO instantiation. Listing 8.2 includes everything, including the NetConnection portion.

Listing 8.2 Basic Remote Shared Object

```
1   function initRSO() {
2      my_rso = SharedObject.getRemote("myRSO", my_nc.uri, true);
3      my_rso.connect(my_nc);
4   }
5   my_nc = new NetConnection();
6   my_nc.onStatus = function(info) {
7      if (info.code == "NetConnection.Connect.Success") {
8         //ready to get the remote shared object
9         initRSO();
10     }
11  };
12  my_nc.connect("rtmp:/my_app/my_instance1");
```

Notice the initRSO() function is declared first, but isn't triggered until the NetConnection is successful (line 9). The basic code for the RSO is in lines 2 and 3. First, we perform a getRemote() and pass three values: the filename we want to use ("myRSO"), the NetConnection uri property (think: the application instance), and true to make it persistent (that is, saved between sessions). Then, we issue the shared object's connect() method to complete the process.

Because the RSO's connect() method is also asynchronous, you really need to define an onSync callback (such as the my_nc's onStatus callback on line 6) to ensure the RSO has successfully connected before proceeding. You'll see onSync in the next section on synchronizing, but for now, we'll just make sure we wait a second before trying to set or get values from the my_rso object.

{ Note }

Persistent Versus Temporary When you issue the getRemote() method (effectively creating an RSO instance), you have to include true or false for whether you want the RSO to be persistent or not. It's really pretty simple: If you want the variables contained to be available later, you say true (for persistent). Persistent RSOs actually reside in an FSO file like LSOs—but in the application folder on the server. Any RSO (persistent or not) keeps up-to-date in real time because all connected users are immediately notified any time contained variables change (as discussed in the next section, "Synchronizing Values"). The decision for persistent or not has to do with the nature of the data you're tracking.

> Suppose you're building an online meeting app that includes a chat feature. In that case, the persistent option might be appropriate if you want to keep an archive—perhaps to allow someone to see the discussion at a later date. If you're building a two-player game, however, it's probably alright if the RSO that tracks the location of each player's game piece later vanishes when both users disconnect. Naturally, persistent RSOs can start to get cluttered while testing if you keep making up new variable names. Remember that any RSO is tied to the app name *and* the app instance. FCS maintains as many same-named RSOs as you have app instances. In the case of persistent RSOs, you'll actually see an FSO file show up in a subfolder to your application folder that matches the instance name (specified in the NetConnection `connect()` method).

After your RSO is connected, you can access and set named properties using the same syntax as for LSOs. That is, they all go inside the `data` property. Here's an example:

```
my_rso.data.someVariable="this value";
trace("value is: " + my_rso.data.someVariable);
```

If one connected user sets a named variable and then another user accesses it, both will see the latest value at the time they check. Luckily, however, you don't need each user to repeatedly check the values to see whether they happen to change. The `onSync` event is triggered every time a contained property changes—you just have to write a callback to handle the `onSync` event.

Synchronizing Values

The idea is simple enough: Any time `onSync` is called, something about the RSO changed. If your RSO contains just a few properties, when `onSync` triggers you can just check the value of each property (and, presumably, respond by presenting the user with a visual representation). Although that technique is easy, it's undesirable when your RSO contains lots of properties—because any time one property changes, you're checking each one.

To take something simple, suppose you have three List components that each maintain a real-time list of users who say they're happy, neutral, or unhappy (see Figure 8.4). Your RSO could contain three named properties (for instance, `happy`, `neutral`, and `unhappy`) that each contains an array of usernames. There are two sides to this application: letting users add their names to the appropriate array, and then displaying the arrays' values to everyone connected. Listing 8.3 goes through such an example that, although not ideal, is a decent solution.

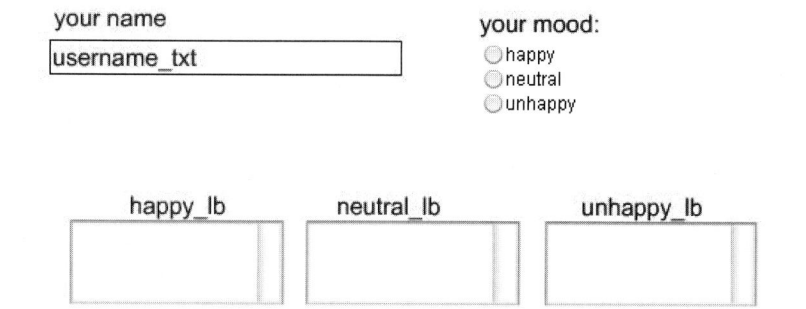

Chapter 8 Foundation Communication Server 243

Figure 8.4 *The mood monitor will let us synchronize many different users' moods.*

Listing 8.3 **Real-Time Mood Monitor**

Changing the RSO

To give the user a way to set their mood, grab three RadioButton components (named happy_rb, neutral_rb, and unhappy_rb) and an input text field (named username_txt). The following code should be added to the code in Listing 8.2:

```
1   happy_rb.addEventListener("click", setMyMood);
2   happy_rb.data = "happy";
3   neutral_rb.addEventListener("click", setMyMood);
4   neutral_rb.data = "neutral";
5   unhappy_rb.addEventListener("click", setMyMood);
6   unhappy_rb.data = "unhappy";
7   function setMyMood(me) {
8     var thisMood = me.target.data;
9     if (my_rso.data[thisMood][0] == undefined) {
10      my_rso.data[thisMood] = [];
11    }
12    my_rso.data[thisMood].push(username_txt.text);
13  }
```

Aside from some component tricks, there's not much RSO stuff here. The setMyMood() function finds the data in the button just pressed and puts it into the thisMood variable. (Notice the parameter me includes a target property that points back to the component that triggered the function.) Then because I'm about to add the username to one of three properties (my_rso.data.happy, my_rso.data.neutral, or my_rso.data.unhappy) but I don't know which, I use the bracket reference with the

continues

Listing 8.3 Real-Time Mood Monitor (Continued)

string `thisMood`. The `if` statement in line 9 just ensures the property in question contains an array (and if not puts an empty array into it in line 10). Finally, line 12 is the meat where I push the `username_txt`'s `text` value into the correct property.

Responding to RSO Changes

The rest of the code just populates the three List components whenever there's a change to the RSO. You can just insert the following code between lines 2 and 3 from Listing 8.2. That is, you're just adding the `onSync` callback between where my_rso is created and gets connected. (The rest is "boilerplate" NetConnection code.)

```
1   my_rso.onSync=function(){
2     happy_lb.removeAll();
3     var total=my_rso.data.happy.length;
4     for(var i=0;i<total;i++){
5       happy_lb.addItem(my_rso.data.happy[i]);
6     }
7     neutral_lb.removeAll();
8     var total=my_rso.data.neutral.length;
9     for(var i=0;i<total;i++){
10      neutral_lb.addItem(my_rso.data.neutral[i]);
11    }
12    unhappy_lb.removeAll();
13    var total=my_rso.data.unhappy.length;
14    for(var i=0;i<total;i++){
15      unhappy_lb.addItem(my_rso.data.unhappy[i]);
16    }
17  }
```

Nothing really special here except perhaps a good opportunity to consolidate the three free-standing loops down to a single nested loop. The main thing you should see, however, is that the approach makes sense: Whenever any property gets changed, all this code runs in order to repopulate the three List components. The inefficient part is that if, say, just one happy person adds his name, all three List components get repopulated—even though just the happy one needs to update. In this case, it's only inefficient because you're redisplaying the List components. (FCS is smart enough not to send data that hasn't changed.) You'll see how you can track just the changes to an RSO next.

Using onSync Efficiently

The good news is that FCS is super efficient because clients are only notified of the properties that get modified in an RSO. The preceding example used `onSync` as the indicator that something changed and then just updated everything. When an `onSync` gets triggered, you can determine exactly what variable or variables changed, who changed them, and what they were changed from. That is, instead of `my_rso.onSync=function(){}`, you can use `my_rso.onSync=function(list){}`. The trick is just sorting out the data contained in the parameter that I'm calling `list`.

Here is a visualization of that parameter:

```
[ {code:"change" , name:"happy"   , oldValue: null},
  {code:"change" , name:"neutral" , oldValue: null},
  {code:"change" , name:"unhappy" , oldValue: null} ]
```

Notice that because more than one variable may have changed, the parameter I'm calling `list` will always contain an array. In each slot of the array, there's a generic object with three properties: `code`, `name`, and `oldValue`. There are several possible values for `code`, but `"change"` is by far the most frequent. A close second is `"success"`. See, if you're the SWF who changed a property you'll get `onSync` triggered like normal, but the `code` (in the first slot of the array) will be `"success"`, whereas all other connected SWFs will see `"change"`. It's interesting that you're told the `name` of the property in question—but not the new value. The thinking is that you only need to be notified that the variable has updated; it's up to you to go check its value—provided you want to check it. Notice that in the preceding example `oldValue` is set to `null` in each slot. This is likely what you would see when the movie first connects. If another SWF changes a property, however, you'll be told what its old value was before the change.

{ Note }

Other Values for the Code Property Just to be complete, let me say that in addition to `"change"` and `"success"`, other possible values for `code` are `"reject"`, `"delete"`, and `"clear"`. If you try to change a property and another client beats you to the punch, you'll see `"reject"`. When you delete a property (for instance, `delete(my_rso.data.happy);`), you'll see `"delete"` for `code`'s value. Finally, `"clear"` primarily applies to RSOs that are not persistent. (That's the third parameter in the `getRemote()` method.) Basically, when you connect to a nonpersistent RSO, all properties are cleared and you start fresh. (You'll see more about the persistent option in the next section.)

246   Part II   Technology

Now that you have an idea of how onSync's parameter is structured, let me show you a modified version of the mood application Listing 8.4—but this time only the property that changes causes an update to its respective List component.

Listing 8.4   Revising the *onSync*

First, consider that the following code extracted from Listing 8.3 (which was repeated for each List component) can be "genericized" by just replacing happy_lb with a dynamic reference to a list.

```
happy_lb.removeAll();
var total=my_rso.data.happy.length;
for(var i=0;i<total;i++){
  happy_lb.addItem(my_rso.data.happy[i]);
}
```

Here is the revised onSync callback:

```
1   my_rso.onSync = function(list) {
2     var totalSOs=list.length;
3     for (var n=0; n<totalSOs; n++) {
4       var thisObj = list[n];
5       if (thisObj.code == "change" || thisObj.code == "success") {
6         var sName=thisObj.name;
7         _root[sName+"_lb"].removeAll();
8         var total = my_rso.data[sName].length;
9         for (var i = 0; i<total; i++) {
10          _root[sName+"_lb"].addItem(my_rso.data[sName][i]);
11        }
12      }
13    }
14  };
```

Notice that lines 7 through 11 are based on the code extracted from the old listing. Instead of .happy_lb, however, you see [sName+"_lb"]; and instead of .happy, you see [sName]. These dynamic references rely on the sName variable containing a string name of the property in question. I suppose I should have done something dynamic such as this in the first example, but the big news here is that while you loop through all the objects passed (that is, totalSOs), you only modify lists that correspond to property names whose code is "change" or "success".

I'll be the first to admit that it's always easier to just go through all variables and redraw everything needed to bring the visual representation into sync, but it's not efficient. It can get really slow depending what's changing onscreen. In addition, it wastes bandwidth for each SWF to contact the server and check values for variables that haven't changed. Although meticulously parsing through onSync's parameter (looking for code properties and such) will render the best results, later you'll see an alternative messaging approach that is arguably simpler. Messaging involves creating your own named events (not unlike onSync, but homemade). This way you just trigger events like you would functions (but all clients will trigger them, too).

In the mood app, for instance, you could have defined callback events such as my_rso.updateHappy() and my_rso.updateNeutral(). However, because FCS controls when variables change and when clients are notified, you can't rely on a message reaching all clients in the sequence you intend. Because of this, it's not easy to design "client-to-client" event messaging. As you'll see in the "Messaging" section of Chapter 9, however, sending messages through the server as a clearinghouse works quite well because (for one thing) the server can lock an RSO, change a property, unlock it, and then send a message to all the clients.

Just remember, the main thing onSync does is tell you something happened to the RSO. If you want to know *exactly* what has happened, you need to parse through onSync's parameter.

Architectural Decisions

In Chapter 4, "Working with Complex Data," when you considered different ways to structure data you could usually pick the option that appeared most convenient for you. That is, the difference between 4 rows of 3 or 3 rows of 4 was like the difference between 6 and half a dozen—I told you to pick the one that made the most sense to you. In the case of structuring RSOs, however, you can't be so selfish. Your first priority needs to be bandwidth efficiency, because you may have thousands of users connected simultaneously; put overall performance second, and then the programmer's convenience last.

Generally, your structure should minimize the amount of data that gets updated (and, hence, sent over the Internet). In short, it's best to have lots of small properties in a shared object (as opposed to fewer, larger properties); and it's best not to let any one shared object file get too big. In the mood app, for example, the single RSO had three properties that each had an array of names. That structure is totally valid and pretty convenient. (After all, arrays are good for such cases where you don't know how many items may get added.) However, each array could get pretty large, and the whole array will get sent to each client any time a single name is added to it. So, although it might look totally goofy to a programmer, here is a much better structure (FCS-wise):

```
my_rso.data.happy_1
my_rso.data.happy_2// and so on
my_rso.data.neutral_1
my_rso.data.neutral_2// and so on
my_rso.data.unhappy_1
my_rso.data.unhappy_2// and so on

my_rso.data.count_happy
my_rso.data.count_neutral
my_rso.data.count_unhappy
```

The idea is that you'll have as many "happy_x", "neutral_x", and "unhappy_x" values as you have people of that mood (replacing "x" with an integer). The three count properties are not only to track how many items are in each list, it also helps calculate a unique suffix for each newly created "happy_x" property. This restructuring means you must adjust the code, and it may get more complex. In this case, one could argue that an array full of strings isn't really *that* much data to be transmitting unnecessarily. In this case, maybe, but just understand why this is a better structure: When someone adds her name to a category, only two small properties are changed in the RSO (her name and the counter for total in that category). Listing 8.5 shows the modified code for both the user input part and the onSync event. (You still need the NetConnection and boilerplate RSO scripts from Listing 8.3). Incidentally, because the RSO's data structure will change, now is a good time to change the app instance name.

Listing 8.5 Using Smaller Properties

```
1  function setMyMood(me) {
2    var thisMood = me.target.data;
3    if (my_so.data["count_"+thisMood] == undefined) {
4      my_so.data["count_"+thisMood] = 0;
5    }
6    var nextUp = my_so.data["count_"+thisMood]++;
7    my_so.data[thisMood+"_"+nextUp] = username_txt.text;
8  }
```

This input portion of the code changed in a few ways. I do check whether there's a value in count_happy (or whichever mood), although it turns out we could be sloppy because the purpose of the count property is not so much to *count* but to ensure each new property has a unique suffix. Anyway, in line 7 I increment the appropriate count as well as store it in the nextUp variable, then set the value of a newly created property (thisMood+"_"+nextUp) to the user's username. So far, so good.

The only other code that changes is how onSync displays information.

```
1   my_so.onSync = function(list) {
2     for (var n = 0; n<list.length; n++) {
3       var thisObj = list[n];
4       if (thisObj.code == "change" || thisObj.code == "success") {
5         var sName = thisObj.name;
6         var prefix = sName.substr(0, sName.indexOf("_"));
7         if (prefix == "happy" ||
8             prefix == "neutral" ||
9             prefix == "unhappy") {
10          _root[prefix+"_lb"].addItem(my_so.data[sName]);
11        }
12      }
13    }
14  };
```

The main difference in this code is that we don't need to perform a removeAll() on the List components. That's because they'll be empty initially, onSync will send all the properties at start up, and then just send the ones that need to be added while the app runs. Notice how the string methods substr() and indexOf() (in line 6) are used to extract just the portion in front of an underscore. Then, line 7 starts the compound if statement that checks whether the property just changed is in fact one of the three moods. If so, that item is added to the list.

It turns out there really wasn't too much extra coding in this revised structure. In this case, you'll probably need to add a ton of usernames to the various lists to see a difference in performance. However, it may very well be worth the effort.

In addition to creating more small properties (instead of a few big ones), you should keep an eye on the size of your FSO file. That is, when you execute a getRemote(), the first parameter you pass refers to the actual filename (minus the extension). It makes sense to group related properties and store each set in a separate RSO. For example:

```
my_scores=SharedObject.getRemote("scores", my_nc.uri, true);
my_users=SharedObject.getRemote("users", my_nc.uri, true);
my_active=SharedObject.getRemote("active", my_nc.uri, false);
```

You just have to decide (and then keep track of) which shared object does what. Notice too, this technique means some RSOs could be persistent and others not (such as the last line in the preceding example). Upon arrival to your app, the user needs to wait for the entire RSO to download. Therefore you don't want any single .fso file to grow too large.

Practical Examples

Although the mood population app might have a use somewhere, I've put together a few examples using RSOs that will have more universal appeal.

Example 1: Geographic Locator

Here's a moderately simple example where each user can click a map to share his or her geographic location with all other connected users. Figure 8.5 shows what the result looks like.

Figure 8.5 *Remote shared objects are perfect to track and display all users' locations.*

Every time a user clicks, the "you are here" movie clip moves to the _xmouse and _ymouse locations and those values are set in the RSO. Every time the shared object's onSync event is triggered, a new "other person" clip instance is created onstage in the updated location. The interesting part is how to separate the "you are here" indicator from all the other clips. That is, you don't want to see one of the "other person" clips where you are—just where the others are. This is solved two ways: If the onSync's code property is "success", it means we were the ones who changed a value; therefore we don't need to refresh the screen. In addition, each user is given a unique ID so that when we *do* display all the other people, we check that the ID doesn't match ours. Listing 8.6 contains some excerpts from the complete code that you can download.

Listing 8.6 Map Code Excerpts

```
owner=this;//so we don't use _root
owner.onMouseDown = function() {
  you_mc._x = _xmouse;
  you_mc._y = _ymouse;
  so.data.locations[owner.myID].x=you_mc._x
  so.data.locations[owner.myID].y=you_mc._y;
};
```

We'll just have one property in the shared object, an array called `locations`, which contains objects with three properties each: x, y, and slot. Every time the user clicks, we set the x and y properties of the appropriate slot in the `locations` array. (The value of `owner.myID` is assigned when the shared object first loads, as you'll see next.)

```
1    init=false;
2    so.onSync = function(list) {
3      if (so.data.locations == undefined) {
4        so.data.locations = [];
5      }
6      if(init==false){
7        init=true;
8        owner.myID=so.data.locations.length;
9        so.data.locations.push({x:-100, y:-100, slot:owner.myID});
10     }
11     var totalSOs = list.length;
12     for (var n = 0; n<totalSOs; n++) {
13       var thisObj = data[n];
14       if (thisObj.code == "change") {
15         refreshDisplay();
```

continues

Listing 8.6 Map Code Excerpts (Continued)

```
16      }
17      if (thisObj.code == "success") {
18          //don't have to (or want to) do anything to ourselves
19      }
20  }
```

In the `onSync`, we first check that `locations` is dimensioned as an array (line 3). Then, if we've never been here (`init==false`), we set the `owner.myID` value to the `length` of the `locations` array, and then stuff a generic object onto the end of the array (lines 6 through 9). In line 12, you see the main loop to go through all the properties in the shared object's list even though `locations` is the only property. Notice that only if the code is `"change"` (meaning someone else modified the shared object) do we trigger the `refreshDisplay()` function (as you'll see next).

```
function refreshDisplay() {
  var thisOne;
  var id;
  var total = so.data.locations.length;
  for (var n = 0; n<total; n++) {
    if(n!=owner.myID){
      owner.attachMovie("star", "star_"+n, n+1);
      thisOne=owner["star_"+n];
      thisOne._x=so.data.locations[n].x;
      thisOne._y=so.data.locations[n].y;
    }
  }
}
```

Basically, this code just goes through every item in the `locations` array and assuming the slot doesn't match `myID`, we create a new instance using `attachMovie()` and position its _x and _y.

You'll find more details in the complete version online, but do notice this example doesn't remove people from the map when they leave. You need a bit of server-side code for that (as discussed in the next chapter).

Example 2: Favorite Movie Vote Counter

The following example can be adapted for all kinds of survey needs. Here, we're just letting people vote for their favorite movies. Everyone can see how many votes each movie has received, and users can even add their favorite movie if it's not already listed. Actually, there are almost no error checks, so users can vote twice or add movies already listed. It's fairly simple and only took about an hour to build. You can see what it looks like in Figure 8.6 or visit www.phillipkerman.com/rias/movie_survey. In addition, the entire code file is available on my site.

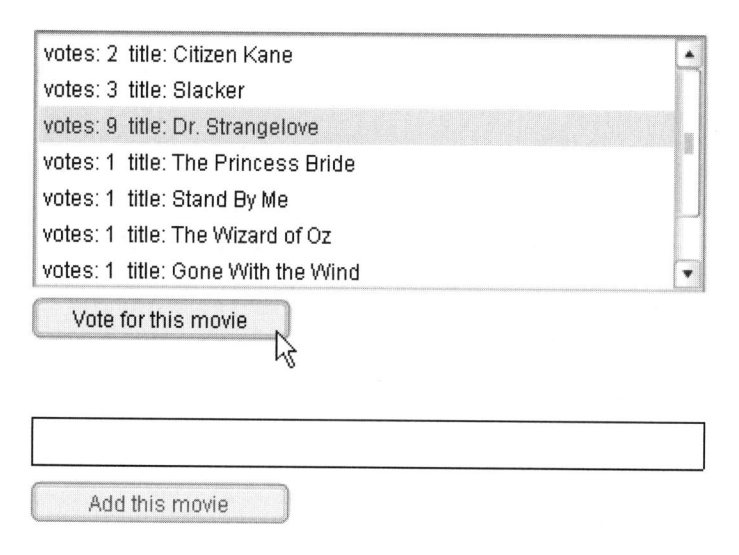

Figure 8.6 *We can quickly track users' votes for their favorite movies using an RSO.*

I structured the shared object's `data` by creating a property for each movie "movie_x" (where x went from 1 to 2 to 3 and so on). In each "movie_x" slot, I stored a generic object with three properties: `title`, `votes`, and `id`. Although I'm not using `id`, I thought it might come in handy later. If, say, I want to sort the movies by rank or name, I need to have a way to identify movies by something other than the order in which they appear in the list. In addition, I have a `counter` property called `total_movies` that tracks how many movies there are. Finally, I used a List component (to hold all the movies) and a regular Input Text field to let users add their own titles. Listing 8.7 shows the key excerpts from the code.

Listing 8.7 Movie Code Excerpt

```
1    function doAddTitle() {
2       var total = ++so.data.total_movies;
3       so.data["movie_"+ total]=new Object();
4       so.data["movie_"+ total].title=movieTitle_txt.text;
5       so.data["movie_"+ total].votes=1;
6       so.data["movie_"+ total].id =total;
7       movieTitle_txt.text="";
8    }
```

The doAddTitle() function is triggered only after the user has filled in the movieTitle_txt Input Text field and pressed a button. Line 2 both adds to the current movie count and sets the local variable total to the new value. (Notice ++ will increment total_movies whether you put it in before or after that variable, but putting it before returns the resulting value—so total becomes the new total.) Anyway, lines 3 through 6 put a generic object in a dynamically named property, set the title and votes properties, and assign a value to id. To ensure every movie gets its own id, I just keep adding to the unique property. I'll never lower that number even if I remove movies.

```
function doAddVote() {
   var movieNum = movies_lb.selectedItem.data;
   so.data["movie_"+movieNum].votes++;
}
```

When users select a movie they want to vote for (by clicking the movies_lb list), they can trigger the doAddVote() function. All I have to do is increment the votes property of the appropriate "movie_x" (dynamically referenced in line 3).

```
1    function refreshDisplay() {
2       movies_lb.removeAll();
3       var total = so.data.total_movies;
4       var thisOne;
5       for (var i = 0; i<total; i++) {
6          thisOne=so.data["movie_"+Number(i+1)];
7          movies_lb.addItem("votes: "+thisOne.votes+
8                       "  title: "+thisOne.title,   thisOne.id);
9       }
10      addVote_pb.enabled=false;
11   }
```

The `refreshDisplay()` function is triggered in the shared object's `onSync` any time the data changes. Basically, it just clears out the list and then loops through all the movies. Line 8's `addItem()` method formats how the data is presented in the list. You can see the resulting presentation in Figure 8.6. Just realize that after you have the data you can present it however you want. You could even make a bar graph or something.

Even when you see the complete code for the previous two examples, you'll see they're pretty simple. No doubt you can probably think of ways to improve them. For example, the favorite movie app lets users vote more than once. You could use an LSO to reduce that issue. However, you may want to wait until you learn a little about server-side ActionScript in Chapter 9, because it makes more advanced features easier to implement (specifically, tracking the user's IP address to prevent multiple votes).

On the surface, RSOs don't seem particularly exciting. Accessing shared variables (and being informed when others change them) doesn't sound like a huge deal, but it really is. Before we move on to audio and video streams (indisputably a sexier topic), let me point out that in addition to multiple users getting access to RSOs, server scripts can too. You'll see in Chapter 9 that just a little bit of server-side coding goes a long way to simplify many tasks. If you want to build a poker game, for example, the server could act as the dealer. Using what you know so far, one user would have to be the dealer and if that user left, the game would halt. Think of server scripts as anonymous robot-users that can make sure everything runs smoothly. Well, maybe it's not that rosy, but I wanted to remind you that RSOs come up again next chapter.

Streams

FCS supports true streaming media. This differs from the way plain Flash movies support progressive streaming. Like so many audio and video formats, Flash movies will play the first part of a movie while the rest of the file downloads. The idea is the rest of the movie will download by the time those end frames need to display. The two big advantages of true streaming are that the quality of the video file can be adjusted as it plays (for example, skipping frames as needed) and, after the movie or sound plays, the native media format is not downloaded to the user's machine (which media producers desire because it protects their content).

Of course, there are less esoteric features to media streams. Clients can play recorded videos or sounds and they can publish audio (from their microphone) or video (from their webcam) to share with other users live or, optionally, record it for later playback. That's pretty much everything. Naturally, there are lots of details. But for as cool as it is, there's not too many.

A Channel Inside Your NetConnection

Just like how an RSO is attached to a particular NetConnection, so are NetStreams. Each NetStream instance can handle one-way avenue over which audio, video, or both travel. If you want to both send audio from your microphone and, at the same time, hear audio from another user, you need two NetStream instances. It's sort of like how a telephone has both a speaker next to your ear and a mic by your mouth. Of course, it doesn't work that way, but remember each stream is a single channel. FCS can handle thousands of simultaneous streams (although, obviously, bandwidth quickly becomes a issue).

There's a second step after you create a NetStream instance. Namely, you have to say whether you want to play or publish. That is, if you want to play a particular stream that's either been recorded earlier or currently being published live, you just have to identify it. In addition, when you play a video steam, you'll want to attach it to a video symbol onstage (so that you can see the video). Alternatively, when publishing, you first need to identify the user's camera and microphone and attach them to the stream. Finally, you need to give this published stream a name (so that others can subscribe to it) and whether you want to optionally record it permanently. It may sound like a lot of details, but it's not that bad. Figure 8.7 shows an overview of the possibilities.

It all starts with a NetConnection, and then a NetStream. From there, you can go on to either play or publish. Making a NetStream is pretty easy, as Listing 8.8 shows.

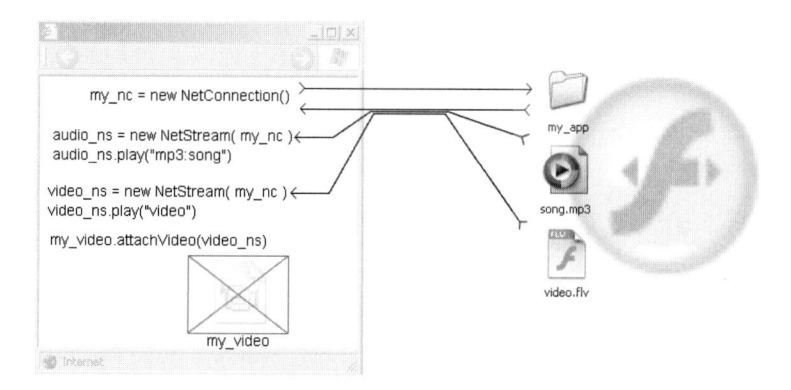

Figure 8.7 *This visualization of NetConnections and NetStreams should help sort things out.*

Listing 8.8 Skeleton NetStream Creation

```
1   my_nc = new NetConnection();
2   my_nc.onStatus=function(info){
3     if(info.code=="NetConnection.Connect.Success"){
4       initNS();
5     }
6   }
7   my_nc.connect("rtmp:/stream_app/r1");
8
9   function initNS(){
10    my_ns = new NetStream(my_nc);
11  }
```

The first 7 lines contain standard NetConnection stuff. It turns out that you don't really have to wait for a successful connection before creating a NetStream, but it makes the most sense to do so. Anyway, line 10 is all you need. In this case, we'll have the my_ns instance onto which we can play or publish a stream. That instance will also have an onStatus event that you can use to trap such events as when a stream stops playing (as you'll see in the next section). If you need more streams, just duplicate line 10, but change my_ns to some other unique variable name.

Take a little time to plan out your use of NetStreams. It's fine to have lots of streams, you just have to keep track of them all. If you're building a video chat application for two people, for example, the SWF will need to create two streams (one for publishing and one for playing the other person's published stream—call the two instances out_ns and in_ns if you want). (By the way, one user can publish both audio and video over a single NetStream.) From FCS's perspective, however, there will be a total of four streams (two for each user). This means that while the variable names for the two streams inside the SWFs can have the same names, user A and user B can't both publish something they call "me" and subscribe to "him". Rather, user A can publish "a" and play "b", whereas user B would *play* "a" and publish "b". Okay, that sounds like two stream names that the server has to track, but in fact, the server will set up four channels of stream. It just so happens each of the two named streams will be used in two channels each. I think visualizing this is easier than explaining it (see Figure 8.8).

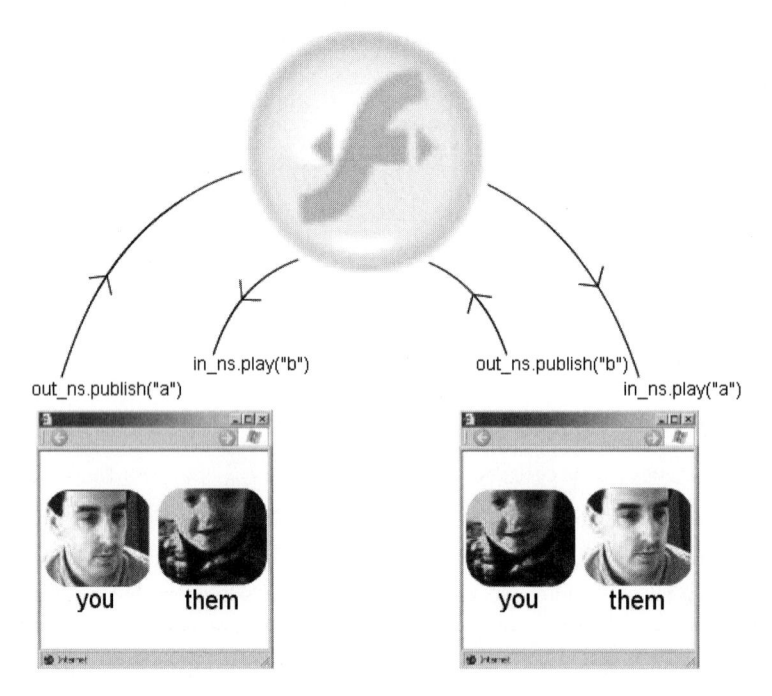

Figure 8.8 *Although there are only two named videos ("a" and "b"), the server needs to maintain four streams.*

Playing FLV Videos and MP3s

Although you may think you have to first record or publish a stream before someone can play it, that's not necessarily true with FCS. You can place MP3 audio or FLV videos in the appropriate folder and connected clients can stream them into their Flash movie.

> **{ Note }**
>
> **What's an FLV Video?**
>
> The only video format that Flash can play dynamically at runtime is FLV. This proprietary format can be produced three ways.
>
> 1. FCS produces FLV files when a user publishes video and audio stream coming from their camera and microphone (and the Record option is specified).
>
> 2. If you embed a conventional video (say, a QuickTime) inside Flash, you can export an FLV (by selecting the Export option when you double-click a video item in the library).
>
> 3. Both third-party video editors that support Flash Video Export (which comes with Flash Pro) or products such as Sorenson Squeeze (sold separately) can produce high-quality FLVs either manually or—in the case of Squeeze—automatically when raw videos appear in a "watch" folder.
>
> Note that although Flash Player 7 can natively play FLVs dynamically, you need FCS to stream them. Without FCS, you're only able to do a progressive download (which means you can see the first part of the video while the last part downloads).

Playing FLV Videos

The script for playing a prerecorded FLV is identical to playing a live video (see Listing 8.9). In fact, playing an MP3 (always prerecorded) is nearly identical—you just include an additional `"mp3:"` in the script. In the case of video, there's an extra step of attaching the stream to a specific video instance onstage so that you can see it. To make the following code work, you need a video instance onstage named my_video. (Create the video instance by first selecting New Video from the Library's menu as shown in Figure 8.9.) You also need an FLV in the right place. In this case, call the app my_app and the instance my_instance, then the FLV (called `"somevideo.flv"`) must reside in the following location *inside* FCS's applications folder my_app/streams/my_instance/somevideo.flv.

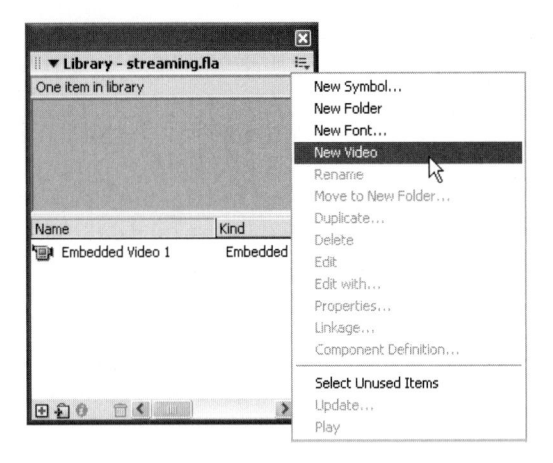

Figure 8.9 *You can create a video symbol (to later drag onstage) via the Library Options menu.*

Listing 8.9   Playing a Video Stream

```
1    my_nc = new NetConnection();
2    my_nc.onStatus = function(info) {
3       initNS();
4    };
5    my_nc.connect("rtmp:/my_app/my_instance");
6    function initNS() {
7       my_ns = new NetStream(my_nc);
8       my_video.attachVideo(my_ns);
9       my_ns.play("somevideo");
10   };
```

Line 7 creates the NetStream instance (and notice it's associated with my_nc). Then line 8 attaches the video portion of this stream to the my_video instance onstage. (If it's pure audio, you don't need this step.) Finally, the play() method is issued in line 9. Incidentally, you leave off video's .flv extension. (It's the default format.) FCS actually looks for a live stream first, and then looks for a saved FLV.

By the way, you can quickly modify this code to work inside Flash (with no FCS). Just change line 5 to my_nc.connect(null); and line 9 to my_ns.play("someVideo.flv");. Finally, you need to store the FLV adjacent to your SWF.

Playing MP3s

It's possible to create audio-only FLVs, but it's not exactly a standard format. Version 1.5 of FSC now supports true MP3 streaming (via the NetStream object). It's pretty much the same as the preceding code listing, except you don't need the `attachVideo()` method, and you need to specify MP3. Just take an MP3 file named somesong.mp3 and put it in the same folder you placed the FLV above. Then comment out line 8 and change line 9 to read as follows:

```
my_ns.play("mp3:somesong");
```

Alright, having the extension in front of the filename is weird. I suspect that because Macromedia added MP3 support after already deciding FLV files will be the default is why it's odd. (It will make more sense later when you see how to play live streams.)

Virtual Directories for Sharing Streams

Not only are the streams played so far hidden deep inside a set of subfolders, they're tied to a particular app instance. If you want several applications (and different instances of those apps) to have access to the same library of songs, you don't have to fill up your server's hard drive with duplicate copies of each song. Instead, you just have to set up a common folder called a Virtual Directory. Virtual directories have two parts: the actual folder location, and an alias that you use from inside Flash to point to this folder.

The way you identify such an alias is by editing the Vhost.xml configuration file (found deep inside the conf folder adjacent to your installed version of the FCS). In Listing 8.10, you'll see how the alias music will point to the folder C:\My Music where the actual FLVs and MP3s reside.

Listing 8.10 Defining and Using a Virtual Directory

Here's the pertinent portion of the Vhost.xml file:

```
<VirtualDirectory>
   <Streams>music;C:\My Music</Streams>
</VirtualDirectory>
```

When you restart the server, you'll be able to play MP3s stored in C:\My Music from any SWF by just referring to the folder music (as shown next).

```
my_ns.play("mp3:music/other");
```

continues

Listing 8.10 Defining and Using a Virtual Directory (Continued)

Basically, you just squeeze in `alias_name/` (or, in this case `music/`) in front of the MP3 filename. The same technique works for FLVs (just leave off the `mp3:`). Now, any application can stream MP3s or FLVs stored in the My Music folder.

There's certainly more to streams than just getting them started. For example, you may want to stop the stream with script:

`my_ns.play(false);`

Notice you don't `stop()`, you just use `play()` and pass `false` rather than a filename.

Next you'll see more advanced controls than just start and stop (or, I should say "play a file" and "play false").

Playback Controls

The advanced controls covered in this discussion include the following:

- Pausing (and resuming) a stream
- Displaying the current position with a progress bar
- Seeking to a particular position
- Ascertaining when a stream has finished playing
- Creating a play list that automatically plays one song after another

Let's go through the scripts for each of these tasks (see Listing 8.11). Because the first four tasks build on each other, you can keep adding to the same file. Start with three homemade button instances (`play_btn`, `pause_btn`, `stop_btn`) and one rectangle clip instance (`bar`) for the progress bar (using the center-left registration option). You also can draw an outline around the bar. Finally, to let the user click right on the progress bar and seek, place an invisible button (the same size as the progress bar). This button should also have the center-left registration option (see Figure 8.10).

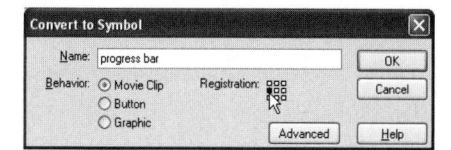

Figure 8.10 *The center-left registration option is used for the progress bar (and the invisible button later).*

Listing 8.11 Pausing and Resuming a Stream

```
1   my_nc = new NetConnection();
2   my_nc.onStatus = function(info) {
3     if (info.code == "NetConnection.Connect.Success") {
4       initNS();
5     }
6   };
7   my_nc.connect("rtmp:/jukebox/ap1");
8   function initNS() {
9     my_ns = new NetStream(my_nc);
10    my_ns.onStatus = function(info) {
11      for(i in info){
12        trace(i+":"+info[i]);
13      }
14    };
15    paused=false;
16  };
17  play_btn.onPress = function() {
18    if (paused) {
19      my_ns.pause();
20    } else {
21      //set up progress bar later
22      my_ns.play("mp3:rock");
23    }
24    paused = false;
25  };
26  pause_btn.onPress = function() {
27    paused = true;
28    my_ns.pause();
29  };
```

I hope most of this looks familiar. Note that I have an application named jukebox and instance ap1. (The MP3 rock.mp3 needs to be in a folder ap1 inside streams inside jukebox.) The onStatus event (starting on line 10) is used later to ascertain the end of

continues

Listing 8.11 Pausing and Resuming a Stream (Continued)

the song (although you'll see interesting information in the Output window until then). The default use of pause() will pause when playing and resume when paused—hence, the simplicity of the pause_btn's onPress callback. However, because play() will always start from the beginning, I came up with the homemade variable paused to track whether it was really time to play() or just (un) pause(). That is, in play_btn's onPress callback, it either plays or pauses and always sets paused back to false.

A NetStream instance has a time property from which you can determine the current position. To show this as a percentage (such as with a progress bar), however, you also need to know the entire duration of the stream. The length property is available only in server-side ActionScript. Instead of making you wait until the next chapter, I've included client-side code that asks the server-side code to get and return the length of a particular stream. The server-side code is just a text file named main.asc and resides in the application folder. Listing 8.12 shows how to make the progress bar work.

Listing 8.12 Displaying Current Position with a Progress Bar

First, the contents of your main.asc should contain this code:

```
Client.prototype.getLength =function (filename){
    return Stream.length("mp3:"+filename);
}
```

Second, you need to insert the following code in place of line 21 in the preceding listing (that is, in the else part of the if statement):

```
21  returnObj = new Object();
22  returnObj.onResult = function(result) {
23    totalLength = result;
24    _root.onEnterFrame = function() {
25      bar._xscale = my_ns.time/totalLength*100;
26    };
27  };
28  my_nc.call("getLength", returnObj, "rock");
```

The server-side code returns the length() of whatever filename was passed. Then the client side code calls the getLength function in line 28. You'll see call() in Chapter 9, but for now, notice that the second parameter is the object returnObj that I previously defined to handle an onResult event. Inside that onResult callback, I set totalLength to the value returned, and then set up the onEnterFrame code that will repeatedly set bar's _xscale to the appropriate percentage (that's time/totalLength).

For the seek code in Listing 8.13, it turns out that actually seeking is very easy (just issue `my_ns.seek(seconds)` and replace `seconds` with a number). Calculating to which point in the song you want to jump is a bit more work. The invisible button instance seek_btn must match exactly the shape of the bar instance (and be right on top of it).

Listing 8.13 Seeking to a Particular Position

```
seek_btn.onPress = function() {
  var percent = (_xmouse - seek_btn._x)/bar._width;
  my_ns.seek(percent*totalLength);
};
```

Because the registration point for the button is at its far left, you can calculate how far over the mouse click was by subtracting the seek_btn's _x from the _xmouse. I first tried using seek_btn._width, but invisible buttons have no width! Notice the totalLength variable was set in the previous code listing.

Finally, use the NetStream object's onStatus event to figure out when the song has finished playing. (I suppose you could just keep checking to see whether time was equal to the totalLength, but Listing 8.14 enables you to explore the onStatus event.)

Listing 8.14 Ascertaining When a Stream Finishes

This code goes within the onStatus event (after line 13 in Listing 8.11).

```
14   if (info.code == "NetStream.Play.Stop") {
15     this.waitingForEmpty = true;
16   } else if ((info.code == "NetStream.Buffer.Empty") &&
17                            this.waitingForEmpty) {
18     trace("song is over");
19     this.waitingForEmpty = false;
20   } else {
21     this.waitingForEmpty = false;
22   }
```

You'd think you could just wait for the code property to equal "NetStream.Play.Stop". However, this information is sent to the onStatus before the song really ends—you stop hearing it when the buffer is empty

continues

Listing 8.11   Pausing and Resuming a Stream (Continued)

(code `"NetStream.Buffer.Empty"`). The preceding script first sets the homemade variable `waitingForEmpty` to `true`; then when the buffer is empty *and* `waitingForEmpty` is `true`, you hit line 18 where the `trace()` executes.

You'll probably want to replace that `trace()` with some code that hides or disables the `stop_btn` and `pause_btn`. If you do that, just remember to re-enable those buttons, say, when the user clicks the `play_btn` again.

Play lists are a lot cooler than you might think at first glance. Basically, you just keep issuing `play()` commands (but with optional parameters) and one song will play after the next. (Listing 8.15 effectively breaks the progress bar and seek features, although you'll find fixes in the online files for this chapter.)

Listing 8.15   Creating a Play List

```
my_ns.play("mp3:song1",-2,-1,false);
my_ns.play("mp3:song2",-2,-1,false);
```

You can put this code in place of your existing `play()` command in the earlier examples. Of course, you need to create the files song1.mp3 and song2.mp3. Translated, the preceding code will play song1.mp3 and, when it finishes, automatically begin playing song2.mp3. The optional second and third parameters are a sort of code system. For example, changing second parameter to `-1` is the code for "play a live stream only." I suggest you look at the Reference panel information inside Flash for this method because there are lots of variations. The fourth parameter (`false` here) means that existing play lists (or, just old `play()` commands) should not be flushed. That is, continuing to issue `play()` will just queue up the requests so that they play in sequence.

Not only does my online version of this code include a working progress bar and seek feature (for play lists), it also includes a nice interface for users to create their own play lists. It's just way more code than will fit here.

Now you've seen there's more to playing back audio and video than just the `play()` command. Virtual directories for sharing media, seeking to specific places in a song or video, and defining play lists are all variations on the main idea behind playing audio and video. It turns out that's only the first half! Now you'll see how to record live media through what's called publishing.

Publishing

This section shows you how to take the image and sound from one user's camera and microphone and publish it to other connected users and optionally record it. Here's the process in a nutshell:

1. Make a variable instance that points to the user's camera using `Camera.get()`.

2. Make another variable instance that points to the user's microphone using `Microphone.get()`.

3. On a free NetStream instance, use both `attachAudio()` and `attachVideo()` to connect the preceding two instances.

4. Issue the `publish()` method on that NetStream instance and specify a stream name (that other clients identify when they `play()`) as well as other options such as whether it will be recorded or just go out live.

Accessing the User's Camera and Microphone

You'll see that grabbing the camera and microphone really is pretty easy. It's probably easiest to see with a simple example.

```
my_cam=Camera.get();
```

The preceding code finds the first available camera (say the user has more than one connected to his machine) and stores a reference to it in the my_cam variable. To access a specific camera, you can pass an index inside the get() method. To best see whether the user does have multiple cameras, however, let the user select, say, from a ComboBox (named camera_cb) as this code shows:

```
my_cam = Camera.get();
if (Camera.names.length>1) {
  camera_cb._visible = true;
  camera_cb.removeAll();
  camera_cb.addItem("Change Cameras",null);
  for (var i = 0; i<Camera.names.length; i++) {
    camera_cb.addItem(Camera.names[i], i);
  }
  camera_cb.addEventListener("change", pickCamera);
} else {
  camera_cb._visible=false;
}
function pickCamera() {
  my_cam = Camera.get(camera_cb.selectedItem.data);
}
```

You'll get an array of all attached cameras using Camera.names (not to be confused with my_cam.name, which returns just the string name of the camera in the instance my_cam). The preceding code uses that array to populate the ComboBox. The ComboBox triggers the `pickCamera()` function, which then selects a different camera.

You can implement nearly the same code to grab a microphone:

```
my_mic = Microphone.get();
if (Microphone.names.length>1) {
      microphone_cb._visible = true;
      microphone_cb.removeAll();
      microphone_cb.addItem("Change Microphones",null);
      for (var i = 0; i<Microphone.names.length; i++) {
          microphone_cb.addItem(Microphone.names[i], i);
   }
   microphone_cb.addEventListener("change", pickMicrophone);
} else {
      camera_cb._visible=false;
}
function pickMicrophone() {
      my_mic = Microphone.get(microphone_cb.selectedItem.data);
}
```

Publishing a Live or Recorded Stream

Now that you've got handles on both the camera and microphone, you can move on to publishing. The code in Listing 8.16 is complete (although it does forgo a few error checks such as checking whether the connection is really made):

Listing 8.16   Publishing Audio and Video

```
1  my_cam = Camera.get();
2  my_mic = Microphone.get();
3  my_nc = new NetConnection();
4  my_nc.connect("rtmp:/video_app/r1");
5  my_ns = new NetStream(my_nc);
6  my_ns.attachAudio(my_mic);
7  my_ns.attachVideo(my_cam);
8  my_ns.publish("live_signal");
```

(Don't forget to make an application folder called video_app.) After you get the camera and microphone, set up a NetConnection (line 3 and 4) and a NetStream (line 5). Then

Chapter 8 Foundation Communication Server   269

lines 6 and 7 attach the `user_mic` and `user_cam` to the NetStream. Finally, line 8 begins publishing this stream called `"live_signal"`. Incidentally, the `publish()` method has an optional second parameter for which you can supply `"record"`, `"append"`, or `"live"`. By leaving it off, you're using `"live"`, meaning there won't be an FLV left on disk when it's over. Line 6 trips the Security dialog box for users (see Figure 8.11).

The creepy thing about this example is that it just begins to broadcast the camera and microphone signal, but because no one is watching, you don't see anything! That is, the stream called `"live_signal"` is out there for anyone to play. (You'll see that code next.)

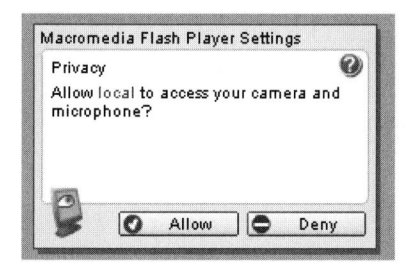

Figure 8.11 *Before you can successfully tie a camera or microphone to a stream (or video instance), the user must "allow" access.*

Once you're broadcasting the live stream, you can do a few things with it. You may want to let the publisher see himself. (That is, whoever is running the movie with the code from the preceding listing may want a picture mirrored back.) To show the user what he *really* looks like (that is, over the Internet), you need to set up another stream, because you're already using my_ns for the signal going out. Remember you have to have a separate stream for each direction. Although into the outgoing stream you can squeeze both the microphone and camera, you need another stream to play (think "download") the published stream. The thing is, you don't really want to let the publisher hear himself with the delay from the Internet, so the code that follows (although it works) isn't ideal. Just place a video instance named my_video onstage and add this code to the preceding listing:

```
in_ns=new NetStream(my_nc);
my_video.attachVideo(in_ns);
in_ns.play("live_signal");
```

Basically, you just set up a whole new NetStream instance (in_ns) to handle playing the live stream. This code should look pretty familiar. It's just like Listing 8.9, which played a recorded video stream—this one just happens to be live. The problem with this is that it also sends the publisher's audio back through the publisher's speakers (where it can get picked up by the microphone to make an echo).

A much easier solution avoids this problem, although it does give the publisher a high-quality image of himself (which may not be accurate). This code should be used rather than the last block showed:

```
my_video.attachVideo(my_cam);
```

To turn all this code into a practical application, consider the idea that you might want to broadcast video to a bunch of students. For the teacher, you could use the preceding listing (with the additional line that displays the video). For the students, create a different movie with a video instance onstage named my_video and the following code:

```
my_nc = new NetConnection();
my_nc.connect("rtmp:/video_app/r1");
in_ns = new NetStream(my_nc);
my_video.attachVideo(in_ns);
in_ns.play("live_signal");
```

This code *is* identical to the old "play a video" code from much earlier, but it does show you how you can have two separate SWFs connected to the same application (but effectively with different privileges or responsibilities). That is, although there are a teacher.swf and a student.swf, you don't let the students have access to the teacher.swf movie. Really, the only hassle here is testing such an app. It's really easy to get mixed up—I recommend using the App Inspector to monitor what's going on with the streams (see Figure 8.12).

There really isn't much more to say about publishing and playing. There are definitely some neat tricks and performance enhancements that I'll go over next. As I was learning FCS, a few areas of confusion kept popping up. For one thing, you have to remember to use attachVideo() to connect your camera to an outgoing stream as well as to attach an incoming stream to a video instance! In addition, unlike most objects that must be instantiated using the keyword new, the SharedObject, Camera, and Microphone objects all use the get() method instead. On top of these syntax issues, you really have to take on a whole new mind-set when building multiuser applications. I guess the point of this interlude is that you'll want to carefully map out your FCS apps.

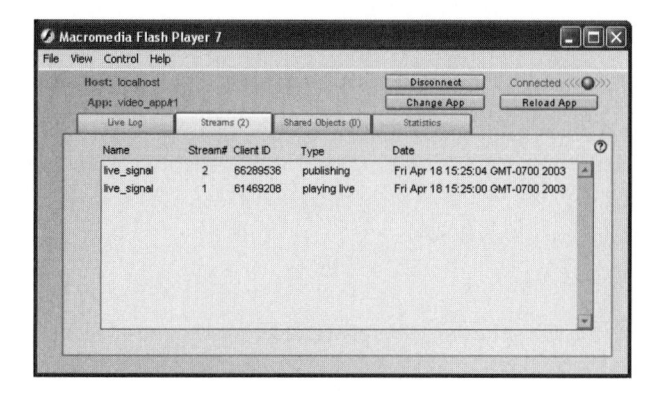

Figure 8.12 *The App Inspector's Streams tab enables you to monitor all network streams.*

Miscellaneous Tips When Publishing

I said there's not much more to say about publishing but, in fact, you can do quite a lot of tweaking with the signal uploaded from a camera or microphone. (Just check out all the properties for both the Camera and Microphone objects, in addition to the NetStream object.) Regarding published streams, FCS pretty much handles that automatically. The big concept to understand is that a video signal can adapt to low bandwidth by dropping frames and lowering picture quality, whereas a sound really can't. Besides lowering the capturing microphone's frequency rate, the best thing you can do for slower connections regarding audio is to increase the buffer time (that is, the amount that must download before it plays). The following list highlights some of the more important properties and methods (which you should look up in Flash's Reference panel) for microphones, cameras, and streams.

Microphone

- setRate()—Sets the frequency rate at which the microphone captures. A mic instance's rate property has a direct impact on quality as well as bandwidth requirements. (The lower the number, the lower the quality and the bandwidth need.)
- setSilenceLevel()—Affects the threshold at which a microphone stops transmitting. That is, when it gets really quiet, there's no point in using bandwidth. You can control this breakpoint.

- `setUseEchoSuppression(true)`—Effectively presses the Reduce Echo option seen in the Settings panel—but it's really such a no-brainer; I'd say always set this to `true`.
- `activityLevel`—Continuously updates to show how much signal is going through the microphone. It's neat because you can use it to make your own VU meter.

Camera

- `muted` (which also applies to Microphone objects)—Is true when the user has chosen Deny on the Security a dialog box (shown earlier in Figure 8.12).
- `setMode()`—Has huge affect on how well the image survives squeezing through the Internet. Use `setMode()` to set the resolution and frame rate for how much data is captured by the Camera object. The thing that messes me up is that this is different from the `_height` and `_width` for a particular video instance onstage.
- `setQuality()`—Confusingly similar to `setMode()`, but controls the quality of each frame in the video by ensuring it doesn't exceed a specified bandwidth (such as controlling the quality with JPG compression).

Stream

- `setBufferTime()`—Enables you to control how much of the stream must preload before beginning to play.
- `liveDelay`—A read-only property that helps you monitor what sort of delay the user is experiencing.

When it comes to balancing quality and bandwidth, the general approach is to try to keep your original streams at their highest practical quality. That is, if you think some people will be able to handle a 300Kbps download, there's no need to make the video any higher quality than that. Remember that audio is a different story: Everyone will experience it at the same quality level (although, perhaps, delayed differently for buffering). The sad part is that people tend to notice audio quality suffering before they notice picture quality. (This is why FCS puts a priority on audio quality.) In any event, a high-quality image can be sent at different quality levels to clients with differing connection speeds.

There's one last tip that's really worthy of a whole chapter, but I'll just mention it here and give you a simple example. The NetStream object's `send()` method is a way to embed event triggers right into a stream. If you record a video stream, for example, you'll be recording images, sounds, *and* any event triggers sent during the recording. Subscribers of these streams have the opportunity to be notified of such events while the video plays (and in perfect synchronization). This holds true even if they're playing a stream recorded earlier.

You just have to set up a callback to handle these expected triggers. Here's a quick example. Just make a clip with a `stop()` in the first frame and a visual change in its second frame—give the clip an instance name clip. Use the code in Listing 8.17 for the recording version.

Listing 8.17 Embedding Events While Recording a Stream

```
1   my_mic = Microphone.get();
2   my_nc = new NetConnection();
3   my_nc.connect("rtmp:/video_app/r1");
4   my_ns = new NetStream(my_nc);
5   my_ns.attachAudio(my_mic);
6   my_ns.publish("recorded_message","record");
7   _root.onMouseDown=function(){
8       clip.play();
9       my_ns.send("clickTime");
10  }
```

Nothing really new here except that line 6 includes the `"record"` parameter (to store the FLV stream permanently) and line 9 is issuing `send("clickTime")`. For the code that *plays* this stream, `clickTime` needs to be defined as a callback.

```
1   my_nc = new NetConnection();
2   my_nc.connect("rtmp:/video_app/r1");
3   my_ns = new NetStream(my_nc);
4   my_ns.clickTime=function(){
5       clip.play();
6   }
7   my_ns.play("recorded_message");
```

Notice that we set up the `clickTime` callback on `my_ns`. This gets triggered while the stream plays. I just think this is the coolest feature. I built a simple guided tour on my main web site, www.phillipkerman.com, that uses this technique. I just launch a separate SWF that connects to the same app and it takes just a minute to rerecord a stream along with my mouse movements and button clicks—and it took less than 2 hours to program!

continues

Listing 8.17 Embedding Events While Recording a Stream (Continued)

By the way, events embedded this way trigger even if you play back the FLV without FCS. That is, you'll need FCS to record as shown in the first block of code. But the second part will work without FCS when using Flash Player 7 for playback. Just replace the RTMP string in line 2 with `null` and add `".flv"` after the filename in line 7.

I could go on an on about little techniques and "gotchas" when doing real FSC apps. Remember, however, this is a book about RIAs. It's enough if you get nothing else from this chapter except a clear idea of what's possible in FCS. Ideally, given the basic concepts you've learned, you will now have a clear place to start when you have an idea for an application.

Why Server-Side ActionScript

Throughout this chapter, I kept saying "just wait until you see server-side scripting" (called server-side ActionScript or SSAS). First, realize there's a lot more you can do with client-side ActionScript (CSAS). It's not that SSAS will solve all your problems, but I think there's an unwarranted—although natural—resistance to learn SSAS. It can actually make things easier. If you're doing FCS apps, you're already having to think in a new way. I think of SSAS as a moderate investment in learning that pays off many times over. Compare this to how it's possible to build an entire Flash app laying out everything by hand in Flash's timeline. But, with a little investment in learning ActionScript, you can do much more. The point is you probably don't want to wait until you're at some advanced level before learning SSAS—you can probably use it right away.

Summary

This chapter touched on nearly every technical concept related to FCS. There was a fair bit of groundwork, such as configuring the server, that really had to come first. The next step, of course, is to think of something cool to build. Although I will certainly try to give you a few ideas next, it's really difficult because no one has yet fully exploited FCS. Most likely, you'll have ideas percolating that no one else will. My big suggestion is don't discount the power of live or recorded video, but realize the underlying power in FCS is based on its capability to share variables between multiple connected users. Also, two connected users can have a different view on the same app (as in the single teacher, multiple student concept).

{Chapter 9}

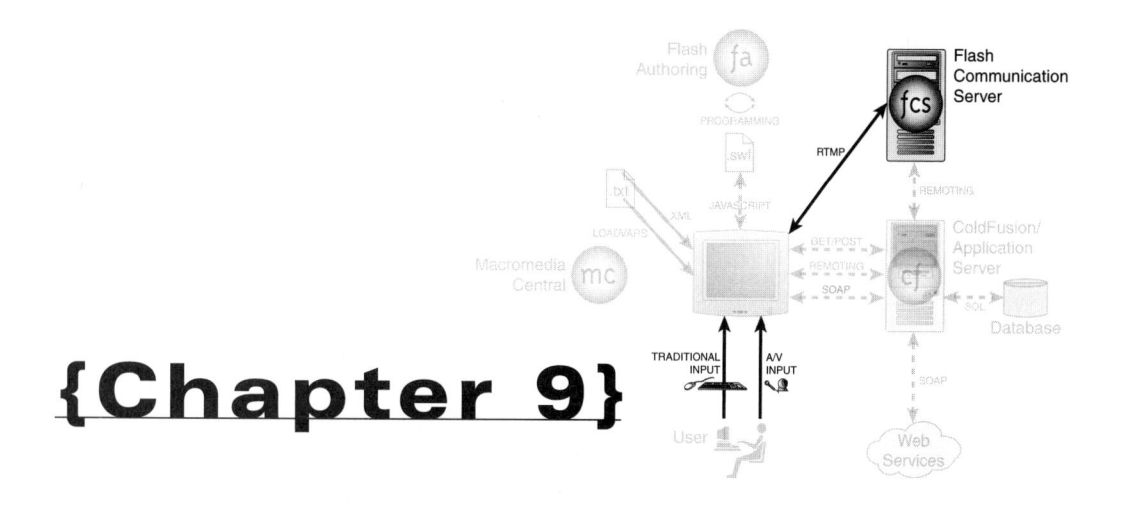

Advanced Communication Server

Designing and building communication applications takes a new way of thinking. It's really a mind twister to think of how to present the same data to several users while any one of them might be changing the data. Instead of thinking of this chapter as "more advanced," I suggest just that you think of it as "more"—more ways to build communication apps.

The primary focus here is on how to use server-side ActionScript (SSAS). As mentioned in the preceding chapter, SSAS may appear to be more complex than client-side ActionScript (CSAS). In fact, a tiny bit of SSAS takes a huge load off the responsibility of your CSAS. That is, it actually makes things easier. The only thing complex in this chapter is the thought process. Now, instead of having multiple client SWFs executing scripts, you also have code on the Flash Communication Server (FCS) acting like a traffic cop or central clearinghouse.

Enough with the analogies, this chapter covers the following topics:

- Storing SSAS in the main.asc file
- Tracking application activity and user behavior with the Application object and Client object
- Messaging using `send()` and `call()`
- The server-side Stream object for logging and sending the same data to multiple clients, almost like broadcasting

In this chapter, you'll also learn plenty of tricks and optimization considerations. In addition, you'll learn some translation techniques, too, because although SSAS is based on ActionScript, in a few places it's *not* identical.

Managing Connections

The best way to understand SSAS is to consider how your application would suffer if it depended on an unreliable client SWF. Imagine, for instance, a card game with one user as the dealer. If the dealer closes his browser, the others are out of luck. If you put the code responsible for dealing in SSAS, however, the game could continue to run regardless of whether anyone was connected.

CSAS is just all the code in a SWF movie. All your SSAS goes into a plain-text file called main.asc that resides in your application directory. Each app maintains up to one copy of a main.asc file. (For example, the previous examples didn't have a main.asc at all.) In addition, you can share code between apps through the include() command (which is nearly identical to Flash's #include directive). Although you can edit the main.asc with any text editor, you really ought to use Dreamweaver because it includes syntax coloring and code hints (see Figure 9.1).

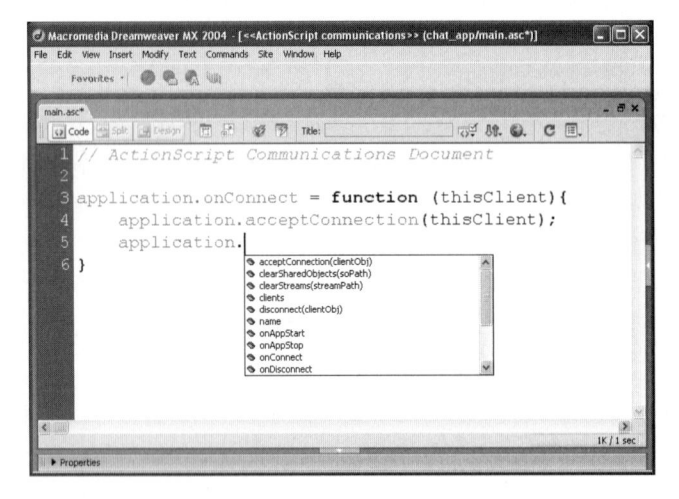

Figure 9.1 *Although you can use any text editor for main.asc files, Dreamweaver MX 2004 includes code hints for server-side ActionScript.*

This section is dedicated to making a main.asc file that can trap server events (such as a user connecting or the application itself instantiating) and include methods that clients or the application can trigger. I suppose there are other details, too, but the point is all SSAS goes into that main.asc file.

Key Events

There are three key events to which you can write a script that responds: the application instantiating, any user connecting, and any user disconnecting. The syntax for each event follows a familiar form:

```
application.onEvent=function(){
}
```

You just have to replace onEvent with the particular event you're trying to trap. For the ones previously mentioned, that would be onAppStart, onConnect, and onDisconnect. These events are part of the Application object, but saying application just refers to the current application for which you're coding. For a quick preview, SSAS also contains the Client object. The upcoming examples show a few properties that give you access to attributes of any one connected client.

onAppStart

When the first user visits your app, an instance comes to life. That app instance name matches what the client SWF specifies in the connect() method (or uses _definst_ if no value gets passed). From that moment, and until the app is unloaded or restarted, that instance lives in FCS's memory. You'll also see it listed in the App Inspector. If there's any code you want executed at the beginning (for instance, perhaps you have some variables to initialize), put the code within the onAppStart event. Listing 9.1 provides a simple example (which, like nearly everything in this chapter, just goes in your main.asc file).

Listing 9.1 *onAppStart* **Skeleton**

```
application.onAppStart=function(){
  trace(this.name+" started at "+new Date().toString());
}
```

Notice that in addition to demonstrating the onAppStart event, this example shows that one of the properties to any application instance is name. In addition to looking through the help files, a good way to find more such events and properties is to type **application.** into a text editor that supports FCS code hints (such as Dreamweaver) and the code-completion drop-down list will appear.

Another thing to notice here is that I'm using trace() and new Date() and toString()—all standard ActionScript supported in SSAS. One slight difference, however, is that trace()outputs a string to the Live Log tab inside the App Inspector (not to your Output window as you might expect).

The easiest way to see the preceding example is to first place the main.asc file in an application folder, perhaps named say my_app, and then manually load the app by typing **my_app/testInstance** into the App/Inst field of the App Inspector. At this point, you'll be too late to have witnessed the application start, but you can select the instance now listed in the App Inspector, click View Detail, make sure you're looking at the Live Log tab, and then you click Reload App (see Figure 9.2). It's a hassle, but you'll get used to reloading apps and, besides, it's just the nature of how an app starts.

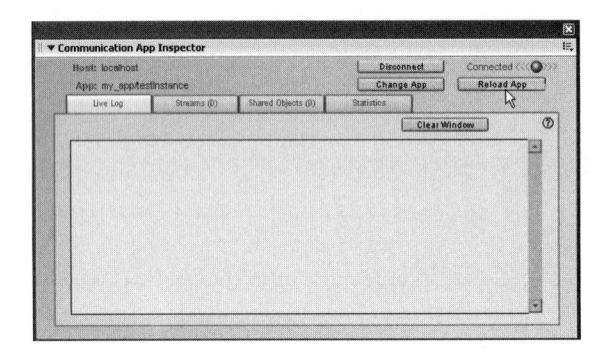

Figure 9.2 *Reloading while already inspecting an app means you'll see trace statements in the* onAppStart *event.*

It may be obvious that code in the onAppStart executes before the onConnect event (that you'll see next) triggers when the first user connects. Probably the most common use for onAppStart is initializing variables. If a slot in my remote shared object (RSO) will have an array (into which I plan to push() values), for instance, I'll use the onAppStart to dimension it as an array (by setting it equal to []). Also, because you can store variables within the application instance, an opportune time to initialize is at app start. (You'll see how to store variables in the application instance in the "Application Object's Additional Features" section and the syntax for RSOs in the "Accessing Remote Shared Objects from the Server Side" section.)

onConnect

Although onAppStart always happens first, you'll see that onConnect is a much more active event. Here you can trigger scripts that notify all other users when someone new has joined the app. In fact, it might be better to think of onConnect as "on attempt to connect" because inside the onConnect you can accept or reject a client. It's weird because if you don't have an onConnect callback defined, everyone is accepted. As soon as you define the `onConnect` event, however, you must include either `acceptConnection()` (to let a client in) or explicitly `rejectConnection()` (which effectively gets triggered anyway if you forget to include `acceptConnection()`).

Although you must remember to accept a connection, it turns out that `onConnect` is mainly a place where you manage connections (for instance, track the active users) and where you assign variables to identify each particular client. Just like how an application can maintain its own set of variables, so can each client instance. Here I'm not talking of how a SWF may have a bunch of its own variables, however, but rather about how the server side can assign variables associated with particular connected clients. It's almost like how you might manage several radio stations on a car radio. Although you program one station under the 1 button and another under 2, each of those stations maintains its own properties such as their call letters and frequency (and they don't care under what button they reside). Ultimately, the server can't reach into a SWF and see its internal variables and a SWF can't reach into the server and see variables assigned to it (not directly anyway). It's not so much that you want to keep everything private (and you'll see how with messaging you can share any data you decide to). It's just that the application (that is, the "server side") has to have a way to keep track of all the connected users who are—otherwise—identical. Such tracking variables need not be available to the SWFs.

Listing 9.2 includes several common tricks. Remember, however, that the one thing you'll always need is `acceptConnection()` somewhere.

Listing 9.2   Example *onConnect()* Callback

```
1   application.onConnect = function(thisClient) {
2     thisClient.user_id=Math.random();
3     if (thisClient.referrer=="http://www.phillipkerman.com/test.swf"){
4       application.acceptConnection(thisClient);
5     }else{
6       application.rejectConnection(thisClient);
7     }
8   }
```

Again, the only part you need inside `onConnect` is line 4. The basic code here assigns to this client a random value for their `user_id` property—a variable name I just made up. Then, if the built-in `referrer` property equals a specific string, they are accepted;

continues

Listing 9.2 Example *onConnect()* Callback (Continued)

otherwise, they're rejected. Notice both the `acceptConnection()` and `rejectConnection()` methods require that you pass an argument pointing to the client instance in question.

Naturally, a random ID for each user isn't practical, but I wanted to show that assigning homemade variables is identical to referring to properties. The variables assigned stay with this client instance while they are connected.

{ Note }

Don't Forget `application.acceptConnection()` I realize I've already said this a million times, but you really must include `acceptConnection()` if you're going to write an `onConnect()` callback. Even after saying this, I just spent 20 minutes hunting down a bug in the examples because I left out this simple line of code! It's particularly elusive because much of your app will continue to work.

Incidentally, `rejectConnection()` accepts a second optional parameter that you can use to explain to the client why they're not being accepted. For example, you may only want to allow 10 users to be connected at a time. To use the standard messaging techniques covered later, you must have a connected client. This technique doesn't require a connection. All you do is pass a generic object with named properties. For example, this can be used in place of line 6 in the preceding listing:

```
var whyObj=new Object();
whyObj.reason="maxUserLimit"
application.rejectConnection(thisClient, whyObj);
```

Then, on the client side, you'll have to know to look for the `reason` property (which, I just made up) that will show up inside the `application` property of the info object received by `onStatus`. (And, you do have to use `application` verbatim.) Here's what it might look like on the client side:

```
my_nc.onStatus = function(info) {
  if (info.code == "NetConnection.Connect.Reject") {
    if (info.application.reason=="maxUserLimit"){
      //tell the user somehow
    }
  }
};
```

You can see that I've been using `thisClient` for the first parameter received. (I could have used anything—and for your information, most of the help files use `newClient`.) The interesting part is that when a client SWF issues `connect("rtmp:/my_app/testInstance")`, `onConnect()` is then triggered and automatically receives a reference to the client doing the triggering. Actually, the client SWF can pass any number of optional parameters when they `connect()`, but the first parameter sent shows up in the second slot (after the client itself). Listing 9.3 shows a more practical alternative to the random `user_id` variable.

Listing 9.3   Passing Values to *onConnect()*

In the SWF, use the following:

```
my_nc.connect("rtmp:/my_app/testInstance", username_txt.text);
```

Then, the main.asc can look like this:

```
1    application.onConnect = function(thisClient, username) {
2        thisClient.username=username;
3        this.acceptConnection(thisClient);
4    }
```

Pretty simple really: Whatever text is found in the SWF's `username_txt` instance gets passed from the client side and then, on the server-side `onConnect()`, assigns that value to the client instance's homemade `username` property. You just have to remember the first parameter passed shows up second, after a reference to the client. Notice that `thisClient` in line 2 is the client instance and the `this` in line 3 is the application.

You'll see that after you have a reference to the particular client instance, you can easily grab any property or homemade variable.

In addition to accepting and setting variables for a connecting client, the `onConnect()` event is a good place to notify others that someone new has connected. Perhaps you only want to tell the teacher in a teacher/student application. It's also possible to send an object full of information back to a client as they're being disconnected. For these tasks, you could use an RSO or an alternative form of messaging (topics that both come up later this chapter). I guess I just wanted to say, you'll see `onConnect()` again.

One last note before moving on: Because SWF files can be decompiled, you'll never want to put the "right" password right in your FLA. However, it's not bad form to store a password in the main.asc; because, after all, you shouldn't make this file directly accessible to web visitors. For example, I could put the following code within the preceding onConnect() listing:

```
if(username=="phillip"){
  thisClient.role="admin";
}else{
  thisClient.role="regular";
}
```

In this case, `"phillip"` isn't a particularly difficult password to crack. The point is, however, that unless a client passes that exact string, the value for the homemade property `role` will be `"regular"`. There are certainly more types of validation schemes such as accessing a database of usernames through an application server. (Macromedia's DevNet site has several articles on this very topic.) However, although this example is hardwired and uses an easy string to crack, this is a legit way to control access. (To carry this through, you'd want to refer to the homemade `role` variable later in the code and treat those with a value of `"admin"` differently than you treat a `"regular"`.)

{ Note }

Using the Component Framework If you use any of the communication components, they will effectively commandeer the onConnect event, so be sure to read the "Integrating the Communication Components" section at the end of this chapter to learn how to get around this.

onDisconnect

To round out the three key events, `onDisconnect()` triggers when a user closes the browser or navigates to another page. In addition, if you boot off a user using `clientInstance.disconnect()`, that user exits via the `onDisconnect()` event. By the way, just like `onConnect()`, you don't have to write an `onDisconnect()` callback. If you do, however, include one important line at the very end: `return true`. It's not as critical as `acceptConnection()` is to `onConnect()`, but by doing so you'll avoid weird situations where FCS thinks a particular client is still connected. Here's a good starter script:

```
application.onDisconnect = function(thisClient) {
  trace(thisClient.username + " has left the app");
  return true;
}
```

This code assumes you assigned a `username` property to this client at some point earlier (for instance, when the client connected). Notice that at the end, I return `true`. This doesn't have to be on the very last line. Realize, however, that when `return` is encountered, it skips the rest of the code.

> **{ Note }**
>
> **Keeping an App Running** Application instances will time out based on a setting in your configuration folders. However, the following code shows how to override that behavior:
>
> ```
> application.onAppStop=function(){
>   return false;
> }
> ```
>
> Basically, every time the app attempts to stop, you say "no."

There's not a whole lot more I can say about `onDisconnect()` except that it's a convenient time to handle certain "housekeeping" tasks. For example, you might actually want to notify all the remaining users that "client *x* has left the building." Also, if you're maintaining an application variable or RSO containing a list of connected users, you'll want to remove the person who just left. These sorts of tasks involve a few things not yet covered, so wait until you get through the next few code listings to see how you would actually pull it off. For now, just realize that these key events are available and you can write code that triggers when they occur.

Application Object's Additional Features

The Application object has more to offer than just a few key events (discussed earlier). There are more events, some built-in properties, and the ability to create your own variables (equivalent to built-in properties). Also, as you'll see in the "Accessing Remote Shared Objects from the Server Side" section later in this chapter, when you `get()` an RSO on the server side, you'll probably want to store the reference in an application variable.

You can think of application variables as global variables. That is, once created, you can access them from anywhere in your main.asc file. The syntax is very straightforward: You just use the form `application.variableName`—including "application" verbatim. (Alternatively, you can use a reference to the active application, such as `this`, when inside an application callback.) The following example uses a couple of homemade application variables to track who's connected. It relies on an Input text field instance username_txt, a button instance connect_btn, and this code inside the SWF:

```
connect_btn.onPress=function(){
  my_nc= new NetConnection();
  my_nc.connect("rtmp:/track_user/r1",username_txt.text);
}
```

Then, the code in Listing 9.4 goes inside your main.asc file inside the application folder track_user.

Listing 9.4 Using Application Variables to Track Users

```
1   application.onAppStart=function(){
2     this.userList=[];
3     this.userCount=0;
4   }
5
6   application.onConnect = function(thisClient, username) {
7     this.userCount++;
8     thisClient.slot=this.userCount-1;
9     this.userList.push(username);
10    trace("total users = " + this.userCount);
11    this.acceptConnection(thisClient);
12  }
13
14  application.onDisconnect = function(thisClient) {
15    this.userCount--;
16    var newList=[];
17    for(var i=0;i<this.userList.length;i++){
18      if(thisClient.slot != i){
19        newList.push(this.userList[i]);
20      }
21    }
22    this.userList=newList;
23    trace("remaining users "+this.userList);
24    return true;
25  }
```

There's a little bit of everything here. First you'll see application.userList and application.userCount is initialized (in lines 2 and 3) as an array and number respectively. (Actually, I use this.userList, but that's the same as application.userList while inside this callback.) Then, anytime someone connects, userCount is incremented (line 7) and, to give each client instance a unique identifier I made up the *client* variable called `slot` (which appears again when the user disconnects). I really couldn't resist including that a bit early (the next section is about the Client object). Anyway, the application variable `userList` contains an array of all usernames, and `userCount` tracks how many items are in that array.

Down in the `onDisconnect` callback, you can see that first `userCount` is decremented (line 14). Then I make a fresh array variable `newList` that will get built up during the loop in lines 17 through 21. Basically, this loop adds each username from `userList` to `newList` unless the index matches the `slot` property for the client who's leaving. Finally, line 22 dumps the temporary `newList` into `userList`.

I should probably mention that not only is the `userCount` variable in the preceding listing unnecessary (after all, I could always just check the `length` property of `userList`), but there turns out to be a built-in property for all application instances called `clients`. It's some sort of weird cross between an array and a generic object. In practice, it's closer to an array, as this example shows:

```
for (var i = 0; i < application.clients.length; i++){
   trace(application.clients[i].username);
}
```

Notice that `application.clients[i]` refers to the actual client instance in that slot (whereas my `userList` was a list of strings). Also, your client instances need a `username` property created for this code to work.

Application variables are just plain convenient. Alternatively, you may find a use to store variables inside RSOs. RSOs offer the following three advantages over application variables:

- They can be set to be persistent, whereas application variables are cleared when the application unloads.
- Clients can be automatically and immediately notified when an RSO's contained variables get modified.
- Clients have direct access to the values inside RSOs.

With all those advantages of RSOs, application variables are still a better choice when appropriate because they're so easy to use.

Finally, although standalone functions aren't really part of the application object per se, I think it makes sense to mention that you can write functions in the main.asc the same way you can in Flash MX 2004.

Now that you've learned about the Application object, it's time to move on to the Client object. Although these are two different objects, they work together and your scripts will nearly always contain a reference to both.

Additional Client Object Information

It turns out that if you're reading this chapter in order, you've already seen a bit about how the Client object works. From the perspective of the server, each connected user is an individual instance of the Client object. Given a reference to a particular instance, you'll gain access to various properties and methods. In addition, you can make your own variables that get treated like properties. (As a reminder, you saw the built-in `referrer` property and a few cases with made-up homemade variables, including `username` and `slot`.)

It's important to understand that unlike how the Application object enables you to use either the literal `application` or a reference such as `this`, you must always use a reference when you intend to address an individual client instance. That is, if you ever use `Client` literally, you'll be referring to *the* Client object—not a particular instance. We'll use `Client` later in this section when attaching functions to its `prototype` (thereby adding the function to every instance). To access properties, methods, and homemade variables, however, always use a reference to a particular client (for example, the parameter I keep naming `thisClient` that gets passed to the `onConnect` event).

Although the sky's the limit for what sorts of homemade variables you assign to client instances, do check out the server-side ActionScript dictionary; in it you'll find some really handy methods and properties. In addition to `referrer`, you'll find properties such as `ip` and `agent`, which are both useful. In addition, `getStats()` and `setBandwidthLimit()` are interesting methods.

There's still more you can do with the Client object. When you read about `call()` in the "Messaging" section of this chapter, you'll see how to let client SWFs trigger functions defined inside the main.asc. Even still, the Client object isn't super exciting—it's just a convenient and necessary way help keep things in order.

Accessing Remote Shared Objects from the Server Side

As you learned in Chapter 8, "Foundation Communication Server," RSOs enable you to share efficiently data among multiple connected users. The application can have access to and read and write RSOs as well as receive notices when others change RSOs. On top of this, a server-side script (that is, your main.asc file) has the additional power to lock an RSO when it's about to change a value so that no one else can mess with it. This means that there's no need to check whether a change succeeded (like you do on the client side). Locking also temporarily pauses any notices going out that could otherwise repeatedly trigger everyone's onSync events. Finally, RSOs offer a gateway over which you can send messages to everyone connected to the RSO.

Syntax Differences

To optimize performance, the syntax for reading and writing data stored in an RSO doesn't use the familiar dot syntax. The two equivalent code samples in Listing 9.5 compare CSAS to SSAS by achieving the same basic task.

Listing 9.5   Remote Shared Objects in CSAS Versus SSAS

In CSAS:

```
my_rso=SharedObject.getRemote("some_so", my_nc.uri, true);
my_rso.data.myProp=my_rso.data.myProp+1;
```

In SSAS:

```
myRSO=SharedObject.get("some_so", true);
current=myRSO.getProperty("myProp");
myRSO.setProperty("myProp", current+1);
```

The client-side code should be familiar from Chapter 8. Basically, the some_so RSO contains a variable called myProp. (Remember, variables are accessed as properties within the data property.)

There are a few things to notice as different in the server-side code. First, there's only a get() method (no getRemote(), because everything is remote). Second, you don't have to include the NetConnection uri property. Finally, the big difference is that instead of accessing the values inside the data property (using dot syntax), you must use getProperty() and setProperty(). These both require you to provide a string version of the property name.

For some, setProperty() and getProperty() will bring back memories of Flash 4; for others, it will just appear funky. It's actually slightly more convenient when identifying property names dynamically (as opposed to using bracket references).

Remember that with dot syntax you can access properties dynamically by generating a string placed in brackets. Anyway, the server-side version always uses strings.

In practice, it makes sense to first get your SSAS to grab a reference to an RSO, store that value in an application variable, and then just apply `getProperty()` and `setProperty()` to that reference. That is, you don't need to `get()` the RSO before each use. For instance, this is a typical example from an `onAppStart` event:

```
Application.onAppStart=function(){
  this.myRSO.SharedObject.get("some_so", true)
  if(this.myRSO.getProperty("myArray")==undefined){
    this.myRSO.setProperty("myArray",[]);
  }
}
```

This code just creates an application variable called `myRSO` and makes sure it starts with a fresh array. From this point forward, you can refer to `this.myRSO` or `application.myRSO` and then continue with `setProperty()` or `getProperty()`.

While on the subject of storing an array in a slot of an RSO, take a look now at perhaps the biggest inconvenience of the syntax differences. Suppose you just want to `push()` a value on the end of the array (in your RSO). You can't just add `".push()"` on the end of your `getProperty()`. You have to do a two-step process (drawn out in Listing 9.6).

Listing 9.6 Accessing an Array in an RSO

```
var temp=application.myRSO.getProperty("myArray");
temp.push("a value");
application.myRSO.setProperty("myArray", temp);
```

The idea is to grab the array, `push()` a value into it, and then put it back into the RSO. On the client side, you could do it in one swoop like this:

`myRSO.data.myArray.push("a value")`. It's just that in the case of RSOs on the server side, you must get and then set.

Although the syntax differences for RSOs on the server side are significant, you'll be happy to know these differences are balanced by the fact that they are powerful and have some special features.

Locking

One really cool feature of RSOs on the server side is that you can lock and unlock them. The main sequence is lock it, change it, and then unlock it. On the server, therefore, you can change values in an RSO with utmost confidence that the change will be successful. You may recall from Chapter 8 that whole deal with the info object (received in the onSync callback) that had various values for the code property. You can still use onSync on the server side, but you won't need to check whether info.code=="success" as you must on the client side.

Mainly, locking gives priority to the server-side script. (That is, clients can't jump in and change the RSO while it's locked.) Another nice feature is that when you finally unlock the RSO, all the changes are sent to clients in a single message. Realize that, normally, each client is notified of each change to each property in an RSO as it changes. Lock just says, "Don't let anyone edit this RSO…do these changes…and now that we're done, tell everyone what's happened in a single message." Listing 9.7 provides a simple example.

Listing 9.7   Simple Lock/Unlock Sequence

```
application.myRSO.SharedObject.get("some_so", true);
application.myRSO.lock();
  application.myRSO.setProperty("myProp","a value");
application.myRSO.unlock();
```

I guess the only thing to add is that you definitely need to remember to unlock the RSO.

Sending Messages on RSOs

So far this discussion has focused on how to use RSOs on the server; now, however, it's time to transition to the topic of using RSOs for more than just storing shared data. Namely, you can send messages over an RSO. That is, one connected client (or the server) can issue myRSO.send("someFunction") and everyone connected to myRSO will have the someFunction() triggered. It's very similar to how messages are sent over the LocalConnection object. However, this isn't "local"; it's over the network. You'll see how send() works in the next section. Just remember it's tied to RSOs.

Messaging

As already mentioned a few times, you can send messages between connected users. The term *messaging* might need some explanation. Here I'm talking about triggering functions defined in the other client's files and, optionally, passing values. The two basic ways are SharedObject.send() and NetConnection.call(). For send(), you use an RSO instance and trigger functions in all connected clients' files. For a single client to trigger a function in the main.asc file and get a result returned, you must use call() on a NetConnection instance. Although it was impossible for me to get this far in the book without mentioning send() and call(), now it's time to go through both in detail.

Using *SharedObject.send()*

You can use RSOs as a channel over which you trigger methods in all connected clients. Like any function or method, there's two parts: the definition and the trigger. For the definition, you just define a callback on an RSO instance. Then, to trigger it, you use the send() method on an instance connected to the same RSO. Listing 9.8 shows a typical example. You just need a my_btn button instance, a message_txt input text field, an other_txt dynamic text field, and an empty application folder called messaging.

Listing 9.8   Using *SharedObject.send()*

```
1   my_nc=new NetConnection();
2   my_nc.connect("rtmp:/messaging/r1")
3
4   my_rso=SharedObject.getRemote("someRSO",my_nc.uri,false);
5
6   my_rso.onMyFunction=function(param){
7      other_txt.text="someone said " + param;
8   }
9
10  my_rso.connect(my_nc);
11
12  my_btn.onPress=function(){
13     my_rso.send("onMyFunction", message_txt.text);
14  }
```

Nothing much new here except in line 6 you see the `onMyFunction` callback defined (on the `my_rso` instance). In addition, it's set up to accept a parameter. Then, in line 13 you see how to trigger that function using `send()` (again, on the `my_rso` instance). When you test this by yourself, you just see the text move from `message_txt` to `other_txt`.

Note that `onMyFunction` can be renamed. And, you can define more callbacks.

Listing 9.8 is more interesting when two people can connect and send messages to each other. However, the fact that it works by itself is a bit interesting—just because now you know `send()` looks for a function attached to the RSO instance in *any* movie connected to that RSO (including the movie that triggered it). Suppose you want to send messages to everyone else except yourself? (Ignore, for the moment, that you could probably pull this off by changing variables inside an RSO.) One solution is to send an additional parameter identifying `me` and only trigger code in the function when that parameter doesn't match `me`. However, you'll need a surefire way to uniquely identify each user. That is, if you just use the user's login name or something, there might be two `Phillips`.

A different tack involves making two or more SWFs—say, `student.swf` and `teacher.swf` or `admin.swf` and `regular.swf`. Then, the contents of one movie's `onMyFunction` callback could contain different scripts. Personally, I try to have as few different source FLAs as possible to maintain—so, even if I want several different roles, I try to squeeze them all into a single FLA that dynamically changes depending on the user. (Say when the teacher logs into the SWF buttons that are normally hidden get revealed.) It's not so bad if you just have two FLAs to maintain. If you want more uniquely identified users, the server-side script can certainly handle giving each client a unique number (see Listing 9.4). However, you'll have to wait until `call()` is discussed to see how the server can pass variables back to the client. Doing it all on the client side would definitely be a hassle. You could have a variable inside the RSO that each user increments when the user connects and that is then used to identify each user. To ensure no two users have the same value, you have to check the success every time a user changes it. Go ahead and work this out if you want. The downloadable files for this chapter contain a solution. Just remember the main point here: A little bit of server-side code will make it much easier.

Before looking at `call()`, it's worth looking at an example of server-side code using `send()`. In fact, it *is* a way for variables to get passed (as parameters) from the server to all users connected to an RSO. Listing 9.9 shows how the server can notify everyone when someone new arrives (without using a data slot in the RSO). This example is like Listing 9.4.

Listing 9.9 Using *SharedObject.send()* on the Server Side

Put this code in your main.asc file in the track_user application folder.

```
1a   application.onAppStart=function(){
2a     application.message_so=SharedObject.get("mso",false);
3a   }
4a   application.onConnect = function(thisClient, username) {
5a     application.message_so.send("onNewUser", username)
6a     thisClient.username=username;
7a     this.acceptConnection(thisClient);
8a   }
9a   application.onDisconnect = function(thisClient) {
10a    application.message_so.send("onLeaveUser", thisClient.username);
11a    return true;
12a  }
```

In the FLA, you need a username_txt input text field instance, a connect_btn button instance, plus a dynamic text field named message_txt, plus this code:

```
1    connect_btn.onPress=function(){
2      my_nc= new NetConnection();
3      my_nc.onStatus=function(info){
4        if(info.code=="NetConnection.Connect.Success"){
5          initSO();
6        }
7      }
8      my_nc.connect("rtmp:/track_user/r1", username_txt.text);
9    }
10
11   function initSO(){
12     message_so=SharedObject.getRemote("mso", my_nc.uri, false);
13
14     message_so.onNewUser=function(who){
15       message_txt.text = "New user: "+who;
16     }
17     message_so.onLeaveUser=function(who){
18       message_txt.text = who + " has left";
19     }
20     message_so.connect(my_nc);
21   }
```

To compare the client side to the server side, first notice that the same name is used to identify the RSO in line 2a and line 12. That is, both client and server share the RSO named mso. Notice that it's unimportant that the server-side code uses application.message_so and the client side uses message_so. (Those are just the name for the local instance.)

Anyway, the main idea here is that lines 5a and 10a of the server-side code use send() to trigger a function defined in the client SWFs. It also passes a parameter. Then in lines 15 and 18 the client SWF displays the received value in a meaningful string onscreen.

> RSO's send() is often more convenient than combining data properties with the onSync event. However, onSync can be more reliably lightweight. Because FCS handles all requests to send messages or change variables, you don't really know exactly when users will receive triggers sent (using send()). At least with data properties (variables in the RSO) you have the info.code property, which enables you to check success. Deciding to use variables or send() is partially a matter of personal preference. I think it really comes down to the nature of your objective. If you want to ensure everyone is in sync with variables, you might as well just share those variables. For an easy way to send out notices (that aren't extremely time critical), however, use send().

Using *NetConnection.call()*

The call() method is particularly useful because it enables you to trigger functions that return values. That is, just triggering a function is useful; sending parameters is still more useful; but, sometimes, you'll want to write a function that returns a result to whoever called it. For example, you may want a function to calculate a value and send the answer back. In Chapter 8, we actually used call() to ascertain the length of a stream. Because only SSAS can find a stream's length, however, the client movie called a function on the server that returned the answer.

Not only does call() have the option for returning values, it's also the only way you can truly trigger scripts in an individual client or just the main.asc file. That is, when you issue send() on an RSO, every client or main.asc currently connected to that object receives the event. Actually, if a particular SWF has no callback defined for the event name in the send(), it is ignored. But with call(), it's possible to target just a single client or the main.asc.

Listing 9.10 shows first how a single client can `call()` a function in the server script, and then how the server calls a particular client's script. In the first example, the client passes a parameter but does not expect any results returned.

Listing 9.10 Using *call()* from the Client

Anywhere in the main.asc file, include this code:

```
Client.prototype.myFunction=function(param){
  trace("client says " + param);
}
```

Then, from inside any SWF, you can issue this script:

```
my_nc.call("myFunction", null, "hello");
```

I suppose it's weird that in the SWF you issue `call()` on your NetConnection instance and that triggers a function in the prototype of the Client object at the server. In any case, notice that the first parameter in `call()` is the function name and the second parameter is for an optional object that you prepare to handle a result (discussed next). That parameter is `null` for now because nothing is being returned from the server-side function. Interestingly, to send parameters, you start with the third parameter (after `null` in the preceding example), and that value will arrive at the server function inside the parentheses.

In Listing 9.11 you can see that the server script can trigger a function defined on the client side in nearly the opposite way: This time, from the server, this example `call()`s on a client instance to trigger a callback defined on the NetConnection instance inside a particular client SWF. It sounds worse than it is.

Listing 9.11 Using *call()* from the Server

You can set up the client-side code first:

```
my_nc= new NetConnection();
  my_nc.onStatus=function(info){
    if(info.code=="NetConnection.Connect.Success"){
      //proceed
    }
  }
  my_nc.onMyFunction=function(param){
    trace("server said: " + param);
  }
my_nc.connect("rtmp:/test_app/r1");
```

Chapter 9 Advanced Communication Server   295

Now you can trigger onMyFunction from the server-side code:

```
application.onConnect=function(thisClient){
  application.acceptConnection(thisClient);
  thisClient.call("onMyFunction",null, "I'm a server");
}
```

Notice that the onStatus callback has been left in the client-side code—not only for good practice, but because it shows how custom callbacks are nearly identical.

The trick with going from the server to the client is to confirm that you have a reference to the client instance. In addition, notice that I don't issue call() until after I've issued the acceptConnection() on the client.

Now that you know the basic structure for call(), it's time to cover the way it returns values. The definition for the function will look familiar: just the keyword return followed by the value you want to send back. When such a function gets called, however, you must first set up a "result object" with an onResult callback defined. That's because such function calls traveling over the network run asynchronously. (Because they may take a second, you don't want Flash to freeze while it waits for the result.) The following practical listing should look familiar from Chapter 8 (where it was also used). However, this time it should make more sense.

Listing 9.12 Using *call()* to Find a Stream's Length

Here's the function on the server side:

```
Client.prototype.getLength =function (filename){
  return Stream.length("mp3:"+filename);
}
```

Here's the client-side part that first sets up the result object and then triggers the call():

```
resultObj = new Object();
resultObj.onResult = function(result) {
  totalLength = result;
};
my_nc.call("getLength", resultObj, "rock");
```

continues

Listing 9.12 Using *call()* to Find a Stream's Length (Continued)

First, `resultObj` is just a homemade variable—you can name it anything. However, you must use `onResult` for your callback—that's what gets triggered when a function called with `call()` returns a value.

As a quick reminder how this works (and, coincidentally, a quick preview of the "Server-Side Stream Object" section coming up), only server-side code can use the `Stream.length()` method. If you translate the last line of the preceding example, it would read, "Trigger the `getLength` function on the server; use the generic object `resultObj` that I predefined to handle the result; and pass the string `"rock"` (because the server-side function needs a stream filename from which to get the length)."

Optimizing

I'm sorry to say that this section won't tell you "everything else" you need to know to make successful FCS apps. There's so much more, and you'll only really begin finessing your apps after you build a few. Most of my suggestions come from the experience of doing things the hard way first. That's not a bad way to learn because you sometimes appreciate things more. This section covers just a few tips and tricks to both enhance your app's performance and reduce the work necessary to build it.

It's Still ActionScript

This may go without saying, but remember that CSAS and SSAS are both ActionScript. Nearly everything from traditional ActionScript is supported in FCS. For example, you can use the Date object, the Math object, and `setInterval()` (just to name a few personal favorites). For example, the auction site I built needed a countdown clock that would keep ticking away regardless of who was connected. Obviously, I had to keep the timer code in the server script. It was pretty simple to define an interval with `setInterval()`.

Note that no ActionScript 2 is supported in FCS.

Defining Functions Inside the Prototype

Because it's possible to have thousands of people connected at one time, it's good to know at least a little bit about extending the prototype of an object—in this case, the Client and the Application objects. When we set up a function on the server side that a particular client could `call()`, we defined that function inside the prototype of the Client object. Obviously, we didn't want to define it for just one client instance. In addition—and, probably not as obvious—we didn't want to define it for each client individually. That is, putting a function definition inside the prototype of an object type makes it available to each client that gets instantiated. However, it doesn't get duplicated with each instance. If you define a function on each individual instance, it does get duplicated and begins to eat up memory unnecessarily. Listings 9.13 and 9.14 shows the difference.

Listing 9.13   Sloppily Defining Functions on Each Instance

```
application.onConnect(thisClient){
  application.acceptConnection(thisClient);
  thisClient.onMyBadFunction=function(){
    //some code
  }
}
```

In this example, every new client instance (new user connecting) is given its own identical copy of the `onMyBadFunction`. Each copy takes up additional memory. *Don't* do it this way!

Listing 9.14   Efficiently Defining a Function in the Prototype

```
1    application.onConnect(thisClient){
2      application.acceptConnectiont(thisClient);
3    }
4    Client.prototype.onMyFunction=function(){
5      //some code
6    }
```

I didn't need the `onConnect` part but included it to show that lines 4 through 6 can stand on their own. The idea here is that `onMyFunction` is now part of the prototype for the Client object—that's big "C" Client meaning the object, not an individual instance. When defining functions this way, you store them in the prototype, meaning the template that is used when any new instance is created. Although in the end, this code works the same as the previous listing, this way is much better because the code resides in just one place.

You can use this same basic technique to extend the Application object. It's a bit touchy because you have to use an uppercase A. And, actually, it's not like it's any better than writing a traditional function in the main.asc file. In any event, Listing 9.15 provides a practical example of a formatted date. Because I might need to call this function from several places in my app, I want it in a function.

Listing 9.15 Extending the Application Object

```
Application.prototype.getTD=function(){
  var now= new Date();
  theString=1+now.getMonth()
  +"/"+now.getDate()
  +"/"+now.getFullYear()
  +" "+now.getHours()
  +":"+ (now.getMinutes()<10 ? "0"+now.getMinutes() : now.getMinutes())
  +":"+ (now.getSeconds()<10 ? "0"+now.getSeconds() : now.getSeconds());
  return (theString);
}
//then call it using: answer=application.getTD();
```

This code is quite useful. It's actually used it in an upcoming example. Basically, it's a function stuffed inside the prototype for the Application (with a big A) object. Remember to include "application." every time you call it.

Using Messaging Sparingly

I think the concept of messaging is much easier to grasp than RSOs. However, RSOs tend to be more efficient because they only broadcast variables that change. (Naturally, you also should structure your RSOs to have lots of small properties instead of fewer large properties—as Chapter 8 explained.) The problem with messaging is that you're really never sure when a message is received. Actually, with call() you should use the optional result object to—if nothing else—confirm a message was received. With RSOs, each user may not be 100 percent in sync every second, but there will always be just one value for any variable in the RSO.

I suppose this section might be better titled "think about it" because my main point is that after you get your rough design planned or an initial prototype built, it's a good idea to take a pause to analyze things. Decide whether you're sending messages unnecessarily. Make sure your RSOs are parsing through the data received in their onSync events so that just the parts that changed update. In traditional Flash apps, less than ideal ActionScript code will have little or no impact on performance. (Usually the impact involves graphic-related issues such as moving a semitransparent clip over text, for example.) However, any time you send data over the Internet, be extra careful that the data is small and that you're not sending it any more frequently than you have to. In addition, there's an extra burden to do error checks that follow-up when failures occur. It's a pretty safe bet that if a client remains connected, the client will get notified when an RSO changes.

Server-Side Stream Object

There's a special version of the Stream object just for the server side. As you recall, on the client side a separate stream is created for each audio/video signal traveling in a particular direction to or from a particular client. So, basically, you may have a ton of client-side streams. The server-side Stream object is different. It's not like your main.asc file wants to watch a stream, nor can it publish the source of its camera signal. However, the server-side Stream can perform the following interesting tasks:

- Begin publishing a prerecorded stream at a specific time so that users who tap in will hear or see it already in progress
- Grab an existing stream (being published by a user) and record part or all of it independent of what the client script is doing
- Record a stream with no sound or video, but just for embedding events as a form of logging or archiving

To understand the server-side Stream object, you almost have to forget how things work on the client side; not quite, but the syntax is a little different—as you'll see in the following examples.

Publishing Existing Streams from the Server Side

For most situations, you'll probably want to give each client the capability to decide when to begin streaming a prerecorded video or MP3. Suppose, however, that you want something such as a radio DJ to select songs to play and let people tune in and out as they want? Although the DJ could connect and begin publishing a live stream, he can't really get each client to begin streaming the same song at the same time. I suppose you could send a message over an RSO and tell everyone to commence streaming—but it's not the same. Listing 9.16 creates a server-side Stream and immediately begins publishing a recorded stream. This is sort of like an individual client publishing a live stream; because once it starts, anyone can receive it by just issuing a `play()` command.

Listing 9.16 Publishing a Server-Side Stream

```
1a   application.onAppStart=function(){
2a     application.s=Stream.get("theStream");
3a     application.s.play("mp3:some_song");
4a   }
```

Then, on the client side, issue the following:

```
1   begin_btn.onPress=function(){
2     my_ns= new NetStream(my_nc);
3     my_ns.play("theStream");
4   }
```

You can think of line 2a as the server-side equivalent to `new NetStream()`. It creates a variable called s (kept inside the Application object, because I figure you might want to access it later—for instance, to stop it). This variable (s) contains a server-side instance of the NetStream object. When you issue `get()`, you specify a name that gets used by those who want to play the stream. (That name is also the name of the saved FLV if you decide to record it.) Line 3a just starts playing the some_song.mp3 even though no one may be listening. (The actual MP3 needs to reside in the appropriate Streams folder—details of which you learned in Chapter 8.) The client-side code pretty much looks as if you're playing a stream called `"theStream"` that you expect someone else is currently publishing. In this case, that "someone else" is the server side. Of course, it won't begin until the `begin_btn` is pressed. And then when it does begin, you'll hear the song already in progress. (So, maybe pick a longish song for this example.)

Most of the same options found on the client side are available for playing a server-side stream. For example, that `play()` command could include the options for making play lists (covered in Chapter 8). You could set up hours of music to stream for whenever anyone happens to log in. It turns out that if you're really planning on creating an Internet radio station, FCS is probably not the ideal tool. What's cool, however, is that you've got the Flash interface, so you can customize the interface and really do whatever you want.

Republishing Portions of Client Streams

You just saw how a server-side stream can play a prerecorded stream. Alternatively, when you identify what stream to play, you can specify a live stream being published by any user. Of course, any client can also identify that same stream and start playing it. For example, I could create an admin application that enables me to type in any stream name that I see in the App Inspector and start listening in (see Figure 9.3).

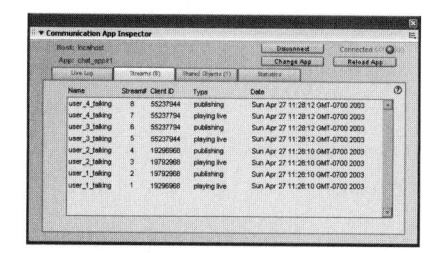

Figure 9.3 *You can tap into any active stream when you know its name.*

You don't need the server-side stream for this—just the stream name. Anyway, it might be neat to automate the process. Suppose, for instance, there are three users, each publishing a stream from their microphone. Listing 9.17 sets up a special server-side stream that, one by one, rebroadcasts (that is, publishes) each user's steam—sort of like a security camera application, but this one cycles through each audio stream. Perhaps this might even be useful for monitoring a large chat application. Keep in mind that you'll hear only one user's microphone at a time (not two people talking to each other). You would just need an extra server-side stream to listen to two people simultaneously.

Listing 9.17 Cycling Though Three Published Streams

```
1    application.onAppStart=function(){
2      application.s=Stream.get("theStream");
3      application.n=0;
4      myInt=setInterval(application.switchNow,5000);
5    }
6
7    Application.prototype.switchNow=function(){
8      application.n++
9      if(application.n>3){
10       application.n=1;
11     }
```

continues

Listing 9.17 Cycling Though Three Published Streams (Continued)

```
12      application.s.play(false);
13      application.s.play("user_"+application.n);
14      trace("now republishing user "+ application.n);
15  }
```

In addition to exploiting the `setInterval()` feature, notice that all I do in lines 12 and 13 is stop playing the current stream and then start playing a new one (based on the `application.n` variable I made up). Notice, too, that I only needed to `get()` the stream once in line 2 (effectively just to give it a name).

This code assumes that someone is publishing each of the following stream names: `user_1`, `user_2`, `user_3`. Then, someone is playing `theStream` stream to hear them cycle through. When I tested it, I created two NetStream instances in my FLA and attached my microphone to one instance and published `"user_1"`. Then I used the other NetStream instance to play `"theStream"`. If I heard myself after seeing that `trace()` in line 14, I knew it was working. Here's the portion of my client-side code that I put inside the `my_nc.onStatus` callback:

```
in_ns = new NetStream(my_nc);
in_ns.play("theStream");
out_ns = new NetStream(my_nc);
my_mic = Microphone.get();
out_ns.attachAudio(my_mic);
out_ns.publish("user_1");
```

While republishing different users' streams may seem sinister, I'm sure you can think of some practical examples. The point is that you can use a single server-side stream to selectively "play" different streams. If anyone plays the server-side stream, that user will hear whatever the server-side stream is playing at the time.

Server-side streams are definitely an interesting concept that allow for some pretty neat applications. For example, you'll see next that you also can specify that a server-side stream gets recorded. I've used that feature to archive online meetings. Because a stream can't mix multiple streams together, in my app I made the stream switch around like the preceding example (although not randomly). This way the archive included only one person at a time, but it switched to the person presenting at the time.

By the way, everything in the preceding two listings also applies to video streams (live or recorded). I say that because the next section focuses on using server-side streams to archive or log events. In such cases, you may not want to include the video or audio portion.

Using Server-Side Streams to Log Events

You're about to see how you can use recorded streams for something other than audio and video: specifically, for logging. For example, you may want to keep an archive of all text sent through a chat application. Although you could probably just store everything inside an RSO, this isn't ideal because the archive code would have to work alongside your existing RSO code. In addition, RSO files are associated to application instances where you can save log streams with unique names—perhaps including the date. What's really wild about streams saved full of events is that you can output all contained events in real time or in one burst. Consider the idea of saving a chat meeting: You could play it back in real time or just output a transcript of everything.

You also can record server-side streams that do contain audio and/or video, but you'll probably want to keep the task of logging separate from saved media streams.

The following listing shows a simple example of a saved server-side stream that can store a record of events triggered while the app runs. For this example, suppose that you have a simple chat application already complete, but you want to keep a record of everything that was said and when it was said. The existing app can have a `message_txt` input text field instance and a button instance, `send_btn`, and this code:

```
my_nc = new NetConnection();
my_nc.onStatus = function(info) {
  if (info.code == "NetConnection.Connect.Success") {
    my_so = SharedObject.getRemote("chat_so", my_nc.uri, false);
    my_so.onSync = function() {
      message_txt.text = my_so.data.archive;
    };
    my_so.connect(my_nc);
  }
};
my_nc.connect("rtmp:/chat_app/r1");
send_btn.onPress = function() {
  my_so.data.archive = message_txt.text;
};
```

This code works as is. Basically each user can change the text in their input text field, press send, and everyone else will see what they entered. The shared object file ("chat_so") contains a single property called archive—and that's the value each user changes.

To extend this super-simple chat application so that archives can be recorded, we're going to write some server-side code (to record a stream) and then some client-side code (to initiate the recording and to play it back later). That is, we need a client interface to both start the stream and to extract data from it later. At first I thought we would automatically start recording when the app started, but then we would have to work out a strategy to uniquely name the streams—and we would need some way to stop the recording. That solution might be okay down the road, but during testing it was just way too hard to constantly restart the app and so on. Figure 9.4 shows what the prototype interface might look like.

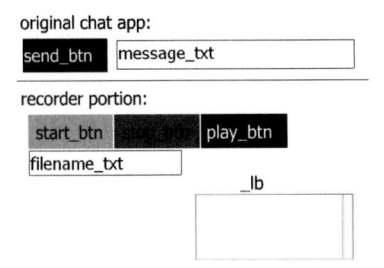

Figure 9.4 *The buttons, text field, and list on the bottom portion enables you to record all text sent through the chat interface (on top).*

In the extended chat app, I have buttons to start and stop the recording (start_btn and stop_btn), and a button to extract the events (really, play the stream) called play_btn. Finally, I've added an instance filename_txt input text field (to specify the stream name) and a List component instance called _lb (to view the data extracted, as shown in Figure 9.5).

The following solution in Listing 9.18 uses the send() feature first explained in Chapter 8—but this time on the server side.

Listing 9.18 Logging Events in a Stream

Here are the contents of the main.asc file:

```
1a   Client.prototype.onStartRecording=function(filename){
2a      application.s=Stream.get(filename);
3a      application.s.record();
4a      application.s.send("newText", "start time", application.getTD());
5a      application.the_so=SharedObject.get("chat_so",false);
6a      application.the_so.onSync=function(list){
7a         for (var i = 0; i < list.length; i++) {
8a            if(list[i].code=="change" && list[i].name=="archive") {
9a               application.s.send("newText",
10a                                 application.the_so.getProperty("archive"),
11a                                 application.getTD());
12a         }
13a      }
14a   }
15a  }
16a  Client.prototype.onStopRecording=function(){
17a     application.s.record(false);
18a     application.the_so.onSync=null;
19a  }
```

For the client-side code, you can add this to the existing chat code (or, at least, make sure you also have the connection code):

```
1   start_btn.onPress = function() {
2      my_nc.call("onStartRecording", null, filename_txt.text);
3   };
4   stop_btn.onPress = function() {
5      my_nc.call("onStopRecording", null);
6   };
7   play_btn.onPress = function() {
8      in_ns = new NetStream(my_nc);
9      _lb.removeAll();
10     in_ns.newText = function(message, timeStamp) {
11        _lb.addItem(timeStamp+"--> "+message);
12     };
13     in_ns.play(filename_txt.text);
14  };
```

continues

Listing 9.18 Logging Events in a Stream (Continued)

The server-side code has two functions: one to start and one to stop the recording. Line 2a creates a new stream with the filename passed in, and then line 3a begins recording. Incidentally, if you also added something such as `application.s.play("some_stream")`, it would include the media from that stream recorded in the archive—but we're just going to include events. Line 4a goes ahead and sends the first event into the stream. Basically, `newText` is the event name, `"start time"` is just text for the first parameter (that will get extracted later), and then we use `getTD()` (from earlier) to create a nicely formatted date string (and this is just another parameter to extract). Finally, we connect to the RSO the clients are using (`"chat_so"`). The `onSync` callback executes only lines 9a through 11a provided the `archive` property has changed. (Who knows, there might be other properties.) Then, you see that lines 9a through 11a are similar to 4a, but after the event name, we stuff the new value of `archive` (line 10a). Finally, the `onStopRecording` code closes the stream file and clears the `onSync` that we were monitoring.

For the client side, realize there are two features: start/stop a recording and then playing one back. Line 2 shows how to trigger the `onStartRecording` method on the server (via `call()`), and line 5 shows how `onStopRecording` is triggered. The idea is that you first type in a name for the recorded stream, and then click the `start_btn`. Do some chatting (typing into the `message_txt` field and pressing the `send_btn`) and finally press the `stop_btn` when you're done. Then, to extract the data from a stream, make sure to fill in the `filename_txt` with the stream you want to "play." The `play_btn` creates a stream (line 8), clears the list (line 9), and sets up the `newText` callback (lines 10 through 12). (Remember `newText` was the first parameter in the server-side `send()`—line 4a.)

Figure 9.5 shows what a typical log might produce when "played."

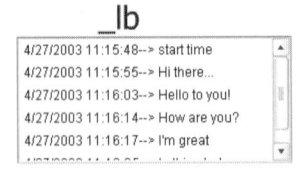

```
                    _lb
4/27/2003 11:15:48--> start time
4/27/2003 11:15:55--> Hi there...
4/27/2003 11:16:03--> Hello to you!
4/27/2003 11:16:14--> How are you?
4/27/2003 11:16:17--> I'm great
```

Figure 9.5 *The list will display the entire log recorded in a data-only FLV file.*

Note that when you play a stream containing events that were recorded on the server side, the events all trigger at once when the stream plays back. This is useful for logging. In this example, for instance, you'll see the whole chat history immediately after you click play. If you want the events to retrigger at playback at the same time they were recorded, however, you need to use client-side code like you saw in Chapter 8.

The technique of using streams for logging events is actually pretty easy considering the power. What's really nice is that you can build a rich Flash interface to view the recorded data (and it's *really* easy). Alternatively, you could connect to an application server and write log data to a database; but then to view that data, you either use the database's viewing tools or have to write another Flash app to extract the data. Events go into streams (via send()) almost as easily as they come out (via callbacks).

Integrating the Communication Components

The communication components enable you to snap together a pretty sophisticated application with nearly no scripting. Although I might normally pooh pooh the bogus claim of "programming without programming," some components are hard to resist. Although I would love to document every detail of the communication components, such an exhaustive discussion is beyond the scope of this chapter. Instead, I'm including just enough information in case you plan to use them alongside your own code.

Generally, you can do all your own homemade scripting and throw in a few components and nothing will conflict. The one minor exception is how the communication components effectively overwrite key methods in your main.asc file. First, if you've succeeded in using any of the communication components, you've learned that you must create a main.asc file with—at least—the following code:

```
load("components.asc");
```

This code is effectively the same as the #include directive found in CSAS—it loads the modular support scripts needed for the communication components. (Alternatively, you can selectively load individual components' ASC files.)

Although you must load the component framework, you're also welcome to write your own code. However, there's one minor workaround you may need to use. Specifically, if you use `application.onConnect`, you can't put any code following `application.acceptConnection()`. Similarly, you can't put any code following `application.rejectConnection()`. Recall, just for one example, that you can't invoke `call()` on the client until the client is accepted—so it's definitely useful to have code that follows the acceptance/rejection. The simple solution is to move all "post-acceptance" code into another callback called `application.onConnectAccept` (and all "post-reject" code into `application.onConnectReject`). These additional callbacks shadow the connection process and will, in fact, get called at the appropriate time. You'll want the parameter in both such callbacks to mirror the `onConnect`. Listing 9.19 should make this clear.

Listing 9.19 Playing Nice with Component Framework

```
1   load("components.asc");
2
3   application.onConnect = function(thisClient, arg1, arg2){
4     if(arg1=="test" && arg2=="condition"){
5       this.acceptConnection(thisClient);
6       //put any post-accept code down in onConnectAccept
7     }else{
8       this.rejectConnection(thisClient);
9       //put any post-reject code down in onConnectReject
10    }
11  }
12
13  application.onConnectAccept = function(thisClient, arg1, arg2){
14    //post-accept code goes here
15  }
16
17  application.onConnectReject = function(thisClient, arg1, arg2){
18    //post-reject code goes here
19  }
```

Basically, if you put any code in line 6—thinking the client was accepted by then—it won't work. Such code that you may intend to go on line 6 must not appear until line 13 (inside `onConnectAccept`). The same goes for code you plan to put in line 9—it needs to go down in the `onConnectReject` callback in line 17.

> **{ Note }**
>
> **Recycling SSAS** By the way, you can build a library of reusable ASC files, save them in the common scriptlib folder, and then include them in any app using `load()`. You'll learn more about building a code library in Chapter 12, "Using Components."

The communication components really are useful. I think the SimpleConnect and SetBandwidth are my favorites. They're well documented, and you can find several articles on them at www.macromedia.com. Incidentally, for a detailed explanation of the general framework (including the specific workaround previously discussed), check out www.macromedia.com/devnet/mx/flashcom/articles/framework.html.

Summary

With the skills you now have using server-side ActionScript, you probably understand that the division between client- and server-side script is really somewhat artificial. Like I keep saying, "A little bit of SSAS goes a long way to reducing your CSAS."

The general skills you picked up in this chapter include the following:

- How to trap key events such as `onAppStart` and `onConnect` in the main.asc file
- Basic approaches to control access to your app
- How to extend the SSAS application and Client classes so that you can write functions that automatically become available to each instance
- The differences in the way SSAS accesses RSOs
- The way to use `send()` and `call()` for messaging (between server and client)
- The details of using the server-side Stream object to both play media and log events
- Starter tips on using the communication components

On top of all these specific techniques, the most valuable thing you can take away from this chapter is a clear understanding of what's possible. With the framework under your belt, you should be able to select the right tool for the job as you gain experience. Obviously, you may want to dig deeper in some areas, but you're definitely ready to build some killer apps.

{ Part III }

Productivity

10 Production Techniques   313
11 Quality Assurance and Debugging   339
12 Using Components   371
13 Building a Code Library   401

{Chapter 10}

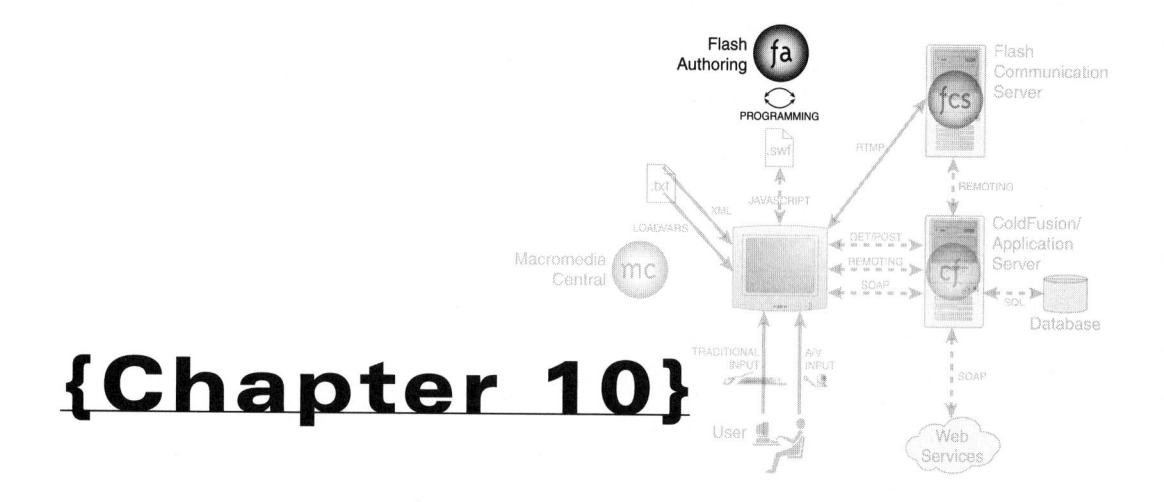

Production Techniques

Now that you've gotten through the bulk of technical details, the next part of this book deals with productivity. Although it may seem late to begin being efficient, think of it more like a time to refine, finesse, and improve what you already know. When you're learning, it's okay to be sloppy. When you embark on a large project, however, it's best to move forward in a well-mannered and deliberate way. This part of the book deals with how to be productive.

This first chapter in the production part of the book covers a variety of general techniques. It's more than just a list of common-sense practices, however. You'll learn specific approaches that I've either learned the hard way or developed during real projects (invariably with the help of others). I've also borrowed traditional "scientific approaches" and applied them to Macromedia Flash MX 2004 application development.

This chapter covers the following topics:

- How to exploit some of the newer productivity features in Flash
- The basics of editing Flash's external configuration files
- How to use shared library items and runtime shared libraries
- Ideas for prototyping and using components
- How to use Flash MX Professionals 2004's Project panel

Exploiting Flash MX 2004 Features

In the last two revisions, Flash has grown up to become a formidable development environment. It really pays to take the time to learn how the newer features can save you time. Every minute you spend learning a new trick will pay back in hours of time saved down the road. The following sections cover some of my favorite newer features and what they mean to your productivity.

Find and Replace

It sounds so innocuous, but the new Find and Replace feature is a super time saver. On the one hand, you should strive to keep your files simple and—if nothing else—modular. A big complex file is difficult to update, troubleshoot, and can also negatively affect performance. On the other hand, there are times when the nature of your project requires lots of discrete elements. For example, you may need to import hundreds of small icon graphics. If you were displaying large images, you would probably want to look at `loadMovie()` to import at runtime—but importing many small items is best handled in one swoop. Find and Replace provides a slew of hidden gems that avoid repetitive tasks.

I haven't personally had too many occasions to use Flash 2004 in actual projects, but I have enough experience in older versions to see how Find and Replace *would* have helped me.

Obviously, you'll have your own occasions to use Find and Replace. In any event, be sure to check it out. Incidentally, to search your scripts, you need to use the Find and Replace option in the Actions panel. More about the Actions panel next!

Actions Panel Tricks

Several features built in to the Actions panel are worth learning. (By the way, most of the following features are also available if you use Flash MX Professional 2004 as a text editor to edit plain AS script files.) It's probably impossible to miss some of these features, but I think it makes sense to touch on a few things that, if you're not, you should be using.

Toolbox

First, realize that although the toolbox on the left side of the Actions panel is useful to hunt down or just explore for elements in the ActionScript language, it's not exhaustive. Interestingly, you can supplement the content that appears in the toolbox by creating and placing XML files in Flash's Configuration folder. I'm not going to document the format, but it's not a huge task to duplicate one of the XML files you find under ActionsPanel/CustomActions and then tinker on your own... trying edits and viewing the results. My main point is the toolbox is extensible.

{ Note }

Finding Your Local Configuration and Application-Level Configuration Files The easiest way to find your configuration files is by looking for the folder named en, adjacent to your installed version of Flash (en standing for English—look for es if you're Spanish, for example). There are two folders: `First Run` and `Configuration`. Everything in the `First Run` folder gets copied into your *local* Configuration folder every time Flash launches. The idea is that if someone else logs on to your machine and runs Flash, the First Run folder gets copied to that user's local Configuration folder. This way it's possible to have personalized settings for each user. Just realize that if you make a change to the First Run folder, you must quit and restart Flash to see the changes. In addition to First Run, you'll find a folder adjacent to Flash called `Configuration`. This is the application-level Configuration folder with items that don't vary from user to user. After you've run Flash MX 2004 at least once you'll find your local Configuration folder (called `Configuration` although it's a copy of `First Run`) in the following paths:

Windows XP/2000:

`C:\Documents and Settings\Phillip\Local Settings\Application Data\Macromedia\Flash MX 2004\en\Configuration`

Replace `Phillip` with your login name. Also, if you can't find the preceding folder, you may need to select the following option from Windows Explorer: Tools, Folder Options, Show Hidden Files and Folder.

Mac OSX:

`Users:phillip:Library:Application Support:Macromedia:Flash 2004:en:Configuration`

Again, replace `Phillip` with your login name.

Code Hints

No doubt you know this one. For example, type **test_btn.** and the instant you type the period, a code-completion tip for Button methods appears (see Figure 10.1). You may also know that like the Actions toolbox, you can customize these code hint suffixes via the AsCodeHints.xml configuration file. What you may not know is that new for Flash MX 2004, you can define your own code-completion triggers inline with your ActionScript.

```
test_btn.
```
```
_xmouse
_xscale
_y
_ymouse
_yscale
enabled
getDepth
onDragOut
```

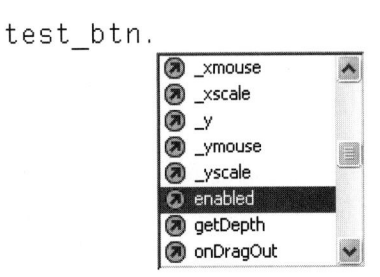

Figure 10.1 *Several objects have designated suffixes, such as _btn for buttons.*

The new way to get code hints builds off the strict data type casting feature in Flash MX 2004 (discussed in Chapter 4, "Working with Complex Data").

When you cast a variable name as a particular data type, the code completion for that data type appears for that name. It's really easy: just start by typing:

`var myVariable:`

As soon as you type the colon casting identifier, you'll see a pop-up list of all the built-in data types—including classes for the components. Pick a data type and then continue on your way (either with a new line or to fill the variable with its default value). Then, anywhere later in that script, you'll get the code-completion hints anytime you use that variable name. Figure 10.2 shows a simple case where I first cast myB as a Button to get all the code hints. In some cases—such as when casting component instances—you'll need to include the path to the class file. For example, to cast myCB as a ComboBox, use `var myCB:mx.controls.ComboBox`. That's because the ComboBox class is in the folder Classes/mx/controls.

Even if you don't fully exploit strong data type casting, it's hard not to take advantage of this gem.

```
var myB:Button;
myB.
```

[code completion dropdown showing: _xmouse, _xscale, _y, _ymouse, _yscale, enabled, getDepth, onDragOut]

Figure 10.2 *After casting your variable as a particular type, the appropriate code-completion hints appear.*

Code Navigator

On the left side of the Actions panel, underneath the "toolbox" of ActionScript references, you'll find a collapsible pane called the Code Navigator. Those familiar with Flash MX can think of this as a Movie Explorer but for code only. The Code Navigator gives you direct access to all the scripts in your movie. Although it's really best to keep your code as centralized as possible, I still find occasions—especially while prototyping—when putting code in separate frames is convenient. For example, Figure 10.3 shows how the Code Navigator enables me to jump around to different keyframes in my application.

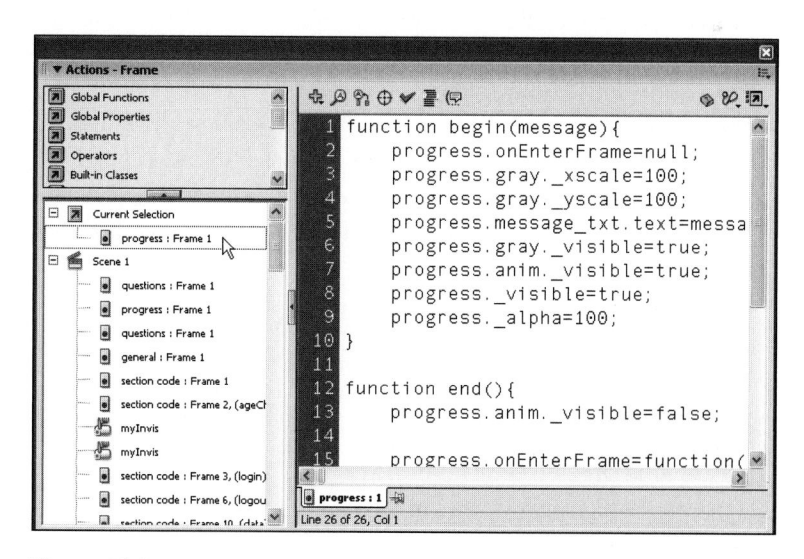

Figure 10.3 *The Code Navigator pane (lower left) provides access to all your application's scripts.*

Single-clicking a script jumps you to that script, whereas double-clicking in addition "pins" the script. Pinned scripts appear as additional tabs to the right of the script current selection (see the bottom of Figure 10.3). Incidentally, you can pin a script manually when you know you'll be returning to a particular script.

Code Cleanup

It's not that programmers are neat nicks. If anything, the reason why we keep code clean is to make it easier to troubleshoot. Do yourself a favor and strive to write clean code even if it seems to slow you down. The Auto Format button in the Actions panel will help by inserting tabs appropriately when your syntax is complete. I usually start by writing code that, although containing no script errors, is somewhat meaningless—but formatted properly. For example, I'll type out the `if` statement as so:

```
if(condition){
//do stuff
}
```

Then, I press the Auto Format button. The word *condition* is legitimate syntax, but will be replaced with my actual condition. The thing is, I don't have to complete that part just to get the basic skeleton formatted right.

Again, you have to have proper syntax before auto format will work. I recently learned a neat trick that will help you balance things such as parentheses, brackets, and curly braces. While editing a script, if you do a Ctrl+' (that's Ctrl and the apostrophe), the entire currently enclosed code block gets selected. Not only does it help identify where you are in your script, but you also can use this to quickly and accurately select a large block of code (for example, the entire `else` part of a huge `if` statement). Check it out; I can't believe I went so long without knowing this one.

There are probably other hidden or underused features for scripting. Just remember taking the time to learn these tricks pays back many times over.

Commands

Flash MX 2004 introduced scripted control of the Flash authoring tool. This means nearly anything you can do with the mouse, keyboard, and a human can be re-created in code. The code is written in JavaScript Flash (JSFL) and only runs at authortime on a machine that has Flash installed. In fact you can set it to run unattended. Normally, you just select and run such scripts from Flash's Commands menu.

Although this feature will unlikely remove the need for humans altogether, it will be quite handy once people write a few nice utility Commands. Initially, your copy of Flash won't have any Commands. You can follow the menu Commands, Get More Commands to browse for some built by others. But they're very easy to create yourself. Chapter 13, "Building a Code Library," walks you through how to create a Command that changes the offstage color. (Basically, the Command draws a shape just in that area.) In fact, making a Command is as simple as selecting a few lines in the History panel and pressing the Save As Command button. For now, just realize that Commands can eliminate mundane, repetitive, or meticulous tasks.

Commands may also run from a custom panel. Such Window SWFs will show up in your Window menu, provided that a SWF is installed inside the WindowSWF configuration folder (not unlike the CustomActions folder discussed earlier). Actually, any movie can serve as a WindowSWF, but only ones that perform some useful task make any sense.

It turns out it's not absolutely necessary that you learn how the various configuration files work and where they get installed. When installing extensions built by other developers, the Macromedia Extension Manager (free from `www.macromedia.com/exchange/em_download/`) takes care of installing the right files. When you want to quickly create your own extensions, however, it helps to have a working understanding of the various configuration files. If nothing else, snooping through these files can be very enlightening.

Although this section would spin out of control if I were to try and document *how* to write advanced Commands, let me make a few suggestions in case you want to venture into custom Commands. First, anyone can make a simple Command using the History panel. Just do the steps manually and select the appropriate rows in the History panel and then press the Save As Command button (see Figure 10.4).

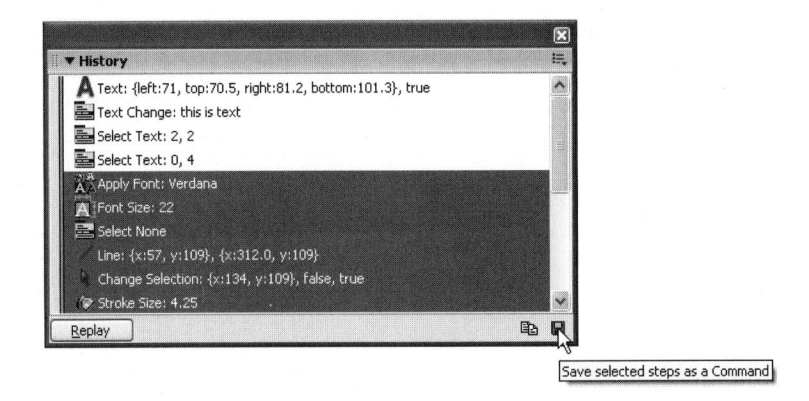

Figure 10.4 *You can make a Command by just saving steps recorded in the History panel.*

For more about the JavaScript Flash (JSFL) language used for Commands, check out Chapter 13.

Project Panel

Flash MX Professional 2004's Project panel has two main benefits:

- An easier way to manage and track projects that involve multiple files
- A version-control tracking system to ensure no two developers are working on the same file

If you're a single developer, the Project panel is nice because it helps you keep all related files in one place. When you create a new project, you create a single FLP file and then add all files related to your project. This can include FLAs, SWFs, HTML, MP3s, JPGs, FLVs, and various text data files. When you return to work on a project, you just open the FLP and all the connected files are available through the single interface (shown in Figure 10.5).

Another management benefit is the Test Project feature. You must identify one file as the default document. The main index.html file is a logical choice. It's the default document that you'll view when testing a project. The cool part, however, is that all your open files from the project also get published according to the publish profile you specify. This feature alone can save you a ton of legwork publishing multiple files.

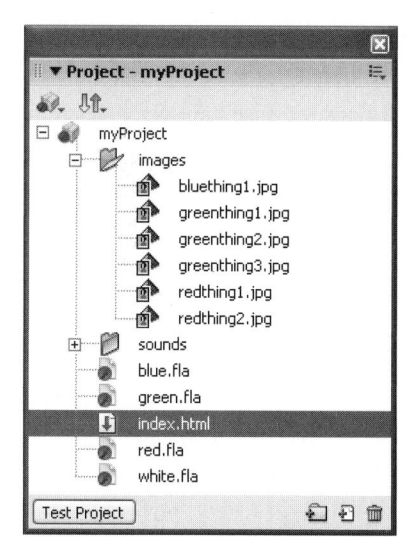

Figure 10.5 *The Project panel enables you to manage all the files related to your project through a single interface.*

The version-control side of the Project panel is more sophisticated. The main idea is that you can have several developers working on the same project and, provided they follow the correct protocol, no two people will think they're working on *the* master version of a file. You need to keep the master files in a single shared location, such as a network drive. After everything is set up, here's how the scenario will play out: Developer one checks out a file, the master version of that file gets copied to developer one's computer, and the copy on the network is marked as checked out. If another developer attempts to check out that file, the developer is told that developer one has it checked out. When developer one is done working, she checks the file back in, making it available for check out by anyone else. In addition, the local copy developer one was working on is also marked as locked; if she tries opening it later, she is notified that she should first check out the master from the network to ensure she has the most up-to-date version.

That scenario is ensured if everyone follows the rule to always check out files and check them back in. Actually, if one developer checks out the file and then decides *not* to save his changes, that developer can "undo check out," which is like checking the file back in (because it's marked as available), but it doesn't upload the file with which he was working.

Setting up and using the Project panel correctly requires that you understand how it works and that you don't expect it to be something it isn't. Because I was familiar with Dreamweaver's Site panel, I had the false impression the Project panel helped you deploy sites. In Dreamweaver, every file you work on is part of your site. In Flash, however, your primary files are FLAs, which you don't want to post. For this reason, you need to handle any deployment manually.

The following subsections provide a quick rundown of how you can use the Project panel for both management and version control.

Managing Files

If you just want to manage a bunch of related files, just select New Project and save a FLP file. Then select Add File for all the files you want to track. You also can specify separate publish profiles for each FLA in your project. Of course, you must first define profiles from the Publish Settings dialog box. Then you can select Settings from the Project panel's main menu (see Figure 10.6).

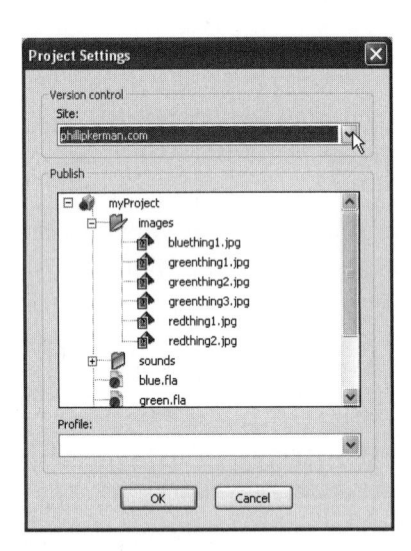

Figure 10.6 *After you define site profiles, you can associate a project with any site.*

The top section of the Settings dialog box (as well as the second menu in the Project panel) is only needed for version control.

Setting Up Version Control

To use version control, you first need to define a site and then associate your project file with a particular site. Actually, Flash MX Professional 2004 automatically displays any sites you've previously defined with Dreamweaver MX 2004. You can define sites by first selecting Edit Sites from the Version Control menu (the second one in the Project panel). Sites include a given name, a local location for files, your email and name (so other developers can contact you if you have a file checked out), and a remote location for the master version of each file (see Figure 10.7).

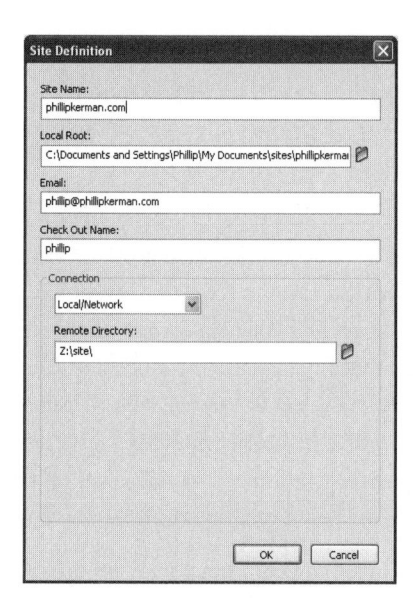

Figure 10.7 *Site definitions include a local and remote directory plus a name and email so that others know who has a file checked out.*

You'll see options to store remote files on an FTP site, a network, or in Microsoft Visual SourceSafe. (You may likely find a third-party extension to support other tools such as CVS—but nothing else is available at this time.) Because there are additional restrictions on FTP, I recommend you perform initial tests using the Local/Network option.

After you have a site defined, you can associate your project to one via the Settings dialog box (shown in Figure 10.6). Actually, you'll be prompted to do this as soon as you attempt to check out any files.

Using Version Control

With your project associated with a site, you can start using version control. The first step should be to check in each and every file in your project. This might sound strange, because you would expect to first check the files *out*. To make the files available to others on your team, however, you need to check them in for the files to upload. To begin working, select the file and choose Check Out (from the Version Control menu or right-click the context menu). Perform all your edits on that file and when you're done, save and then Check In. Realize that if you ever click Test Project, you'll see the published versions of all checked out files, but only the most recent local copy of any files you haven't checked out. If you have a bunch of JPGs that load dynamically, it may not be an issue that you may be viewing old versions of those files. If you want to bring your local copies into synchronization, just check out all the files and immediately Undo Check Out so that others can check out those files.

For others to start accessing your project files, they must first define their own site that uses the same remote folder. However, each of your coworkers won't have to define his or her own project file (and point to files) like you did initially. All they need to do is select File, Open from Site. That dialog box enables them to select any of their site definitions, and then it connects to get a list of files available in the remote folder. Then they can select just the FLP file. Flash then prompts the users that they can update "missing" project files. This just downloads a local copy of all the files in the project. For me, it's a lot easier to use the Project panel in a real project after first walking through several test scenarios.

Finally, remember that after you check in a file, your local copies are marked as read only—forcing you to first check out files before working on them again. I think the best tip I can give is not to try to make the Project panel something it's not. It's a very convenient way to keep related files together and it can prevent two coworkers from working on the same file simultaneously.

Library Management

Flash has three general ways to manage media in its internal library. Normal items are those items you either create inside Flash or import directly from file. Shared library items arrive in your Flash movie via another file. Shared items can be set to automatically update each time you publish so that they reflect changes made to their original. Finally, runtime shared libraries (RSLs) contain items that get imported at runtime. This way, items in RSLs are always up-to-date as they get imported at runtime (not unlike SWFs that get loaded via `loadMovie()`).

There's not a whole lot I can say about the plain library items created while in Flash. Similarly, a type of media not mentioned yet is external native files (specifically, MP3s, JPGs, and FLVs). Flash support for these native file formats means that, at runtime, you can import and present them. With both normal items and external media, being productive means being smart with your naming strategy. Because you know that libraries and file folders can sort alphabetically and numerically, for example, you might name your files clip_1.mp3, clip_2.mp3, and so on. However, this section covers the intricacies of shared items and runtime shared libraries.

Shared Library Items

Perhaps the easiest way to remember this feature is to call it "authortime" shared library items. That is, all the magic happens while authoring. The idea is you can store items in one (source) FLA's library and use them in another (user) FLA. Every time you publish the user movie, it updates the item by effectively re-importing from the source. It's really easy to do.

The benefit of shared items is you can keep a library of common media in one place even if you plan to use those items in several files. For example, you can store your company logo as a shared item. Then, if you get bought out, for instance, you can edit the original, republish all your movies, and they'll all reflect the change. Although there's a slight hassle republishing everything, after you do, the new media is actually *in* the user files. In addition, you don't have any download considerations (like RSLs do).

You need to know how you get shared items into a movie's library. First realize you need one source FLA that contains library items you intend to use elsewhere. In addition, you need one or more "user" files that share items from the source file. Start with the source file and make a symbol. Save the source FLA in a known location. Then, there are two ways to let the user files share the item (symbol) you just made. The easiest but perhaps less intuitive way is to just copy an instance of that symbol from the stage of the source and paste it into a new file. Then, find the symbol in the new file's library, and select Properties. When viewing the advanced portion of the Symbol Properties dialog box, select the Always Update Before Publishing check box (see Figure 10.8). You'll see additional details in the Source section because Flash knows the item was copied from another file.

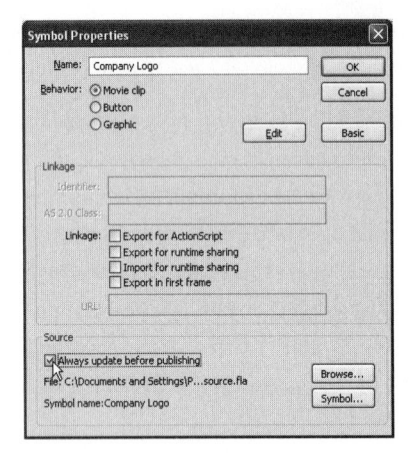

Figure 10.8 *Flash knows whether a library item was copied from another file, and you can force it to re-import when you publish.*

Now, every time you test the movie or publish, the latest version of the original symbol is re-imported. In addition, the library item in the user file has an extra option, Update, available in the library's menu to force the re-import.

The other way to get shared items into a user file is to select File, Import, Open Library for Import. This enables you to point to the source FLA, and its library will open in Flash ready to drag and drop instances onstage. As these symbols get added to your file, they will automatically have their Source property set as in Figure 10.8.

Incidentally, the equivalent to Flash's swap symbol—as applied to shared library items—is the button labeled Symbol, also in Figure 10.8. It enables you to swap this item with any item in the source file.

Shared library items is not necessarily a super production saver or particularly useful in every project. However, there are key situations that really call for it.

Runtime Shared Libraries (RSLs)

Runtime shared libraries are like an automated version of `loadMovie()`. That is, Flash has the power to load in and play SWFs at runtime. RSLs are effectively doing that, but in a way that's seamless to you, the developer. Basically, you make a movie with the library items to be shared and export a SWF. Then, in the files you intend to use as the resources of the shared movie, you point to that exported SWF. The cool part is that because you'll likely have one source and many user files, only the source needs to get updated, because the shared media loads at runtime. (Recall, with shared items each user file had to be republished to reflect a change to the source.)

RSLs get a bad rap because they have some issues you must contend with. For certain situations, however, they're great. Suppose you have a seasonal background image—maybe a picture of the beach for the summertime. You can store that asset in a RSL. Then, when fall rolls around you could update just that RSL and all subscribed user movies would reflect the change the next time the users visited. Perhaps the single static image isn't a great example because you could also just use loadMovie() to load a JPG and then swap out the JPG. If your background includes animations, you can see how a static JPG won't suffice. Although this chapter deals with "productivity," RSLs also offer another huge benefit: Files will be smaller because shared assets download only once (in the RSL file).

Before I show you the basics of RSLs, I should probably point out a couple limits. In the movies that use the shared items, you'll never see the real thing until you test or publish the movie. Because the item loads at runtime, you won't see it until then. In addition, the default behavior is for shared assets to download before the first frame of the movie displays. As a result, the user sees nothing until that media downloads. For this reason, it's usually best to use RSLs for media that's relatively lightweight.

The thing is, RSLs are so attractive for their efficiency both in reducing the total download across a site and ease of making updates. Interestingly, the entire set of user interface components made for Macromedia Central are contained in a RSL hosted at Macromedia.com. The first time Central runs, the shared assets download to Central's cache. This way, all subsequent apps that use the components won't force any extra download because the shared library is already present. In addition, when Macromedia updates, the components changes will be seen immediately. The only catch is that while authoring, you don't really "see" the components.

Here's a quick walkthrough of creating a RSL. Start with the item to be shared: Save a new movie as **shared.fla** and draw a shape. Select the shape and convert to symbol (F8), and then in the Linkage section of the Convert to Symbol dialog box check Export for Runtime Sharing. Set the Identifier to MyShape and fill in the URL to read **shared.swf** as in Figure 10.9.

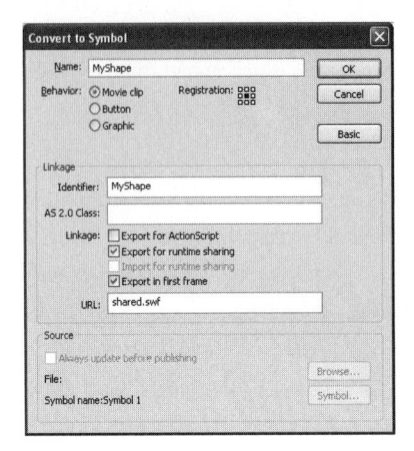

Figure 10.9 *When you make an item available for runtime, you specify the filename where Flash will look for that item.*

As it stands, the URL `shared.swf` is going to be relative to the movie that will use it—but that can be an explicit path including your entire domain and path to where you plan to store this RSL. Now, when you're ready to use the RSL, you just need to note the identifier (myShape) and URL (`shared.swf`). Before you can do that, however, the `shared.swf` must exist. So, just test the shared.fla movie.

Now, start a new file, name it **`user.fla`**, and save it adjacent to the `shared.swf`. Next, make a shape that will get linked to the RSL. (You could even copy the contents of the myShape clip to get the matching size.) Finally, convert it to a symbol (F8), but this time select Import for Runtime Sharing and specify an identifier of myShape and URL `shared.swf` (see Figure 10.10). Basically, this says, "Make this symbol import the clip with the identifier myShape that's inside the `shared.swf`."

That's it. Again, the funky part is you can easily get mixed up when editing the user.fla. Suppose you go and edit shared.fla (for instance, change the color of the myShape symbol—and be sure to export a SWF by testing the movie). If you go back to user.fla, you'll still be looking at the proxy. Do a test movie in user.fla and you'll then see the updated version. However, the normal sequence is that you'll upload everything, and then later change the shared.fla and make a SWF to upload. From that point forward, all visitors to user.swf will see the new shared symbols. The key to testing this sort of feature is keeping your folders and files clean and working deliberately.

Figure 10.10 *Setting this item to Import for Runtime Sharing means Flash will look in the specified SWF for a clip with this identifier.*

Finally, it's not as though either RSLs or shared library items are better. Instead, they both have their place. I guess my main point in this whole section is that you've got several useful ways to manage the library. RSLs are a way to automatically reflect the up-to-date media and share the download across several files. Shared items are a way to force the latest media into each file as its published.

Prototyping

After you define the objectives for a project and specify the features, it's best to first create a prototype before you build the real thing. A prototype will really clarify *exactly* what your application will be like. It helps team members reach a consensus and exposes flaws in your idea, which, up to that point, has been nothing but an idea in your head. A prototype appears in the final form of your application (say, a Flash movie). People can touch it and really feel how things flow. After you build a prototype, you can quickly identify issues that must be resolved.

Hopefully, you agree that prototypes have a real value. In any event, the following section covers specific techniques worth using when building prototypes.

Being Sloppy

If ever there were a place where being sloppy is okay, it is while prototyping. The goal of prototyping is to get something up and running quickly. Therefore, a prototype doesn't have to look pretty. Not only are blocky "holder" graphics perfectly suitable, they're quicker to produce. In addition, the risk of presenting a halfway decent-looking prototype to a graphic designer is that the designer may mistake your visual elements for having some purpose. Ideally, the graphics won't be influenced by anything visual in your prototype. It's not like you have to be intentionally messy, but realize that prototyping goals include getting a feel for your application, identifying all the interactions necessary, and getting sign-off from all interested parties.

I could list quite a few general tips for prototyping, but most are either common sense or specific to the way I work. One universal suggestion I can make is to always think modularly. That is, even though you may not need a lot of the code you're developing, you may need *some* of it. If it's all wrapped up into a few huge functions, it'll be harder to extract. If you break things apart (as you're building), however, it will be easier to grab select routines. It's like I'm saying "follow good code practices while you're being messy." Obviously, that's a contradiction. I'm just saying time saving sometimes has a higher value than pretty code.

Using Components

I used to advise using user interface components only while prototyping. However, they're so darn useful I'll admit using at least the Buttons and List components in real projects. In any event, they're still quite useful for prototyping. I guess my main point here is that it's worth the investment to learn how to populate components and to tie them in so that they trigger your code.

In the case of Flash MX 2004, there's a new set of version 2 components that require a slightly different procedure. Chapter 12, "Using Components," provides more details on these. For now, just realize that they can save a lot of time while prototyping, too.

Staging and Deployment

Long after prototyping but still before your application is ready for prime time, you'll want to stage it. *Staging* refers to viewing your application in its final form, but not in its target location—that is, not on the public server or wherever you intend for it to reside. It's like the last step of testing before you go live.

Staging probably sounds easier than it really is. The thing is, you can't always test your application on your hard drive. Many applications use application servers that abide by a different set of restrictions. When you test a Flash SWF on your hard drive, for example, it's allowed to reach out and load data from web services on remote servers—something that's restricted when you view your movie in the browser from a web server. Every time you test a movie, it will work, but it will fail when you deliver.

In addition to my previous dire warnings, I have a few specific recommendations to make your staging go smoothly:

- Perform reality checks or proof-of-concept test runs throughout the production. That is, do mini-stagings along the way. This way, you're more likely to find (and resolve) problems before you get too deep.

- Use variables as constants for base values. For example, if you're delivering to `http://www.phillipkerman.com/realthing/` but want to do your testing at `http://www.phillipkerman.com/test/`, store one of those URLs in a variable (for instance, `BASE="http://www.phillipkerman.com/test/"`). Then, when you go live, you can just change that variable. Consider if you had written out that URL in multiple places in your code—you'd have to be sure to fix each instance. (By the way, using all capital letters for variable names, like `BASE`, is a convention that means you're treating the variable as a constant—you intend to set it once and not change it.)

- Try to come up with scripted solutions. For example, I use the following code to determine whether my file is on a web server or running on the desktop (or inside Flash itself):

```
if(_url.charAt(0)=="f"){
  online=true;
}else{
  online=false;
}
```

   This works because the `_url` property begins with an `f` only when running locally (for example, `file:///C|/folder/file.swf`). The big clue that you should have either a constant variable or a scripted solution is that you find yourself editing.

- Install a local web server. There are a variety of free web servers you can install to run on your computer. I don't know how long it took me before I really understood that it's totally different to run an HTML page in a browser on the hard drive than to point to a page on a web server. Web servers aren't limited to servers set up to host pages publicly. For example, you can install the free developer version of ColdFusion, and it comes with a web server perfect for testing. To run files, they need to be in the server's wwwroot folder. You launch them by typing `http://localhost/`... instead of just double-clicking the HTML file. Also, know that if you install ColdFusion to run parallel to another application server on your computer, it uses a different port number. For example, I have a couple of web servers installed locally for testing; so when I need to point to ColdFusion's wwwroot folder, I use `http://localhost:8500/`.... That's because my installed version of ColdFusion "listens" to port 8500.

- Publish to your stage. Although the Project panel is really your best option here, you also can just set Flash's Publish settings to target a folder (for instance, on your web server). For instance, Figure 10.11 shows how every time I publish, the SWF goes into my test server. The idea is that I can have all the HTML and related files ready and waiting on the local server—even have a bookmark in my browser. So if I make a change, I just republish and then go test. I don't have to meticulously copy files and so forth.

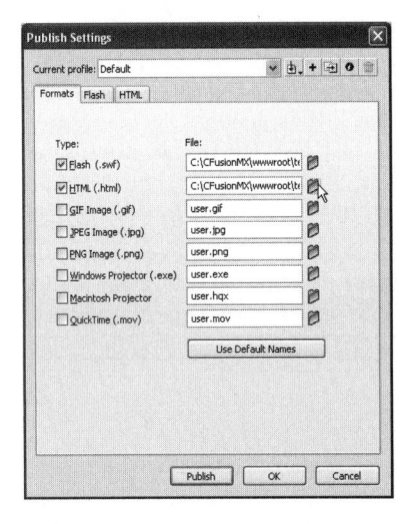

Figure 10.11 *You can direct Flash to publish in any folder you want. (Notice that the folders are now buttons to browse.)*

I'm sure there are countless other tips for staging, many of which you'll learn (perhaps the hard way). In any event, I'll say it again: The time spent coming up with production time-saving tricks is usually worth the investment.

Multimode Applications

Although not specifically a staging issue, I think multimode applications fit well here. The idea of having multiple views on a single application is quite common despite *multimode* being a term I made up. A familiar example is when you want both a public view and an administrator view. The point is that you probably don't want to actually make two different applications (one for the admin and one for everyone else) but rather one application that adapts to perform appropriately depending on who the user is. Multiple files mean more maintenance and so on.

Here's a real example. When you visit my answering machine (www.phillipkerman.com/machine), you can only view messages you left or those left by others who agreed to make them public. However, I wanted a way for me to view *all* the messages plus a way to change the outgoing message. Instead of creating two different versions of this app, I just made one multimode app. There's a single variable admin and it's set to true or false depending on whether I'm the one viewing the app.

{ Note }

How It Really Works   In case you're wondering, the approach I used on the answering machine is both simple and secure. I placed a different HTML file in a password-protected area of my web site (that is, a folder I protected using my ISP's administration tools—not unlike traditional .htaccess and .htpasswd files). So the HTML page I use to launch the app is inaccessible to you, and it's slightly different in content. Specifically, is uses the FlashVars tag (covered in Chapter 6, "Basic Data Exchange") to set a variable called username to the secret password that I can't disclose here. Anyway, because I didn't want to store the correct or expected value for that variable *in* the Flash movie (because SWFs can easily be hacked), what I do is pass that variable to the Flash Communication Server when I connect. If the main.asc file receives the expected value in the onConnect() method, I trigger a function in the SWF that just sets the admin variable to true. Then throughout my app, there are several places where you're taken on a slightly different course if admin is true or if it's false. Okay, so my answering machine isn't used by international spies, but it was a good exercise nevertheless.

It's not that multimode applications have to be super sneaky or secure. You may just have the need to reveal or hide specific buttons that don't apply to the user's interests. That is, you don't have to protect one mode with a password as I did with the answering machine. The thing is, when you design your application so that code and data are well separated, adding a multimode feature becomes much easier. Although I suppose it's best to plan ahead for such a feature, it should be fairly easy to add later in a project.

Incidentally, the reason I put this discussion under staging is that many of the same basic techniques apply to both staging and multimode apps. For example, you may set up your application to run differently while testing locally than when on a server. That's similar to how the app might have to work differently in one mode or the other. You can think of staging/not staging as two modes in your app. Anyway, I don't mean to push the multimode concept on every app you build. When appropriate, however, it can really add some value to your project. Here are just a few examples of multimode features I've built in real projects:

- The live cattle auction I programmed for stampedecattle.com has both an auctioneer view and a bidder view. The bidder view has several modes depending on how you log in—spectators are restricted from bidding, whereas registered buyers can bid. Also, if you log in as the second auctioneer, you're able use your microphone to call the bids—this way the auctioneer can log on from anywhere in the world. For the main administration console, I did create a separate SWF only because the window size had to be larger because there was so much information to present onscreen. It's still a form of multimode because the `admin` connects to the same Flash Communication Server application.

- The site allsteeloffice.com/number19 includes several linked videos in both Windows Media and QuickTime format. When visitors pick their first video to view, they must choose a format preference. From that point forward, they're in a slightly different mode. (That is, I know their preference.) Anyway, for testing I built it so that if you hold Shift when you click to view a video, it will ask your preference again.

- I built a graphing application that had two modes: data entry and visualization. You could either get in and edit the values to be plotted, or you could view the graphs. In this case, I just built a toggle option for the user—it wasn't as if one mode was a secret.

- Whenever I give a presentation, I like to make an online version available. Although I want to make sure the navigation is clear to users, I prefer to keep buttons and such hidden while I give the presentation. That is, I know where the buttons are but I don't want them to remain hidden. Again, I built a multimode feature that will hide the buttons when I'm running it locally but not online. (I also added speaker's notes to many such presentations that are only viewable by those viewing the presentation online.)

- Although Flash has some remote debugging features, your `trace()` statements become lost forever when you deploy. You'll learn in Chapter 11, "Quality Assurance and Debugging," however, how to use the local connection object to send trace strings from your app to a homemade output window. The idea here is that you can have a "debugging mode" to your app in which you can test things online.

It's not like you'll probably sit down and decide to build a multimode application. Instead, it's just a type of feature that's nice to add. Even if just for testing or your convenience during production, multiple modes are quite useful.

Creating Dummy Data

Chapter 3, "Technology Overview," and Chapter 4, "Working with Complex Data," covered manipulating and presenting data. During production you may not have a supply of data handy, however. What if your app is supposed to display the current standings in a sports event that hasn't taken place yet, for instance? The answer is you're going to have to make up data.

Just like how designers use *lorem ipsum* to display the layout before they get the actual copy, programmers need to build dummy data before the real thing is available. However, it's probably better if the data you derive is truly representative of the real thing. Herein lies the challenge. In the real app your data will, for the most part, be pretty consistent. (For instance, most people's first names have fewer than 12 letters.) However, you really need to prepare for any possibility (perhaps someone's first name contains 24 letters).

The thing is that you don't need to start by worrying about such outliers (that is, individual cases where values are out of the normal range). Although you will need to come up with a range of data that could possibly break your code, it's fine to start with "nice data." Start by stocking your app with data that fits what you expect. Work out your data structure and parsing routines. Then come back through and try to break it with oddball values. A secondary advantage of fixing the data is that you can readily see whether your code is working correctly. If you're plotting student scores as a percentage of 100, for example, you could start with nice round numbers (100, 90, 80, and so on).

Here's an example of what I call "nice" data (and the code to populate it):

```
function init(){
   users=[];
   users.push({name:"Tom"  ,score:100});
   users.push({name:"Dick", score:80});
   users.push({name:"Harry", score:50});
}
```

Notice that, even while the movie plays, you can reset all the values by triggering the `init()` function.

If you need a ton of data, you could create a loop to do the populating, as this example shows:

```
users=[];
for(var i=0;i<1000;i++){
   users.push(({name:"username"+i, score:random(100)});
}
```

The interesting point here is that basic scripting skills can come in handy when creating sample data. Although it's best to start with "nice data," it's also important to test for a full range of data. Although this is really a debugging step that gets covered in the next chapter, it's worth touching on here. First, realize that *all* the data doesn't have to try to strain your code, just a few outliers to prove it's still working. In the preceding examples, for instance, you could try adding one oddball user to the beginning or end of the array. For example, above or below the existing "nice" population code, you could add something like this:

```
user.push({name:"a_very_very_long_name",score:0});
user.push({name:"s",score:101});
```

Exactly how you fashion data to stress-test your app depends on the nature of the application. In the preceding example, there may be no way for `score` values to reach beyond 100—so the second line of code would be unnecessary. Also, we haven't discussed how you respond to a case where whacked data breaks your app (for instance, if the long `name` in this example wraps or gets cut off). Generally, you just want to make sure you're testing everything. To begin, you just need something to work with. The idea of dummy data is to get you rolling.

Incidentally, often your app will need to import data from outside sources. So, to fully test your system, store the data in its native format externally. You can still start by creating dummy data internally. Just be sure to fully test with data when it comes from outside, too.

Creating dummy data is a basic production technique. The concept applies to other portions of your work, too. It's impossible to do everything at once, so instead, hard-wire parts of your work and then come back and finish it later. Quite often I write a function that always returns the same value (for instance, `true`). In the real project, however, it will have to return a range of values (even if that's just `true` or `false`). The point is that I can keep rolling even though parts of my project are not complete. Without such mock ups, you'd be forced to do everything "in order," and that may not be possible or practical. The good news with these techniques is that you also can apply the skills needed to debugging, as discussed in the next chapter.

Summary

Although you may not associate productivity with a slacker, that's really what it's all about: Do as little work as possible. The name of the game is efficiency. In this chapter, you've seen a range of techniques that can save you time or frustration. No doubt you'll pick up many more techniques along the way. Also, feel free to try applying productivity techniques you have acquired elsewhere. For example, designing a range of dummy data is not unlike how a photographer brackets exposures (by shooting several photos at different settings to get at least one that's right on). Even if that analogy isn't perfect, do realize that there are many ways to be efficient. This chapter just touched on a few tricks I've come across.

{Chapter 11}

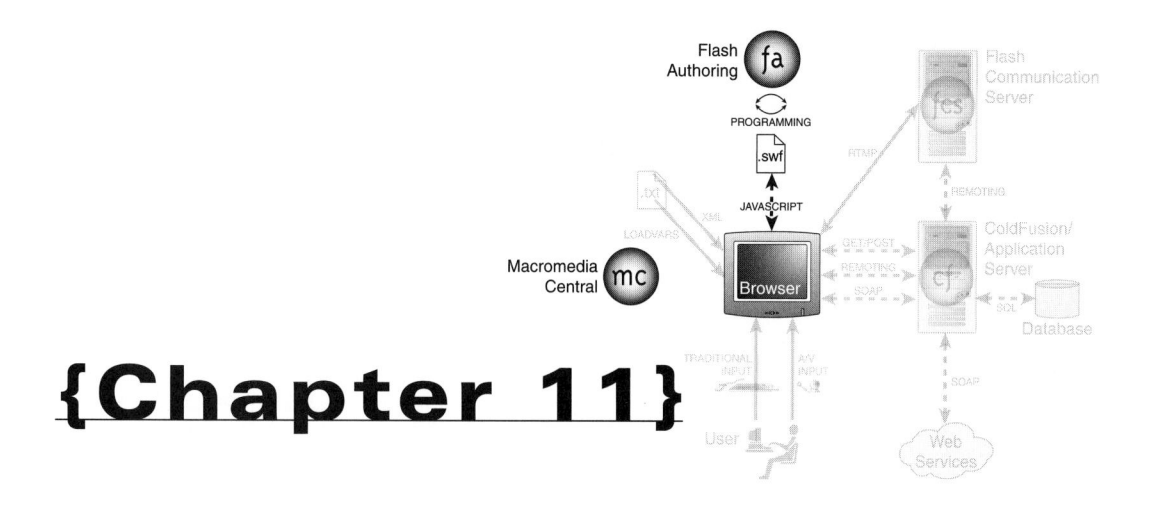

Quality Assurance and Debugging

Obviously, if you could ensure quality there would be no bugs to remove. But it isn't that easy. What constitutes a "bug" is arguably anything from an onscreen typo to code that causes the user's machine to crash. A range of things can certainly go wrong and, in a perfect world, we would avoid all of them. I've heard people say, "All software has bugs," as if this is supposed to placate a client stuck with a show-stopper bug in a project. In fact, it's possible to build an application free of critical bugs. This chapter gives you philosophical approaches as well as practical tools so that you can make your application as bug free as possible.

This chapter covers debugging in a sort of chronological order: how to evaluate the seriousness of your bugs, ways to avoid bugs in the first place, and ways to actually squash bugs.

Specifically, this chapter covers the following topics:

- Techniques to manage your bugs so that you can address them systematically
- How to build systems that reduce or eliminate the chance for bugs
- Practical methods to hunt down and resolve bugs, including the use of the Macromedia Flash MX 2004 Debugger panel

Evaluating Quality

On the surface, saying you want a bug-free app is a no-brainer. Because many of the approaches proposed in this chapter have an associated cost, however, it's best if everyone understands the cost. That is, to judge whether an investment is worthwhile, you want to be sure you see the entire value.

Naturally, a known "show-stopper" bug that renders your app useless must be fixed or your app isn't really an app. If you look beyond such critical bugs, however, you'll see bugs of varying degrees. The question is what sorts of bugs can you avoid at what cost. You'll ultimately reach a point of diminishing returns, where the last bug might take months to crush. The key is to always assess bugs before attempting to address them.

Benefits to Client and Developer

Although both programmer and client *should* be on the same side, they tend to value quality for different reasons. A client might be able to associate a dollar figure with the downtime while an application (bugs) gets repaired. From the developer's perspective, time going back to fix bugs might delay another project or cost the developer money if the developer bid the first project at a fixed price. Finally, although the "pain and suffering" cost (due to stress) may be difficult to calculate, it's real nevertheless.

Ultimately, the idea that time is money is something both developer and client can agree on. Keep in mind also that with projects involving a large team, redoing work at one stage might ripple through and require others to redo their work, too. Fixing a particular bug might not seem so important if the cost is many people's time plus a delay in the overall schedule. Although, obviously, everyone wants quality, you have to consider the cost/benefit from each party's perspective. Also, because avoiding bugs costs money, everyone in a position to benefit should "pay." Even though the client is the only one who really pays, it's best if everyone understands and places a similar value on quality. As you'll see in the "Ensuring Quality" section later in this chapter, avoiding bugs costs money, too, so you need to make sure everyone is willing to pay.

Finding and Assessing Bugs

My personal opinion is that the person who created a bug in the first place (the programmer) is the person least able to find it later. However, you can develop some skills to become a better bug finder. The first step is self-criticism. For instance, you may need to walk through code you wrote—code that made sense when you wrote it—but you have to question every line, effectively calling yourself a liar. Walking through code is more likely to occur while fixing bugs (covered later), but the concept is the same when *looking for* bugs. You want to find bugs, but that means you did something wrong in the first place.

Programmers often miss their own bugs because they almost tiptoe around the app. If nothing else, it's common to repeatedly test an application by following the same steps. If you're testing the third screen in an app, for example, you'll probably find the quickest way to navigate to that screen every time you test. However, a bug may pop up when you take a slightly different route to get to that screen. The reason clients inevitably discover bugs immediately is not their uncanny sensitivity but just because they play your app differently than you do. When it comes to testing, you really need to break out of the cycle you followed during most of the development.

Another issue that may be human nature—but makes no sense when hunting for bugs—is how some programmers would rather find no bugs. In your dreams! First, accept the fact you're going to have bugs. I sometimes rationalize it by accepting a few bugs as inevitable, figuring I must have been working so swiftly when I created them. (As discussed in the "Ensuring Quality" section later in this chapter, there are ways to avoid making bugs in the first place, but there is no way to write bug-free code.)

You should try to limit your reaction to finding a bug to two responses: happiness and pride. When someone else finds a bug, be happy because you're that much closer to a quality app. When you find a bug, be proud that you were the one to find it. Suppose you're testing your app and you see something happen (a bug, that is). Don't ignore it and hope it never comes back. Document it! Try to remember the exact steps that caused it. Although it might be a big distraction to stop everything and go into bug documenting mode, at least make a note of it. Don't, however, just try to fix the bug when you find it. (As discussed in the next section, you need to take a deliberate approach to fixing bugs.)

Even if you feel like cringing when a client points out a bug, you really need to accept it graciously. Consider that someone else finding a bug is doing you a favor. It's certainly much better to find it early than later. And, besides, you need all the help you can get. Bug finders should be thanked, if not also rewarded.

Just finding a bug is only part of the identification process. The key to effectively fixing a bug is having a clear understanding of the bug. You need to understand the full scope of a bug, because you don't want to fix just part of the bug. Suppose, for instance, that a user describes the bug as "I can't enter my name in the Name field." If there are other related issues—for instance, the user can't enter his number in the Number field either—you need to know about those other issues (so that you don't waste time fixing just part of the bug).

A full understanding of a bug also means that you will be able to reproduce it. After all, how can a programmer fix something she can't see? Documenting the exact steps to exhibit a bug is critical for several reasons. You want to make sure the programmer is seeing the same thing as the bug finder. Also, you'll often find that the steps that caused the bug may almost serve as instructions for fixing the problem. (Many times, as someone is explaining how he got a bug to occur, a light goes off in my head.) You also can use those same steps that caused a bug to test later whether the bug has been fixed.

You can categorize each bug you find. The following are typical categories:

- Causes a crash
- Incorrectly functioning
- Wrong data appears
- Data lost
- Usability issue
- Cosmetic issue
- Typo(s)

To give you an idea of what's possible, Figure 11.1 shows a fairly sophisticated bug-reporting tool used in a large project I worked on.

Of course, you can come up with appropriate categories for your own app. You also may want to include other notations, such as in which portion of the app each bug was found. You may find it helpful to work up a little table into which the bug finder can document these things. Depending on the size of your project, it may be worth creating an online data-entry app to streamline the bug-collecting process. Again, it doesn't have to be super fancy or formal—you just want to make sure bugs are found and that people's efforts in finding bugs are not wasted.

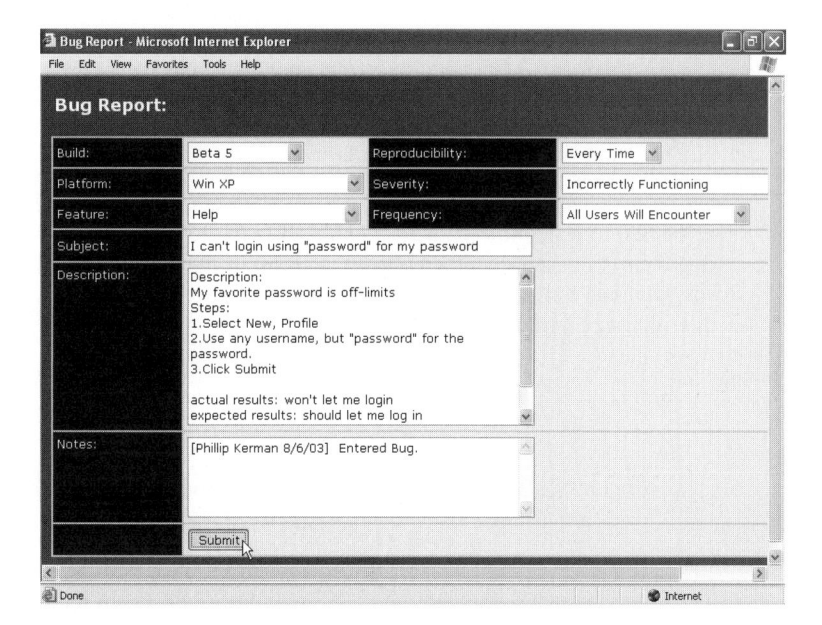

Chapter 11 Quality Assurance and Debugging *343*

Figure 11.1 *A web application itself, this bug-reporting tool made reporting bugs easy and consistent.*

Now that you know a bit about finding bugs, the next step is to decide how to address them (which, perhaps surprisingly, isn't always to fix them).

Taking a Deliberate Approach

One of the biggest mistakes programmers make is fixing bugs as they find them. That is, a client calls up and provides a perfect explanation of the problem; the developer realizes the cause and goes and makes the fix. Although this may sound like the correct process, it's actually a bit dangerous. When a bug is found, you really ought to answer the following questions before attempting to fix it:

- **How important is the bug?** After answering the following questions you'll be able to associate a cost with the fix, and it may, in the end, not be worth fixing.

- **How easy do you expect the fix to be?** You can even do a little bit of offline research to see whether you can fix it. Of course, if you succeed, you can use that code when implementing the fix.

- **What are the possible side effects?** Fixing one thing may cause other bugs to crop up. Incidentally, this is a perfectly legitimate rationalization that you can use when a client suggests a fix. I'm not really suggesting you use it as an insincere scare tactic, but it is an important consideration nevertheless.

- **How will you ensure the bug was fixed?** It's best to have a way to measure success worked out ahead of time. At a minimum, document the steps to cause the bug so that you have steps to follow when testing the fixed version.
- **When should you schedule the fix?** Considering that you really ought to retest *everything* after making a fix (to see whether other bugs surfaced), it may be best to wait until you have a few bugs to fix before going in and fixing them. Consider, too, there's often a deployment step necessary that takes time (and introduces more possible bugs).

You may think from the preceding list that I'm living in a dream world and that your clients won't accept anything other than all bugs being fixed. I've been there, too. The truth is, you're doing your clients a favor if you take a well-structured approach to quality assurance. For really large projects, apply the concepts introduced in this chapter (as well as those from Chapter 10, "Production Techniques") and expand on them. You also can apply knowledge from traditional software development, too (and from any other sort of production process for that matter). Just remember: Haste makes waste.

Client Management

Because this discussion may imply that clients are easy to persuade, I want to share the little I know about client management as applied to debugging. I think it really comes down to education. It's not so much to avoid conflict—although that's nice, too—but the goal is really just an efficient production. Everyone wants all the bugs removed, but I think most would also agree that it's better to leave in a few minor bugs if it means you can fix all critical bugs (as opposed to fixing every bug as you find it and not getting to them all).

{ Note }

Avoid "Groupthink" One downside to being too persuasive is the concept of groupthink. You don't want to fall into this cycle where everyone helping each other rationalizes his or her way out of fixing anything. It may sound funny, but groupthink is a real phenomenon. (For more about groupthink, check out the writings of Irving L. Janis and others on the topic of organizational behavior.)

After answering the questions found in the "Taking a Deliberate Approach" section earlier in this chapter, you have a number of ways to approach problems. There's often more than one way to fix a bug. If a button is taking the user to the wrong screen under certain conditions, for example, you could just disable or hide the button when that condition occurs. You might immediately think the "fix" is to make the button take you to the right screen—but turning off the button might be a fix. One time when I rented a car, I pointed out a bug in the computer the rental company had set up to print door-to-door directions for any destination. The service person walked up and unplugged the computer, saying "that fixed it." I couldn't dispute that the problem was gone.

I think the best way to manage bug fixes is to think about schedule. Obviously, I don't suggest waiting to fix a critical bug in "version 2" of your application. However, addressing bugs in a logical order is important. Also, you can consider bugs that affect the overall function of an app as critical (as compared to bugs related to features). For enhancement requests, however, it really makes sense to say, "Add that to the list of features for the next revision." Not only does this help you stay focused on the important bugs, it also helps the client to scope out future variations of your app. The concept of "feature creep" is where you keep adding every feature as requested. Feature creep often causes missed deadlines and may result in unusable applications.

Ensuring Quality

Before you worry about fixing bugs, it makes more sense to figure out a way just to avoid bugs. After all, if you don't create any bugs, you won't have to fix them. In practice, this will probably never happen. However, you can follow approaches that tend to reduce or nearly eliminate bugs. This section covers such techniques that should lead to higher-quality apps.

Building Proofing Systems

A proofing system is an application itself that helps you review your application. Usually it's a hidden feature built in to your app that gives you the additional power to help step through all the content. Not only can you use such features to "proof" your content (by making sure it's all there), it also helps ensure you viewed every screen. The idea is that instead of manually stepping through every conceivable combination of settings available in your app, you have a script that does this for you.

Here's a simplified example from a real project. I helped build a catalog-maker tool for representatives of a clothing manufacturer. The database included just more than 3000 items. For each piece of clothing, there were about a dozen additional fields of data, such as retail price, discount price, size information, description, and so on. The representatives were able to view or display (for a printed copy) any item and any corresponding data. One of the proofing tools we built presented each item with all the additional data onscreen simultaneously (shown on the right side of Figure 11.2). If the quality assurance person found an item with funky data, he could print the screen; all the data and any pertinent variables from my app would display. In the real app, no one would ever want to see *all* the data for any item simultaneously—although he could individually select each field. For the quality assurance person to use the finished app to proof the data, he would have to click to see each additional field. Not only would this be a ton of clicking, the quality assurance person would likely miss a few. This is just one proofing tool, basically creating displays that would never be needed in the finished app.

Figure 11.2 *This proofing tool used a modified version of the real app to enable the quality assurance person to check each item in a large database.*

Chapter 11 Quality Assurance and Debugging 347

One serendipitous outcome of proofing scripts is that they sometimes turn out to be so useful, you may decide to turn them into features for the end user. For example, I made a simple script that automatically stepped from one screen to the next (loading external JPGs). This way, my client could ensure the image files they created were all in order. We ended up adapting the script (originally tied to a button) to automatically engage on a timed basis, and the client used it for a "kiosk mode," in which they could just leave it running at tradeshows and such. In basic form, Listing 11.1 shows what the code looked like before (when it was used as a proofing tool) and after (when it was turned into a slide-show feature):

Listing 11.1 Image-Proofing Script

Part A: Initialization (common to "before" and "after")

```
1    //populate variables
2    sections=["outdoor", "architecture", "portraits"];
3    photos=new Object();
4    photos.outdoor=["beach", "mountain", "hills"];
5    photos.architecture=["house", "bridge", "office"];
6    photos.portraits=["kids", "family", "baby"];
7
8    //init
9    sectionNum=0;
10   photoNum=0;
```

We actually had way more than nine images, but this is how the data was structured.

Part B: Proofing Script ("before")

```
11   //proofing button:
12   next_btn.onPress=function(){
13     //trace(photos[sections[sectionNum]][photoNum]+".jpg");
14     my_mc.loadMovie(photos[sections[sectionNum]][photoNum]+".jpg");
15     photoNum++;
16     if(photoNum>=photos[sections[sectionNum]].length){
17       photoNum=0;
18       sectionNum++;
19       if(sectionNum>=sections.length){
20         sectionNum=0;
21       }
22     }
23   }
```

continues

Listing 11.1 Image-Proofing Script (Continued)

The only gnarly part here is line 14—and that's more a factor of the way the data was structured. (If you want to test it without actual photos, just uncomment line 13.) I didn't want to modify how the data was structured just for this proofing script. The if statements are just to make sure we don't go past the last photo in any section, and they ensure that we loop around after the last section.

Part C: Combined Slide-Show/Proofing Script ("after")

```
11   //proofing button:
12   next_btn.onPress=function(){
13     advance();
14   }
15
16   function advance(){
17     //trace(photos[sections[sectionNum]][photoNum]+".jpg");
18     my_mc.loadMovie(photos[sections[sectionNum]][photoNum]+".jpg");
19     photoNum++;
20     if(photoNum>=photos[sections[sectionNum]].length){
21       photoNum=0;
22       sectionNum++;
23       if(sectionNum>=sections.length){
24         sectionNum=0;
25       }
26     }
27   }
28
29   startShow_btn.onPress=function(){
30     showInt=setInterval(advance, 10000);
31   }
32   stopShow_btn.onPress=function(){
33     clearInterval(showInt);
34   }
```

Notice the entire "proofing script" was moved into the advance() function. This way the same code could get triggered both by the proofing button and the setInterval (triggered every 10 seconds while the slide-show feature played). I guess it's sort of rare that the same exact script can get recycled into your project—but it usually doesn't take much modification.

> In addition to providing a feature for your users, a proofing script might also come in handy during production. Although this tip probably may seem like Chapter 10 material, it actually fits well here. As a simple, quick, and dirty

production helper, I use the Output window all the time. For example, I made a little wheel-of-fortune app that helps me pick a random number (say, for book giveaways). For the different colored slices in the wheel, I had code that picked colors randomly, but I would often see dark muddy colors that didn't really match the look and feel I wanted. The solution was to randomly pick colors from a pool of "good" colors. Because I wanted lots of colors in the pool and I didn't want to type them all in by hand, I wrote a script that enabled me to quickly point to a color on Martin Naas's Color Picker component (downloadable from www.flashcomponents.net). I would click an Add It button (which would push() the selected color onto the end of an array). Then I would pick a bunch of colors and click a See It button that just did a trace(colorArray). I then copied the Output window and pasted it into my real app (see Figure 11.3).

Figure 11.3 *I gathered a variety of suitable colors using a free Component and a little bit of code.*

Even though the wheel-of-fortune example was a production tip, it also ensured there were no color bugs—getting a random color that I didn't like. To carry it a bit further, I could have written a proofing script that—one by one—went through and colored a clip of each of the colors in the array. In either case, these sorts of tricks save a lot of typing!

In many situations, you'll want your proofing script to report the results after you have finished. The idea is you want to avoid the human element every step of the way. Suppose, for example, that you're just checking whether all the linked JPGs are present—you don't care whether the content is correct; you just want to see whether each file is in the appropriate folder. In this case, you just need a report of the results. This can be as simple as doing a trace() and viewing the report in the Output window. A more permanent way to save the results is to send an email containing the results of the test. It's pretty easy. Suppose you've collected an array called myArray, for instance; you can use this code with a Send button:

```
send_btn.onPress=function(){
  var theString=myArray.toString();
  getURL("mailto:bugs@phillipkerman.com?subject=data&body="+theString);
}
```

Like I said, easy. Just stuff the results after body=, and it will appear in the email body. This approach means your bug finder can be running the test remotely; users just click the button to send you the results. They don't even need Flash! You'll see a similar application later in this chapter as you learn how to build a homemade debugger.

On some occasions, you may need to use an outside tool to help you proof your app. (For instance, although Flash can do a lot, other tools can write text files directly to disk. An application server such as ColdFusion MX can do this sort of operation, too.) Outside tools may prove valuable to you because beyond the Output window, onscreen text fields, and triggering an email, Flash can't really get data into other forms without the help of outside tools. One advantage, however, of writing all your proofing scripts inside Flash is that you can readily recycle the code into something useful for your app. Don't feel obligated to use just Flash if you have some other needs or you have existing skills with other tools.

Leaving Tracks As You Go

The idea of leaving tracks won't necessarily prevent bugs, but it will help you recover when you do find a bug. It's like Hansel and Gretel's well-intentioned plan of leaving bread crumbs to help find their return path. Of course, you'll use a more secure method, but the idea is the same: You need an easy way to go back to an earlier (functioning) version of your app. This section shows you ways to plan for such backtracking.

Save As

Your tracking system need not be terribly fancy. For example, the easiest way is with version numbering. All you need to do is periodically do a Save As and rename the file with a higher number. I combine the date with the version number. For example, here are a few filenames from a work in progress:

```
cows_12_APR_r1.fla
cows_12_APR_r2.fla
cows_13_APR_r1.fla
cows_13_APR_r2.fla
cows_13_APR_r3.fla
```

Basically, I can see the latest version of my cow project is revision 3 on the 13th of April. This is just the way I do it; you can come up with another system if you prefer. For example, my approach makes it slightly difficult to determine which is the latest version—you always have to look for the highest number. Regardless, it's definitely easy to go back and view older versions when you find that some recent addition causes a bug.

If you're really organized, you'll want to document exactly what features were added to each version. You don't have to be super detailed, but knowing when each feature was added can help you backtrack. Here's what I'm talking about: Every time you do a Save As, write down the new version number. Then, for every general feature you add, write it down under the version number—as general as "sorting feature," "fixed double-entry issue," or "added back button," for instance. Continue to do this so that in the end you can easily see all the features that were added to each revision. This may seem overly detailed, but it does offer two additional benefits in addition to recovery. Namely, you have a document to let the client see all the new features. Also, if you have some disaster and lose files, going back and adding features is much easier (even without the code) when you have a list to remind you of what all you added. Honestly, I don't usually use this technique until a project starts getting really hairy and deadlines are looming. Even though it might seem that's the time to hunker down and work (instead of spending time documenting), it's exactly the time you need to become even more careful because you're more likely to make mistakes.

There's an obvious fact that's easy to forget. You should always save, and then do a Save As. Otherwise, the most recent changes won't be in the old file, but rather in the new file. This process will more accurately mimic the concept I have in mind: "Okay, let's save what we have so far and begin adding some new features."

Carrying the Save As technique a step further, I always keep a backup of my source files on a separate computer. At least twice a day, I back up the latest revision onto my web space. (I did the same with the manuscripts for this book—talk about paranoid!) The thing is, I've never had a hard disk failure, but it's definitely possible. I'm just not going to be the one who says, "The computer lost my file." If you do back up to a web space, you'll see that separating your code from your content is an extra benefit because your backups will be nice and small.

You might not think there's much more to say about Save As, but it's worth noting that Flash MX 2004 has a new feature called *Save and Compact*. A nasty fact about Flash files is that they always grow when you save—even if you've removed items. Now, instead of needing to Save As, you can select File, Save and Compact. This effectively defragments your file by discarding unused elements.

Documenting Inline

Again, a simple tracking system involves putting tracking information right inside your code files. Generally, I'm talking about comments in the code, such as keywords that make it easier to search through the code. For example, I usually put //HW next to any hard-wired scripts. The idea is that I can later search my scripts for "HW." You can come up with your own keywords. Also, if you work on a team, you should probably put your initials next to any code you add to someone else's file.

{ Note }

Check In/Check Out If you're working on a team and have Flash MX Professional 2004, you can take advantage of the Project panel's Check In and Check Out features. You can learn more about the Project panel in Chapter 10. Basically, you can check out a file, and others on the team will see an indication that the file is unavailable to them while you edit it. Like a lot of these techniques, it's more of a habit that you develop than anything else. But it's a habit that becomes critical as your project size grows.

Your inline documentation can also be right onscreen. Often I keep a list of known issues—bugs or missing features that I plan to fix later. This saves bug finders' time because they know something isn't complete yet. Also, it helps you, the developer, because you're reminded of the remaining work. Similar to how I suggested you approach fixing bugs in a deliberate manner, you should approach adding features carefully, too. You would never program anything if you tried to program everything at once. Keeping a "to do" list right onscreen is a good way to (almost subconsciously) plan for the upcoming work.

Document Fixes

I suppose this is a repeat of the tip in the "Save As" section, but it bears repeating here: Document the changes added to each revision. Because we're nearly ready to look at how to fix bugs, I thought I should remind you that the same technique of documenting added features can be applied to fixing bugs. That is, every time you fix a bug, you may consider doing a Save As—or at least documenting all the fixes in each revision. All the additional benefits apply here, too: You have documentation for your client and a list of reminders if you have to start all over.

Defining Testing Procedures

Measuring success is an important component to any project. If your application is supposed to save time for the user, for instance, it's best if you can prove that with data. Similarly, measuring an application's quality takes place while you test it. Although you can't really test until you have something built, you can identify how you plan to test in advance. Ideally, you should identify the testing procedure before you even build. Without a way to test, how can you tell whether you've reached your goals? It may seem I'm mixing the concept of testing for bugs and testing for success, but the best way to find bugs is to test whether the app reaches its goals.

It's not critical that you define how you're going to test before you begin programming. Actually, as you're working you may become suspicious that something you're building may be prone to fail. Obviously, the programmer should do what he can to ensure the app works—but he can't test everything. There's nothing wrong with the programmer saying, "Be sure to test this feature; I think it may be buggy."

Although some people's idea of bug testing is to just pound on an app, it's best to have a formal process in place. A good testing procedure means that you test for things you otherwise may not when just poking around. Then, when the time comes to retest, you have a procedure to follow so that you retest everything.

I think the best way to judge how much effort is warranted for any quality assurance plan is to look at the size or importance of your project. It's not always easy to calculate the value of quality assurance. Like *insurance*, it's a ripoff until you need it. In any event, it makes sense to analyze this question early in a project—often before you have anything to test.

Practical Debugging

A whole chapter on debugging and only now does debug come up? Yes. The easiest bug to remove is the one that doesn't exist. Ultimately, you *will* create bugs. This section shows you how to hunt them down and remove them.

Basic Approaches

Before considering more formal debugging approaches (namely using debuggers), it makes sense to look at the general approach to finding bugs.

Know Your Enemy

If the bug that doesn't exist is the easiest to fix, the one you clearly understand is only slightly more difficult. As mentioned earlier in the "Finding and Assessing Bugs" section, a clear description of a bug is often the prescription to fix it. So, of course, the general concept of "know your enemy" applies to fixing bugs.

At this point, I should mention that compile-time errors are so critical that there's no point in continuing until they're resolved—that is, the errors that appear in the Output panel when you do a test movie. They're bugs in your syntax. Your movie is not even worth testing if you don't resolve these first. In Flash MX 2004, a whole new set of detailed error messages will appear when using AS2 (ActionScript 2). However, it's the existing compile errors that can be unclear. Here's a rundown of the standard messages (and how to resolve them):

- **Balancing errors** always cause a script error. That is, anything you start you have to finish. Every open parenthesis needs a closing parenthesis (). Same goes for quotes "", curly braces { }, and brackets []. Recall from Chapter 10 the keyboard shortcut Ctrl+' to help find the end of the currently enclosed bracket, curly brace, or parenthesis.

- **Right church, wrong pew** is what I call putting a script on the wrong type of object. You should put all your code on keyframes, but it's actually possible to put code on clips and on buttons. If you do, however, you must surround them with on events (for buttons) or `onClipEvent` (for clips). Usually when you see these errors, it means you accidentally put code on a button or clip rather than in a keyframe. The error displayed will read either "Statement must appear within on handler" or "Statement must appear within `onClipEvent` handler."

- **Type mismatch** now appears in Flash MX 2004 when you supply a variable of the wrong data type. For me, it shows up most often when I refer to a function before it has been declared. The bottom line is that AS2 is now a typed language—meaning, for example, you can't put a number in the place of a string or vice versa.

- **Syntax error** is sort of a catchall where there's something wrong, but that's all you're told. In fact, the error will include the line number to help you find the bug.

If your code compiles (that is, no error appears in the Output panel), you can move on to regular old functional bugs—that is, instances where your application doesn't work right. The first step is always to identify the bug clearly. Ideally, you've figured out how to repeat the bug. It might take a few steps to cause the bug to appear. However, try to reduce the steps necessary to the fewest possible. At a minimum, try to remember what you were doing just prior to experiencing the bug.

Another part of identifying your bug is to narrow down the description of the bug. For example, "the app doesn't work" is too general. Something like "the save feature doesn't save" is better, even though saving might be your app's number one feature (and, without it, the app doesn't really work). It's definitely better to have more detailed bugs as opposed to a few all-encompassing bugs.

Scientific Approach

When you have your list of bugs prepared, you'll be able to clearly see your goal: to fix the bugs. You need to take a scientific approach to the process for several reasons. First, you want to be efficient by clearing out bugs as swiftly as possible. Second, you don't want to be careless by accidentally introducing more bugs. Finally, you don't want to overlook any bugs. A similar issue occurs when you think you fixed a bug but only changed it.

The scientific approach comes down to fixing one thing at a time. You have to act like a machine, staying focused on one bug at a time. If you see another bug while working, don't ignore it, but don't fix it either. Just add it to the list (and follow the steps of identifying and categorizing bugs discussed earlier).

Realize that most bugs have several ways to fix them. The best fix requires the least amount of work—more specifically, the least amount of disruption. The less "stuff" you add to the file, the easier you'll be able to maintain your file. In addition, try to avoid writing `if` statements to handle every specific exception. Here's a simplified excerpt to show what I'm talking about. First the buggy code:

```
function go(direction){
  clip.gotoAndStop(clip._currentframe+direction);
  if(clip._currentframe==10){
    next_btn.enabled=false;
  }
}
```

This code contains no syntax errors. However, that `if` statement was added to disable the `next_btn` when we reached the tenth frame. Actually, this code contains two problems. First, it has hard-wired 10 frames. It's better to use a dynamic reference. That is, change the `10` to `clip._totalframes` so that if the clip is longer, it still works. The second problem is almost like fixing the symptom rather than the cause. It definitely makes the button disable when frame 10 is reached. However, what happens when they jump back to frame 9? The button is still disabled. Here's the modified code that both disables and enables the button as needed:

```
function go(direction){
  clip.gotoAndStop(clip._currentframe+direction);
  if(clip._currentframe==clip._totalframes){
    next_btn.enabled=false;
  }else{
    next_btn.enabled=true;
  }
}
```

The idea is that you want to add as little code as possible to have the greatest impact. Also, when you fix one thing, be careful not to break something else! This happens often.

Finally, even though the ultimate fix to a bug should involve only a little bit of code, you'll still generate quite a bit of code attempting various solutions. I recommend solving bugs "offline." That is, first back up the source file so that you're working with a copy. Then go wild trying to find the solution. When you do find what you think is the solution, go back to the original (make *another* backup), and then try to incorporate your fix. If after testing it still works, consider this copy your source. The idea is that when you're investigating a solution, you may forget to remove some of your failed attempts. Starting fresh and going directly to the solution will keep your source clean. Compare this to an artist who investigates a technique with many "studies."

Just as with a lot of techniques, you're welcome and likely to find more approaches to bug fixing.

Homemade Debuggers

When you have a clearly identified bug, there's nothing to do but fix it. Often, however, the bug is more ambiguous. A debugger, despite its name, is only a tool to help find bugs. "Bug finder" isn't even a good name because you're still the one to find the bugs. Think of a debugger more as a runtime code viewer.

You can use a range of debuggers, everything from a low-tech homemade debugger to the built-in Debugger panel. This discussion focuses first on homemade solutions. Don't discount these; they can offer much more than the real Debugger. Not only can they be customized, they're also easier to use at runtime.

Simple Debug Mode

You may be familiar with the old-school approach to using a dynamic text field's Var: option to monitor a variable. The problem with that is it can tend to cast your variables as a string. Here's a more advanced debug feature that you can use to monitor any variable's value. You need an input text field named toAdd_txt, a button instance name add_btn, and a List component named my_lb. Put all those items inside a movie clip so that it's easy to turn invisible or move to another file. Finally, put the code in Listing 11.2 all in the first keyframe of the clip.

Listing 11.2 Homemade Variable Watcher

```
1   indexCounter=0;
2   add_btn.onPress=function(){
3      doAddWatch();
4   }
5   function update(id, oldVal, newVal,index){
6      my_lb.replaceItemAt(index, id+"="+newVal);
7      return newVal
8   }
9   function doAddWatch(){
10     my_lb.addItem(toAdd_txt.text+"="+_root[toAdd_txt.text]);
```

continues

Listing 11.2 Homemade Variable Watcher (Continued)

```
11      _root.watch(toAdd_txt.text,
12                  update,
13                  indexCounter);
14      indexCounter++
15      toAdd_txt.text="";
16   }
```

Basically, this code sets up a watch for any variable the user types into the `toAdd_txt` field. Line 10 adds an item to the list containing the variable's name and current value. Then the `watch()` method in line 11 takes 3 parameters (`toAdd_txt.text`, `update`, and `indexCounter`). The function `update()` executes every time the variable changes. Line 6 replaces the text shown in the appropriate index of the list. (Notice the value for that index is passed as the third parameter of `watch()` on line 13.)

In practice, this homemade variable watcher enables me to monitor any variables I identify while the movie plays, as shown in Figure 11.4.

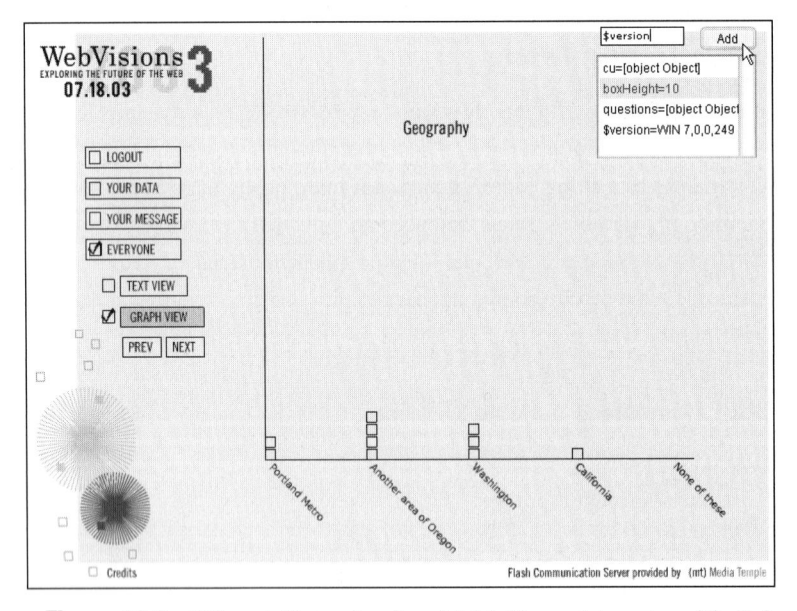

Figure 11.4 *This variable watcher (top right) is like a mini-version of the Debugger— but it runs in the Flash Player.*

The big advantage of this approach is that it works during runtime. You could hide this clip initially and then use a sequence of key presses to reveal it. This way, even your client could pop it open and type in a couple of variables. This is what makes it more useful than the built-in Debugger: It can even work in the browser.

Although this example is all right, you may want to add more features to make something even more useful. For example, watched variables don't update if they contain arrays. An approach using onEnterFrame could redisplay the current values of arrays even if they haven't changed. This wouldn't be as efficient as watch(), so you may want to be sure to remove it upon delivery.

Another issue is that you might get tired typing in several specific variables every time the movie plays. You could prepopulate the list with a few of the variables you know you want to monitor.

The main point is that you can build an entire mini-application just for testing. In my experience, just a few watch() variables is usually enough, but I can see the need for something more powerful. Like everything, you just have to judge how much investment it's worth.

Building a Runtime Trace Window

Wouldn't it be nice if your trace() statements worked even after you delivered the project and you were watching it online? Maybe most users wouldn't be impressed, but I know I get pretty dependent on seeing that Output panel while authoring. The following example creates a runtime Output panel that you can use with any app you build even after it's delivered. It's all done through the magic of the LocalConnection object (covered in detail in Chapter 6, "Basic Data Exchange").

You build a separate file that serves as the runtime trace window. Then, for any application you build, you can add the code in Listing 11.3.

Listing 11.3 Runtime Trace Window (Sender)

```
function myTrace(theValue){
  //trace(theValue);
  //return;
  my_lc=new LocalConnection();
  my_lc.send("_phillipTrace", "onGetTrace", theValue);
  delete(my_lc);
}
```

continues

Listing 11.3 Runtime Trace Window (Sender) (Continued)

Now the only trick is you have to remember to start using `myTrace()` in place of `trace()`. That is, any of your apps can issue `myTrace()` and pass a value; then this code makes a LocalConnection instance and connects to "_phillipTrace"; sends the value received; and finally, deletes the LocalConnection instance.

Two important notes: While testing locally, you can just uncomment the first two lines and `myTrace()` will redirect to `trace()` so that it works like normal. Also, you don't have to use "_phillipTrace" for your LocalConnection channel. However, you need to start with underscore! This overcomes some of the issues when you send data between a remote web site and your local machine.

Okay, so the preceding code goes into any new app you build. Then, to use it, you create the following file once. Just create a multiline dynamic text field instance named onscreen_txt, and include a scrollbar in case you receive a lot of text. Listing 11.4 shows the code for the runtime Output panel.

Listing 11.4 Runtime Trace Window (Receiver)

```
1   my_lc=new LocalConnection();
2   my_lc.allowDomain = function(sendingDomain){
3       return(true);
4   }
5   my_lc.onGetTrace = function(theString){
6       onscreen_txt.text+=theString+newline;
7       onscreen_txt.scroll=onscreen_txt.maxscroll;
8   }
9   my_lc.connect("_phillipTrace")
```

This movie will run locally on your hard drive. However, lines 2 through 4 will allow any outside domain access to talk to your movie. Finally, you just set up the LocalConnection instance to handle onGetTrace (sent from your app) and identify the common channel "_phillipTrace".

Unlike many examples, this one is pretty solid as is. Just make a SWF containing the preceding receiver code and launch it through the standalone Flash Player. (That is, double-click the SWF.). Then visit any web application you created that uses `myTrace()` (from the preceding sender code). The only enhancement I can think of is a clear button. Pretty easy, however: `onscreen_txt.text=""`.

Additionally, this the only reasonable way to debug Macromedia Central apps because they must run in the Central environment. But, because you can use the LocalConnection object, this homemade debugger works great.

Now it's time to look at the "real" Debugger. Again, however, I want to stress that homemade debug tools such as the runtime trace window are very useful. It doesn't even make sense to compare because they're used for different purposes. The homemade tools enable you to monitor things, whereas (as you'll see next) the Debugger enables you to step through the code and provides several additional monitoring features.

Using the Debugger Panel

Unfortunately, the Debugger panel does not "de-bug" your movie. Instead, it can help you view what's going on in your code—almost at a subatomic level. Specifically, you can monitor the value for any property or variable and step through your code one line at a time. This section shows you how to use the Debugger.

Watching Variables and Properties

The Flash Debugger enables you to view and set both properties and variables—while the movie plays. To view the Debugger, select Control, Debug Movie (rather than Control, Test Movie). When the Debugger first appears, your movie pauses until you click the Continue button (see Figure 11.5). Actually, while it's paused you can navigate through your code and add additional (temporary) breakpoints.

While debugging, you'll see four panes. In the upper left, a hierarchy of all your movies appears. To view properties or variables, first select the Movie Clip instance that you want to analyze. Then in the middle-left pane, you'll see four tabs—click Properties or Variables to reveal details about the selected clip. For example, Figure 11.6 shows that the selected text field's text property is "".

One thing about watching variables and properties is that you can edit their values right as the movie plays. You can't really use this to fix bugs because it only works while you're debugging. However, it's nice to preview possible values for your variables and properties.

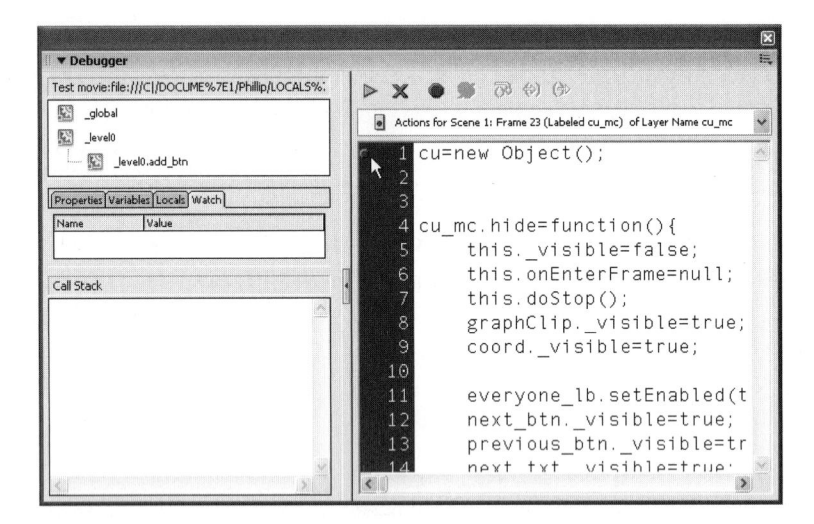

Figure 11.5 *Before clicking the Debug panel's Continue button, you can navigate through the code to add breakpoints.*

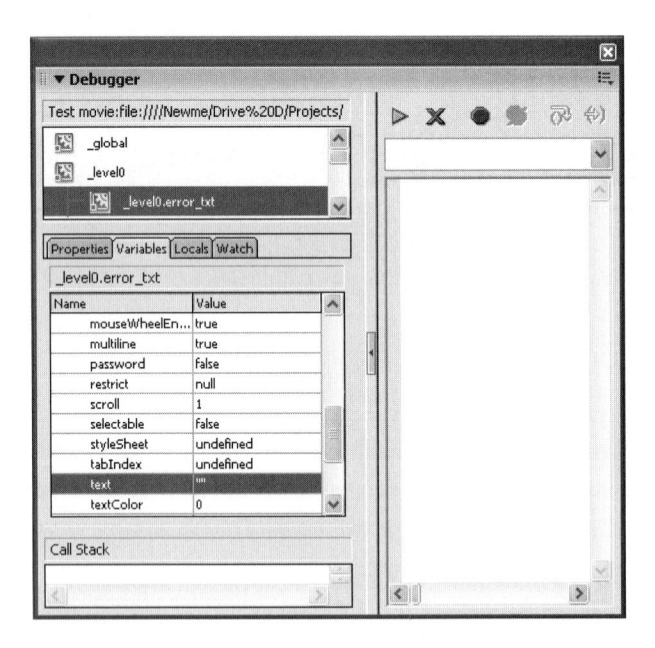

Figure 11.6 *The Debug panel enables you to inspect any property or variable of any clip in your movie.*

By the way, if you find your movie has a ton of variables and you only want to monitor a few of them, you can select that/those variable(s) (under Variables in the Debugger) and then right-click and select Watch. This adds the selected variable(s) to the list under the Watch tab. Not only does this save a bit of hunting around, it also keeps watching those variables the next time you debug the movie.

At this point, I should say 90 percent of my work with the Debugger panel has now been described. That is, viewing properties and variables is quite useful. If I'm loading data and want to see whether the values have been received, I can use the Debugger. Also, as you saw in Chapter 6, the easiest way to see the tree of data in an XML object is through the Debugger.

Stepping Through Code

It's almost as though you can make the frame rate come to a halt while you step through one line of code at a time. As you step, you can watch variables and see the sequence of events in slow motion. The way it works is you first set a breakpoint on any line of code you want to analyze. While debugging, if that line of code is encountered, the Debugger pauses the movie and displays the line of code in context in the right-side pane (see Figure 11.7).

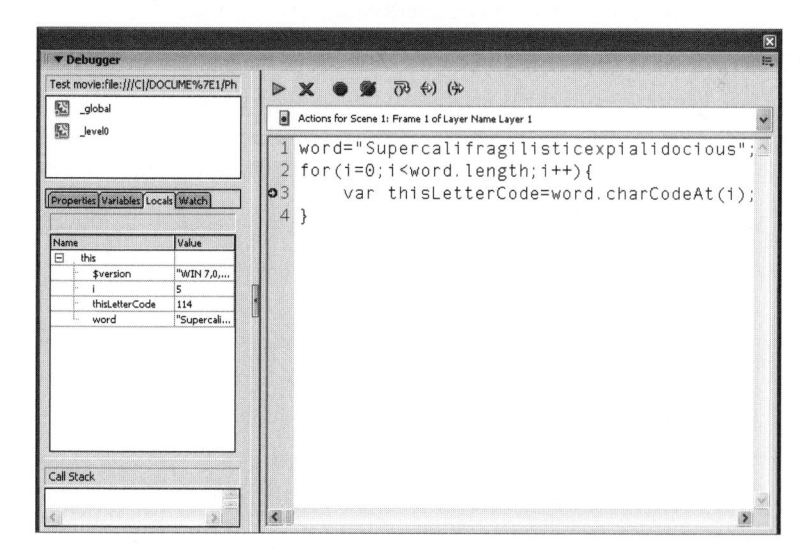

Figure 11.7 *Stepping through code is the most focused way to track bugs.*

When your movie is paused on a breakpoint, several additional pieces of data may be revealed. You'll always see the line of code in question on the right side. If your breakpoint is inside a function, you'll see additional variables listed under the Locals tab. These variables are specific to the function in which you've just paused. For example, some functions may operate on a temporary variable just while inside the function. Or, if your breakpoint is inside a loop, the itinerant variable could be local; this way, you can reveal its current value. Finally, if you're paused inside a function and you arrived at that function by way of another function, the Call Stack pane will be filled with a history—or "how you got here" information.

To see how this all works, you can debug the code from the homemade variable watcher code in Listing 11.2 and add a breakpoint to line 6 (inside the update() function). Add and remove breakpoints by clicking in the gutter to the left of your code in the Actions panel. The Debugger pauses when the line of code with the breakpoint is encountered. To have a variable that changes, trigger the update() function (so, you can in turn reach the breakpoint) and put this code in the main timeline:

```
count=0;
_root.onMouseDown=function(){ count++ };
```

Select Control, Debug Movie (click the green Continue button) and type **count** into the homemade variable watcher. Now, every time you click onstage you should encounter the breakpoint. When paused on a breakpoint, click the Locals tab; I will walk through what you see (also shown in Figure 11.7).

Notice a yellow arrow on the breakpoint line of code. Also, the Locals section shows temporary variables such as the parameters newVal and oldVal. There's really no other way to see temporary variables unless you do a trace() or store them in regular variables. The pane at the bottom left (Call Stack) is pretty neat. It shows you (in reverse order) the sequence of functions that got you to the breakpoint. It all started with an onMouseDown(), and then the update() function was triggered. The function that you're currently "in" is always on top of the stack. The Call Stack can become much taller and more interesting when you have a complex app. While still paused, check out the code exposed in the right pane. In addition to Continue, you'll see Step Over, Step In, and Step Out. Basically, these give you the option (when stopped at a breakpoint) to step through one line of code at a time. When a breakpoint is encountered, a little yellow arrow points to the line of code in question (the breakpoint). Clicking

Continue makes the movie play until the next breakpoint is reached. If you click the Step In button (think "baby step"), however, the arrow moves to the very next line of code, at which point you can keep clicking Step In and monitor how variables or properties are changing. Step Out is slightly different, because when you're paused within a homemade function, it steps right outside the currently enclosed function. Step Over is similar, but it just jumps over the very next line of code. In any event, your code isn't really skipped. (Every line will always execute no matter what.) However, the little yellow line can jump a little bit further ahead and pause if you want. In practice, I find myself clicking Step In first, but then if I find that I'm stepping into a repetitive loop, I might use Step Over or even Step Out. The differences are really subtle, but the general idea is the same: You can step through one line at a time and check out what's happening.

Remote Debugging

One of the coolest features of the Debugger is that you can debug movies playing in a browser. This means that even after you upload a finished movie, it's possible to debug it remotely. When you see the steps involved for this to work, you might think it's a pain, but the steps are necessary for good reason. For example, you might not want others to be able to debug your movies.

To debug a movie remotely, the following conditions must be met:

- The original FLA needs to have its Publish settings set to Debugging Permitted. Optionally, you can also specify a password (see Figure 11.8).

- You must store an SWD file adjacent to the SWF on your server. (You'll create an SWD file automatically any time you test, debug, or publish a movie with the Debugging Permitted option selected in Publish settings.)

- Finally, the Debugger must have the Options menu set to Enable Remote Debugging (see Figure 11.9). (This makes Flash act like a server, so you might need to adjust firewall settings.)

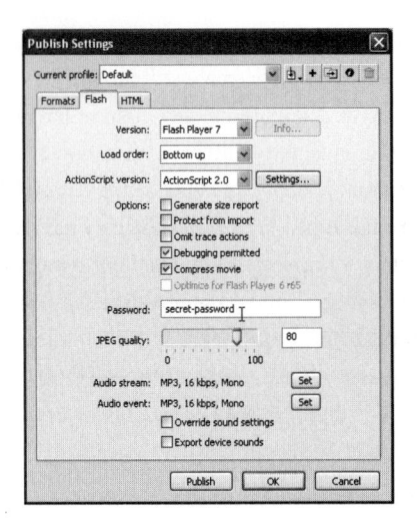

Figure 11.8 *A public SWF with Debugging Permitted can be password-protected from other Flash developers.*

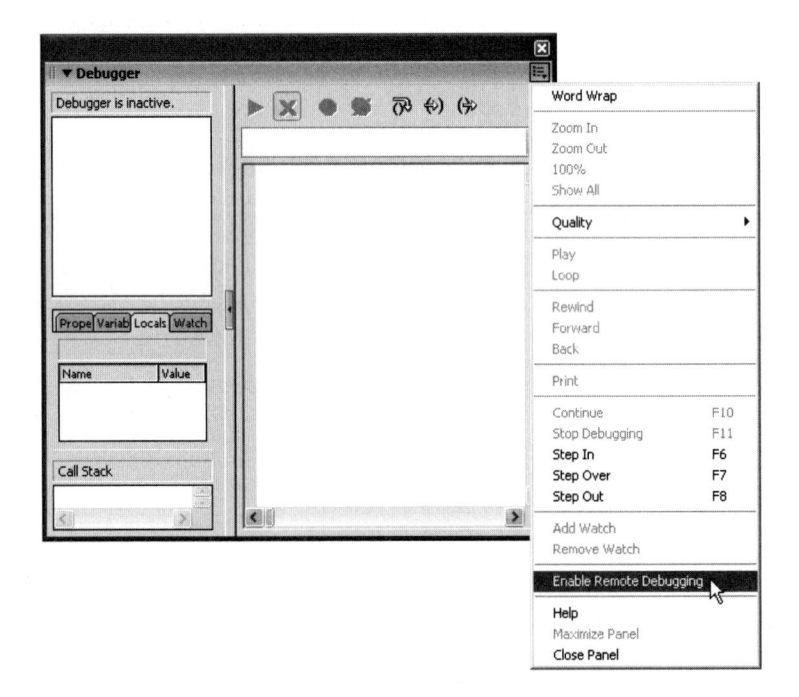

Figure 11.9 *You must enable remote debugging from the Debug panel.*

To debug a movie, first open Flash, start a new movie, and then select Window, Debugger. From the Debugger's Options menu, select Enable Remote Debugging. Then just launch your browser and right-click a movie that has been set to permit debugging when it was published. If you're running the correct version of the Flash Player (the default version that gets installed when you install Flash), you can select Debugger from the menu that appears. (Users who have downloaded the free player from Macromedia won't see this option.) First you need to specify where your version of Flash is running (that is, the one with its Debugger set to Enable Remote Debugging). Normally, you'll just accept the default Localhost option. Then you can return to Flash, enter the password (or just click OK if you have no password), and you'll be able to debug the movie like normal.

The Error Object

Flash MX 2004 includes an Error object that makes it easy to set up traps for various conditions *while your app runs*. That is, it's basically a glorified `if` statement that will trigger code if certain conditions are met. The reason I made this like an epilogue at the end of the chapter is that it's really not a tool for debugging. It's an error trap—equivalent to trapping an event. In addition, it only triggers at runtime (when your bugs should be well out of the way). In any event, I think it's worth documenting here.

The benefit is that for several different places in your code, you may have the same condition you're checking. Suppose, for instance, that you build a calculator. When the user attempts to divide by zero, you want to give the user some meaningful feedback instead of just displaying `NaN` (not a number). You can define an Error object that specifies off-limit conditions, what to do when those conditions occur, what do to do otherwise, and—optionally—what to do in all cases.

The structure is `try`, `catch`, `finally`. You'll always have some code that you want to try to execute. You can include conditions (such as `if` statements) that throw errors. If any errors are thrown, the code is diverted to the catch you've defined. Finally, you can include code that will execute regardless of whether an error was encountered. Reread this paragraph after you see the actual code in Listing 11.5 because it might help explain the syntax.

First, you'll see a hard-wired `try`, `catch`, `finally` structure.

Listing 11.5 Basic Try, Catch, Finally

```
1   try {
2     if (Number(denominator_txt.text)<=0) {
3       throw new Error("Can't divide by zero");
4     }
5     trace("okay");
6   } catch (theError) {
7     trace(theError.message)
8   } finally {
9     trace("always");
10  }
```

Notice first that lines 1, 6, and 8 are aligned because, like an if-else statement, there are three parts. Actually, just like how the else is optional, you could forgo the finally by ending things at line 8 with a closing curly brace: }.

Note that this entire listing would likely go inside an event (for instance, a button's onPress). Mainly, it's line 5 that triggers when everything's okay. Think of line 5 as the else of the if statement in line 2. More specifically, line 5 will never be encountered if line 3's throw is reached. It's like return—it skips the rest of the code. You could have several other if statements that throw different errors. You could even throw errors from within a loop. Suppose, for example, that you are looping through an array of usernames checking for any that match what the user typed (in which case you'd throw an error).

Any time an error is thrown, it gets redirected to line 6. You can think of line 6 as a function that waits to be invoked—it just gets invoked whenever an error is thrown. The weird thing is that the passed argument "Can't divide by zero" gets stuffed inside the message property, a built-in property containing whatever parameter is sent when the error is thrown.

The trace() in line 9 triggers every time—with or without an error. This is just a place you can put code that gets triggered regardless.

> I guarantee you could pull off the same effect of the preceding code by using a more traditional (or familiar) approach. The Error object excels when you consolidate code and share exceptions and catches among several different places in your application. For this, you need to define a constructor function for each error you plan on using. By having several different parts of your code throwing the same error, you can later edit and refine that error to control all instances that

throw it. In addition, you have an opportunity to use more than just the default message property. Listing 11.6 shows an applied example involving two input text fields (top_txt and bottom_txt) plus a dynamic text field for the result of dividing two numbers (result_txt).

Listing 11.6 Advanced Error Object

```
1    function StringError(){
2       this.errorString="need numbers";
3       this.extra="you can't do math on words";
4    }
5    function NumberError(){
6       this.errorString="can't divide by 0";
7       this.extra="it's just not allowed";
8    }
9
10   my_btn.onPress = function() {
11      try {
12         // try
13         if (isNaN(top_txt.text)||isNaN(bottom_txt.text)) {
14            throw new StringError();
15         }
16         if (Number(bottom_txt.text)<=0) {
17            throw new NumberError();
18         }
19         //otherwise
20         result_txt.text = Number(top_txt.text)/Number(bottom_txt.text);
21
22      } catch (theError) {
23         result_txt.text =theError.errorString;
24         trace("extra info: "+ theError.extra);
25      }
26   };
```

The two constructor functions (StringError() and NumberError()) have two properties that I made up: errorString and extra. Way down on lines 23 and 24, you can see I'm using errorString for what the user sees and extra for the trace() statement. I'm sure you can get more creative by modifying this code. Anywhere else in this application, you can throw either of these two errors. Keep in mind that you only throw inside the try portion. In addition, you need a catch defined uniquely for every try.

As mentioned previously, the Error object is a glorified `if` statement. Of course, it's much more than that. However, mainly you just specify what you want to happen, what the exceptions are, and how to handle exceptions.

Summary

There's a saying that salespeople don't begin selling until they hear their first "no." If that's the case, debugging is where programming begins. In any event, debugging is as important as any part of programming.

This chapter has shown that debugging is more than just fixing bugs. It's also about finding ways to avoid bugs in the first place. It's identifying bugs clearly, approaching the process efficiently, and even classifying the importance of bugs. I can't say that I like debugging, but the relief I feel having addressed a bug is worth the stress involved hunting it down.

{Chapter 12}

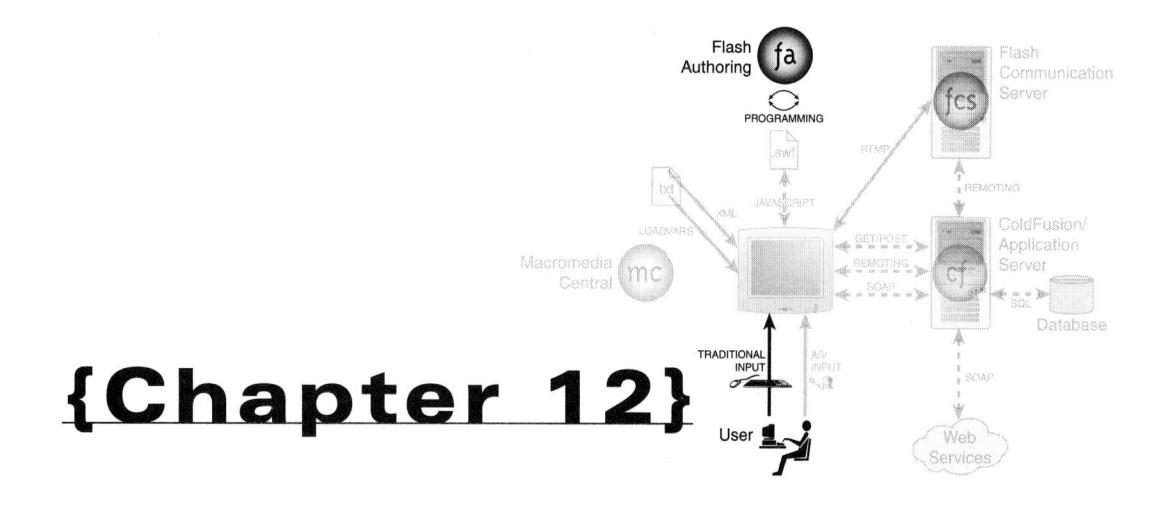

Using Components

Although you have most likely seen and used some of the components that ship with Macromedia Flash MX 2004, you probably can't say that you've fully exploited them yet. In fact, even the developers who created components are just now scratching the surface. They're built with extensibility in mind. Almost like an erector set, components are cool because you know you can build something cool with them. In the case of components, however, it's their ease of use that makes them even more compelling. This chapter covers *using* components. Specifically, this chapter covers the following topics:

- Populating components with your content
- Accessing component properties and methods to control their behavior
- The `dataProvider` data structure
- Tying components to your applications so that they can trigger your code
- A few neat tricks that save tons of time

Note that this chapter deals only with the user interface (UI) components that ship with Flash MX 2004. You'll be able to apply this knowledge to any future components that use the same architecture as these.

V2 Components

The components that ship with Flash MX 2004 are called *V2* for version 2. (In fact, they started life as "smart clips" in Flash 5—so one could argue they're really V3.) Every time they get better. And, every time there's a new set of usage rules. Before getting into advanced topics or details of any specific components, it's important to consider the general advantages of V2 components.

The advantages range from practical usage benefits to under-the-hood optimizations. In use, they're nicer because nearly every property is accessible using standard dot syntax. Whereas before you might have said `myList.setSelectedIndex(1)`, now you can just say `myList.selectedIndex=1`. Not only is this more logical, it also means that you don't need a separate method for getting as well as setting. Check out how long this old way of increasing the selected index value is:

```
myList.setSelectedIndex(myList.getSelectedIndex()+1);
```

Using the new direct property access, it's just as follows:

```
myList.selectedIndex++;
```

When you attempt to explore the code behind these components, you'll quickly realize they're compiled. That is, you can't edit the code. The main idea behind compiling is to prevent users from accidentally messing up the code. You'll find the compiled SWC files inside the Components folder. (That's located in the First Run folder adjacent to Flash MX 2004.) This is also where you can install old components (which involves moving FLA files into that folder or letting the free Macromedia Extension Manager do it for you).

If you're using Flash MX Professional 2004, you can use the new components to take advantage of the new validation and formatting controls (for example, to confirm a user enters a qualified phone number). In addition, there's the whole concept of binding values from one component to another (covered in Chapter 7, "Exchanging Data with Outside Services") that's available in V2 components.

Although V2 components may be the best thing since V1 components, there are a couple of disadvantages. Most notably, file size. Adding just one button in an app that has no other components adds about 74K to the SWF's file size. This is relatively huge. However, the good news is that you can add several more components, and the size only grows marginally. That's because one component may include a variety of connected class files that make up its underlying framework.

That framework is shared among several components—so it's not like each new component adds another 74K.

> **{ Note }**
>
> **Class-Based Means Code Is Exposed and Extensible** You may think the primary reason behind compiling is securing the component programmer's intellectual property. In fact, SWC files are not exactly hack-proof. In addition, the new class-based structure makes V2 components easier to extend. That is, the code behind Flash UI components is all exposed through AS class files located in First Run\Classes\mx\controls. Don't edit those files, but—if you really need to—learn how you can extend them. You can create a new class file that either overrides current methods or adds new methods to the component, and then import that into your Flash movie. Chapter 13, "Building a Code Library," touches on this subject. (Incidentally, the components in this chapter will be extended, but just not via the class files.)

Another disadvantage is the investment you make learning the "new way." Of course, this applies only if you're familiar with V1 components (in which case, try to forget much of what you know). Given the choice between Macromedia coming out with a better way every 18 months or having them stagnate so that I don't have to learn anything, I would much rather have the new stuff. Besides, in the case of V2 components, the investment in learning is paid back in productivity. Also, the rest of this chapter will give you a good start.

Foundation Skills

This section moves from the ground level up through all the standard ways to use components. Basically, the process is you populate them, associate them so that they can trigger your code, and optionally customize their look. For a simple example, consider a button. You'll want to populate its label (so that it reads Click Me, for example), you'll want to link it to your code so that something happens when the user clicks it, and you might even want to change the typeface or highlight the color. You'll learn all of this.

Populating Manually

The basic idea of a component is that it's a movie clip containing code and graphics. With any movie clip, you can set individual properties for each instance onstage through the Properties panel. When the instance is a component, the Properties panel includes an additional tab called Parameters (see Figure 12.1).

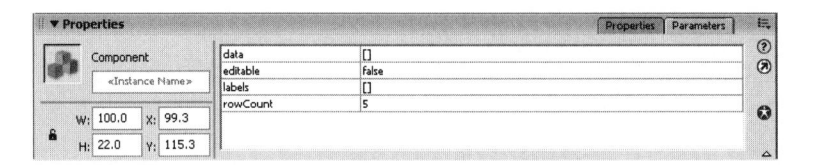

Figure 12.1 *In addition to the normal settings available for clips, components have the Parameters tab in the Properties panel.*

Through this interface, you, the author, can assign initial values for any property you decide to expose. Actually, most components include more properties you can access, but they require scripting (which you'll do in the next section).

Just drag two Button components from the Components panel onto the stage. Select one instance, and through the Properties panel's Parameters tab, change the Button's value for labels. That is, type something other than Button in the labels field. In the Button component's case, it uses LivePreview, so you'll actually see the label you set without testing the movie. (You can turn Live Preview on and off via the Control menu.) To see the button behave like a button, however, you need to test the movie. Feel free to tinker with the other properties exposed in the Parameters tab.

{ Note }

Parameters Versus Properties Think of them all as properties. It's just that the Properties panel had to have a different name for the additional properties added to a component, so Macromedia called it *Parameters*. Actually, the property names visible in the Parameters tab (for instance, `data` or `label` in Figure 12.1) are not necessarily the same as the property names the component author is using. That is, some components use more presentable names in the Parameters tab than the underlying property names to which they're linked. In addition, you can't just set those property values using script unless the component author designed it that way. (You'll see how to check next.)

Although the Button is a quite useful component, you can't do much using just the Properties panel. Before moving on, however, it might help to look at one that's a bit more exciting. Drag a ComboBox component onstage. To populate this component, click the [] to the right of the labels parameter. Then click again (or click the little magnifier) and you'll see the dialog box from which you can add multiple values (see Figure 12.2).

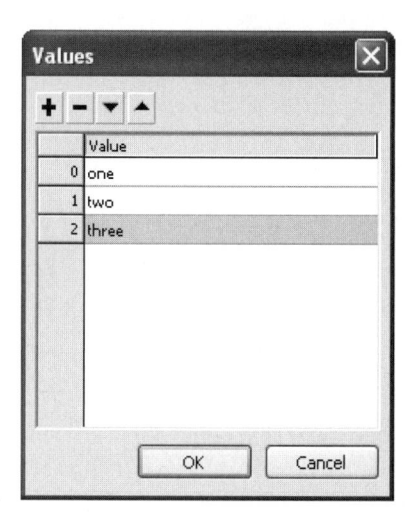

Figure 12.2 *For parameters that accept multiple values, this dialog box is accessible.*

Click the plus button a few times, and then replace each `defaultValue` with something like "one," "two," "three," and so on. Click OK, and then test the movie. Pretty cool. Almost no work, and you have a sophisticated ComboBox. Naturally, you'll need to read on to learn how to make it *do* anything.

Populating with Script

It's possible to do everything—and more—that the Parameters tab can do by using script. The first step is to ensure your components have instance names. Then you just use "object dot property" or "object dot method." That is, when you know the supported properties and methods, you can use very standard-looking code.

Using Properties and Methods

Some attributes of components are settable directly through properties. In the case of setting a Button component's label, for example, name the instance **my_pb** and just use the following:

```
my_pb.label="Click me";
```

That is, "instance dot property." (I just happen to know buttons have a `label` property.)

In the case of the ComboBox, it doesn't actually have a `label` property. You need to use the `addItem()` method to populate it. Also, the `removeAll()` method clears any labels currently in the ComboBox. Consider this simple code for a ComboBox with the instance name my_cb:

```
my_cb.removeAll();
my_cb.addItem("one");
my_cb.addItem("two");
my_cb.addItem("three");
```

There's not a whole lot to this except that you'll have to learn what properties and methods are available for the particular component you're using.

Learning Properties and Methods

It's sometimes difficult to see why some cases warrant using a method and others use properties. I think it's easy to understand why `removeAll()` is a method—it's more of a procedure than a static attribute. (That is what properties are.) It's just that when you can, it's easier to use properties because you can "get" their values using the same syntax you use to "set" their values. This isn't up to you, however; it just depends how the component was designed. Take the ProgressBar component. You may want to say my_bar.value=50, but you must use my_bar.setProgress(50,100).

Again, you just need to look up the properties and methods available. In the Help panel, search for the component name (for instance, ComboBox), and then find the following matching categories:

    1 ComboBox component

    2 Using the ComboBox component

    3 Customizing the ComboBox component

    4 ComboBox class

Because these four categories show up for most all components, let me explain each one. In 1, you can find what the component is useful for and how the *user* will interact with it. Under 2, you can find how you can populate via the Properties panel. Under 3, you get details about how to skin the component (covered later this chapter). Finally, under 4 you can find all the properties and methods accessible to you via ActionScript.

Another "how to help yourself tip": In lieu of designated code hints suffixes (like how I use _pb for Buttons and _cb for ComboBoxes), Flash MX 2004 supports an improved method. At the top of your script, just identify your component instances using the new strict data type casting. For example:

```
var mybutton:Button;
```

Then, you'll find anytime you type `mybutton.`, you'll trigger all the supported properties and methods. Remember to start with `var` or the preceding technique won't work. Also, you'll need to include the full path to a component's class file (for example, `var myCombo:mx.controls.ComboBox`).

Component Data Structure

Most of the components support the idea of maintaining both labels and data. This is classic code-data separation. That is, the user sees the label, but deep inside the component there is a corresponding value for the data. For example, Figure 12.3 shows a manually populated ComboBox that displays wordy labels but maintains actual web addresses in the data.

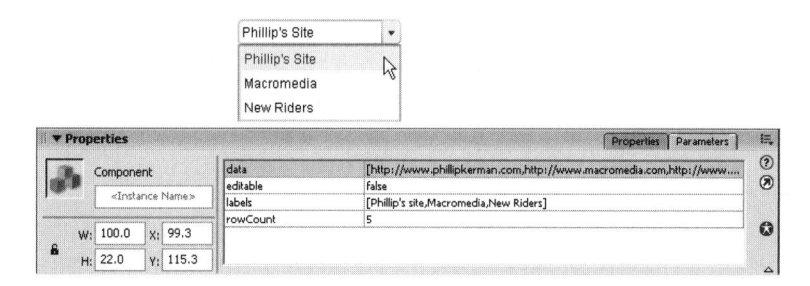

Figure 12.3 *Once populated, this ComboBox has three labels and three matching values for data.*

The user doesn't need to see the data, but your scripts may need access to it. In this example, the script that triggers when the user selects an item will need to ascertain the corresponding data if you are to navigate to that URL.

Naturally, you can populate a component's data and value via ActionScript. Some components just have one `label` and one `data`—such as Buttons, CheckBoxes, and RadioButtons. In those, you just set each property directly. For example:

```
my_button.label="Click me";
my_button.data=101;
```

You can put anything you want into the `data`. The idea is that you're the one who can grab the `data`'s value, so put whatever you want. In fact, you can store any data type you want: string, number, array, generic object.

Earlier, I left out the fact `addItem()` has room for two parameters (one for `label`, the other for `data`). To repeat what Figure 12.3 shows, for example, the all-script version is shown here:

```
my_cb.removeAll();
my_cb.addItem("Phillip's Site", "http://www.phillipkerman.com");
my_cb.addItem("Macromedia", "http://www.macromedia.com");
```

Notice the first parameter is the `label` and the second parameter is the `data`. In fact, you don't have to use this syntax. For one reason, you have to remember the `label` goes first and the `data` goes second. A more extensible variation involves providing just one parameter—namely, a generic object that contains both a `label` and a `data` property. For example:

```
my_cb.addItem({label:"Macromedia", data:"http://www.macromedia.com"});
```

You'll see this syntax is nicer because it also provides a way for you to add additional properties that are effectively hidden from the user (but still accessible through code) like the `data` property.

Visualizing a Button component with a label and data is fairly easy. For multi-value components that support multiple labels with corresponding data (ComboBox, DataGrid, and List), each label/data pair is stored in what can be thought of as a slot of an array. In fact, the array will become what's called a DataProvider, as you'll see next. I still think it's easiest to think of a component's `addItem()` method as being like and Array's `push()`. For example, this actually populates the ComboBox as was done earlier—but this time without `addItem()`:

```
myArray=[];
myArray.push( {label: "Phillip", data: "http://www.phillipkerman.com"});
myArray.push( {label: "Macromedia", data: "http://www.macromedia.com"});
my_cb.dataProvider=myArray;
```

The only twist thrown in is the last line about the ComboBox's `dataProvider` property (covered next). The part you should really understand, however, is that each item in a multivalue component contains a `label` and a `data` property, and all the items are stored in what can be thought of as an array.

dataProvider

On the surface, a `dataProvider` is just an array that contains generic objects—each with a `label` and a `data` property. It's actually a special type of array because when you associate a component instance with a `dataProvider`, the component remains synchronized any time the `dataProvider` changes. By just saying `someInstance.dataProvder=`, you'll trigger a bunch of underlying code to keep things synchronized.

It's really as easy as shown earlier, but you should use `addItem()` rather than `push()`. Either way will work while populating your array, but after it's been identified as a particular component's `dataProvider`, you'll have to use `addItem()` for the component to remain synchronized. So, just think of `addItem()` the same as `push()`. Just be sure you're inserting a generic object with `label` and `data` properties. There are other useful methods—for example, `addItemAt(1, {label:"1", data:1})`, which inserts this object into index 1. Check out the help on the List class.

Finally, you can definitely store more than just a `label` and `data` property. Those are just the ones the component wants. You'll see in the "Applied Examples Using Components" section that follows (see Listing 12.5) that when you build a survey, you'll store additional properties such as the text of the question as well as an array of possible responses. It's really up to you what you store in the `dataProvider` array.

Ascertaining Values

Although the user sees only the label in a component, you need a way to grab the data as well as any other homemade properties you add. It's pretty simple to get it from a single label/data component such as a Button:

```
trace("value of button is "+my_pb.value);
```

In the case of multivalue components, you first need to grab the item, and then ascertain the value. For example, the following code first gets the item in the 0 index (of my_cb) and then finds the `data` property:

```
trace("first url is "+my_cb.getItemAt(0).data);
```

A few terms are important to understand. First, an *item* in a component is the entire generic object in that particular slot. So when you have the whole item, you can use dot syntax to grab its `data`, `label`, or any other homemade property you stuffed into that slot. There are also two properties to know: `selectedIndex` and `selectedItem`. Take the ComboBox. When the user makes a selection, the `selectedIndex` is the selected slot (0, 1, 2, and so on). However, the `selectedItem` is the whole generic object from which you can grab properties. Suppose, for instance, that you want a button that will take the user to whichever site he has selected in the ComboBox. Just grab a Button component (named my_pb) and a ComboBox (named my_cb) and put the code in Listing 12.1 in the keyframe.

Listing 12.1 ComboBox Jump Menu

```
1  var myArray=[];
2  myArray.addItem({label:"Phillip", data:"http://phillipkerman.com"});
3  myArray.addItem({label:"Macromedia", data:"http://macromedia.com"});
4  my_cb.dataProvider=myArray;
5  my_btn.label="Go";
6  my_btn.onRelease=function(){
7      getURL(my_cb.selectedItem.data);
8  }
```

Ignore for the moment how `onRelease` serendipitously works (because you'll see a better approach next). The main thing to notice is line 7 where my_cb's `selectedItem`'s data property is used to provide the actual string to the `getURL()` command.

Incidentally, if you want to store any additional properties in the `dataProvider`, you would have done so in lines 2 and 3. Then, at the place you intend to ascertain those values, just grab the property in the same manner as line 7 grabbed the `data`.

The key to ascertaining values stored inside a component is just to get a reference to that component instance. In the example above, we just used the instance name. Later, you'll see how to get a reference to the instance that triggered the event (using the `target` property). In either case, after you have a reference to the component, you get any property inside an index.

Triggering Code

We totally lucked out when the Button component responded to the `onRelease` event—just like conventional Flash buttons. That certainly isn't the preferred approach. There are two general ways to handle it now. They both deal with a new set of events specifically supported for particular components. For example, Button components have a `click` event, and ComboBoxes a `change` event. In fact, some components have multiple events for which you can trap. For example, ComboBoxes additionally have such properties as `"close"`, `"open"`, and `"scroll"` (to name just a few), all of which you can trap. The first step is deciding for which event you plan to have code respond.

The two general ways to trap code are as follows:

- The on method (much like code you place right on conventional buttons).
- Use `addEventListener()` to point to an object that contains definitions as to how to handle one or more events.

The *on* Method

Real quick, let me explain the on method. Even though I don't recommend using it, it's bound to become popular because it's implemented this way when you use behaviors. To make it work, you have to put the code right on the component instance. That is, select the component and open the Actions panel. Ensure you see the movie clip instance icon for the selected component at the bottom of the Actions panel, as Figure 12.4 shows.

Figure 12.4 *To explore the built-in "on" events, select a Component and ensure you see its name in the tab at the lower left as shown here.*

If you have a Button component selected, you can type this code:

```
on(click){
  trace("You clicked");
}
```

As soon as you type **on(**, the code completion displays to help you select from the available events for this component. Obviously you'll want to put some more useful code on the component depending on what you want the button to do. One little note, if you want access to the component's properties, be sure to start with `this.`, as in `trace("the label is "+this.label)`. That's about it. You just need to find an appropriate event name for the component you select (and behavior you want).

I don't like the `on` method because you end up with code scattered about (not just in the keyframe). The code-completion help offers a quick reference, however. I suppose the on method is also nice because you don't even have to give your components instance names; without instance names, however, recall that you can't set many properties. I advise you to learn to use `addEventListener()`.

Using *addEventListener()*

With `addEventListener()`, you specify an object that contains properties that match the specified events you want to trap. The function you define gets triggered when the event occurs. Here's the basic form:

```
1  myObj=new Object();
2  myObj.event=function(){
3    //some code
4  }
5  someInstance.addEventListener("event", myObj);
```

Just replace `someInstance` with your component instance name. Also replace both `"event"` (the string in line 5) and `event` (the property in line 2) with the event you're trapping (with, for instance, `click` or `change`). Also, be sure to define your object first before executing the `addEventListener()` method.

> **{ Note }**
>
> **Better Than Flash MX** If you're familiar with the Flash MX methods `setChangeHandler()` and `setClickHandler()`, you'll like `addEventListener()` because it consolidates both of these and makes it much easier. That is, you always use `addEventListener()` but then you specify a different event, depending what you want to trap.

So, instead of lines 6 through 8 in Listing 12.1, I should have used the following code:

```
myReaction=new Object();
myReaction.click=function(){
  getURL(my_cb.selectedItem.data);
}
my_btn.addEventListener("click", myReaction);
```

Although this may seem like more code (okay, this *does* have two extra lines), it actually starts to consolidate when you have several components triggering the same function. Naturally, if you do add event listeners to several components that all point to the same function, you need a way to sort things out inside the function. That is, if several buttons all point to the myReaction object, inside the myReaction.click function you'll probably want to figure out who triggered it. That comes up next, but first consider this more elaborate variation:

```
1  myObj=new Object();
2  myObj.change=function(){ trace("change triggered"); };
3  myObj.open=   function(){ trace("open triggered");   };
4  myObj.close=  function(){ trace("close triggered");  };
5  my_cb.addEventListener("change", myObj);
6  my_cb.addEventListener("open",   myObj);
7  my_cb.addEventListener("close",  myObj);
```

Lines 1 through 4 should look pretty familiar despite each one appearing in a single line. The part that I find weird is how the event listener appears both in the string ("change" in line 5) as well as the property name of the object (change in line 2). I guess my expectation would have been that you could say addEventListener(myObj) and not specify which event—however, that's not how it works. You identify the event name in both places.

Let me show how you can redefine how an event is handled. That is, even after you've defined the functions that will trigger for specific events, you can change what happens when, for instance, "change" triggers. For example, later you could add the following code that would redefine how the script reacts to the change event:

```
myObj.change=function(){trace("something different");};
```

The idea here is that by storing all your events inside properties of an object (here, myObj), it's easy to wipe them away or redefine them.

Event Objects

When any component invokes a function identified through `addEventListener()`, it sends as a single parameter a generic object full of interesting properties. This parameter is called the Event object. For those of you familiar with V1 components, you'll want to know about the `target` property because this is a reference back to the instance that triggered the function. (This is equivalent to the entire first parameter received by V1 components—here you just have to use `target`.) In fact, for anyone the `target` property is probably the most useful. With it, you can ascertain any property of the component (for instance, its `label` or `data`).

It's easiest to see in a simple example (see Listing 12.2). Suppose you have two instances of the RadioButton component (male_rb and female_rb). Instead of having each one trigger a different function, you can make them point to the same function. Then, when inside the function, you can sort out which button was pressed.

Listing 12.2 Using Event Objects

```
1   genderObj=new Object();
2   genderObj.click=function(who){
3      if(who.target.data==1){
4         trace("you clicked male");
5      }else{
6         trace("you clicked female");
7      }
8   }
9   male_rb.label="male";
10  male_rb.data=1;
11  male_rb.addEventListener("click", genderObj);
12  female_rb.label="female";
13  female_rb.data=2;
14  female_rb.addEventListener("click", genderObj);
```

The new part here is that line 2 identifies the parameter who. Then, inside the function I can get a handle on the button by saying `who.target`. In this case, I just grab the `data` property from the button that's calling it, but I could have grabbed anything (even ascertained or set its _x or _y properties).

The other properties besides `target` vary depending on the component type. You can search the Help for "event object." Alternatively, you can insert this (now familiar) tracing code between lines 7 and 8:

```
for(var i in who){
   trace(i+":"+who[i]);
}
```

That will show you all the properties in the `who` parameter. In the case of my radio button, this is what I saw in the Output window:

```
relatedTarget:undefined
button:0
metaKey:false
shiftKey:false
altKey:false
ctrlKey:false
clientY:3
clientX:29
screenY:100.35
screenX:276.35
detail:undefined
view:undefined
type:click
target:_level0.male_rb
```

Don't ask me what all those properties are—just learn how to find them and research them.

Now that you have the foundation skills necessary to use components (populating them, ascertaining their values, triggering code, and figuring out who triggered the code), it's time to move on to a few examples.

Applied Examples Using Components

The following examples are intended to review the concepts already covered and point out a few more details. In addition, they should give you an idea of how you can use components in your apps.

Text (Label, TextArea, and TextInput)

These three components are little more than dynamic and input text fields that come in the form of components. However, that little bit of extra makes them worth learning. The three features in particular are as follows:

- They adopt the text styles defined in the theme or skin defined for all components. This means you can reformat all text using one style definition. This is similar to how we defined our own styles in Chapter 5, "Presenting Data." Doing it with themes and skins is covered later in this chapter.
- TextArea includes an automatic horizontal or vertical scrollbar when the text grows.
- Using Flash Pro, you can apply the binding features that link components to data.

Here's a quick example to make scrolling text. Grab a TextArea and TextInput component and resize them using the FreeTransform tool so that they're wide (not terribly tall, however). Name the TextArea **area_txt** and the TextInput **input_txt**. Put the code in Listing 12.3 in the keyframe.

Listing 12.3 Using TextArea and TextInput Components

```
myListener=new Object();
myListener.enter=function(who){
  area_txt.text+=who.target.text+newline;
  who.target.text="";
}
input_txt.addEventListener("enter",myListener);
```

The first thing to notice is that TextInput components have an enter event (when the user clicks Enter). Also, when the area_txt instance gets too much text to display, it should begin to scroll (see Figure 12.5).

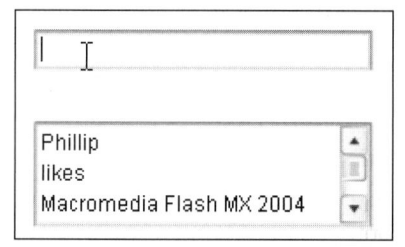

Figure 12.5 *Both the TextArea and TextInput components enable you to trap events. In addition, the TextArea automatically scrolls.*

ComboBox

Although the earlier Jump menu example was useful, here's a slightly more advanced example using the ComboBox. Basically, you need two ComboBoxes (instance names colors_cb and shapes_cb). Also, make a movie clip inside of which you make nine keyframes into which you draw red, green, and blue circles, lines, and squares. Label the keyframes accordingly. So...you'll need a `"red_circle"`, `"green_circle"`, `"blue_circle"`, `"red_line"`, and so on. Make sure you have an instance of this clip onstage with the instance name content. Finally, put the code in Listing 12.4 into the first keyframe of the main movie:

Listing 12.4 Using Two ComboBoxes

```
1    navigate=new Object();
2    navigate.change=function(){
3      content.gotoAndStop(colors_cb.selectedItem+"_"+
4                          shapes_cb.selectedItem);
5    }
6    colorLabels=["red", "green", "blue"];
7    shapeLabels=["circle", "line", "square"];
8    colors_cb.dataProvider=colorLabels;
9    colors_cb.addEventListener("change",navigate);
10   shapes_cb.dataProvider=shapeLabels;
11   shapes_cb.addEventListener("change",navigate);
12   content.stop();
```

In a way, this code is playing loose with the rules, but because it works I thought it'd be good to leave. First, notice the `dataProviders` (defined in lines 6 and 7) are not arrays full of objects (each with a `label` and `data`) but rather arrays full of strings. Well, that works okay, but it doesn't give you a chance to embed additional properties for each

continues

Listing 12.4 Using Two ComboBoxes (Continued)

item. In fact, if you notice in lines 3 and 4, I am grabbing the `selectedItem` of each ComboBox. Normally, that returns an object from which you would grab the `label` or `data` property. In this case, the items are those strings from the `dataProvider` array.

In many ways, the preceding example is bad because it shows how `dataProviders` can break the normal mold. However, sometimes you just don't want to stuff your `dataProvider` full of data. That is, the ComboBox doesn't *really* need anything more than a few labels. You always have the `selectedItem` and `selectedIndex` properties if you need them. Having said all this, do know that one array can be the `dataProvider` for several different components. So, it's not like you should avoid storing data "in" components via their `dataProviders`.

Using the List

The List component is probably my favorite (second only to the DataGrid, but that's only included in Flash Pro). The List is quite useful for storing data and giving the users access to it. Listing 12.5 gives an example for a survey. You'll need one List component (instance name ListBox), one Label component (instance name `question_txt`), and eight RadioButton components (named rb_0 through rb_7). Make all the components pretty wide to accommodate lots of text and lay it out something like that shown in Figure 12.6.

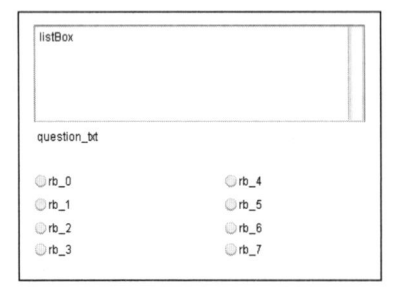

Figure 12.6 *The List, Label, and eight RadioButton components are all you need for this mini-app.*

Listing 12.5 Survey Using the List Component

```
1   questions=[];
2   questions.push({topic:"Geography",
3                   question: "Where are you from?",
4                   options:["Oregon",
5                            "Washington",
6                            "California",
7                            "None of these"]});
8   questions.push({topic:"Software",
9                   question: "What software do you use most?",
10                  options:["Dreamweaver",
11                           "Fireworks",
12                           "Flash",
13                           "Director"]});
14  //add a label property
15  for(var i=0;i<questions.length;i++){
16    questions[i].label=questions[i].topic;
17  }
18  myObj=new Object();
19  myObj.change=function(me){
20    //handle situation that they deselected list item
21    if(listBox.selectedItem==undefined) {
22      question_txt.text="";
23      for(var i=0;i<8;i++){
24        owner["rb_"+i]._visible=false;
25      }
26      return;
27    }
28    question_txt.text=listBox.selectedItem.question;
29    var options=listBox.selectedItem.options;
30    for(var i=0;i<maxQuestions;i++){
31      var thisOne=owner["rb_"+i];
32      thisOne.value=false;
33      thisOne.data=i;
34      thisOne.addEventListener("click",myObj);
35      if(options.length>i){
36        thisOne._visible=true;
37        thisOne.label=options[i];
38        if(theirAnswers[listBox.selectedIndex]==i){
40          thisOne.value=true;
41        }
42      }else{
43        thisOne._visible=false;
```

continues

Listing 12.5 Survey Using the List Component (Continued)

```
44        }
45      }
46    }
47    myObj.click=function(me){
48      theirAnswers[listBox.selectedIndex]=me.target.data;
49    }
50    //init
51    var owner=this;
52    var maxQuestions=8;
53    var theirAnswers=[];
54    //connect
55    listBox.dataProvider=questions;
56    listBox.addEventListener("change", myObj);
```

The first 13 lines just populate the questions array. The for loop on lines 15 through 17 inserts a label property on each object in the questions array. Naturally, I could have used label in place of topic in the original structure, but I wanted to demonstrate that you can just extend your data structure instead of reformatting it.

Line 18 shows how myObj gets a change event defined where most of the work will take place (lines 19 through 46). Real quick: Lines 20 through 27 just bypass the rest of the code if they happen to be *de*-selecting the List. From there, a lot of data is accessed by using listBox.selectedItem. For example, line 28 grabs the question property for the current item, and line 29 the options property. The for loop on lines 30 through 45 goes through all potential slots for answer to set details for all the RadioButtons. Notice the value is set initially to false (line 32) but if it turns out they've been to this question already and set this option, the RadioButton's value is set to true (line 40). Also notice line 34, where each RadioButton has a click event listener added.

The click event (also part of myObj) is relatively simple. Notice, however, that we set the appropriate slot in theirAnswers to the data in the target of the parameter I used (me).

Lines 51 through 56 just set a few initial variables as well as link the listBox instance to a dataProvider (questions) and add the change event listener.

Advanced Components

By no means have we looked at all the components. The good news is they're very consistent. For example, the idea of a label the user sees and data hidden in an item is used widely. Here are a couple images and ideas about how you can use other ones. There's not enough room to walk through the code for each, but you can find the code for these figures on my website (www.phillipkerman.com/rias). Note that because the license agreement forbids anyone from distributing the source component code, I've only posted the code (not an FLA with the component). Anyway, here are a few of my favorite components.

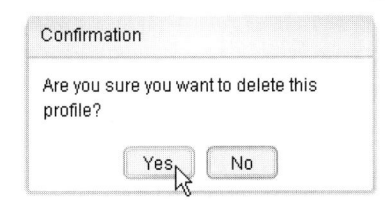

Alert Component: You can invoke Alert dialog boxes using script. Additional options include a way to make the dialog box modal (meaning the user must respond before the rest of the app proceeds).

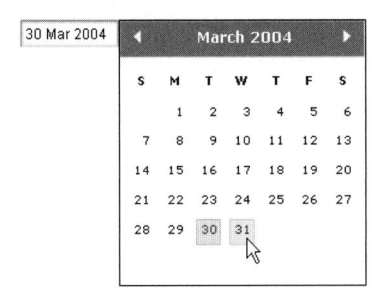

Date Field and Date Chooser Component: You can use this component with no scripting whatsoever. Advanced options include restricting users from selecting certain dates.

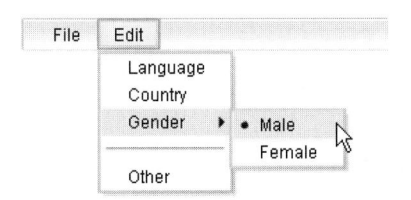

Menubar Component: This component is pretty sweet. You can make hierarchical menus, separators, and even exclusive (radio button type) options. You can use just the pop-up portion (the Menu component) without the horizontal bar.

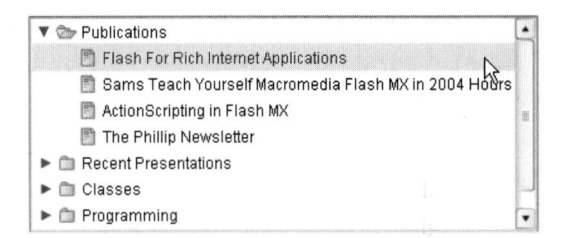

Tree Component: The Tree and XML data were made for each other. You can import XML files to describe the structure or build nodes (think folder) on-the-fly using script inside Flash.

DataGrid Component: This component is the perfect way to visualize all your arrays full of objects. You can even edit entries provided you set the `editable` property to `true`.

Rest assured that when you have a need for one of these components, they'll save you a ton of time. Also, let me suggest that you don't bang your head too long trying to figure out how to populate them. Some require a particular format. (That is, you may not be able to just take any array and expect it to work as a `dataProvider`.) However, if you just take a sample (for instance, the ones you can download from my website) and then try modifying the content, you'll be on your way quickly. Realize that populating a component is only half the process. You also need to figure out how to use it—that is, set properties and trap events.

Styles, Skinning, and Themes

Components are cool, but customizing components by changing their look is really very useful. It's possible to modify a component's default graphics, colors, fonts, and general look through styles, skins, and themes. All the underlying code is unaffected when you make a change.

A *style* is a single attribute for a component (such as the font or font color). *Skinning* is just the process of replacing or adding the graphics used by the component. Finally, a *theme* (of which there are only two right now) is a collection of various skins that work together for an overall look. For example, changing a style can be as simple as changing a button's font to Courier. Skinning a

CheckBox can mean replacing the check mark with an "x" graphic (which we'll do). Making a theme involves identifying all the visual attributes: maybe specifying Courier font but also that all highlights appear in gray and all corners are sharp edged.

Changing styles is the least involved, skinning is a bit more involved, and making themes is the most work even though it's not necessarily very technical.

Setting Styles

When you change a component's color or text, you can do so entirely in script. Such style changes are not much more involved than first identifying the attribute you want to change, coming up with a replacement, and then deciding how global a change you intend to make. For example, you can change any of the following:

- A single instance of a component
- One component type (say, all Button components)
- All components containing the attribute you're affecting (for instance, changing the text color on every component containing text)

Instance Versus Component Versus Global Styles

Suppose you've decided you want to change the text color. (You learn how to pick a style in the next section—but let's do this part with the idea you're going to change the text color.) Ultimately, you must decide whether you want to affect one instance, all instances of a certain component type, or all components containing text. The syntax varies. Consider a sample for each:

Affecting a single instance:

```
myInstance.setStyle("theStyle", value);
```

Replace `myInstance` with the instance name, replace `"theStyle"` with the supported style, and replace `value` with an actual value. If I had a RadioButton instance named rb, for example, I could use the following code to change the text color (style name `"color"`) to red:

```
rb.setStyle("color", 0xFF0000);
```

Affecting a single component type:

```
var myStyle = new mx.styles.CSSStyleDeclaration();
myStyle.color = 0x0000FF;
_global.styles.CheckBox=myStyle;
```

Maybe I should have worked up to this one, but most of this you just copy verbatim every time. The first line creates a new style declaration and stores it in a variable `myStyle`. Next you set the `color` property (directly, not via `setStyle()`). Finally, you associate all CheckBox components with that style. This example causes all CheckBoxes' text color to appear blue.

Affecting all components:

```
_global.style.setStyle("color", 0xFF0000);
```

Notice this syntax is nearly identical to skinning a single instance. Instead of saying "some instance set style," however, you say "global style set style." In fact, I use this setting the most frequently because it's equivalent to creating a theme. If I want a silvery blue look to all my components, text, and highlights, for example, I can set several global styles and it will affect everything.

After you decide what you want to affect, it's just a matter of identifying the styles you want to change. Next you'll learn how to find the different styles you're allowed to change. Let me first remind you that it's not just a matter of picking colors. Styles include things such as `fontWeight` (`"normal"` or `"bold"`) and `textAlign` (`"left"`, `"center"`, or `"right"`).

Picking Styles

The available styles vary among components, but you can find a list of which styles are available by searching Flash's help for "supported styles." You'll notice most of these are based on standard CSS styles. This is probably your best resource for finding which styles you're allowed to set.

For one particularly influential style, check out `"themeColor"`. This style mainly affects the rollover highlight color. You can set it to any color you want, but three specific color schemes are available: `"haloBlue"`, `"haloOrange"`, and the default `"haloGreen"`. For example, I can make a button instance (myButton) adopt the `"haloBlue"` look by using this code:

```
myButton.setStyle("themeColor", "haloBlue");
```

You'll no doubt find other styles that prove useful. I find an interesting way to not only find the available styles but also to see how they affect my components is to use the Debugger panel. That is, just put a few components onstage and select Control, Debug Movie. Then start digging through the styles by first selecting _global and the Variables tab as shown in Figure 12.7.

You can change the values of many of these styles right in the Debugger and see the results onstage. Digging through the plethora of options is a bit overwhelming, but when you find the style you want to affect, you can see the results immediately. Also, it's a drag because colors have to be represented as a number between 1 and 16,000,000 or so. I guess I point out this process because it can help you see the structure behind styles.

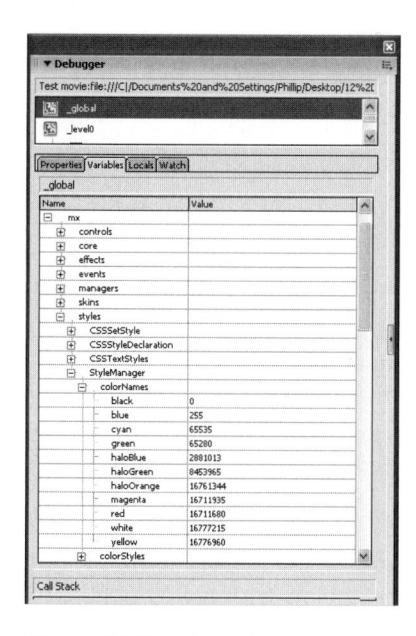

Figure 12.7 *Although not recommended for the faint-hearted, you can see all the style names using the Debugger panel.*

{ Note }

"borderStyle" Style Without picking favorites, there's one style I feel compelled to point out. That's `"borderStyle"`. If you use the TextArea or TextInput (for instance, to get the scrolling text), you may find that you don't want that border (no matter how beautiful it may be). Just use the following code (on an TextArea instance named my_txt):

```
my_txt.setStyle("borderStyle", "none");
```

Replacing Skins

Whereas setting styles involves changing an attribute, replacing skins involves replacing actual contents of movie clips. For example, we'll replace the check mark the CheckBox uses with one that looks like an "x." One notable difference from styles: In the case of skins, all instances are affected. In addition, any component that uses the skin element you changed will also be affected. If you change the down arrow, for example, you'll see the results in both the ComboBox and the TextArea (when it scrolls) because they both use the same down arrow.

You can skin several different ways: Just apply a theme (which means you'll be skinning everything with the same look), edit the theme for one movie, or edit and create your own theme to use with other movies.

Applying a Theme

Flash only ships with a couple themes (`Halo` and `Sample`). The assets for these are stored in a folder called ComponentFLA inside the First Run folder adjacent to Flash MX 2004. Perhaps by the time you read this book, other themes will be available.

To apply the theme, just open the source FLA file as an external library. That is, select File, Import, Open External Library. Point to the file SampleTheme.fla. Copy the contents of that library into your file. To do so, open your movie's library so that you can see both the internal and external library (see Figure 12.8). Then drag the folder Flash UI Components 2 into your movie's library.

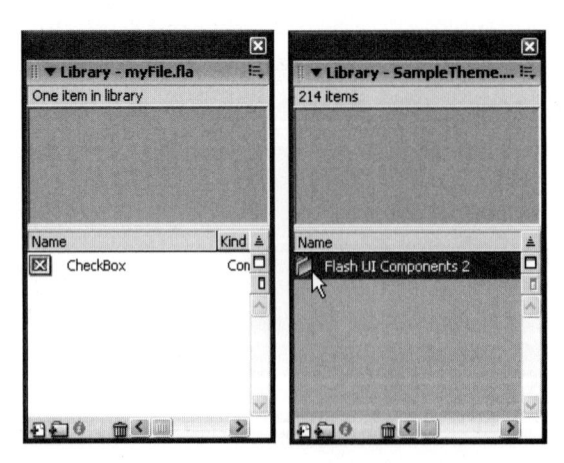

Figure 12.8 *You can drag the entire Flash UI Components 2 folder into your movie and then edit the graphics it contains.*

Put a few components onstage (using the standard method of dragging from the Components panel). Test the movie. By just having that folder in your library, all components adopt an entirely new look.

Editing a Theme for One Movie

The applying a theme exercise you just completed will affect only that movie. Although you may like most of that theme, however, you may want to make a minor change to it—for example, the check mark the CheckBox uses (see Figure 12.9). If you want, you can replace that check mark.

☒ CheckBox

Figure 12.9 *You can edit the check mark graphic for the CheckBox component.*

If you're going to be editing a theme, this means you'll be changing the contents of specific movie clips. It's basically a process of hunting down the element you want to change and editing it. The only warning is that you need to make sure you get all variations. In the case of that little check mark, there are four variations to edit. Luckily, both the Halo theme and the Sample theme are well organized. In fact, every component includes a clip named CheckBoxAssets (or similar) that includes all the various states in one clip. You don't really need that clip during runtime, but it includes the clips you do need. They're easy to find this way.

Go ahead and open as external library either the Halo or Sample theme as you did in the preceding section. Drag the Flash UI Components 2 into your movie. Now you can dig in to find the check marks. You want to edit CheckBoxAssets, which is in the path Flash UI Components 2/Themes/MMDefault/CheckBox Assets/. Double-click to edit that clip and zoom way in to see everything (see Figure 12.10).

Now just carefully double-click the check mark until you get to its base shape. Delete the onscreen graphics and draw your own "x" check mark. Test the movie.

Saving a Theme

Making edits to a theme is just a tad bit touchy. You have to dig deep and you don't want to be sloppy for fear of breaking everything (which, actually, isn't very easy to do). It's certainly more work than you'll want to do for every project if there's a change you commonly make (for instance, changing the check mark).

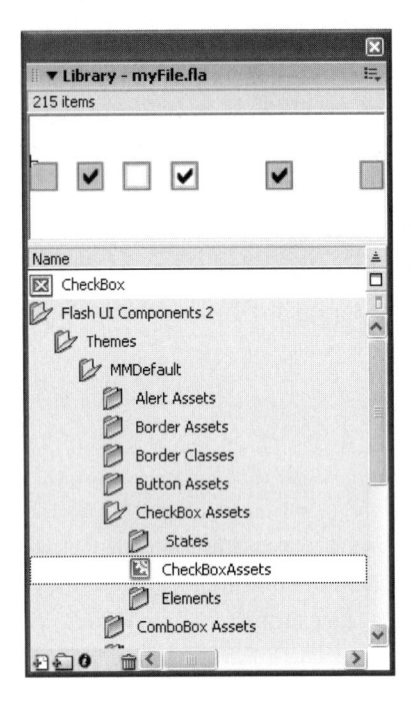

Figure 12.10 *The CheckBoxAssets clip includes all the pieces you may want to edit.*

Making your own theme is so easy, you'll kick yourself. Just start a new file and import as an external library the theme on which you want to base yours. Make the edits, and then just save the FLA in a safe place (for instance, with the other themes). Easy.

If you have visions of making your own theme from the ground up, I still recommend starting with one of the completed themes, but just change everything. I think you'll do the least amount of work if you make changes starting with the most specific. Because so much is shared, you'll see that changing something specific may affect several other (more general) attributes. In addition, try to edit the contents of clips instead of replacing clips. Naturally, clip instance names are used, so your replacement needs the same name. That's not an issue if you just edit clip contents. Finally, you'll find that components also use linkage settings—meaning that even if a particular symbol isn't used within any other clip, it may still be part of a component that effectively uses the `attachMovie()` method. Again, edit contents and you should be fine.

Summary

I'll admit I'm a reformed component naysayer. I used to think they homogenized applications by making them all look and act the same. In fact, this is a good thing because the user won't have to continually relearn every developer's interface components. Components have come of age for several reasons:

- They're well thought out and conform to a consistent behavior.
- They can get bound to data in your app via `dataProviders`.
- You can skin them to match your app's look.

{Chapter 13}

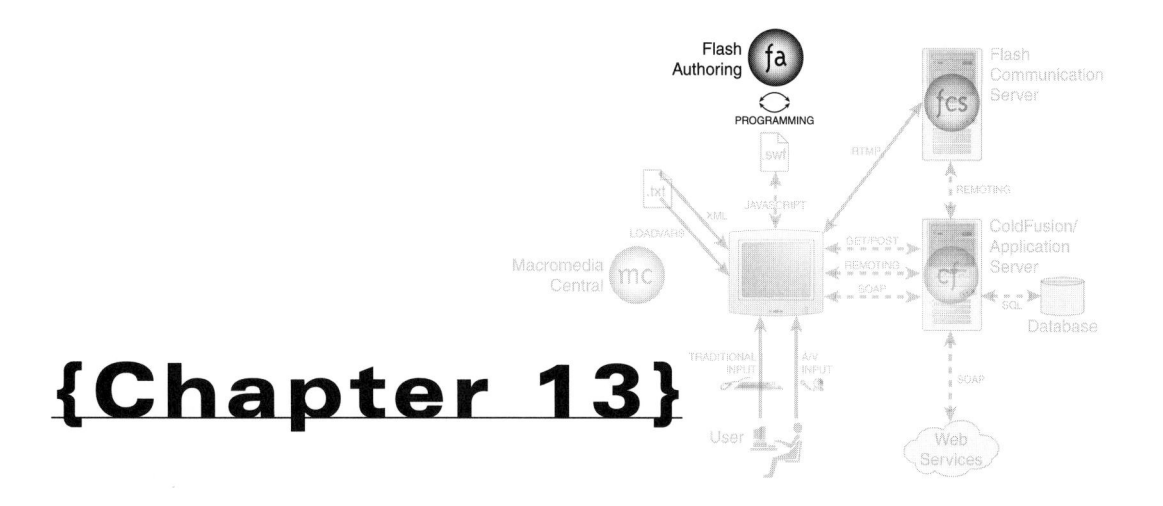

Building a Code Library

As your experience grows, it makes sense that you'll start recycling approaches and techniques that have proven useful. The best techniques are often the ones you developed on the job. In any event, the true craftspeople continually add to their toolsets. This chapter is dedicated to developing and maintaining your bag of tricks.

I tend to think it's more important to learn how to develop useful skills than just to be good at archiving them. Often something you find useful early in your career turns out to be not as useful as you grow to develop more skills. It's sort of like how you might be embarrassed of the clothes you thought were cool a decade ago. At least in my experience, I tend to look at my old projects the same way: "What was I *thinking* when I wrote that code?" For this reason, you want to be careful not to dedicate too much time-saving code for posterity and more time living in the here-and-now. Having said that, I find some tricks and code algorithms as useful today as the day I picked them up years ago. In this chapter, you'll learn how to "generic-size" code to make it transferable as well as learn techniques to store that code in a convenient form for easy access.

Specifically, this chapter covers the following topics:

- Making your own simple components
- Recognizing and addressing places to modularize your code
- Saving code snippets as behaviors for quick access

- The foundation of JavaScript Flash (JSFL) and "XML to UI" for writing commands that extend Macromedia Flash MX 2004
- The basics of constructor functions, the `prototype` property, and class files

Homemade Components

In the preceding chapter, you learned how to *use* the second-generation (V2) components. They're useful, and you're likely to see even more handy components published over time. Although this chapter doesn't attempt to deconstruct the UI components, you will see how modest components that you build yourself can be very easy to make and useful throughout your projects. If nothing else, this section walks you through the first steps in making any component.

Designing a Component

Like any project, building a component starts with design. First understand what a *component* is: a movie clip for which initial values are assigned—by the author using it—via the Parameters tab. Any movie clip can have contained variables, but each instance starts with the same initial values for those variables. Obviously, you can refer to a clip's instance name to change its variables using ActionScript, but sometimes it's more convenient for authors to set such variables in a similar manner as they set properties—right in the Properties panel.

Components are just clips with code inside them. But so are movie clips. What makes a component different is that although each instance contains the same base features, each instance also has the capability to behave slightly differently. Take the Button component. Each one acts like a button, but one might be labeled "start" and another "stop," and they both result in a different behavior when clicked.

The component I designed for the example that follows is a title/subtitle display—basically, just two lines of text in a given font style and layout. The idea is that authors can place this on any page of an app and manually modify the words that appear. Although they could have done this with separate blocks of text, this will be better because the font and other formatting can be updated in one place (the master symbol). In addition, this is better than a regular movie clip because authors can set the displayed text by just typing into the Properties panel's Parameters tab (instead of writing code). Above everything else, this, and all components, insulates the using authors from the code. They don't have to worry about code, and you don't have to worry about them messing with your code.

Making a Component

Let me walk you through making the text component just described. First, create two dynamic text fields with nice large margins. Type `title_txt` into one and `subtitle_txt` into the other, name their instances the same, and then spend as much time as you want stylizing the text. (I just made my subtitle italic.). See Figure 13.1.

```
title_txt
subtitle_txt
```

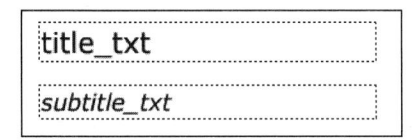

Figure 13.1 *These two dynamic text fields will become a component.*

Select both blocks of text and convert to a clip (press F8), call the symbol MyComponent, and make sure it's a movie clip. Double-click the instance of your symbol now onstage so that you can edit its contents. Put the following code in the first keyframe of the clip:

```
title_txt.text=title;
subtitle_txt.text=subtitle;
```

Pretty simple; as long as the `title` and `subtitle` variables have a value, the two fields will be populated properly. Turning this clip into a component enables you to establish `title` and `subtitle` as variables (called parameters) the using author can edit via the Parameters tab. You can return to the main timeline (Ctrl+E) and then open the library (Ctrl+L). Select the MyComponent symbol from either the library's Options menu (top right), or right-click and select Component Definition. From the Component Definition dialog box, click the plus button twice, and then fill in the Name, Variable, and Value fields as follows.

Name	Variable	Value
Title	title	Title appears here
SubTitle	subtitle	Subtitle appears here

Name is what the using author will see, but Variable is the actual name of the variable they're setting. If you leave Variable blank, it will just use whatever you have under Name. The idea is that you can further insulate the using author from your potentially cryptic variable names. Finally, Value is really the default value. In this case, the using author will always change these. In any event, make sure these default values are acceptable in case the using author fails to populate the component.

This component is ready (although we'll add to it later). Take the instance onstage, and using the Properties panel Parameters tab, replace the values for Title and SubTitle. Test the movie and you'll see your values appear. If you build a simple paging app, you can put a new instance of this component on each page with different content. The cool part is you can later edit the master symbol (perhaps change the font color), and all instances will update despite the fact that they contain different words.

Although this isn't the next killer component, it's actually fairly useful. However, next we'll improve it by giving using authors a preview of their text (without the need for testing the movie) and also build in some alignment.

Enhancing Components

The component just built was pretty basic. Tons of additional features are available when building a component. Here's a list of the big ones:

- **Live Preview** enables you to present a separate SWF in place of any component instance onstage. This SWF runs code while authoring, so using authors can get a preview of how it *will* look when they test the movie.

- **Compiled clips** are a simplified addition to Live Preview. Basically, a compiled clip is like a mini–test movie right inside the component onstage. Like Live Preview, this means you'll see the clip as it will look when published—but compiled clips are based on the same clip (making them identical); whereas because Live Preview is a separate file, it can optionally present a slightly different presentation. Compiled clips are also much simpler to produce.

- **Custom UI** is still another SWF that serves to replace the name/value pair interface found in the Parameters tab. It's misguided to use these to just spice up the Parameters tab. Use them only for guided wizard-type interfaces or for when a visual interface makes it easier for the using author to populate values. Imagine, for instance, if the Align panel looked like that shown in Figure 13.2 rather than the more intuitive graphic solution.

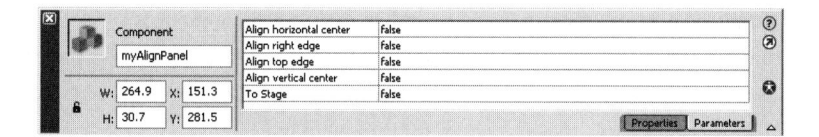

Figure 13.2 *This mock-up of what the Align panel would be without a graphic interface emphasizes the value of images.*

ActionScript 2 (AS2) isn't so much a feature of components but rather a new implementation of the ActionScript language. However, some specific features (such as associating your component symbol with an AS2 class definition) apply specifically to components. You'll read about just some of these in the last section of this chapter.

Making a Compiled Clip

Now it's time to make a compiled clip out of the title/subtitle component. The hooks to Live Preview and custom UIs are found in the Component Definition dialog box (although you also need to read up on how to make these). In addition, the Component Definition dialog box includes options for how your component is to appear in the Components panel when distributing (the next section's topic).

Before you make a compiled clip based on your component, add scripts that respond to the using authors making changes to the parameters. Specifically, there's an event triggered called onUpdate that enables us to update what the using authors see any time they make a change to the parameters. We'll add such a script to the MyComponent component built earlier. You can't just double-click a component instance (because that would increase the chances of your using authors messing up the code). To edit its contents, you must either select Edit from the library symbol or right-click an instance and select Edit in Place. Add the following code under the two lines currently in the first keyframe of the symbol:

```
function onUpdate(){
  title_txt.text=title;
  subtitle_txt.text=subtitle;
}
```

Basically, every time onUpdate triggers, we'll push the two variables (title and subtitle) into the text field—and onUpdate triggers when the using authors edit the parameters.

Return to the main timeline (Ctrl+E) and select the MyComponent in the library. From the library's Options menu (or right-click), select Convert to Compiled Clip. Not only does this create an authortime SWF into the library, it also swaps any instances onstage. Now you should be able to edit the parameters and see the results while authoring—that is, no test movie required. You shouldn't Convert to Compiled Clip until you're really sure the component is complete, because you can't make any changes to the original (unless you compile it again).

By the way, your onUpdate handler doesn't have to be literal and direct. That is, this example showed both parameters having a direct visual result in the onscreen text. Often the parameters you give to the using author don't have an immediate visual result. Similarly, you can have as many variables and functions inside your components—they don't all have to be available to the using author. Although it's not quite the same, exploring your own components is a good introduction to object-oriented concepts such as private and public properties.

Distributing Components (MXI)

Obviously, this chapter cannot cover all the ways to enhance your component. Suppose, however, that you've built a great component that you want to share with the world. The way to distribute it is as an MXP file (Macromedia eXtension Package). You can download an MXP file and then use the free Extension Manager software to open it (see Figure 13.3).

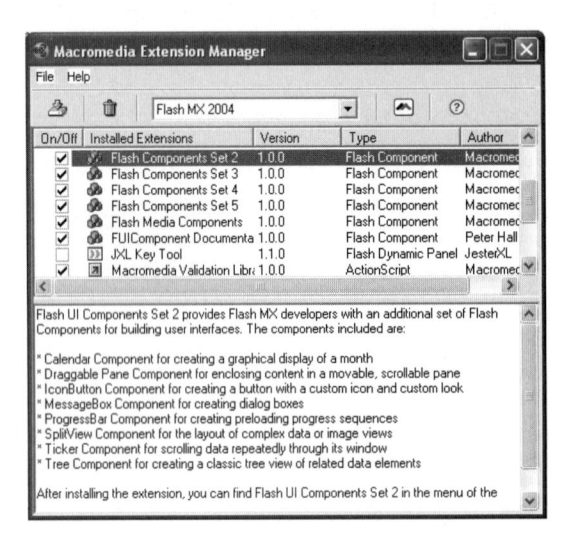

Figure 13.3 *The Extension Manager makes it easy to install, disable, and remove components.*

The Extension Manager gives users a convenient way to install and manage multiple component sets. To create an MXP file, start with either an FLA containing your component or an SWC packaged version of your component. The new compressed SWC format (created via the Export SWC option in the library) enables you to distribute a component along with its AS2 class files (described later). An MXP is basically your component (either FLA or SWC) along with an XML file (.mxi extension) that provides instructions as to where the components are to be installed and descriptive information such as its name and instructions. Finally, the Extension Manager can combine the component and MXI description file to make an MXP that you can distribute and share. For complete details, refer to this document:

`http://download.macromedia.com/pub/exchange/mx1_file_format.pdf`.

Although the extra steps to make an MXP are worthwhile when you distribute your component, you can also install them manually so that they appear in the Components panel while you're authoring. After all, because we're talking about building a code library, it might be nice for you to have quick access to your favorite homemade components. It's really easy. First go back to the MyComponent's Component Definition dialog box and select the check box Display in Components Panel. Find the Components folder inside the First Run folder adjacent to your installed copy of Flash inside the en (for English) folder. Make a new folder: My Components. Finally, from the library select MyComponent and choose Export SWC and save it inside the My Components folder you just created. (Alternatively, just save the FLA containing your component in that same folder.) Restart Flash and you will see your beautiful component along with the components that ship with Flash (see Figure 13.4).

There you go—everything you need to know about components in a few pages. In fact, there's a lot more you can do, but this is a good start. Try to design components that are as generic as possible, especially with regard to look and feel (not so much the underlying code). For example, I recently built an interminable busy indicator (for operations that I don't want to show 0-100, but just "busy doing something"). I took the idea from macromedia.com (where they use a rotating circle). Anyway, it works great, but the second client for whom I used it wanted to change it from a circle to a square. Naturally, I could have planned for such changes, but it demonstrates that components tend to embed the visual elements with the code (although, of course, that is *not* a rule). The rest of this chapter focuses on building a library of pure code.

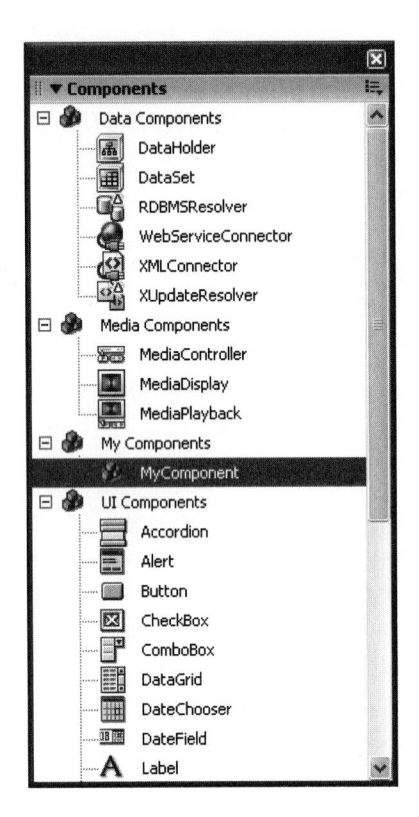

Figure 13.4 *You can manually add components to the Components panel.*

Your Script Style

Your scripting style should continue to improve forever. That is, you never know it all and you're never too old to learn more. Before you start archiving the greatest scripts of all time, however, you just want to improve your style. That is, you can start by improving a single script in part of your movie, then move on to improving the whole movie…and then maybe improve an entire project and so on. Start with the details. This section examines ways to improve the way you write scripts.

It would be great if I had a set of absolute rules to follow, but it's more ambiguous than that. Even when there are accepted "best practices" defined, you may not be ready to fully use them. Regardless of your experience level, it makes sense to always look for ways to improve, even if that means being self-critical of the way you've solved a problem.

Think Modularly

A few general approaches, when taken, should alert you that a better way exists. If you ever copy and paste the same block of code, for example, you know something is wrong with your approach. You should instead take that code and put it inside a function. Then in the two places you were going to paste it, trigger the function. Not only does this mean you can modify the code in one central place, it also means that if later you need to trigger the same code, you can do so by invoking the function (instead of copying and pasting again).

Often you may be copying and pasting when you intend to make minor changes to the copy. That is, you're not really duplicating the code exactly, but with minor adjustments. For example:

```
button1_btn.enabled=false;
button2_btn.enabled=false;
button3_btn.enabled=false;
```

In this case, you can't just trigger the same function three times because you're doing three different things. But you can generalize the code. Instead of thinking, "I've got to disable button1, button2, and button3," think, "I've got to disable buttons 1 through 3." Pretty much the same thing, but by thinking in these terms the adjusted code is easier to derive:

```
owner=this;
for(var i=1;i<4;i++){
   owner["button"+i+"_btn"].enabled=false;
}
```

Although this is more code, you'll see the benefits when you have, say, 100 buttons to disable. Actually, if you think even more generally, it might make sense to put this inside a function that you can use to both enable or disable all the buttons:

```
owner=this;
function changeButtons(active){
  var total=3;
  for(var i=0;i<total;i++){
    owner["button"+Number(i+1)+"_btn"].enabled=active;
  }
}
```

Now you can just say `changeButtons(true)` or `changeButtons(false)`. Notice another enhancement I made: I'm using a variable `total` that's more exposed because, frankly, it's the only hard-wired part of this script. Notice, too, that because I'm using a more popular technique of starting with 0 in the `for` loop, I need to add 1 when building the button's instance name.

This example isn't supposed to be revolutionary, but rather descriptive of the process where you continually improve the scripts you have. Way before code is worthy of recycling, it has to be as generic as possible. Although it is sometimes more complex, the best code is very specific in its purpose and very general in its application. For example, one function may be in charge of disabling buttons (that's a specific goal), but you should write the function so that it can disable as many or few buttons as needed (that is, you can apply it generally). I can assure you that many scripts in this book are not ideal. Although they should all work, most of the time I was just trying to show a particular subject. In many cases I opted for clearer code rather than optimized, elegant code. When you try improving your scripts (for possible use in your code library, for example), it makes sense to capitalize on making it as generic as possible.

Advanced Techniques

The good news about ActionScript is that because there's so much you can learn, you'll never feel like you know it all and become bored (at least I'm nowhere near that point). Here are some pointers for the direction you might take to enhance your scripting ability as well as develop more useful code snippets.

Functions as Constructors

Most functions behave like subroutines where you can trigger the contained code by using the form `functionName()`. By just changing the way you design and implement the function, however, it can serve to produce custom object instances while the movie plays. This enables your code to adapt by spawning many instances of the same code template. For example, you could give your users the ability to add entries into an address book where each entry was based on the same object that contained a standard set of properties and methods. The funkiest thing when learning to use constructor functions is that you're just making variables containing code—it's not like you necessarily "see" anything onstage. (Obviously, if you tie it to `attachMovie` where you're creating clips on-the-fly, you'll see something; however, that's not a requirement by any means.)

Here's a before-and-after example where constructor functions were used. The example requires the following components: a Button (`add_btn`), a List (`all_lb`), and a ComboBox (`option_cb`) populated with some labels. Plus, an input text field (`name_txt`) and a multiline dynamic text field (`results_txt`). See Figure 13.5.

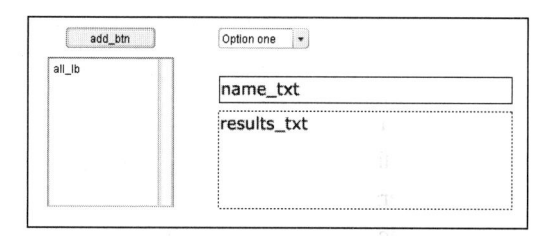

Figure 13.5 *The following code sample uses the components shown.*

```
allEntries=[];
function addEntry(){
  var thisObj=new Object();
  thisObj.name=name_txt.text;
  thisObj.option=option_cb.selectedItem.label;
  thisObj.creationDate=new Date();
  all_lb.addItem(thisObj.name+" : "+thisObj.option,
              allEntries.length);
  allEntries.push(thisObj);
}
add_btn.onPress=function(){
  addEntry();
}
all_lb.addEventListener("change",doClickList);
function doClickList() {
  var thisObj=allEntries[all_lb.selectedItem.data];
  results_txt.text=thisObj.creationDate+newline;
  results_txt.text+="name: " + thisObj.name+newline;
  results_txt.text+="option: " + thisObj.option;
}
```

Although there's nothing wrong with this code—it works after all—things are spread out. I'm using an array (allEntries) to store all the saved data, and the List's data array (the second parameter) contains the entry's index in the array. Also, the doClickList() function needs to directly grab properties of the appropriate object from within the allEntries array.

The following alternative uses a constructor function to create objects that contain homemade methods to give outside functions indirect access to their contained properties:

```
function Entry(name, option){
  this.name=name;
  this.option=option;
  this.creationDate=new Date();
```

```
    this.getName=function(){
      return this.name;
    }
    this.getOption=function(){
      return this.option;
    }
    this.getAll=function(){
      var retString="";
      retString+=this.creationDate+newline;
      retString+="name:  "  + this.name+newline;
      retString+="option:  " + this.option;
      return retString;
    }
}
function addEntry(){
    thisOne=new Entry(name_txt.text,option_cb.selectedItem.label);
    all_lb.addItem(thisOne.getName()+" :
              "+thisOne.getOption(),thisOne);
}
add_btn.onPress=function(){
    addEntry();
}
all_lb.addEventListener("change",doClickList);
function doClickList() {
    results_txt.text=all_lb.selectedItem.data.getAll();
}
```

This accomplishes the same thing as the first solution. However, this example centralizes all the data handling in one place: the `Entry()` constructor function. That is, when a new entry is needed, the `Entry()` function is invoked with the keyword new. This returns an object fashioned however `Entry` is defined—in this case, including methods to get the name, get the option, or get a formatted string with all properties. Having all this data handling in one place means that outside scripts never directly touch an object's properties—they always go through the methods. This way, if you change the name or behavior of any property, you don't have to go searching all the places that may be accessing the old properties. Everything is in one place.

There are a couple other approaches in this example, but to learn more I highly recommend a book called *Object-Oriented Programming in Flash*, by Brandon Hall et al.

Extending the Prototype

The concept of extending the prototype is covered in much more detail other places. However, I think it's worth showing you a technique that's really practical even if it doesn't fully explain the subject. Real quick: Every object type has a `prototype` property where all of its methods are stored. If you add more methods to an object's `prototype`, you'll be adding to all instances of that object type in your movie. The following example adds to the `prototype` of the MovieClip by defining a method that will adjust any clip's scale:

```
MovieClip.prototype.setScale=function(toWhat){
  this._xscale=toWhat;
  this._yscale=toWhat;
};
```

The `setScale()` function is now automatically embedded in every MovieClip instance in our movie. Because the two lines inside the function affect `this`, we can use `setScale()` to affect any clip. For example, `myClip.setScale(50);` will scale the instance named `myClip` to 50 percent (both _xscale and _yscale).

This is really powerful, but you don't want to override built-in methods. For example, you don't want to replace `setScale` (above) with `play` or something built-in. Here are just a couple more examples to give you an idea how useful it is.

Here is a method that makes it possible to set a clip's right-side location directly:

```
MovieClip.prototype.setRight=function(toWhat){
  //assuming top left registration
  this._x=toWhat-this._width
};
//e.g. myClip.setRight(400);
```

This method enables you to build a functional time string based on a sound that's playing:

```
Sound.prototype.getTimeString=function(){
  var p=this.position;
  var m=Math.floor(p/60000);
  var s=Math.floor((p-m*60000)/1000);
  var d=Math.floor((p-m*60000-s*1000)/100)
  if(m<10){m="0"+m;}
  if(s<10){s="0"+s;}
  return m+":"+s+"."+d;
}
//e.g. myField_txt.text= s.getTimeSring();
```

It turns out that Flash MX 2004's support for ActionScript 2.0 gives you a more elegant way to extend objects. It's actually called "extends." The equivalent to `MovieClip.prototype` is `class myClass extends MovieClip{}`. You'll learn the basics of AS2 later in this chapter.

After you get the hang of it, extending the `prototype` is very, very convenient. My only recommendation is to always start with a clear objective instead of extending the `prototype` just for the sake of doing it.

It's important to remain practical. If using constructor functions or the `prototype` concepts are confusing, for instance, there's no point in using them immediately. It makes sense to attempt to apply them—perhaps just not in the heat of a project. Ultimately, this way you'll recognize what code to save by recognizing what's familiar. After a few projects (or revisions of the same project), try to identify patterns in your approach. Not only will this help you see places for improvement, it will also enable you to identify the sorts of code worthy of archiving. Now it's time for you to explore different ways to store your favorite scripts.

Storing Scripts

Often, I'm sad to say, when I think to use an old script, I usually hunt it down in an old project's source file. This works fine, but it's not exactly ideal. There are many ways to store your favorite scripts so that they're available to you when you need them. This section shows you how to include external ActionScript (AS; extension .as) text when you publish your movie and how to grab your own homemade code snippets from the Behaviors panel.

AS Text Files

Flash supports a feature called `#include`, which enables you to store your scripts in an external text file. The way it works is that in lieu of writing scripts right inside the Actions panel, you can instead point to an external file. For example, I can put the following script in the first frame of my movie:

```
#include "somefile.as"
```

Then, when you publish or test the movie, the contents of the file somefile.as is effectively copied into the SWF.

{ Note }

No Semicolon Notice that lines of code using `#include` do not include a semicolon at the end.

Not much more to it. Realize that this is done at publish time (not runtime). So if you make a change to the AS file, you must republish all movies that use it.

On the surface, storing your scripts outside Flash may seem like a big pain. It may be worth the hassle, but there are ways to make it not such a hassle. First, the advantage is that you can easily use the same script file in multiple movies or projects. This is much more logical than my technique of copying scripts from old files. You can build a library of AS files—each one with a different purpose. By the way, AS files can also `#include` other AS files. So you might have a few generic-utility AS files, but one applied script that uses `#include` to use several of the utilities. Finally, the `#include` call can use relative references such as `#include "../filename.as"`, where `filename.as` is up one folder from where the Flash movie resides. In this way, you can point to a common library of AS files.

The fact that AS files are just plain-text files might seem to suggest you need to use a plain-text editor to produce them (which you can). However, you have many better alternatives. Flash MX Professional 2004 supports direct editing of AS files, meaning you can use all the code hinting and stay in the Flash environment with the Help panel and so on. In addition, Dreamweaver MX 2004 enables you to edit AS files and gain code-completion help inline. Finally, there are a host of third-party text editors for which other developers have written syntax coloring, code hints, and code-completion support files. So, although maintaining both the FLA and the AS files takes a moderate effort, it's really not too bad. The hardest thing I find is that I have to remember to save the AS files before I test my movie (or the latest saved version is used instead).

Before moving on to homemade behaviors, let me point out there's a new option confusingly similar to `#include`; it's called `import`. You'll see it in the section "Basic Class Files in AS2" later, but just realize the two differ.

Homemade Behaviors

Building a library of utility AS files makes perfect sense. When you have code that's generic enough to externalize, it can keep your FLA files very simple. The idea of such a library is that you (or someone else) wrote the code once, made it accessible through a few methods and functions, but you never really need to go in an edit those AS files because they're complete. Sometimes your needs aren't that orderly—maybe you find yourself frequently typing the same basic code but with significant modifications each time. For such situations, there are behaviors.

Behaviors just paste a snippet of code into your Flash movie. This is similar to how a word processor can run a simple macro. If you've explored the behaviors that came with Flash, you probably found that some are slightly more involved because they let you set a few options to modify certain parameters. But at their core, they just paste a block of code into your scripts. In addition, if you don't mess with the code pasted in, you'll be able to use the Behaviors panel to remove entire blocks of added scripts without breaking the rest of your code. In any event, it's easy to write your own behaviors, and doing so can prove useful for blocks of code you find yourself using a lot.

Here's a great example of code that I find myself typing all the time:

```
for(var i in obj){
    trace(i+":"+obj[i]);
}
```

Let's turn that into a behavior. Without documenting the entire XML format, let me just show you how easy it is by example. Listing 13.1 shows the content of a file I saved as Phillips_object_trace.xml inside Flash's Behaviors folder (then restarted Flash):

Listing 13.1 Simple Behavior

```
<?xml version="1.0"?>
<flash_behavior version="1.0">
<behavior_definition
  dialogID="my_id-dialog"
  category="Phillips"
  name="Phillip's object trace script">
<actionscript>
<![CDATA[
  //BEGIN
    for(var i in obj){
      trace(i+":"+obj[i]);
    }
  //END
]]>
</actionscript></behavior_definition></flash_behavior>
```

You can test it out. It simply pastes the text in the CDATA portion of the XML file. In use, I might paste this, and then replace *obj* with a name of an object—for instance, _root—to see all the clip's in the main timeline.

In the behavior example in Listing 13.1, I didn't define a dialog box; it just pasted the same code no matter what. You can make custom dialog boxes with real live buttons, text entry fields, list boxes, sliders, and more. The example in Listing 13.2 prompts the author for an object name; then that name will be used (in place of obj above). Here's the code for a file named Phillips_object_trace_advanced.xml.

Listing 13.2   Advanced Behavior

```xml
<?xml version="1.0"?>
<flash_behavior version="1.0">
<behavior_definition
  dialogID="my_id-dialog"
  category="Phillips"
  name="Phillip's object trace script advanced">
<properties>
  <property id="loopObj"/>
</properties>
<dialog id="my_id-dialog" title="Object Trace" buttons="accept, cancel">
<hbox>
  <label literal="false" value="Enter Object Name."/>
  <textbox id="loopObj" tabindex="1" required="true"/>
</hbox>
</dialog>
<actionscript>
<![CDATA[
  //BEGIN
  for(var i in $loopObj$){
    trace(i+":"+$loopObj$[i]);
  }
  //END
]]>
</actionscript></behavior_definition></flash_behavior>
```

Notice there's an entire dialog section to the XML where you lay out the elements to the dialog. Basically, the dialog makes the user set a property (think variable) named loopObj. Then, notice each instance of that property is surrounded by dollar ($) signs indicating the value for that variable should be used rather than the string "loopObj".

For a feature that I thought was pretty cheesy at first look, behaviors may become the big cheese. Oh, and to call this an "advanced" example is a bit of a stretch, because when you study the documentation for these XML files (called XML to UI), you'll see there's a ton more you can do.

Beyond Flash

The way Flash turns XML into user-interface dialog boxes is through an implementation they call *XML to UI*—based on a standard called XUL ("zool"). Luckily, the time you invest learning it for behaviors comes in handy when building commands (which are covered next). Commands' only similarity to behaviors is they both use a dialog box for user input. Commands also have the power to run still *another* language called JavaScript Flash (JSFL), which can effectively run Flash on autopilot (making changes to your document, for example).

If it feels like your head is about to explode, don't worry. First off, I'm only going to give you an overview and a few tips to get started with JSFL. Second, the good news with most of this stuff is the community of developers is already building tools to share. A great place to start after reading the next section is www.actionscript.nl.

Intro to JSFL (JavaScript Flash)

JSFL is scripting language that runs only in the Flash authoring environment. Instead of addressing clips or buttons the way ActionScript does, JSFL can address the currently selected shape or timeline's layer. What's wild is that JSFL can then execute nearly any command that you would normally do while authoring. In this way, you can use JSFL to help you author an FLA.

It may seem daunting to jump into JSFL, but it's actually *really* easy to start. That's because nearly every move you make while authoring is being recorded in the History panel using JSFL! Check it out: Draw a few simple shapes in a movie, and then open your History panel, select a few rows, and then click the Copy to Clipboard button at the lower right of the panel (see Figure 13.6).

Now, paste into the Actions panel. You'll see the exact steps you performed but written in pure JSFL. The way it records everything you do would be creepy if it weren't so cool. I should note there's no JSFL for complex bending operations like the pen tool.

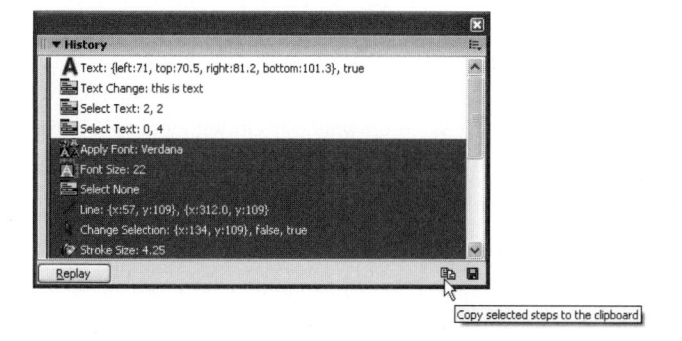

Figure 13.6 *You can grab some killer JSFL by just copying it from the History panel.*

So JSFL is cool. I find it interesting to study the data structures Macromedia developed to describe your moves. But just admiring JSFL only goes so far; you'll probably want to know how to make it run inside Flash. There are a few basic ways:

- **As a command.** The simplest way is to just run JSFL as a command accessible through the Commands menu (as we'll do next).
- **In a WindowSWF.** You can write JSFL that gets executed by a SWF that runs as a custom panel (also called a WindowSWF).
- **As a custom draw tool.** Finally, you can also run JSFL as a drawing tool that you add via Edit, Customize Tool Panel.
- **Externally.** It's even possible to set up batch scripts to run on an unattended version of Flash—although you need Flash Pro for that.

Before we go any further, I want to reiterate that JSFL does one thing: modifies Flash files. It can do anything you can do while authoring (such as open files, edit contents, import media, break apart images, export movies, and so on), but it only runs inside the Flash authoring environment—not the browser.

Homemade Commands

You can take a few steps (that get recorded in the History panel), select them, and then save the steps as a command. Using the History panel's Save Selected Steps as a Command does the work of actually pasting the JSFL into a text file and saving it in your Configuration folder. From that point forward, you can select your homemade script from the Commands menu. Alternatively, you can just create a text file into which you paste the script and then select that file directly when selecting the menu Command, Run Command. That's the way it's done in the following exercise. It's just cleaner because while we're testing we don't want to manage a bunch of homemade commands.

The background for the following task is the fact that some artists don't like Flash's gray background. Often they'll draw a large fill with a rectangle removed in place of the stage. My script now does that automatically. The process I took to develop that script was as follows:

1. I cleared the History panel and drew a large shape.
2. Because I couldn't just select a rectangle in the middle of a shape, I clicked off the shape and dragged until I was on the shape, and then pressed Delete. Although this wasn't exactly what I was going to need, it was close enough to start making edits.
3. I selected the steps, clicked Copy Steps to Clipboard, and then pasted into a text file eventually saved as stageMask.jsfl (see Figure 13.7).

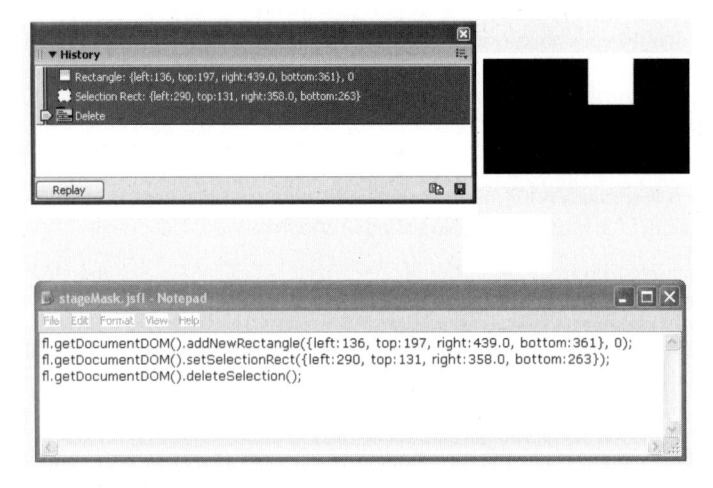

Figure 13.7 *Take the raw script for clearing a rectangle within a shape from the History panel into a text file.*

All I needed to do was make sure the original rectangle was big enough to cover the stage and then the selection (to be cleared) had to be the exact size and location of the stage. Here is the next incarnation of my script:

```
1  width=550;
2  height=400;
3  fl.getDocumentDOM().addNewRectangle({left:-500, top:-500,
                  right:width+500, bottom:height+500}, 0);
4  fl.getDocumentDOM().selectNone();
5  fl.getDocumentDOM().setSelectionRect({left:0, top:0,
                  right:width, bottom:height});
6  fl.getDocumentDOM().deleteSelection();
```

Notice how line 3 draws a rectangle that goes exactly 500 pixels past the edges of the stage by using a nice -500 as well as expressions such as width+500. Then line 5 makes a selection the exact size of the stage (something, by the way, not possible to do manually). I tested it (by selecting Command, Run Command), and it worked pretty well!

To make it a bit more practical, I wanted the first two lines to dynamically adapt to whatever the current stage size was. It took about 30 seconds to find in the JSFL documentation that the stage has two properties (width and height). So lines 1 and 2 changed as follows:

```
width=fl.getDocumentDOM().width;
height=fl.getDocumentDOM().height;
```

One last touch was another cool method I found in the JSFL docs—setFillColor. So I added the following code to what I had:

```
fl.getDocumentDOM().setFillColor("#000000");
```

At this point, you could keep improving on this command. For example, you can make it automatically insert a new layer and then lock it (whereas the current script just draws into the current layer). In addition, you could present the user with a dialog box where, perhaps, the user could select a color to use. Before you go that far, let me suggest that the easiest way to build a custom dialog box is to use Flash itself (as opposed to using XML to UI). The next section shows how you can use a SWF as the user interface to a command—just as long as the SWF runs inside the Flash authoring environment.

WindowSWF Custom Panel

Making a custom SWF appear as in a panel (called a WindowSWF panel) is just a matter of publishing your movie to the configuration folder WindowSWF. Once installed, your SWF can be accessed from the menu Window, Other Panels.

These WindowSWFs have all kinds of uses (beyond triggering JSFL commands as we'll do in a minute). For example, the App Inspector used for maintaining Flash Communication Server apps in Chapter 8, "Foundation Communication Server," is just a WindowSWF. I've seen homemade WindowSWFs for anything from a tool to retrieve key codes (Key.getCode()) to a color picker to help find nice color combinations. Anyway, to make your WindowSWF execute JSFL, you just trigger the function called MMExecute().

To trigger some JSFL, you need to store the entire set of steps as a string and pass that string to `MMExecute(theString)`. For example, the following example flips upside down any item the user has selected. Just make a new movie (somewhat small stage size, such as 200×200) put a button (`my_btn`) onstage and this code in the first frame:

```
my_btn.onRelease = function() {
  var command="fl.getDocumentDOM().rotateSelection(180);";
  MMExecute(command);
};
```

Finally, publish this to your WindowSWF configuration folder. You won't even need to restart Flash if you chose the WindowSWF folder inside your user Configuration folder (as opposed to the First Run version). Pop open the SWF via Window, Other Panels, and test it out.

The only thing tricky about executing JSFL this way is that you need to format your code as a string. When you need quotation marks inside the string, remember how you can use single quotes or `\"` for literal quotes. Also, variables and expressions need to be concatenated to the string. To separate multiple lines of code in a more complex command, simply use semicolons. Just be sure you supply a single command for the `MMExecute()` method. These are the same sorts of issues encountered when building a `getURL()` string dynamically.

Other Uses for JSFL

Hopefully, you feel empowered rather than overwhelmed. In any event, I feel obligated to mention a couple other ways you can use JSFL. The biggie is as custom tools. If you haven't noticed, the menu Edit, Customize Tools Panel preference enables you to change and *add* additional tools (see Figure 13.8).

It turns out that Flash ships with just one special tool: the PolyStar! The expectation is that developers will create and share more tools. I've seen a few cool ones already, such as a 3D cube maker and a variety of arrow heads that automatically apply to lines you draw. Well, you guessed it: Creating such tools is done using JSFL. The best way to learn how to write such a tool is to look at how the standard tools that do ship with Flash work. You can find their JSFL files (along with the .png icon) in the Tools folder.

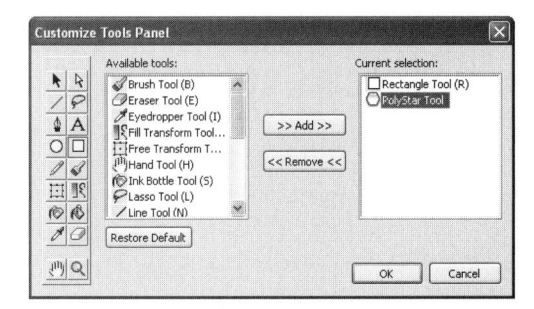

Figure 13.8 *The new Customize Tool Panel dialog box supports tools written in JSFL.*

Finally, you can take a JSFL file and drag it onto Flash, and it will run. This means you can execute Flash from the command line. If you want to run a script on an unattended copy of Flash, you need to add additional lines of code, such as a command to close Flash at the end. For example, take the file stageMask.jsfl (from earlier) and add this line of code above the first line you currently have:

```
doc=fl.createDocument();//to make a new document
```

Then put this code after the last line:

```
doc.exportSWF("file:///c|/temp/test.swf");
fl.closeDocument(doc);
fl.quit(true);
```

Now you just have to make sure that you have a folder called temp. Save the JSFL file, quit Flash, and then just double-click stageMask.jsfl. You'll see the test.swf show up automatically. To see the mask, launch the SWF, go full screen (Ctrl+F), and then right-click and select 100%.

I believe extensibility through JSFL will surprise even Macromedia. Consider how simple that mask script was. Add to that the fact you can make an interface as a Flash SWF, and I think you're going to see some creative solutions. I know I'll be making a few utilities for my own use.

Basic Class Packages in AS2

Ah, the last section of the last chapter. And I'm bringing up a topic that will easily fill another book twice the size of this one. I do want to orient you to AS2, but not as some afterthought or futile attempt to cram it all in. Rather, the best thing I can offer is an introduction to how AS2 is structured and how you can get started putting it to use. For me, the hardest aspect of learning is taking the first steps to apply all the tidbits I gather by reading or looking at others' solutions. This section attempts to put things in perspective so that you can get a good idea where things fit.

Anyway, AS2 is a formalized set of rules for ActionScript. The intention is for ActionScript to be more like other object-oriented languages such as Java and C#. It's not quite AS1 with more stuff (although, there are several added script elements). Instead, AS2 enforces syntax rules to even your old AS1. If you set your Publish settings to AS2, for example, you'll be able to use things such as strong data typing and the new Error object. However, with this setting, something that may have worked in AS1 will no longer work. For example, in MX you could use the following:

```
var myName="Phillip";
trace(myname);   //and see "Phillip"
```

In contrast, AS2 is case sensitive, so you will see `undefined` unless you use the following:

```
trace(myName);
```

Obviously, the idea of AS2 isn't just to make things difficult. Some would argue `myName` is different from `myname`, which when you use AS2 and publish for Flash Player 7, it is. It's hard to demonstrate the differences because it's more than just AS1 versus AS2. You've given Publish options for AS1 or AS2 as well as what version of Flash Player you will require. For example, you use AS2 even if you're delivering to Flash Player 6. You'll have to select this option if you want to use the V2 components. You'll only encounter the case-sensitive issue when using AS2 and delivering to Flash Player 7.

Subtle details of AS2 have already popped up a few places in this book. The following section describes the topic of class files. *Class files* are a modular way to keep generic functions external to your application. That is, you can make a library of useful classes, store them adjacent to your installed version of Flash, and use them in any project.

Structure

True to the modular nature of AS2, each class appears in its own class file. The filename is the class's name plus .as. (By convention, classes are capitalized.) You'll find all the installed classes that ship with Flash in the global class path—that is, a folder in your Local Settings Configuration folder. On my machine it's in this path:

```
C:\Documents and Settings\Phillip\Local Settings\Application Data\
Macromedia\Flash MX 2004\en\Configuration\Classes\
```

You'll find this "global class path" specified when you select Edit, Preferences, ActionScript tab. Figure 13.9 shows `$(LocalData)/Classes`, which is a dynamic reference to the long folder path above. (You should also see a period on the second line so that the folder where you save your FLA is also included in the class path.)

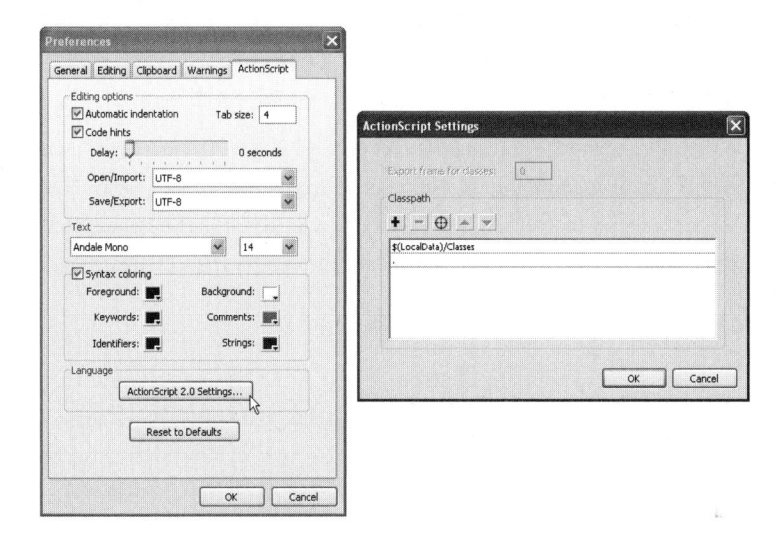

Figure 13.9 *The default class path is set globally through Edit, Preferences.*

You can import any of those class files into your application using `import`. For example, components that need the `DepthManager` class include this line of code:

```
import mx.managers.DepthManager;
```

This means that the file DepthManager.as is inside the folder managers inside the folder mx, which is inside the global class path. Notice dots are used rather than slashes. Also, all folders and filenames are case sensitive!

To make your own class, first create a file (for instance, MyClass.as). If you make a folder called mine inside the Classes folder, you need this code in your movie:

```
import mine.MyClass;
```

This is similar to the old `include()` directive that enables you to embed code from an external file. Using `import` gives you access to all the code inside the class file. Also, you can import all classes in the mine folder if you use the following:

```
import mine.*;
```

Incidentally, you can add additional class paths. The settings made in Edit, Preferences affect all applications you create. In addition, you can specify document-specific class paths through the Publish settings. Finally, you can also store AS files adjacent to your FLA and you don't even need to `import` them. Although this is convenient, you'll encounter a downside when you see how the first line of code *in* a class file refers to the class itself—and its path.

The structure of class files is detailed and unforgiving. It's necessary, however, so that that classes can import and share code from other classes. The Flash UI components rely on that structure as a way to eliminate repeated code. Be sure to read all the Help files in Flash; they cover the subject effectively.

Basic Skeleton

You're welcome to explore the contents of any of the classes that appear in your Local Settings folder. You can open them with any text editor, including Dreamweaver and Flash MX Professional 2004. Start by considering the following simple example of the contents of a class file named MyClass.as:

```
class mine.MyClass
{
  function repeatMe(param:String):String{
    return ("you said "+param);
  }
}
```

Notice the name of the class (`MyClass`) appears after the path to that class (that is, inside the folder mine). Also notice I'm using strict data typing with colons that cast as strings both the parameter received and the value returned. Basically, `repeatMe()` becomes a method of every instance of this class. For example, the following code imports the class, makes an instance, and then triggers the `repeatMe()` method:

```
import mx.mine.MyClass;
var myInstance:MyClass=new MyClass();
var reply:String = myInstance.repeatMe("hi");
trace(reply);
```

Of course, I expect your class methods to get a bit more involved.

You can go in several directions from this point:

- You can add more features to this class, such as additional methods and implied get/setter properties.

- You can separate private methods from public methods by using what's called an *access modifier*. This reduces the access given to developers, which is primarily to reduce the amount of effort to use the class.

- You can "extend" other classes. That is, your class can be a subclass of another. This means the subclass can do anything its parent class can (called the *super class*). The subclass has extended capabilities: either additional methods or methods that override same-named methods in the super class (called *specialization*). For example, you could make a clip that's a subclass to the Movie Clip class. Your clip will begin life with all the same methods and properties of movie clips, but you can add more or override methods as needed. This is equivalent to how you can extend the prototype property of an object.

Implied *get/set* Methods

By now you've seen how true properties available in V2 component instances make setting and getting properties easy and direct. In the past, you could access properties only via methods, which made code messy. The properties you define for your class instances can also use this same protocol. You still define methods (one for how to set a property, and one for how to get a property). However, implied get/set methods include an extra word (not surprisingly: get and set). The code in Listing 13.3 shows you a getter/setter property called area.

Listing 13.3 Implied *getter/setter* Property

```
1   class mine.MyClass
2   {
3     var width:Number=10;
4     var height:Number=10;
5     function get area():Number {
6       return width*height;
7     }
8     function set area(val:Number):Void {
9       width=Math.sqrt(val);
10      height=Math.sqrt(val);
11    }
12  }
```

continues

Listing 13.3 Implied *getter/setter* Property (Continued)

This example is pretty simple compared to the old `addProperty()` technique required in AS1.

Notice that I created a property called `area`, but that doesn't appear anywhere like the width and `height` properties. In fact, an implied getter/setter property can't. It's really not so much a property as a function for which there is both a `get` and a `set` version. The `get` version (line 5) has the job of just returning a value in place of anyplace the developer uses `myInstance.area`. The set version (line 8) can perform any operation you want. In this case, I'm setting the `width` and `height` properties. Realize that for the simple properties `height` and `width`, I don't have any `get/set` functions defined. When the user sets one (for instance, `myInstance.height=100`) or gets one (perhaps, `myVar=myInstance.height`), nothing happens internal to the class. Basically, for the properties you expect to affect other properties or display an immediate visual change, you'll want to set up `get/set` functions.

Here's how you could use the preceding class from inside Flash:

```
import mx.mine.MyClass;
var myInstance:MyClass=new MyClass();
trace(myInstance.area);
myInstance.area=50;
trace(myInstance.width);
```

{ Note }

***getter/setter* Properties Can't Match Internal Property Names**

The weird part in the preceding listing is that you can't use the property name `area` inside the class. For this reason, you may need to maintain separate properties that use different names. If I want direct access to `area` inside the class, for example, I would make a different property (for instance, `myArea`) and insert a line after line 10, such as `myArea=val`, so that it would mirror the `area` property.

Modularizing by Extending

You can do just a few other general things with classes—but they can get pretty advanced. Let me define some topics so that, when you do encounter them, you'll have a good basis of understanding.

Modularizing your classes can be as simple as making a separate class for every little thing and then importing several classes as needed for your app. In fact, class files can import other class files to leverage code written elsewhere. A much more elaborate version of the same idea is extending and implementing.

When one class extends another, it means it will have all built-in methods and properties of the class it's extending, as well as any you define in the class itself. To make one class extend another, you just add `extends otherClass` at the end of the first line, like this:

```
class myClass extends otherClass;
```

This means that any method in `otherClass` is available to all instances of `myClass`. This way you can write generic methods for the `otherClass` that are available to any class that extends it. Here's a simple example:

```
class MyDate extends Date
{
  function formattedDate ():String{
    return this.getDate()+"/"+
           Number(this.getMonth()+1)+"/"+
           this.getFullYear();
  }
}
```

With this code, I can say `today=new MyDate()`, and then later do everything I would normally do with the `today` instance as if it were an instance of the Date object. In addition, I could do something like `trace(today.formattedDate())`.

Overriding is when one class can write its own version of a method found in its super class. If I want `MyDate` instances to respond to `getDate()` differently than normal, for example, I could just write a function like this:

```
function getDate(){}
```

If later I want to use the *real* `getDate()` method (that is, the one in the super class), all I need to do is use `super.getDate()`. You can think of the `super` keyword as a pointer to the super class.

Finally, class definitions can include properties or methods designated as `public` or `private`. The idea is that you may have the need for properties or methods that you want to shield from the developer using the class. Items designated as `private` are almost like local variables because there is no chance a subclass will override them—even if they use the same name.

Implementing an Interface

An interface is like a regular class except it has methods only—no properties. And those methods are empty. An interface is basically a list of all the methods you expect to get overridden. One class can "implement" an interface. It looks the same as one class extending another:

```
class MyClass implements MyInterface{}
```

Unlike the hierarchy of subclass/super class, however, this arrangement just ensures `MyClass` uses the same method names found in `MyInterface`. (That is, its behavior is implemented the same.) This way, you might have several classes that each has its own implementation of the `cleanUp()` method. When you structure your classes, an interface defines how developers using the class will interact. It's like you're setting up the methods that will become available even before you define how they work.

Summary

There are certainly a lot of avenues open to developing and archiving your code library. Components, behaviors, commands (as well as the entire JSFL programming language) are all available as ways to reduce rework. The one tip I can offer is that you don't have to use them all from the start. First, just understand what all is available and how it might help you. Then, when a need arises later you should be able to take the time necessary to build your code library.

Regardless of what you expected from this book, I hope you feel better off than when you started. I wanted to include a mix of details as well as an overall thought process or attitude behind building rich Internet applications. I figure technical details are nothing without a good idea, and a great idea is nothing without a way to apply it. At this point, I hope you don't think this is the last word. I'm sure, for me, my best RIA is yet to be built.

Finally, do feel free to send me links to things you build: ria@phillipkerman.com.

{ Index }

Symbols

\ (backslash) escape character, 118

A

a href code
    creating hyperlinks, 120
    invoking Flash functions, 120
a:hover tag, 124
absolute connections, 237-238
access modifiers, 427
accessibility
    hearing issues, 56-57
    motor skills issues, 55-56
    overview, 52-53
    vision issues, 53-55
Actions panel
    Flash Remoting methods, 196
    productivity features, 314
        code cleanup, 318
        code hints, 316-317
        Code Navigator, 317-318
        toolbox, 315
ActionScript
    NetServices library, 191
    web services
        listing, 224

ActionScript 2 (AS2), 405
   class files, 423
      exploring contents, 426-428
      implementing an interface, 430
      modularizing classes by extending, 428-429
      structure, 424-426
ActionsPanel.xml document, 201
adaptors, conf folder (FCS), 230
addEventListener( ) method, triggering code to respond to events, 382-383
addItem( ) method, 211
   populating components with script, 376, 379
advance( ) function, 348
Alert component, 391
alternatives, consideration of, 32-33
AMF packet encoded data, loading, 68
API (Application Programming Interface), 22
application development features, 19-20
Application object, 277, 283-285
application servers, 23, 37
   database access, 77
   Flash integration with, 78
   overview, 73-77
   web services, gateway to, 77
applications
   history of, 13
      milestones, 13-15
      multimedia computer, 14-15
      plug-ins, 15-16
      users having modern browsers, expectation of, 15
   killer apps, 13, 22
   multimode, 332-335
   overview, 12
   prototyping, 329
      components, 330
      modular thinking, 330

quality assurance and debugging, 339
   assessing bugs, 340-342
   avoiding bugs, 345-354
   client management, 344-345
   deliberate approach to addressing bugs, 343-344
   Error object, 367-370
   finding and removing bugs, 354-367
   types of bugs, 342-343
   scripts
      code cleanup, 318
      Code Navigator, 317-318
      staging, 330-332
applications folder (FCS), 229-230
architectural decisions, RSOs, 247-249
Array.CASEINSENSITIVE parameter, 212
Array.DESCENDING parameter, 212
arrays
   associative arrays. See generic objects
   benefits of, 99-100
   buttonList, 152
   contacts, 213
   frameList, 152
   generic objects, 96-98
   objects used like, 100
   overview, 95
   parsing imported data into (LoadVars object), 170-172
   questions, 170
AS text files, storing scripts, 414-415
AS2. See ActionScript 2
ascertaining values, populating components with script, 379-380
AsCodeHints.xml configuration file, 316
asfunction technique, 120
   creating hyperlinks to Flash functions, 120-121
associative arrays. See generic objects
attachMovie( ) method, 129-130

attributes
  Schema tab, 218
    Encoding option, 219
    Formatters option, 219-221
    Kind option, 219
    Validation option, 219, 222-223
  XML, 180
audio, 39
author time, 22
authoring components on Macintosh, 229
authortime shared library items, 325-326
Auto Format button (Actions panel), 318
AVI files, 40
avoiding bugs, 345
  defining testing procedures, 353-354
  leaving tracks, 350
    documenting fixes, 353
    inline documentation, 352-353
    version numbering, 351-352
  proofing systems, 345-350

B

Back button
  listing, 160-164
  local connection objects, 158-160
    FlashVars tag in HTML, 160-165
backslash (\) escape character, 118
balancing errors, debugging, 354
bar instance, 168
base values, staging, 331
begin property, 128
behaviors
  listing, 416-417
  storing scripts, 415-418
Bindings tab (Component Inspector), 198, 201-207
BMG files, 38
body_ta instance, 206
borderStyle style (components), 395

bottom.swf files, 157
Bound To dialog box, 200
bracket reference, 101-102
Breeze, 36
Breeze Live, 37
Broadmoor Hotel example of RIA standard, 24
bugs, quality assurance and debugging, 339
  assessing bugs, 340-342
  avoiding bugs, 345-354
  client management, 344-345
  deliberate approach to addressing bugs, 343-344
  Error object, 367-370
  finding and removing bugs, 354-367
  types of bugs, 342-343
Button component, 374
  saving usernames (LSOs), 144
buttonList array, 152
buttons
  Auto Format (Actions panel), 318
  Back
    listing, 160-164
    local connection objects, 158-165
  Copy to Clipboard (History panel), 418
  navigate_btn, 156
  off_btn, 156
  on_btn, 156
  Plus (Bindings tab), 200
  Save (slide-show maker), 147-148
  Save As Command (History panel), 319
  Save Selected Steps as a Command (History panel), 419
  setInterval, 348
  sfx_btn, 156
  Step In, 365
  Step Out, 365
  Step Over, 365
  Symbol, 326

C

Call Stack pane, 364
camera, accessing, 267-268
Cascading Style Sheets. *See* CSS
categories of bugs, 342-343
Central. *See* Macromedia Central
Central folder, 87
CFCs (ColdFusion Components), 194
cfoutput tags, 173
#CGI.SERVER_NAME# variable, 173
Check In feature (Project panel), 352
Check Out feature (Project panel), 352
CheckBox component, saving usernames (LSOs), 144
class files (AS2), 423
    exploring contents, 426-427
    implementing an interface, 430
    implied get/set methods, 427-428
    modularizing classes by extending, 428-429
    structure, 424-426
class-based structure, components, 373
cleanUp( ) method, 430
client management, debugging, 344-345
Client object, 286
client side, 22
client streams, republishing portions of, 301-302
clients, benefits of bug assessment, 340
code
    building a code library
        AS2, 423-430
        JSFL, 418-423
        scripting style, 408-414
        storing scripts, 414-418
    data kept separate from, 62-63
code cleanup (Actions panel), 318
code hints (Actions panel), 316-317
Code Navigator (Actions panel), 317-318
code-data separation, populating components with script (label and data properties), 377-379
ColdFusion, 74-76
ColdFusion Components. *See* CFCs
collaboration, 23
ComboBox component, 375, 387-388
    listing, 387
commands
    Control menu, Debug Movie, 361
    Edit menu, Preferences, ActionScript tab, 425
    File menu
        Import, Open External Library, 396
        Import, Open Library for Import, 326
        Publish, 156
    Insert menu, Convert to Symbol, 168
    JSFL homemade commands, 419-421
    Tools menu, Folder Options, Show Hidden Files and Folder, 315
    Version Control menu, Edit Sites, 323
    Window menu
        Debugger, 367
        Other Panels, 191
Commands menu, productivity features, 318-320
communication components, overview, 307-309
compiled clips, enhancing components, 404-406
complex data, Flash Remoting, 195
Component Definition dialog box, 405
Component Inspector, 198
    Bindings tab, 198, 201-207
    Parameters tab, 198
    Schema tab, 198, 201-207, 218
        Encoding option, 219
        Formatters option, 219-221
        Kind option, 219
        Validation option, 219, 222-223

components, 372-373, 385, 390
   Alert, 391
   class-based structure, 373
   ComboBox, 387-388
   creating, 402
      design, 402-403
      distribution, 406
      enhancements, 404-406
      text components, 403-404
   customizing, 392
      skinning, 392, 396-398
      styles, 392-395
   data components, 81, 197-199
      Component Inspector, 198, 201-207
      connectors, 197, 201
      managers, 197, 207-215
      resolvers, 197, 215-218
   DataGrid, 392
   Date Field and Date Chooser, 391
   direct property access, 372
   disadvantages, 372-373
   List, 388-390
   Menubar, 391
   overview, 79
   populating manually, 374-375
   populating with script, 375
      ascertaining values, 379-380
      data structure, 377-379
      dataProvider property, 379
      properties and methods, 376-377
   prototyping, 330
   providing data to, 81
   Remoting, 189
   Text components
      Label, 386
      TextArea, 386
      TextInput, 386
   TextInput, 219
   Tree, 392
   triggering code to respond to events, 381
      addEventListener( ) method, 382-383
      Event objects, 384-385
      on method, 381-382
   using, 79-81
   V2 components, 79-80
   validation and formatting controls, 372
Compose String formatters (Schema tab), 219-220
composed_txt instance, 220
conf folder (FCS)
   adaptors, 230
   editing configuration files, 231-232
   overview, 230
   virtual hosts, 230
configuration (FCS)
   authoring components, 229
   folders, 229-232
   overview, 228
   production, 232-236
configuration files
   AsCodeHints.xml, 316
   editing, 231-232
   locating in Actions panel, 315
      Configuration folder, 315
      First Run folder, 315
Configuration folder (configuration files), 315
configuration folders, 85-86
   Central folder, 87
   FCS
      applications folder, 229-230
      conf folder, 230-232
      overview, 229
   First Run folder, 85
connect( ) method, 152
connections (NetConnect)
   absolute connections, 237-238
   basic connecting, 236-237

HTTP tunneling, 238-239
overview, 237
ports, 238-239
connectors (Data components), 197
WebServiceConnector, 197-200
XMLConnector, 197-201
constructors
functions as, improving scripting style, 410-412
new, 138
contacts array, 213
contacts.push( ) method, 211
contents, AS2 class files, 426-427
Control menu commands, Debug Movie, 361
Convert to Symbol command (Insert menu), 168
Convert to Symbol dialog box, 327
convert( ) method, 193
Copy to Clipboard button (History panel), 418
createEmptyMovieClip( ) method, 130
createTextField( ) method, 130
creating components, 402
design, 402-403
distribution, MXP files, 406
enhancements, 404-405
compiled clips, 404-406
custom UI, 404
Live Preview, 404
text components, 403-404
CSS (Cascading Style Sheets), 116
formatting text, 122
formatting inside Flash, 124-125
importing CSS definitions, 122-124
Ctrl+' (code cleanup), 318
custom UI, enhancing components, 404
Customize Tools Panel (JSFL), 422

customizing components, 392
skinning, 392
replacing skins, 396-398
styles, 392-393
single instances versus global styles, 393-394
supported styles list, 394-395

D

data
dummy data, 335-337
formatting (schema tab attributes), 218-223
parsing, 115
data access (RSOs), 240-242
data components, 81, 197-199
Component Inspector, 198
Bindings tab, 198, 201-207
Parameters tab, 198
Schema tab, 198, 201-207
connectors
WebServiceConnector, 197-200
XMLConnector, 197, 201
managers
DataHolder, 197, 207-210
DataSet, 197, 210-215
resolvers
RDBMSResolver, 197, 215-218
XUpdateResolver, 197, 215-218
data exchange, 135
errors in, known, 71
flat data, 165
formatting, 166-167
LoadVars object, 166-172
server interaction, 172-176
loading data, 66-69
AMF packet encoded data, 68
SOAP encoded data, 68
URL encoded data, 67
XML encoded data, 68

DataGrid component 437

local connection objects, 149
    Back button, 158-165
    creating a guided tour Help feature, 151-154
    downloading media into a single window, 154-158
    structure, 151
LSOs (local shared objects), 137, 143
    flushing data to disk, 141-143
    limitations, 148-149
    return users versus new users, 139
    saving a password with username, 146-147
    saving a username, 144
    skip-intro feature, 143
    slide-show maker Save feature, 147-148
    structure, 138
    where to save files, 139-140
outside services, 187-188
    Data components, 197-199
    Flash Remoting, 188-197
overview, 66
parsing data, 69
protocols, 135-136
success of, ensuring, 71-72
synchronizing data, 70-71
timeouts, 71
web services, 72-73
writing data, 69-70
XML structured data, 177-178
    browsing Amazon through Flash, 182-185
    loading data, 178-179
    parsing data, 179-182
data handling
    code and data, separation of, 62-63
    overview, 62
    presentation of data, 65-66
    structuring data, 64-65
        arrays, 95-100
        data types, 93-95
        DataProvider object, 104
        functions, 102-103
        objects, 100-102
        overview, 92
        slide-show maker example, 108, 112
        sorting data, 105-108
data presentation, 115-116
    CSS, 122
        formatting inside Flash, 124-125
        importing CSS definitions, 122-124
    HTML, 116-119
        hyperlinks to Flash functions, 120-121
        img src tags, 119-120
    layout options, 129-134
        attachMovie( ) method, 129-130
        createEmptyMovieClip( ) method, 130
        createTextField( ) method, 130
        MovieClip object's drawing methods, 130
    TextFormat object, 126-129
data property, 138
    components, 377-379
    DataHolder component, 207
    determining presence of properties (new users versus return users), 139
data structure, populating components with script (label and data properties), 377-379
data types
    overview, 93-95
    primitive variables, 94-95
    reference variables, 94-95
    strong data typing, 93
database access, application servers, 77
DataGlue object, 196
DataGrid component, 392

DataGrid instance, 217
DataHolder component, 197, 207-210
    accessing nested data, 207
    creating schema, 207-209
    data property, 207
DataProvider object, 104
dataProvider property, populating components with script, 379
dataProviders, recordsets, 195
DataSet component, 197, 210
    iterating data, 210-211
    saving collection, 214-215
    sorting and searching, 211-214
Date Field and Date Chooser component, 391
Debug Movie command (Control menu), 361
Debugger command (Window menu), 367
Debugger panel, 361
    properties and variables, 361-363
    remote debugging, 365-367
        conditions, 365
    stepping through code, 363-365
debugging, 339
    assessing bugs, 340
        acceptance, 341
        benefits to client and developer, 340
        categories of bugs, 342-343
        clear understanding of the bug, 342
        self-criticism, 340
    avoiding bugs, 345
        leaving tracks, 350-354
        proofing systems, 345-350
    client management, 344-345
    deliberate approach to addressing bugs, 343-344
    Error object, 367-370
    finding and removing bugs, 354
        homemade debuggers, 357-367
        scientific approach, 355-357
        standard messages, 354-355

defining testing procedures, avoiding bugs, 353-354
deliberate approach to addressing bugs, 343-344
deltaPacket, 215
deployment
    in-browser applications, 42-46
    overview, 41-42
    standalone applications, 46-48
deprecate property, 205
DepthManager class, 425
description property, 191
design time, 22
designing components, 402-403
developers, benefits of bug assessment, 340
dh instance, 209
dialog boxes
    Bound To, 200
    Component Definition, 405
    Convert to Symbol, 327
    Publish Settings, 322
    Settings, 322
        Local Storage tab, 141
    Symbol Properties, 325
    System Settings, 141
        System.showSettings( ) method, 143
direct property access, components, 372
Director and Flash compared, 17-18
disk space checker (listing), 142
displaying
    download progress (LoadVars object), 168-169
    text (HTML), 116-119
displayText( ) function, 123
distribution of components (MXP files), 406
doClickList( ) function, 411
document type descriptions, 177
document.title property, 164
document.write( ) method, 160, 163

documenting fixes, leaving tracks, 353
doDisplay( ) function, 133
doMyFunction( ) function, 192
doSave( ) method, 148
downloading
    displaying download progress (LoadVars object), 168-169
    media into a single window (local connection objects), 154-158
Dreamweaver, 37
ds.addSort( ) method, 211
ds.applyUpdates( ) method, 215
ds.getItemId( ) method, 212
ds.hasSort( ) method, 211
ds.next( ) method, 211
ds.previous( ) method, 211
ds.removeSort( ) method, 212
DTDs (document type descriptions), 177
dummy data, 335-337

E

Edit menu commands, Preferences, ActionScript tab, 425
Edit Sites command (Version Control menu), 323
editing themes, component customization, 397
embedding images (HTML), img src tags, 119-120
Encoding option (Schema tab), 219
end property, 128
enhancements, creating components, 404-405
    compiled clips, 404-406
    custom UI, 404
    Live Preview, 404
Entry( ) constructor function, 412
error messages, known errors in data exchange, 71

Error object
    listing, 369
    quality assurance and debugging, 367-370
errors, debugging
    balancing, 354
    syntax, 355
escape characters, 118
escape( ) function, 167
event handlers
    onResult, 191
    onStatus, 191
event logs, server-side streams used for, 303-307
Event objects, triggering code to respond to events, 384-385
events
    onChanged, 144
    onMusic, 156
    onMyMethod, 150
    onSFX, 156
    onStatus, 142, 157
    onSynchronize, 161
    onUpdate, 405
    SSAS
        Application object, 277, 283-285
        Client object, 286
        onAppStart event, 277-278
        onConnect event, 278-282
        onDisconnect event, 282-283
        overview, 277
    triggering code to respond (components), 381
        addEventListener( ) method, 382-383
        Event objects, 384-385
        on method, 381-382
examples (RSOs)
    favorite movie vote counter, 253-255
    geographic locator, 250-252
    overview, 250

exchanging data, 135
    flat data, 165
        formatting, 166-167
        LoadVars object, 166-172
        server interaction, 172-176
    local connection objects, 149
        Back button, 158-165
        creating a guided tour Help feature, 151-154
        downloading media into a single window, 154-158
        structure, 151
    LSOs (local shared objects), 137, 143
        flushing data to disk, 141-143
        limitations, 148-149
        return users versus new users, 139
        saving a password with username, 146-147
        saving a username, 144
        skip-intro feature, 143
        slide-show maker Save feature, 147-148
        structure, 138
        where to save files, 139-140
    outside services, 187-188
        Data components, 197-199
        Flash Remoting, 188-197
    protocols, 135-136
    XML structured data, 177-178
        browsing Amazon through Flash, 182-185
        loading data, 178-179
        parsing data, 179-182
exporting data, 135
    flat data, 165
        formatting, 166-167
        LoadVars object, 166-172
        server interaction, 172-176

local connection objects, 149
    Back button, 158-165
    creating a guided tour Help feature, 151-154
    downloading media into a single window, 154-158
    structure, 151
LSOs (local shared objects), 137, 143
    flushing data to disk, 141-143
    limitations, 148-149
    return users versus new users, 139
    saving a password with username, 146-147
    saving a username, 144
    skip-intro feature, 143
    slide-show maker Save feature, 147-148
    structure, 138
    where to save files, 139-140
outside services, 187-188
    Data components, 197-199
    Flash Remoting, 188-197
protocols, 135-136
XML structured data, 177-178
    browsing Amazon through Flash, 182-185
    loading data, 178-179
    parsing data, 179-182
Extension Manager. *See* Macromedia Extension Manager
external native files, 325

F

FCS. *See* Flash Communication Server
features, productivity, 314
    Actions panel features, 314-318
    Commands menu, 318-320
    dummy data, 335-337

Find and Replace feature, 314
Library management, 324-329
multimode applications, 332-335
Project panel, 320-324
prototyping, 329-330
staging, 330-332
File menu commands
Import, Open External Library, 396
Import, Open Library for Import, 326
Publish, 156
files
bottom.swf, 157
configuration, locating in Actions panel, 315
index.html, 155
main1.html, 157
main1.swf, 157
main2.html, 157
management (Project panel), 322
my_script.cfm, 173
path.to.cfc, 192
tempconverter, 193
Find and Replace feature, 314
find( ) method, 214
finding bugs, 354
Debugger panel, 361
properties and variables, 361-363
remote debugging, 365-367
stepping through code, 363-365
homemade debuggers, 357
runtime trace windows, 359-361
Simple Debug mode, 357-359
scientific approach, 355-357
standard messages, 354-355
Fireworks, 37
First Run folder, 85
configuration files, 315
Flash
Director compared, 17-18
HTML compared, 18

Java compared, 17
JavaScript compared, 19
RIA standard, 16
Broadmoor Hotel (example), 25
XML News Aggregator (example), 25
upgrades, 19
application development features, 19-20
when to use, 20-21
Flash Communication Server (FCS), 36, 82-83
configuration
authoring components, 229
overview, 228
production, 232-236
configuration folders
applications folder, 229-230
conf folder, 230-232
overview, 229
cost of, 228
NetConnection
basic connecting, 236-237
connections, 237-239
overview, 236
optimization
ActionScript, use of, 296
messaging, use of, 298-299
prototype, defining functions inside, 296-298
overview, 227-228
production
overview, 232
remote production, 235-236
restarting server, 232-234
revisions, 234
subdomains, 235
RSOs
architectural decisions, 247-249
data, accessing and setting, 240-242

examples, 250-255
overview, 240
value synchronization, 242-247
streaming media
   FLV videos, 258-260
   MP3s, 261
   NetStreams, 256-257
   overview, 255
   playback controls, 262-266
   publishing, 267-274
   sharing streams with virtual
      directories, 261-262
Flash MX 2004, 36. *See also* Flash
Flash MX Professional 2004, 36.
   See also Flash
Flash Player, 15
Flash Player folder (SOL files), 139
Flash Remoting, 188
   basic script, 190-193
   complex data, 195
   described, 36
   manual scripts, 223-224
   NetConnection Debugger, 224
   proxy scripts, 225
   sequence, 189-190
   Service Browser, 224
   when to use, 196-197
   writing the Remote method, 194
Flash Studio Pro, 48
FlashVars tag, Back button solution,
   160-165
flat data, 165
   formatting, 166-167
   LoadVars object, 166-167
      displaying download progress,
         168-169
      parsing imported data into an array,
         170-172

server interaction, 172
   loading data from a server script,
      172-173
   retrieving data from a server script,
      175-176
   saving data to a server script,
      174-175
flush( ) method, 138, 141-142
flushing data to disk, LSOs (local shared
   objects), 141-143
FLV files, 40
   overview, 258-259
   playing, 259-260
Folder Options, Show Hidden Files and
   Folder command (Tools menu), 315
folder property, 205
folders
   Flash Player (SOL files), 139
   localhost, 149
font tags, 118
Formatters option (Schema tab), 219
   Compose String, 219-220
   Rearrange Fields, 220-221
formatting controls (components), 372
formatting data
   flat data, 166-167
   Schema tab attributes, 218-223
formatting text
   CSS, 122
      formatting inside Flash, 124-125
      importing CSS definitions, 122-124
   HTML, 116-119
      hyperlinks to Flash functions,
         120-121
      img src tags, 119-120
   TextFormat object, 126-129
frameList array, 152
Freehand, 37
functionName( ) form, 410

functions. *See also* methods
  advance( ), 348
  as constructors, improving scripting style, 410-412
  displayText( ), 123
  doClickList( ), 411
  doDisplay( ), 133
  doMyFunction( ), 192
  escape( ), 167
  event properties, associating with, 102-103
  init( ), 335
  MMExecute( ), 421
  navTo( ), 161
  Number( ), 172
  NumberError( ), 369
  sayHello( ), 194
  setRememberMode( ), 146
  setScale( ), 413
  StringError( ), 369
  unescape( ), 167
  update( ), 358

G

generic objects, 96-98
GET method, 174
getBytesLoaded( ) method, 167
getBytesTotal( ) method, 167
getDate( ) method, 429
getLocal( ) method, 139, 149
getNextHighestDepth( ) method, 134
getSummary method, 203
getTemperature method, 200
GIF files, 38
global class path (AS2 class files), 424
global styles, customizing components, 393-394
glossary, 22-23

groupthink, 344
guided tour Help feature (local connection objects), 151-154

H

Halo theme (components), 397
.headline style (CSS), 122
hearing issues (accessibility), 56-57
Help feature (local connection objects), 151-154
Help panel (component properties and methods), 376
helper files, guided tour Help feature (local connection objects), 153
  listing, 153-154
hierarchical structure (XML files), 177
History panel
  Copy to Clipboard button, 418
  creating Commands, 319
  Save Selected Steps as a Command button, 419
homemade debuggers, 357
  runtime trace windows, 359-361
  Simple Debug mode, 357-359
HTML (Hypertext Markup Language), 116
  Flash compared, 18
  FlashVars tag, Back button solution, 160-165
  formatting text, 116-119
    hyperlinks to Flash functions, 120-121
    img src tags, 119-120
  JavaScript compared, 19
html property, Render as HTML option, 116
htmlText property, 116
HTTP tunneling (NetConnection), 238-239
hyperlinks, asfunction technique, 120-121
Hypertext Markup Language. *See* HTML

I

IDE (Integrated Development Environment), 22
identifier names, 156
image-proofing script (listing), 347-348
images, embedding (HTML img src tags), 119-120
img src tags, embedding images or SWFs, 119-120
implied get/set methods (AS2 class files), 427-428
Import, Open External Library command (File menu), 396
Import, Open Library for Import command (File menu), 326
importing data, 135
    flat data, 165
        formatting, 166-167
        LoadVars object, 166-172
        server interaction, 172-176
    local connection objects, 149
        Back button, 158-165
        creating a guided tour Help feature, 151-154
        downloading media into a single window, 154-158
        structure, 151
    LSOs (local shared objects), 137, 143
        flushing data to disk, 141-143
        limitations, 148-149
        return users versus new users, 139
        saving a password with username, 146-147
        saving a username, 144
        skip-intro feature, 143
        slide-show maker Save feature, 147-148
        structure, 138
        where to save files, 139-140
    outside services, 187-188
        Data components, 197-199
        Flash Remoting, 188-197
    protocols, 135-136
    XML structured data, 177-178
        browsing Amazon through Flash, 182-185
        loading data, 178-179
        parsing data, 179-182
in-browser applications, deployment, 42-46
#include call, 415
incoming instance, 175
index.html file, 155
indexOf( ) method, 163
info parameter, 158
init( ) function, 335
inline documentation, leaving tracks, 352-353
Insert menu commands, Convert to Symbol, 168
installation, Flash Remoting, 189
instanceName.load( ) method, 167
interfaces, AS2 class files, 430. *See also* UI components
items property, 195
    DataSet component, 210
        iterating data, 210-211
        saving collection, 214-215
        sorting and searching, 211-214
iterating data (DataSet component), 210-211

J-K

Java, 37
    Flash compared, 17
JavaScript, 37
    testing main file (guided tour), 154
JavaScript Flash. *See* JSFL
JPG (external) files, 38
JPG (imported) files, 38

JSFL (JavaScript Flash), 319, 418
   Customize Tools Panel, 422
   executing Flash from command line, 423
   homemade commands, 419-421
   PolyStar! tool, 422
   running in Flash, 419
   WindowSWF custom panel, 421-422

killer apps, 13, 22
Kind option (Schema tab), 219

L

Label component, 386
label property, 221
   components, 377-379
last property, 214
layout options (data presentation), 129-134
   attachMovie( ) method, 129-130
   createEmptyMovieClip( ) method, 130
   createTextField( ) method, 130
   MovieClip object's drawing methods, 130
legacy, 23
length property, 178
library, building a code library
   AS2, 423-430
   JSFL, 418-423
   scripting style, 408-414
   storing scripts, 414-418
Library management, 324
   RSLs (Runtime Shared Libraries), 326-329
   shared library items, 325-326
limitations, LSOs (local shared objects), 148-149
linkage identifier name, 156
List component, 388-390
   listing, 389-390

listings
   ActionScript web services, 224
   adding Save feature to slide-show maker, 147-148
   advanced Error object, 369
   Back button, 160-164
   basic remoting script, 191
   behaviors, 416-417
   ComboBox component, 387
   disk space checker, 142
   displaying
      download progress, 169
      text with TextFormat object, 128
   exchanging variables (LoadVars.sendAndLoad( ) method), 175
   helper files (guided tour Help feature), 153-154
   image-proofing script, 347-348
   importing
      Amazon product details, 182
      and displaying CSS styles, 123
      flat data into an array, 171-172
   List component, 389-390
   loading data from a server script, 173
   LoadVars.load( ) method, 168
   local connection objects structure, 150
   LSO skeleton, 138
   main files (guided tour Help feature), 151-152
   playing sounds in separate frames, 155-156
   populating data, 131-134
   runtime trace windows, 359-360
   saving
      passwords with usernames, 145-146
      usernames, 144
   searching for transfer objects in a DataSet collection, 213

skip-intro feature (LSOs), 143
TextArea and TextInput components, 386
try, catch, finally structure (Error object), 368
XML.load( ) method, 178
Live Preview, enhancing components, 404
live stream, publishing, 268-270
load( ) method, 173
loadFromSharedObj( ) method, 214
loading data, 66-69
    AMF packet encoded data, 68
    SOAP encoded data, 68
    URL encoded data, 67
    XML encoded data, 68
LoadVars object, 166-167
    displaying download progress, 168-169
    parsing imported data into an array, 170-172
LoadVars.getBytesLoaded( ) method, 168
LoadVars.getBytesTotal( ) method, 168
LoadVars.load( ) method, 167
    listing, 168
LoadVars.onload( ) method, 167
LoadVars.sendAndLoad( ) method (listing), 175
local connection objects, 149
    Back button, 158-160
        FlashVars tag in HTML, 160-165
    creating a guided tour Help feature, 151-154
    downloading media into a single window, 154-158
    structure, 151
        listing, 150
Local Settings Configuration folder (AS2), 424
local shared objects. *See* LSOs
Local Storage tab (Settings dialog box), 141

localconnection.connect( ) method, 150
localconnection.send( ) method, 150
localhost folder, 88-89, 149
Locals tab, 364
locking feature of RSOs, 289
loopObj property, 417
LSOs (local shared objects), 137, 143
    flushing data to disk, 141-143
    limitations, 148-149
    return users versus new users, 139
    RSOs compared, 137, 240
    saving a password with username, 146-147
        listing, 145-146
        multiple usernames, 147
    saving a username, 144
        listing, 144
    skeleton listing, 138
    skip-intro feature, 143
        listing, 143
    slide-show maker Save feature, 147-148
        listing, 147-148
    structure, 138
    where to save files, 139-140

M

Macintosh authoring components, 229
Macromedia Central, 36, 327
    direct web service support, 225
    overview, 49-51
    web services, 73
Macromedia Extension Manager, 319
    distributing components, 406
Macromedia eXtension Package files. *See* MXP files
main files, guided tour Help feature (local connection objects), 151
    listing, 151-152

.main style (CSS), 122
main.asc file, 276
main1.html files, 157
main1.swf files, 157
main2.html files, 157
management
   files (Project panel), 322
   Library, 324
      RSLs (Runtime Shared Libraries), 326-329
      shared library items, 325-326
managers (Data components), 197
   DataHolder, 197, 207-210
      accessing nested data, 207
      creating schema, 207-209
      data property, 207
   DataSet, 197, 210
      iterating data, 210-211
      saving collection, 214-215
      sorting and searching, 211-214
manual scripts, 223-224
manually populating components, 374-375
maximum property, 206
media
   downloading into a single window (local connection objects), 154-158
   playing sounds in separate frames (listing), 155-156
media formats
   audio, 39
   overview, 38
   raster graphic, 38
   video, 40
Menubar component, 391
menus
   Commands, productivity features, 318-320
   Version Control, 323
messages, sending on RSOs, 289

messaging
   NetConnection.call( ), 293-295
   optimization, 298-299
   overview, 290
   SharedObject.send( ), 290-293
methods. *See also* functions
   addEventListener( ), triggering code to respond to events, 382-383
   addItem( ), 211
      populating components with script, 376, 379
   attachMovie( ), 129-130
   cleanUp( ), 430
   connect( ), 152
   contacts.push( ), 211
   convert( ), 193
   createEmptyMovieClip( ), 130
   createTextField( ), 130
   document.write( ), 160, 163
   doSave( ), 148
   ds.addSort( ), 211
   ds.applyUpdates( ), 215
   ds.getItemId( ), 212
   ds.hasSort( ), 211
   ds.next( ), 211
   ds.previous( ), 211
   ds.removeSort( ), 212
   find( ), 214
   flush( ), 138, 141-142
   GET, 174
   getBytesLoaded( ), 167
   getBytesTotal( ), 167
   getDate( ) method, 429
   getLocal( ), 139, 149
   getNextHighestDepth( ), 134
   getSummary, 203
   getTemperature, 200
   implied get/set (AS2 class files), 427-428

indexOf( ), 163
instanceName.load( ), 167
load( ), 173
loadFromSharedObj( ), 214
LoadVars.getBytesLoaded( ), 168
LoadVars.getBytesTotal( ), 168
LoadVars.load( ), 167
    listing, 168
LoadVars.onload( ), 167
LoadVars.sendAndLoad( ) (listing), 175
localconnection.connect( ), 150
localconnection.send( ), 150
on method, triggering code to respond to events, 381-382
onGetSection, 152
onGo, 152
onSetSection, 154
onShow, 152
onSynchronize, 163
populating components with script, 376-377
POST, 174
Remote, writing, 194
removeAll( ), 376
repeatMe( ), 426
saveToSharedObj( ), 214
send( ), 152, 157, 174
sendAndLoad( ), 174
    listing, 175
setFillColor (JSFL), 421
setInterval( ), 169
setNewTextFormat( ), 127
setStyle( ), 125
setTextFormat( ), 127
showSettings( ), displaying System Settings dialog box, 143
split( ), 172
substring( ), 163
System.showSettings( ), displaying System Settings dialog box, 143

tempconverter.cfc, 193
useSort( ), 211
watch( ), 358
windowopen( ), testing main file (guided tour), 154
XML.load( ) (listing), 178
microphone, accessing, 267-268
mission critical, 23
MMExecute( ) function, 421
modular thinking
    improving scripting style, 409-410
    prototyping, 330
modularizing AS2 class files, 428-429
motor skills issues (accessibility), 55-56
MOV files, 40
MovieClip object, drawing methods, 130
MP3s, 261
MPG (imported) files, 40
multimedia computer, 14
    standards for, 15
multimode applications, 332-335
MXP files (Macromedia eXtension Package), 406
    distributing components, 406
myArray property, 209
myGateway variable, 192
myService variable, 192
my_css variable, 123
my_lc variable, 150
my_script.cfm file, 173
my_ta instance, 199
my_ws instance, 199
my_xml instance, 179

N

name-value pairs, 165
native files, external, 325
navigate_btn, 156
navTo( ) function, 161

NetConnection
    basic connecting, 236-237
    connections
        absolute connections, 237-238
        HTTP tunneling, 238-239
        overview, 237
        ports, 238-239
    overview, 236
NetConnection Debugger, 191, 224
NetConnection.call( ), 293-295
NetServices library (ActionScript), 191
NetStreams, 256-257
new constructor, 138
new users, LSOs (local shared objects), 139
newVal parameter, 364
nodes (XML), 180
nodeValue property, 181
noteboard sample (editing a database with Flash Remoting), 194
ns instance, 206
Number( ) function, 172
NumberError( ) function, 369
NumericStepper instance, 205

O

Object-Oriented Programming in Flash, 412
objects. *See also* generic objects
    DataGlue, 196
    dynamically referencing properties, 101-102
    Error, quality assurance and debugging, 367-370
    Event, triggering code to respond to events, 384-385
    LoadVars, 166-167
        displaying download progress, 168-169
        parsing imported data into an array, 170-172

local connection objects. *See* local connection objects
local shared objects. *See* LSOs
looping through properties, 100
MovieClip, drawing methods, 130
TextField StyleSheet, 123
TextFormat, formatting text for presentation, 126-129
thisObj, 172
off_btn, 156
oldVal parameter, 364
on method, triggering code to respond to events, 381-382
onAppStart event, 277-278
onChanged event, 144
onConnect event, 278-282
onDisconnect event, 282-283
onGetSection method, 152
onGo method, 152
onMusic event, 156
onMyMethod event, 150
onResult event handler, 191
onSetSection method, 154
onSFX event, 156
onShow method, 152
onStatus event handler, 191
onStatus event, 142, 157
onSync, 245-247
onSynchronize event, 161
onSynchronize method, 163
onUpdate event, 405
on_btn, 156
Other Panels command (Window menu), 191
outgoing instance, 175
Output panel, 359
outside services, data exchange, 187-188
    Data components, 197-199
    Flash Remoting, 188-197

P

panels
- Actions
    - Flash Remoting methods, 196
    - productivity features, 314-318
- Customize Tools (JSFL), 422
- Debugger, 361
    - properties and variables, 361-363
    - remote debugging, 365-367
    - stepping through code, 363-365
- Help, component properties and methods, 376
- History
    - Copy to Clipboard button, 418
    - creating Commands, 319
    - Save Selected Steps as a Command button, 419
- Output, 359
- Project
    - Check In feature, 352
    - Check Out feature, 352
    - productivity features, 320-324
- Properties, Parameters tab, 374
- WindowSWF custom, 421-422

parameters
- Array.CASEINSENSITIVE, 212
- Array.DESCENDING, 212
- info, 158
- newVal, 364
- oldVal, 364

Parameters tab
- Component Inspector, 198
- Properties panel, 374

parsing, 23, 69, 115
- imported data into an array (LoadVars object), 170-172
- XML structured data, 179-182

passwords, saving (LSOs), 146-147
- listing, 145-146
- multiple usernames, 147

password_txt field, 146
path.to.cfc file, 192
PCT files, 38
persistent RSOs, 241
playback controls for streaming media, 262-266
players, 87-88
playlists for streaming media, 266
plug-ins, 23
- Flash Player, 15
- overview, 15-16

Plus button (Bindings tab), 200
PNG files, 38
PolyStar! Tool (JSFL), 422
populate, 23
populating components
- manual, 374-375
- scripts, 375
    - ascertaining values, 379-380
    - data structure, 377-379
    - dataProvider property, 379
    - properties and methods, 376-377

populating data (listing), 131-134
ports, NetConnection, 238-239
POST method, 174
Preferences, ActionScript tab command (Edit menu), 425
presenting data, 65-66, 115-116
- CSS, 122
    - formatting inside Flash, 124-125
    - importing CSS definitions, 122-124
- HTML, 116-119
    - hyperlinks to Flash functions, 120-121
    - img src tags, 119-120

layout options, 129-134
    attachMovie( ) method, 129-130
    createEmptyMovieClip( ) method, 130
    createTextField( ) method, 130
    MovieClip object's drawing methods, 130
TextFormat object, 126-129
primitive variables, 94-95
production (FCS)
    overview, 232
    remote production, 235-236
    restarting server, 232-234
    revisions, 234
    subdomains, 235
productivity features, 314
    Actions panel features, 314
        code cleanup, 318
        code hints, 316-317
        Code Navigator, 317-318
        toolbox, 315
    Commands menu, 318, 320
    dummy data, 335-337
    Find and Replace feature, 314
    Library management, 324
        RSLs (Runtime Shared Libraries), 326-329
        shared library items, 325-326
    multimode applications, 332-335
    Project panel, 320-321
        managing files, 322
        Test Project feature, 320
        version control, 323-324
    prototyping, 329
        components, 330
        modular thinking, 330
    staging, 330-332
ProgressBar component, 376

Project panel
    Check In feature, 352
    Check Out feature, 352
    productivity features, 320-321
        managing files, 322
        Test Project feature, 320
        version control, 323-324
prompt_txt field, 153
proof-of-concept test runs, staging, 331
proofing systems, avoiding bugs, 345-350
properties
    begin, 128
    data, 138
        DataHolder component, 207
        determining presence of properties, 139
    Debugger panel, 361-363
    deprecate, 205
    description, 191
    document.title, 164
    end, 128
    folder, 205
    html, Render as HTML option, 116
    htmlText, 116
    items, 195
        DataSet component, 210
    label, 221
    last, 214
    length, 178
    loopObj, 417
    maximum, 206
    myArray, 209
    nodeValue, 181
    populating components with script, 376-377
    prototype, 413
    remember, 146
    search, 163

section, 152
seenIntro, 143
sharedobject data, 138
target, Event objects, 384
tiptext, 206
updatePacket, 216
updateResults, 216
username, 144
XMLDocTypeDecl, 177
Properties panel, Parameters tab, 374
protocols (data exchange), 135-136
prototype, defining functions inside, 296-298
prototype property, 413
prototyping, 329
    components, 330
    improving scripting style, 413-414
    modular thinking, 330
proxy scripts, 225
proxy.cfm template, 184
Publish command (File menu), 156
Publish Settings dialog box, 322
publishing
    overview, 89-90
    streaming media
        camera and, 272
        camera and microphone, accessing, 267-268
        live or recorded stream, 268-270
        microphone and, 272
        overview, 267
        tips for, 271-274

Q

quality assurance, 339
    assessing bugs, 340
        acceptance, 341
        benefits to client and developer, 340
        categories of bugs, 342-343

        clear understanding of the bug, 342
        self-criticism, 340
    avoiding bugs, 345
        defining testing procedures, 353-354
        leaving tracks, 350-353
        proofing systems, 345-350
    client management, 344-345
    deliberate approach to addressing bugs, 343-344
    Error object, 367-370
    finding and removing bugs, 354
        Debugger panel, 361-367
        homemade debuggers, 357-361
        scientific approach, 355-357
        standard messages, 354-355
questions array, 170, 390
quiz node (XML), 180

R

raster graphics, 38
RDBMSResolver, 197, 215-218
reality checks, staging, 331
Rearrange Fields formatters (Schema tab), 220-221
receiver files (local connection objects), 150
recorded stream, publishing, 268-270
recordsets, 195
reference variables, 94-95
remember property, 146
remote debugging, Debugger panel, 365-367
    conditions, 365
Remote method, writing, 194
remote production, 235-236
remote shared objects (RSOs)
    application variables compared, 285
    architectural decisions, 247-249
    data, accessing and setting, 240-242

examples
- favorite movie vote counter, 253-255
- geographic locator, 250-252
- overview, 250

LSOs compared, 137, 240
overview, 240
persistent RSOs, 241
server side, accessing from, 286
- locking feature, 289
- sending messages, 289
- syntax differences, 287-288

temporary RSOs, 241
value synchronization, 242-244
- onSync, 245-247

Remoting (Flash Remoting), 188
- basic script, 190-193
  - example, 193
- complex data, 195
- manual scripts, 223-224
- NetConnection Debugger, 224
- proxy scripts, 225
- sequence, 189-190
- Service Browser, 224
- when to use, 196-197
- writing the Remote method, 194

Remoting components, 189
removeAll( ) method, 376
removing bugs, 354
- Debugger panel, 361
  - properties and variables, 361-363
  - remote debugging, 365-367
  - stepping through code, 363-365
- homemade debuggers, 357
- runtime trace windows, 359-361
- Simple Debug mode, 357-359
- scientific approach, 355-357
- standard messages, 354-355

Render as HTML option (html property), 116
repeatMe( ) method, 426

replacing skins, customizing components, 396
- applying themes, 396-397
- editing themes, 397
- saving themes, 397-398

resolvers (Data components), 197, 215-218
- RDBMSResolver, 197, 215-218
- XUpdateResolver, 197, 215-218

restarting server, 232-234
return users, LSOs (local shared objects), 139
revisions, 234
RIA (rich Internet applications) standard, 16
- Broadmoor Hotel (example), 25
- user benefit identification and, 34-35
- XML News Aggregator (example), 25

rich media, 14, 22
RSLs (runtime shared libraries), 324-329
RSOs. *See* remote shared objects
runtime, 22
runtime trace windows
- debugging applications, 359-361
- listing, 359-360

S

Sample theme (components), 397
Save and Compact feature, 352
Save As, leaving tracks with version numbering, 351-352
Save As Command button (History panel), 319
Save button (slide-show maker), saving data into an LSO, 147-148
Save Selected Steps as a Command button (History panel), 419
saveToSharedObj( ) method, 214
saving
- data
  - flat data, 165-176
  - local connection objects, 149-165

LSOs (local shared objects), 137-149
XML structured data, 177-185
DataSet collection, 214-215
themes, component customization, 397-398
sayHello( ) function, 194
sayhello.cfm server script, 176
scalable, 23
Schema tab (Component Inspector), 198, 201-207, 218
    Encoding option, 219
    Formatters option, 219-221
    Kind option, 219
    Validation option, 219, 222-223
scientific approach, finding and removing bugs, 355-357
Screenweaver, 48
scripts
    basic Flash Remoting script, 190-193
        example, 193
    code cleanup, 318
    Code Navigator, 317-318
    custom validate scripts, 222-223
    improving scripting style, 408
        functions as constructors, 410-412
        modular thinking, 409-410
        prototyping, 413-414
    loading data from a server script, 172-173
    manual, 223-224
    populating components, 375
        ascertaining values, 379-380
        data structure, 377-379
        dataProvider property, 379
        properties and methods, 376-377
    proxy scripts, 225
    retrieving data from, 175-176
    saving data to, 174-175
    storing, 414
        AS text files, 414-415
        behaviors, 415-418

SDK (Software Development Kit), 22
search property, 163
searches, DataSet component, 211-214
section property, 152
seenIntro property, 143
selectedIndex property, 380
selectedItem property, 380
self-criticism, finding and assessing bugs, 340
send( ) method, 152, 157, 174
sendAndLoad( ) method, 174
    listing, 175
sender files (local connection objects), 150
sequence (Flash Remoting), 189-190
server interaction, flat data, 172
    loading data from a server script, 172-173
    retrieving data from a server script, 175-176
    saving data to a server script, 174-175
server side, 22
server-side ActionScript (SSAS), 274
    Application object, 277, 283-285
    Client object, 286
    events
        onAppStart event, 277-278
        onConnect event, 278-282
        onDisconnect event, 282-283
        overview, 277
    main.asc file, 276
    messaging
        NetConnection.call( ), 293-295
        overview, 290
        SharedObject.send( ), 290-293
    RSOs, accessing, 286
        locking feature, 289
        sending messages, 289
        syntax differences, 287-288
server-side Stream object
    event logs, 303-307
    overview, 299

publishing existing streams from server side, 299-300
republishing portions of client streams, 301-302
Service Browser, 224
setFillColor method (JSFL), 421
setInterval button, 348
setInterval( ) method, 169
setNewTextFormat( ) method, 127
setRememberMode( ) function, 146
setScale( ) function, 413
setStyle( ) method, 125
setTextFormat( ) method, 127
Settings dialog box, 322
    Local Storage tab, 141
sfx_btn, 156
shared library items, 325-326
sharedobject data property, 138
SharedObject.send( ), 290-293
Shockwave, 23
short objects. *See* generic objects
show variable, 148
showSettings( ) method, displaying System Settings dialog box, 143
Simple Debug mode, 357-359
single instances, customizing components with styles, 393-394
skinning, customizing components, 392
    replacing skins, 396-398
skip-intro feature, LSOs (local shared objects), 143
    listing, 143
slide-show maker example, 108, 112
    Save feature, LSOs (local shared objects), 147-148
SOAP encoded data, loading, 68
SOL files (Flash Player folder), 139
sort( ) method, 105-106
sorting data
    DataSet component, 211-214
    overview, 105

sort( ) method, 105-106
sortOn( ) method, 106-108
sortOn( ) method, 106-108
specialization class, 427
split( ) method, 172
staging, 330-332
Stampede Cattle example of RIA standard, 27
standalone applications, deployment, 46-48
standard messages (bugs), 354-355
Step In button, 365
Step Out button, 365
Step Over button, 365
stepping through code (Debugger panel), 363-365
storing scripts, 414
    AS text files, 414-415
    behaviors, 415-418
streaming media
    FLV videos, 40
        overview, 258-259
        playing, 259-260
    MP3s, 261
    NetStreams, 256-257
    overview, 255
    playback controls, 262-266
    playlists, 266
    publishing
        camera and, 272
        camera and microphone, accessing, 267-268
        live or recorded stream, 268-270
        microphone and, 272
        overview, 267
        tips for, 271-274
    sharing streams with virtual directories, 261-262
string property names, 101-102
StringError( ) function, 369
strong data typing, 93

structure
    AS2 class files, 424-426
    local connection objects, 151
        listing, 150
    LSOs (local shared objects), 138
structuring data, 64-65
    arrays, 95
        benefits of, 99-100
        generic objects, 96-98
        objects used like, 100
    data types, 93-95
    DataProvider object, 104
    functions, associating with event
        properties, 102-103
    objects
        dynamically referencing properties,
            101-102
        looping through properties, 100
    overview, 92
    sorting data
        overview, 105
        slide-show maker example, 108, 112
        sort( ) method, 105-106
        sortOn( ) method, 106-108
    styles, customizing components, 392-393
        single instances versus global styles,
            393-394
        supported styles list, 394-395
subdomains, 235
substring( ) method, 163
success, measuring, 31-32
super class, 427
supported styles list, customizing
    components, 394-395
swap symbol, 326
SWF files, 87
SWF Studio, 48
Symbol button, 326
Symbol Properties dialog box, 325
synchronization of data, 70-71

syntax differences in CSAS and SSAS,
    287-288
syntax errors, debugging, 355
System Settings dialog box, 141
    displaying system settings,
        System.showSettings( ) method, 143
System.showSettings( ) method, 143

T

tabs
    Bindings (Component Inspector), 198,
        201-207
    Local Storage (Settings dialog box), 141
    Locals, 364
    Parameters
        Component Inspector, 198
        Properties panel, 374
    Schema (Component Inspector), 198,
        201-207, 218-223
tags
    a:hover, 124
    cfoutput, 173
    FlashVars (HTML), Back button
        solution, 160-165
    font, 118
    img src, embedding images or SWFs,
        119-120
target property (Event objects), 384
technology map, 84
technology selection
    deployment
        in-browser applications, 42-46
        overview, 41-42
        standalone applications, 46-48
    media formats
        audio, 39
        overview, 38
        raster graphic, 38
        video, 40
    overview, 35

tools, 36
    Application Server, 37
    Breeze, 36
    Breeze Live, 37
    Dreamweaver, 37
    Fireworks, 37
    Flash Communication Server, 36
    Flash MX 2004, 36
    Flash MX Professional 2004, 36
    Flash Remoting, 36
    Freehand, 37
    Java, 37
    JavaScript, 37
    Macromedia Central, 36
tempconverter file, 193
tempconverter.cfc method, 193
temporary RSOs, 241
Test Project feature (Project panel), 320
testing procedures, avoiding bugs, 353-354
text, formatting
    CSS, 122-125
    HTML, 116-121
    TextFormat object, 126-129
text components, creating, 403-404
Text components
    Label, 386
    TextArea, 386
    TextInput, 386
text fields
    password_txt, 146
    prompt_txt, 153
    username_txt, 146
TextArea component, 386
    text property, 116
TextField StyleSheet object, 123
TextFormat object
    formatting text, 126-129
    listing, 128
TextInput component, 219, 386
    text property, 116

theField variable, 118
themeColor style (components), 394
themes, customizing components, 392, 396-397
    editing, 397
    saving, 397-398
theObj variable, 118
thin client, 23
thisObj object, 172
timeouts, 71
tiptext property, 206
title/subtitle component, 403-404
    compiled clips, 405-406
toolbox (Actions panel), 315
Tools menu commands, Folder Options, Show Hidden Files and Folder, 315
totalQuestions variable, 171
tracks, avoiding bugs, 350
    documenting fixes, 353
    inline documentation, 352-353
    version numbering, 351-352
transfer objects, 210
Tree component, 392
triggering code to respond to events (components), 381
    addEventListener( ) method, 382-383
    Event objects, 384-385
    on method, 381-382
try, catch, finally structure (Error object), 367
    listing, 368
Tufte, Edward, 34
type mismatch, debugging, 355

U

UI (user interface) components, 372-373, 385, 390
    Alert, 391
    class-based structure, 373
    ComboBox, 387-388

UI

customizing, 392
    skinning, 392, 396-398
    styles, 392-395
DataGrid, 392
Date Field and Date Chooser, 391
direct property access, 372
disadvantages, 372-373
List, 388-390
Menubar, 391
populating manually, 374-375
populating with script, 375
    ascertaining values, 379-380
    data structure, 377-379
    dataProvider property, 379
    properties and methods, 376-377
Text components
    Label, 386
    TextArea, 386
    TextInput, 386
Tree, 392
triggering code to respond to events, 381
    addEventListener( ) method, 382-383
    Event objects, 384-385
    on method, 381-382
validation and formatting controls, 372
unescape( ) function, 167
Unicode support, importing flat data, 166
update( ) functions, 358
updatePacket property, 216
updateResults property, 216
upgrades, 19
    application development features, 19-20
URL-encoded strings
    formatting flat data, 166
    loading, 67
user benefit identification
    alternatives, consideration of, 32-33
    objectives, 30-31
    overview, 30

RIAs and, 34-35
success, measuring, 31-32
user interface components. *See* UI components
username property, 144
usernames, saving (LSOs), 144-147
    listing, 144-146
    multiple usernames, 147
username_txt field, 146
users having modern browsers, expectation of, 15
user_vars variable, 174
useSort( ) method, 211

V

V2 components, 79-80, 372-373, 385, 390
    Alert, 391
    class-based structure, 373
    ComboBox, 387-388
    customizing, 392
        skinning, 392, 396-398
        styles, 392-395
    DataGrid, 392
    Date Field and Date Chooser, 391
    direct property access, 372
    disadvantages, 372-373
    List, 388-390
    Menubar, 391
    populating manually, 374-375
    populating with script, 375
        ascertaining values, 379-380
        data structure, 377-379
        dataProvider property, 379
        properties and methods, 376-377
    Text components
        Label, 386
        TextArea, 386
        TextInput, 386

Tree, 392
   triggering code to respond to events, 381
      addEventListener( ) method, 382-383
      Event objects, 384-385
      on method, 381-382
   validation and formatting controls, 372
validation controls (components), 372
Validation option (Schema tab), 219
   custom validate scripts, 222-223
value synchronization (RSOs), 242-244
   onSync, 245-247
variables
   #CGI.SERVER_NAME#, 173
   Debugger panel, 361-363
   myGateway, 192
   myService, 192
   my_lc, 150
   saving
      flat data, 165-176
      local connection objects, 149-165
      LSOs (local shared objects), 137-149
      XML structured data, 177-185
   show, 148
   totalQuestions, 171
   user_vars, 174
   var_string, 163
var_string variable, 163
version control (Project panel), 323-324
Version Control menu, 323
   Edit Sites command, 323
version numbering, 351-352
video, 40. *See also* FLV files
virtual directories, streaming media and, 261-262
virtual hosts, conf folder (FCS), 230
Visicalc, 13
vision issues (accessibility), 53-55

W

watch( ) method, 358
web pages, 12
web servers, 73
   loading data from a server script, 172-173
   retrieving data from a server script, 175-176
   saving data to a server script, 174-175
web services, 72-73
   ActionScript (listing), 224
   application servers as gateway to, 77
   direct support from Macromedia Central, 225
   exchanging data, 187-188
      Data components, 197-199
      Flash Remoting, 188-197
WebServiceConnector, 197-200
when to use Flash, 20-21
Window menu commands
   Debugger, 367
   Other Panels, 191
window.location search, 163
windowopen( ) method, testing main file (guided tour), 154
WindowSWF configuration folder, 319
WindowSWF custom panel, 421-422
work environment
   configuration folders, 85-86
      Central folder, 87
      First Run folder, 85
   localhost, 88-89
   players, 87-88
   publishing, 89-90
writing
   data, 69-70
   Remote method, 194
WSDLURL field (Component Inspector, Parameters tab), 199

X-Z

XML
- attributes, 180
- nodes, 180

XML News Aggregator example of RIA standard, 25-27

XML structured data, 177-178
- browsing Amazon through Flash, 182-185
- loading data, 178-179
- parsing data, 179-182

XML-encoded data, loading, 68

XML.load( ) method (listing), 178

XMLConnector, 197, 201

XMLDocTypeDecl property, 177

XUL (XML to UI), 418

XUpdateResolver, 197, 215-218

informIT

www.informit.com

YOUR GUIDE TO IT REFERENCE

New Riders has partnered with **InformIT.com** to bring technical information to your desktop. Drawing from New Riders authors and reviewers to provide additional information on topics of interest to you, **InformIT.com** provides free, in-depth information you won't find anywhere else.

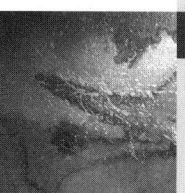

Articles

Keep your edge with thousands of free articles, in-depth features, interviews, and IT reference recommendations—all written by experts you know and trust.

Online Books

Answers in an instant from **InformIT Online Books'** 600+ fully searchable online books.

POWERED BY
Safari

Catalog

Review online sample chapters, author biographies, and customer rankings and choose exactly the right book from a selection of over 5,000 titles.

New Riders
www.newriders.com

HOW TO CONTACT US

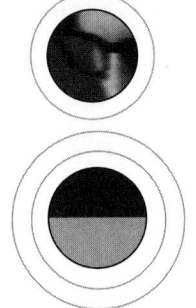

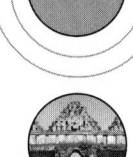

VISIT OUR WEB SITE
WWW.NEWRIDERS.COM

On our web site, you'll find information about our other books, authors, tables of contents, and book errata. You will also find information about book registration and how to purchase our books, both domestically and internationally.

EMAIL US

Contact us at: **nrfeedback@newriders.com**

- If you have comments or questions about this book
- To report errors that you have found in this book
- If you have a book proposal to submit or are interested in writing for New Riders
- If you are an expert in a computer topic or technology and are interested in being a technical editor who reviews manuscripts for technical accuracy

Contact us at: **nreducation@newriders.com**

- If you are an instructor from an educational institution who wants to preview New Riders books for classroom use. Email should include your name, title, school, department, address, phone number, office days/hours, text in use, and enrollment, along with your request for desk/examination copies and/or additional information.

Contact us at: **nrmedia@newriders.com**

- If you are a member of the media who is interested in reviewing copies of New Riders books. Send your name, mailing address, and email address, along with the name of the publication or Web site you work for.

BULK PURCHASES/CORPORATE SALES

The publisher offers discounts on this book when ordered in quantity for bulk purchases and special sales. For sales within the U.S., please contact: Corporate and Government Sales (800) 382-3419 or **corpsales@pearsontechgroup.com**. Outside of the U.S., please contact: International Sales (317) 428-3341 or **international@pearsontechgroup.com**.

WRITE TO US

New Riders Publishing
800 East 96th Street, 3rd Floor
Indianapolis, IN 46240

CALL/FAX US

Toll-free (800) 571-5840
If outside U.S. (317) 428-3000
Ask for New Riders
FAX: (317) 428-3280

New Riders

WWW.NEWRIDERS.COM

VIEW CART ▸ search
▸ Registration already a member? Log in. ▸ Book Registration

Voices that Matter™

| web development | design | photoshop | new media | 3-D | server technologies |

OUR AUTHORS

PRESS ROOM

EDUCATORS

ABOUT US

CONTACT US

You already know that New Riders brings you the **Voices That Matter**. But what does that mean? It means that New Riders brings you the Voices that challenge your assumptions, take your talents to the next level, or simply help you better understand the complex technical world we're all navigating.

Visit www.newriders.com to find:

- **10% discount** and **free shipping** on all book purchases
- Never-before-published chapters
- Sample chapters and excerpts
- Author bios and interviews
- Contests and enter-to-wins
- Up-to-date industry event information
- Book reviews
- Special offers from our friends and partners
- Info on how to join our User Group program
- Ways to have your Voice heard

New Riders

WWW.NEWRIDERS.COM

0735713766
Tom Green, Chris S. Flick, and Jordan L. Chilcott
US$45.00

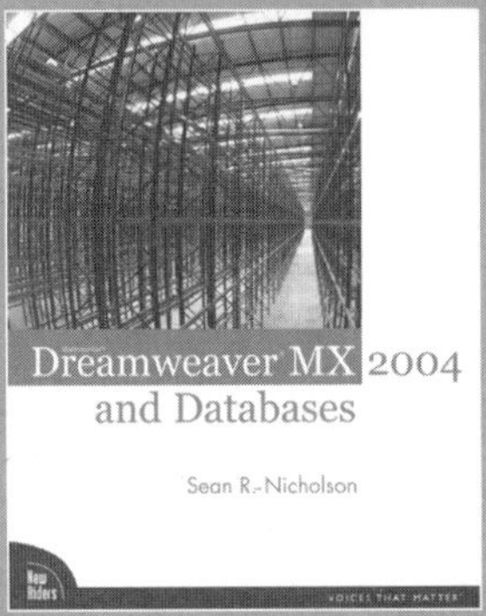

0735713839
Shane Elliot
US$39.99

0735713774
Michelangelo Capraro and Duncan McAlester
US$35.00

0735713782
Massimo Foti, Angela C. Buraglia, and Daniel Short
US$29.99

0735713707
Sean R. Nicholson
US$45.00

0735713820
Nate Weiss
US$45.00

VOICES THAT MATTER™

New Riders

WWW.NEWRIDERS.COM